Frances Willard   A *Biography*

Frances Willard

A Biography
by Ruth Bordin

The University of North Carolina Press

Chapel Hill and London

Library of Congress Cataloging-in-Publication Data

Bordin, Ruth Birgitta Anderson, 1917–

  Frances Willard: a biography.

  Bibliography: p.
  Includes index.
   1. Willard, Frances Elizabeth, 1839–1896.
2. Social reformers—United States—Biography.
3. Woman's Christian Temperance Union. I. Title.
HV5232.W6B67   1986   322.4′4′0924 [B]   86-7029
ISBN 0-8078-1697-3

Chapter XI of this text appeared in somewhat different form as "Frances Willard and the Practice of Political Influence" in the *Hayes Historical Journal: A Journal of the Golden Age* 5 (Spring 1985): 18–28.

For Martha and Charlotte

Contents

Illustrations

Preface

A hundred years have passed since Frances Willard, national president of the Woman's Christian Temperance Union, reigned as temperance queen of the United States and was revered as the beloved St. Frances of American womanhood. Over forty years have elapsed since the most recent biography of the nineteenth-century heroine and leader was published. Three recent developments underline the need for a new "life."

First of all, important original sources—unavailable since early in the twentieth century—were rediscovered after 1980 by Rosalita Leonard, librarian of the Willard Memorial Library in Evanston, Illinois. These include Willard's diaries, some correspondence, and all but one of the twenty scrapbooks missing when the microfilm edition of the *Temperance and Prohibition Papers* was made.[1] They are now accessible by purchase or loan as a supplement to the original microfilm edition as well as being available at the Willard Library. Thus, Anna Gordon, Willard's secretary and companion, always loyal and true in her devotion to Willard, did not destroy, as earlier legend had it, any of her papers but preserved all the memorabilia and private writings of her friend and cohort for posterity to assess.

We now probably have access to all the existing Willard diaries. Although we know of no volumes for many of her adult years, Willard herself explains that there were long gaps in her journal keeping. She did not find time to produce a diary during much of the seventies and eighties, but her autobiography, *Glimpses of Fifty Years*, shows that a diary for 1874 once existed that covered the period of her resignation from Northwestern University. No such volume is now among her papers. However, forty volumes of journals and diaries are newly available and provide a wealth of firsthand information on the inner workings of Willard as a child and young woman as well as valuable information, hitherto unavailable in any form, on her last decade. These late diaries are supplemented by the recently available private papers of Willard's associate and friend, Hannah Whitall Smith.[2]

Willard's diaries were last used by Rachel Strachey, British feminist who published a biography of Willard in 1913.[3] When Willard wrote her autobiography in 1889 she used the diaries extensively, but the materials from the 1890s were not part of that memoir.[4] Anna Gordon in her eulogistic tributes published after Willard's death had full access to the diaries but seems to have used and quoted primarily from Willard's published works.[5] Mary Earhart Dillon in her 1944 biography had access to the correspondence file and scrapbooks that have recently become reavailable but did not see the diaries.[6] The diaries were found too late for Susan Dye Lee to make use of them in her dissertation, and my recent study of the WCTU was completed before I learned of these materials.[7]

The first five chapters of this volume were in draft before I became aware that access to the manuscript diaries was possible. Thus, I had relied heavily on the excerpts quoted in Willard's autobiography in attempting to explain the forces and influences in her early life that shaped the mature Willard. The diaries were important in reconstructing this period, permitting a deeper understanding of the continuum that led from girl to woman. On occasion, firm documentation replaced informed speculation. Willard was remarkably open in the use she made of her journals in *Glimpses of Fifty Years*. It is a tribute to her honesty that no startling reinterpretations flowed from the diaries when they became available in the original. Her editing was relatively minor. She did omit, however, and often the passages she omitted were revealing.

On the other hand, the two diaries for the 1890s break new ground and contribute much to our understanding of Willard's relationship with Lady Henry Somerset and her movement onto the world stage. More importantly, they contribute significantly to our knowledge of the transatlantic interconnections between the woman movement in the United States and Great Britain in the last years of the nineteenth century.

Newly available sources are only one of the reasons that another study of Willard is appropriate. Mary Earhart wrote her biography when temperance was a discredited cause. She reflected the scholarship of her time, which regarded the temperance movement as an antilibertarian, last-ditch fight of fundamentalist Protestant rural America to hang on to its eroding power base in an urban society. The tide of scholarship now runs in another direction. Contemporary scholars have explored the problem of alcohol abuse in the nineteenth century and found its presence very real indeed, and lay public opinion is again concerned about drinking as a contemporary threat. As one commentator put it, "Not so long ago that problem was scarcely larger than a human hand against the horizon, but now it makes good newspaper copy."[8] In fact, *Time* magazine devoted an issue in the spring of 1985 to the "new temperance."

Concurrently, the women's movement of the late 1960s and 1970s and the accompanying growth of women's studies have inspired an impressive burst of scholarship in women's history. This has given us large accretions of fresh knowledge as well as stimulated new conceptual frameworks through which we can attempt to understand past generations of women and the roles they played in society. Again, no previous biography of Willard makes use of these new insights.

INEVITABLY the biographer becomes involved in a touchy interplay of objectivity, self-analysis, and self-indulgence. Biography by its very nature is a subjective medium, and the biographer must sort out personal needs of identification and aspiration from those of the biographee. My life experience quite naturally influenced my attraction to Frances Willard as a subject for research. My training and work as both a historian and an archivist have shaped the way I approached my task. As a manuscript librarian I became familiar with a wide range of nineteenth-century personal papers, an experience I hope has added perspective to my understanding of Frances Willard and nineteenth-century women. As a historian, I trust I have been able to capture some of the larger picture and adequately relate Frances Willard to the society in which she lived. Also, in a personal sense Frances Willard touched many chords in me. Much of her life was close to my early life—her religious commitment, her belief in the equality of women to men, but also her love for the family. The points of communality in our views of the world cannot be denied.

No biography has ever told the whole truth or recreated the person who actually existed. Nonetheless, Anna Gordon, writing soon after Willard's death, told us much about the way Frances Willard was viewed by her colleagues and contemporaries. Rachel Strachey saw the Willard her grandmother had known when they worked together in the Anglo-American woman movement. Mary Earhart showed us Willard at the end of another era when women's values were fast changing. Hopefully this volume helps to provide new insights for a later feminist age.

In *Woman and Temperance* I advanced the thesis that the Woman's Christian Temperance Union became the first mass organization of

American women, and that it was their work in the temperance cause—
and its congeniality with the nineteenth century's doctrine of spheres—
that enabled women to move widely into public life by 1900. In my
view, Frances Willard's contribution to this process was twofold. She
combined skillful leadership, broad social vision, and keen intelligence
with the womanly virtues so dear to the nineteenth-century white middle class, love of home and family and that special quality called
womanliness. She also understood and used American women's unique
place in the evangelical Protestant church. Frances Willard was a successful leader because she did not appear to challenge her society's
accepted ideals, especially the tenets of the cult of domesticity, as she
simultaneously offered women a range of goals and activities that led
them into legislative chambers, union halls, and a host of helping
professions.

She also had a peculiar charisma that doubly enhanced her ability to
lead. In the words of Hannah Smith, her longtime friend and colleague, writing to Olive Schreiner as they consoled each other on
Willard's death, "She was almost pure spirit in very truth—more so
than anyone else I ever knew, and I see from thy words how it was that
she was so wonderfully uplifting and ennobling in all her influence. She
had that indefinable power that spirit always exercises that was entirely
independent of the words she said or the things she did, and one
was always uplifted in her presence without knowing at all how it
happened."[9]

THE genesis of this project dates back over ten years to the time when
I first began work on the woman's temperance movement and decided
that two books would have to be written. Frances Willard played a
much larger role in nineteenth-century America than her leadership of
the temperance cause, and women's part in the temperance movement
was much larger than Willard. Each deserved a separate volume. A long
project results in many obligations. The people and institutions that
made this book possible are beyond acknowledging.

My major debt is to my friends and colleagues at the Bentley Historical Library of the University of Michigan. Francis Blouin, Diane Hat-
field, Mary Jo Pugh, and Kenneth Scheffel should be singled out for
their special contributions. But credit should also be given to the library itself. Without the microfilm edition of the *Temperance and Prohibition Papers*, this project would never have occurred to me, much less
have been possible.

An equal debt is owed to the staff of the National Woman's Christian
Temperance Union who made possible the microfilm edition's WCTU

series and the supplement encompassing the Willard diaries. Martha Edgar, national president, has cooperated in every way, as did Rosalita Leonard, librarian of the Willard Memorial Library in Evanston. Their part in arranging the filming of Willard's diaries and certain related papers that composed the supplement to the microfilm edition will prove a boon to scholars for many years to come. Both understand Willard's importance to the history of American women, as does their organization.

I also owe an important debt to Barbara Strachey Halpern for generously providing access to the papers of Hannah Whitall Smith.

Evelyn Brooks, Joan Brumberg, Jean Campbell, Allen Davis, Jacqueline Goggins, Marjorie Lansing, Judy Papichristou, Lena Ruegamer, Rosemary VanArsdale, and Martha Vicinus have read all or parts of the manuscript and made helpful suggestions and sometimes substantial contributions.

I have also been assisted by a Beveridge grant from the American Historical Association and by Continuing Education for Women at the University of Michigan, which sent me to the 1983 workshop on the biography and autobiography of women sponsored by Smith College's Project on Women and Social Change.

A number of other manuscript libraries and individuals have helped my research in various ways and are acknowledged in the notes and bibliography.

Ruth Bordin

Frances Willard   A *Biography*

Frances Willard in 1889 at the height of her influence. (Reprinted from Willard, *Glimpses of Fifty Years*, and Bordin, *Woman and Temperance*)

Chapter I  Perspective

On 17 February 1898 in a hotel room in New York City, Frances Willard died quietly in her sleep. When her body was brought to Chicago six days later, crowds of mourning admirers met her casket, and when the coffin was placed on the podium of Willard Hall in the Chicago Loop's Temple office building, it was escorted by a guard of honor, Illinois women singing the old hymn, "Rock of Ages, Cleft for Me." The flags of the nation's second largest city floated at half mast. Throngs of silent Chicagoans, thirty thousand in one day, filed by the bier for a parting look at their city's most famous citizen. Crowds stood for hours on the wet, windy pavement outside Willard Hall waiting in fallen snow for their turn to pay homage to this slight, middle-aged woman.

Chicagoans were not the first to honor Willard at her death. Funeral services had already been held at the Broadway Tabernacle in New York City. Seven clergymen officiated. A slow-moving procession, lasting for hours, filed past her casket before the dove gray box was placed in a special railroad carriage for the journey west. The funeral car stopped for a memorial service at Churchville, New York, Willard's birthplace. And at Buffalo "a large delegation of white ribboners [members of the Woman's Christian Temperance Union] . . . passed sorrowfully through the car, leaving 'lilies of love and loyalty.'"[1] The flags of Washington, D.C., as well as Chicago were lowered on the day of her funeral.[2] Final services took place in Willard's home church, the First Methodist Episcopal Church of Evanston. Hundreds of students from nearby Northwestern University filled the galleries, and the white silk flag that had been carried at the head of the dedicatory procession for the 1893 Columbian Exposition was displayed behind the pulpit. Willard's coffin rested on a rug of roses and violets and was crowned by a rainbow arch of flowers. Her funeral was a Victorian stage setting worthy of a woman unsurpassed in dramatizing the social movements she supported. Willard had been a superb showwoman. Also, her leadership of reform causes was symbolized in her decision to be cremated, "to help forward progressive movements even in my last hours."[3]

This woman, widely hailed in the nineteenth century as America's "heroine," had never been elected to public office. Most of the ideas for which she fought represented as yet unachieved goals. But the nation mourned her with the grief, admiration, and respect it would have bestowed on a great national hero or a martyred president. No woman before or since was so clearly on the day of her death this country's most honored woman. Never before had an American woman evoked such an outpouring of reverence and affection.

Willard was as well known to her countrymen in the last decade of the nineteenth century as Eleanor Roosevelt was to be in the 1930s and 1940s. She was a major subject of press attention. Newspaper and magazine interviews with the great lady and those close to her featured vignettes from her life story as well as her opinions on public issues. Willard's every going and coming was reported in the press. Her picture, clipped from a newspaper, purchased from some reform organization, or awarded as a prize for services rendered to a temperance union, graced many American homes, humble and prosperous alike. The list of names of people who sent letters of condolence on her death totals over a hundred pages.

Some of this adulation was frivolous and trivial. For example, the children of Chicago voted to name two lion cubs at the zoo Frances Willard and Martha Washington. But much of it represented the genuine renown and respect in which she was held. No less an arbiter of nineteenth-century American values than Edward Everett Hale stated that he invariably read two annual messages, that of the president of the United States and Frances Willard's yearly presidential address to the WCTU.[4] In the 1880s and 1890s her annual message to temperance women nationally assembled was a widely read and consulted document. Invariably it was an overview of the nation, a summary of the United States' strengths and weaknesses, and not incidentally an assessment of the current status of American womanhood. Edward J. Wheeler, editor of the *Literary Digest*, a popular magazine, observed in an editorial obituary that Willard was "a woman suffragist, and woman suffrage has not prevailed. She was a Prohibitionist and Prohibition has not prevailed. But beyond and above all these she was an awakener of women to the possibilities of true womanhood and she has probably done more than any other person who ever lived to bring to those of her own sex the world over, an adequate realization of their own powers."[5] Wheeler's tribute expressed well the attitude of the liberal political community toward Willard when she died.

> She is coming! Said the angels in heaven,
> As they pressed to the crystal gate.
> There's a hush of the golden symbols,
> And the stars of the midnight wait.
> "She is coming! We heard the summons,"
> And the Seraphim guards are in flight,
> Afar as their flashing pinions,
> As they move through the deepening night.[6]

Willard seriously was called "Saint Frances" or our "Queen of Temperance" by the press and from the pulpit. The *New York Independent*
wrote, "No woman's name is better known in the English speaking
world than that of Miss Willard, save that of England's great queen. . . .
it is the simple truth to say that in the death of Miss Willard the
foremost woman in the public life of this country has been removed."
Another obituary referred to Frances Willard as "next to Queen Victoria the most influential woman of the age," and went on to predict
that "generations to come will honor her more and more."[7]

   That prediction was not to be fulfilled. A hundred years have passed
since Frances Willard, national president of the Woman's Christian
Temperance Union, reigned as temperance queen of the United States
and was revered as the beloved St. Frances of American womanhood.
She is a forgotten leader. Although in recent years Willard has received
considerable scholarly attention, especially from historians of women,[8]
she is no longer a folk hero. Her distant cousin by marriage, the educator Emma Willard, is more likely to be mentioned in secondary school
books. Carrie Nation, the flamboyant Kansas foe of drink, is more
often associated in the popular press with the temperance crusade led
by Willard for a quarter of a century. Susan B. Anthony and Elizabeth
Cady Stanton, unlike Willard, are household words today, but in the
1890s Willard's fame eclipsed that of both of them.

   Why did Willard receive such widespread and fervent acclaim in her
own time, only to have it prove short-lived? Two episodes from my
own experience provide a clue to this dilemma. On my first visit to
Washington, D.C., as an adolescent in 1930, I remember taking with
my family the usual tour through the Capitol Building, and the uni-
formed male guide pointing out the marble figure of Frances Willard in
Statuary Hall. In his set spiel, he stressed how Willard was the only
woman so honored by her state. I stood by and felt a strong surge of

pride in my sex, that one of us had made it to that illustrious company. Prohibition was still in force. Willard was still taken seriously as a reformer and national heroine, although her preeminence had begun to slip. However, I also remember another occasion over twenty years later—in the 1950s—when I accompanied my own children on the same tour. This time the guide facetiously remarked that Illinois, the home of Lincoln, had chosen a teetotalling woman, the president of the WCTU, as its representative in Statuary Hall.

Between these two visits to the Capitol Building and Statuary Hall, prohibition, the crown jewel of many a nineteenth-century reform program, had been repealed as well as associated with crime, lawbreaking, and gunfire in the streets rather than with the perfection of society. Hopes for prohibition had been high. Its failure was seen as so ignominious that public disillusionment could be handled only by translating the idealism of the temperance cause into a national joke, the epitome of midwestern pious provincialism. When Willard's statue was placed in the Capitol in 1905, Senator Albert Beveridge, speaking at the dedication ceremony, described Willard as "the first woman of the nineteenth century, the most beloved character of her time."[9] Fifty years later she was an anomaly among the great and distinguished because the cause with which she was most closely associated had been overwhelmingly rejected. She had been removed from America's panoply of heroes.

Prohibition, the Eighteenth Amendment to the Constitution of the United States, was in part the direct result of Willard's labors. Prohibition also caused her eclipse. Willard's beliefs and contributions, which spanned a wide variety of reform causes, were reduced after her death to a single dimension, temperance, and that dimension of her life's work was repudiated unequivocally by a later generation. The causes to which she made lasting contributions—for example, the vote for women, the public kindergarten, separate correctional institutions for women, Protestant ecumenicism—became part of the permanent fabric of American life. But these causes were later dissociated from Willard because for much of her public career, and almost always in her public utterances, she saw temperance as the seedbed where other reforms would be nourished.

In this ordering of her priorities, Willard reflected prevailing values. For example, Richard Ely, the respected Wisconsin economist and reformer, saw the "deep, wide movement of social reform" as centered "in temperance," and from that center "spreading out in ever more inclusive circles until it touches the entire life of society."[10] Terence Powderly, the nineteenth-century labor leader, told his followers in the

Knights of Labor, "Workingmen, shun strong drink as you would a scorpion. . . . I draw no line between drinkers. They are all in danger."[11] Sidney Webb, the British Fabian socialist, wrote to Beatrice Potter in 1892, when they were courting, "what I see in the Deptford slums does make me feel that drink is one *great* enemy."[12]

Drink *was* one great enemy. Americans had wrestled with the personal and social dislocation produced by their society's tendency toward excessive use of alcohol for over half a century when Willard adopted it as her cause. Temperance advocates, using prohibition laws passed by state legislatures, had succeeded in reducing American dependence on drink in the 1850s, only to watch consumption figures rise again with the Civil War. But all through the nineteenth century Americans were heavy users of alcohol, heavier users than they have ever been since. Reformers zealously attempted to find remedies for what they saw as an alarming characteristic of a republic where the people, drunk or sober, presumably occupied the seat of power. Although the advocates of the "drink reform" also concerned themselves deeply with the personal and family misery caused by alcohol abuse, the threat to the republic's great experiment with self-government was a major motivating force. As industrialization accelerated toward the end of the century, safety factors also came to the fore. Could machinery be entrusted to tipsy operators or railroads left in any but sober hands?

Commitment to the cause of temperance among political liberals was widespread even into the twentieth century. New York State cider, not champagne, was served at Alice Roosevelt's White House debut in 1902. No reform president could have encouraged or condoned the use of intoxicants by young people during the Progressive Era. Some twenty years later, bathtub gin was being made in the basement of Alice Roosevelt's home in Washington while her husband, Nicholas Longworth, was serving as speaker of the House of Representatives and the Eighteenth Amendment and the Volstead Act were the law of the land.[13] So quickly did American mores change. But in the 1890s prohibition (or at least the drastic regulation of the liquor trade) was the articulated goal of most of the membership of the Protestant churches, the business community, and the upwardly mobile middle class. Temperance also had strong support in many Catholic circles, especially among the Irish. In 1890 the WCTU alone had nearly 150,000 dues-paying members; it was the first mass organization of women in the United States and probably the world. As a temperance leader, Willard epitomized prevailing establishment values.

Until recently historians of women have not appreciated fully the strong pull of the temperance cause in reform circles. Although Mari Jo

Buhle recognized Willard's tactical genius in moving women step by step into a broad reform program via temperance, as well as the importance of the temperance movement in recruiting and training women activists, she regarded the WCTU's goal of "ending the liquor traffic" as "unusually anticlimactic" compared with the breadth of the Union's other aims.[14] Mary Earhart, in her biography of Willard written in the 1940s, was almost embarrassed by Willard's devotion to temperance, a cause that seemed too trivial to be worthy of the talent, energy, and commitment of this remarkable leader.[15] As recently as 1979, a study of Julia Ward Howe excused her devotion to the temperance movement as Howe adopting "the tenets of her father's creed."[16] He was a temperance man, as if this were somehow an unworthy plank in Howe's political credo. Actually Howe embraced temperance as essential to reform and would have done so regardless of her father's beliefs. Temperance was seen as crucial to social change by most nineteenth-century reformers. Howe, Mary Livermore, Susan B. Anthony, Clara Barton, and other candidates for "revered woman" status in the late nineteenth century all actively supported the temperance movement, although temperance was for each of them a secondary commitment with which they were less readily identified. Each was widely admired and respected in her own time, but did not attract Willard's level of fame or adoration. Willard, as the undisputed queen of temperance, was the undisputed queen of American womanhood.

Willard's fame among her contemporaries rested partly on her being a temperance stalwart in a felicitous time, but her attitudes about women also reflected the values of her era and contributed in no small measure to her stature among her contemporaries. The United States was a society that cherished the idea of women's special sphere of responsibility, the home and the nurture of children.[17] Frances Willard enthusiastically shared this belief in the tenets of the cult of domesticity. She extolled its celebration of women's special virtues, and she added her own corollary, a corollary shared by increasing numbers of women as the century moved into its final decades, that women must use their special virtues to uplift the public sphere and imbue politics and citizenship with the righteousness and purity so peculiarly their own. Students of women's history are in general agreement that the doctrine of spheres took women by inexorable steps into the public arena. The first step was of course to emphasize women's role in the church, where they had always been.[18] If women were the cornerstone that upheld moral character in the home and a major vehicle for supporting the work of the church (the church by its very nature being a quasi-public institution), the rationale for extending women's sphere to other public

activities was already there, and in one way or another the spheres
doctrine was so used throughout the nineteenth century.[19]

However, Frances Willard greatly accelerated and popularized the
process.[20] If woman was the embodiment of moral superiority and the
acknowledged repository for the true, the good, and the beautiful,
Frances Willard more than any other woman became in the popular
mind by 1890 the apotheosis of that ideal. Her obituaries confirm this.
The *Brooklyn Eagle* wrote that "her mental faculties were not cultivated
at the expense of the gentler side of her nature"; a Canadian newspaper
stated that "She was above all a good woman"; other obituaries mentioned "her womanly feelings," "her lofty exemplification of womanly
virtue."[21] Willard's canonization as St. Frances was the result of her
careful manipulation of the doctrine of true womanhood as well as her
association with temperance. Had she been less willing to embrace
eagerly the accepted values of the day, her fame in her own lifetime
would hardly have surpassed that of Anthony, Stanton, or Howe. Part
of the reason for her almost universal acceptance by men and women
alike was that Willard herself, despite her devotion to public service,
always preached "Womanliness first—afterwards what you will."[22] This
was a key verse in the gospel according to Saint Frances. A generation
later Charlotte Perkins Gilman saw things differently. To her the priorities went, "the world's life first—my own life next. Work first—love
next."[23]

Historians of women have been quicker to grasp the importance of
Willard's use of the doctrine of spheres to move women into public life
than they have been to understand the centrality of temperance. Ellen
DuBois early attributed the WCTU's popular success to the fact that
women felt comfortable with activism and protest only if it was based
in the private sphere, if it took as its starting point women's position
within the home.[24] Barbara Epstein believed that Willard's use of woman's sphere was important, but she also believed (somewhat ambiva-
lently) that Willard's dual support of conventional morality and wom-
en's equality was inconsistent because eventually female equality would
require restructuring the family, and Willard's home protection doctrine implied defense of the male-dominated family structure.[25] Mari Jo
Buhle recognized the importance of sphere ideology to women's activism, pointing out that even socialist women "clung to" the home "as
the traditional source of women's power."[26]

Perhaps the affinity women historians felt for the importance of the
sphere doctrine in moving women into public life reflects a phenome-
non they observed in conservative women of their own time. It is
possible to argue that, in her emphasis on the "womanly" approach to

public activity, Willard was an antecedent of Phyllis Schlafly, and that the WCTU, with its emphasis on a closely delineated moral code and the glorification of womanhood, was the ancestor of Schlafly's following.[27] But was Frances Willard a conservative? Or was her emphasis on womanliness a way to clothe new answers in old garments? Willard differed from Schlafly in that she kept women pushing for equal rights rather than retreating into domesticity by forging a major link, temperance, between devotion to the home and public work by women. She resembled Schlafly in that she repeatedly emphasized that women's home role was important. Also like Schlafly she made public life her own sphere and urged other women to join her in her organizing efforts while at the same time she celebrated domesticity.

Willard's devotion to home and womanliness was paired with radical social ideas. Like many of the women in her movement, she was on the cutting edge of reform. Edward J. Wheeler did not call her a Christian Socialist without good cause, nor was her cremation an odd note in a medley of nostalgia for the good old days. Willard used conservative values to promote radical ends.

Nevertheless, the respect for conservative values was there. Willard did not phrase her demand for the expansion of women's public role in terms of equal rights until late in her life when her own movement pushed her in that direction, and when activist women generally were more ready to embrace that position. By 1894 the WCTU clearly advocated the women's ballot, and the impetus had come first from the state unions.[28] But the home protection ballot, as Willard popularized it in the 1870s and 1880s, was hardly a call for women to exercise their inalienable right to vote as citizens of the republic. Instead, she asked that "the mothers and daughters of America" have a voice in the decision by which "the door of the rum shop is opened or shut beside their homes."[29] When Willard championed the ordination of women and their equal participation with men in church governance, she spoke of the "refinement, sympathy, and sweetness of the womanly nature" that "fits women especially for the sacred duties of the pastoral office."[30] The clothes she wore at her public appearances were always modestly appropriate, but she was quite amenable to a becoming touch of lace at the neck or a subtly flattering color. Men as well as women noticed and responded to these concessions to femininity. She eschewed strident language. One of her speeches was described as "almost a poem."[31] Her addresses extolled the home and women's work in it.

Willard co-opted the domestic sphere and skillfully manipulated it to serve her broader ends. But her vision, unlike Schlafly's, was not conservative. She had no interest in maintaining the status quo or turning

back the clock to some simpler time. Instead she was, if anything,
overoptimistic in her zeal to find innovative solutions to age-old problems. It was this meld of womanliness, Christian Socialism, equal
rights, and concern for nurturance that made the Willard ethos tick.
Here lay the key to her political success, her ability to make public work
by women acceptable, even desirable, to large numbers of men and
women. Temperance like church work was considered a proper womanly arena, one in which women's role had always been accepted. By
tying suffrage, women's rights, prison reform, and a dozen other causes
to temperance Willard made it possible for large numbers of women to
move easily into the public sphere by 1890.

The career of Frances Willard illustrates the nineteenth-century
woman's dependence on family. Nineteenth-century middle-class wom-
en felt secure in their positions as part of the domestic sphere. Willard
encouraged them to do so. Dependence on family, the need for family
support, and in turn the support of home and family were woven into
the very movement Willard personified. She provided women with the
means to link family needs with the public sphere. She gave to her
organization the ultimate lever to wrest the public voice from the quiet
private admonition in her rallying cry, "Home Protection." And she
echoed women's everlasting dilemma in the slogan, "Do Everything."

Willard achieved her fame for very good reason. She rode the crest of
women's rising ambitions in the nineteenth century, women's need to
share in the increasing democratization of the great republican experiment; at the same time, she recognized women's need for the security
women's special place in the domestic sphere could provide. She gave
women and the men who sympathized with them the best of two
worlds. She preached and personally exemplified a womanliness and
domesticity that did not challenge existing cultural values, but through
the vehicle of a militant temperance organization designed as a vital
protection for the home and children she permitted women to do
whatever they wished in the public sphere and compelled men to praise
them for it.

Willard struck a lesser note that also contributed to her place in the
late nineteenth-century world. Her optimism about society, that society
was capable of being changed for the better, that it could be made just
and equable, unrealistic as these views seemed by the late twentieth
century, was a common credo not only for reformers but also for many
conservatives at the end of the nineteenth century. Her optimism, if not
always her considered belief, was invariably the rhetoric of her public
utterances and also suited the temper of her time.

Nevertheless, Willard's triple emphasis—womanliness, the pivotal role of temperance in her reform program, and her complete faith in progress—doomed her to obscurity by the mid-twentieth century. In the new militant age of the 1960s Frances Willard represented unpopular, almost trivial, causes.

Again by the 1980s the popular attitude toward at least one, possibly two, of the once widely held values that doomed Willard to oblivion had shifted. Society now looked at alcohol abuse with growing concern, even alarm, and recognized drug addiction generally as a major social problem demanding a public as well as a private solution. Whereas in the 1950s and 1960s Prohibition was viewed as legislation of morality and an invasion of individual rights, by 1980 legislative solutions were again being considered as an aid to alcohol regulation. As early as 1979 testimony before the United States Senate Subcommittee on Alcoholism and Drug Abuse recommended that alcohol marketing and distribution practices be examined with a view to legislation, and argued that alcohol regulation was not a threat to civil liberties or personal rights.[32] Witness also the campaign for toughening laws against drunk driving, much of it spearheaded by grass roots women's organizations. The very name of the largest, Mothers Against Drunk Driving (MADD), called on motherhood to put things right. New legislative restraints on personal habits were not confined to alcohol. Smoking received its share of regulatory consideration. Simultaneously, the nineteenth-century temperance movement was the recipient of almost more than its share of scholarly attention and again treated as an integral part of the reform tradition.[33] The American campaign against demon rum was no longer an embarrassment, but a possible source of lessons to learn on how and how not to proceed as a society in addressing a major social problem.

At the same time feminists began to reexamine their attitudes toward women's role in the home and family. Betty Friedan's *The Second Stage* supplied the popular version of this feminist soul-searching.[34] Jean Elshtain's *Public Man, Private Woman*, along with her other writings, provided a more theoretical and scholarly look. These two books were part of a growing literature that reexamined the male-female equation and women's role in the family with much more sympathy for traditional values, reaffirming the nineteenth century's willingness to accept differentiation between men and women and rediscovering traditional feminine qualities, especially those associated with mothering and protection of the family.

The rhetoric of the new conservative feminism, as one critic has called it, was more restrained.[35] For example, what the nineteenth century called a "maternal struggle" or "organized Mother-love" Friedan

saw in 1981 as the "feminine mode."[36] But Willard and Friedan shared
the hope that both men and women would make use of supposedly
feminine qualities, "the sensitive, tender, intuitive, life-cherishing values," as Friedan called them, to improve society.[37] In a similar strain
Willard spoke and wrote frequently about her fervent hope that "in the
larger home of Society and Government, women's powers will be most
beneficently exercised to help bring in the reign of universal peace,
purity and brotherhood."[38]

Meanwhile, Frances Willard had proved during her lifetime that it
was possible to use successfully the prevailing values of her time to
advocate change and movement rather than further entrenchment of
the status quo. She used these prevailing values to maximize her influence. The extent of her success can be measured by the way society
celebrated her life at her death. Willard's canonization by her contemporaries was the result of her successful manipulation of the doctrine of
true womanhood, her leadership of the popular temperance cause, and
her optimistic world view.

Chapter II   Origins

Frances Willard was born in Churchville, a small village near Rochester, New York, in September 1839. In her autobiography,[1] she labeled herself "a welcome child," a fair assessment considering that her thirty-five-year-old mother had recently lost two infant children, including a fourteen-month-old daughter who died a year before Frances was born. Mary Hill Willard idealized this baby and mourned her deeply, describing her later to Frances as a "vision of delight," with "eyes full of light and comprehension" and a "disposition without a flaw."[2] Because she was seen as a replacement for the beloved child who had died, Frances must have carried a heavy burden at times, accounting perhaps for some of her lifelong need to strive and excel.

The new daughter was named Frances Elizabeth Caroline, Frances after Frances Burney, the English novelist and member of Samuel Johnson's circle, and Frances Osgood, the American poet. Frances was obviously a name heavily laden with Mary Willard's own aspirations. Caroline Elizabeth (Caroline for her father's youngest sister; Elizabeth for her mother's sister) had been Mary Willard's third baby's name. Possibly reversed for luck, these two names were now bestowed on Frances, who was actually called Frank, a common nineteenth-century diminutive for Frances.[3]

Although Frances Willard was a thorough Midwesterner, she derived from New England stock. She was descended from Simon Willard, an English Puritan convert who at age thirty-one settled in Massachusetts Bay where he became a prominent member of the seventeenth-century colony. But the branch of the family from which Frances was directly descended moved to New Hampshire and embraced the Baptist faith in the eighteenth century.[4]

Her mother's ancestry is somewhat more obscure. The first Hill probably arrived in America as early as 1636. Her maternal grandfather, Nathaniel Thompson, was a Baptist sea captain who settled in New

Hampshire early in the eighteenth century, and Mary Hill Willard was raised in the Freewill Baptist church, a sect that arose on the New England frontier in the late eighteenth century.[5]

Although Frances Willard came from mildly distinguished New England families and some of her ancestors had been among the first Englishmen to settle on American soil, her forebears and immediate family were not the illustrious kin of a Henry Adams, Catharine Beecher, or Charlotte Perkins Gilman. The Willards and Hills produced no revolutionary heroes or Federalist presidents, but they made worthwhile if not impressive contributions to their society and culture. Emma Willard, mid-nineteenth-century educator, was a distant cousin by marriage, as was Elihu Root, jurist, senator, and statesman at the turn of the century. Frances Willard later coveted a bit of distinction for her forebears and carefully investigated her genealogy, making the most of what talent and fame she unearthed. But the relatives she personally knew and who were close to her were essentially solid country folk, not the eminent or wellborn. Moreover, there was no performer or publicist among them who might have served as role model for her later career.

Willard's interactions with her parents point more meaningfully to the directions her life was later to take. Her immediate family was close-knit, especially during the years in rural Wisconsin where the outside world impinged little on the family circle. However, Willard's father, Josiah, was always active in public life.

Originally a Democrat, he joined the Free Soil party at its birth and was elected to the Wisconsin legislature under its banner in 1848. He was instrumental in obtaining legislative support for the State Institution for the Blind, and served on its board of trustees for many years. He was president of the society that ran the county fair and a prominent member of the Wisconsin Agricultural Society, introducing Abraham Lincoln when he addressed its members in 1859. Josiah's interest in horticulture and natural science was lifelong. He always carried a magnifying glass, tape line, and pocket thermometer, constantly measuring the girth of trees, the temperature of air and water, and the microscopic life of the nearby pond, observations he faithfully transmitted to the Smithsonian Institution in Washington, D.C. During most of his life he was a successful businessman and farmer, despite a restless streak that had him changing location and occupation at regular intervals.

Josiah Willard's wife described him as "true in his friendships; devout in religion, honorable and exact in business relations"; "fond of nature and books"; "an amateur artist"; and an "appreciative student of

A.[ndrew] J.[ackson] Downing," a horticulturist who also served as mid-nineteenth-century America's architectural theorist and style setter.[6]

Anna Gordon, Frances Willard's first biographer and lifelong companion, who met Willard after Josiah's death but who certainly was exposed repeatedly to how the adult Willard perceived her father, described him as "elegant in person, and charming in manner," "devoutly religious," "an insatiate reader," and a man of "inflexible will, and unusual powers of thought and speech."[7] All these characteristics later would apply equally well to his famous daughter. Josiah Willard was versatile, intelligent, and certainly an intellectual, but those who knew him also agreed that he was a reserved, undemonstrative, somewhat irritable man whom one of his friends described as audacious in speech but conservative in action.[8]

In her autobiography Frances herself had little to say about her father and her relationship with him. The sketch labeled "Father" at the end of her memoirs began with a description of Josiah by her mother, recounted his public career as a horticulturist and legislator, and discussed most fully the prolonged illness that terminated in his death in January 1868 when Willard was a young woman of twenty-nine. At fifty she found it hard to reminisce freely about him. Willard viewed her father as a more distant figure than her mother, and never seemed to feel very close to or comfortable with him. When she wrote about Josiah she conveyed none of the intimate warmth, understanding, and love she expressed so fluently when writing about her mother.

Willard's diaries provide the key to how she really saw her father. He is revealed there as the manager, sometimes the autocrat, of the household. He made most domestic decisions, did all the family purchasing, and oversaw household expenditures in detail. He bought his daughters' clothes, school supplies, and rubber balls, and their mother's clothes as well. He was provident with books and periodicals. At the same time he held himself apart from his wife and daughters. Day after day Frances's diary records, "Father in forenoon writing, in afternoon at town."[9] He could be generous and he could withhold.

Josiah Willard interpreted open display of affection as weakness and told his small daughters at six and two and a half that they were now too old for bedtime kisses.[10] Willard deplored his coldness later in her life and believed her mother resisted his deprivations.[11] Frances behaved quite differently and quickly expressed physical affection as an adult. Although his daughter perceived Josiah as a man who found it hard to show his love, his wife described him as a "fine caretaker of the children, sharing with me far more than husbands usually do, or did in

Frances (*left*), at age 8 or 9, and her sister Mary Willard—from a daguerreotype made in 1837; shown in the original locket (frame). (Reprinted from Willard, *Nineteen Beautiful Years*)

those days, the work of bringing up our little ones."[12] He warmed and fed his infant daughter her midnight bottle, and both Josiah and his son Oliver took an occasional turn in the kitchen.[13] Male and female roles were not clearly defined in the Willard household, and Frances carried this family pattern into her adult years.

Willard's relationship with her father was complicated. Her childhood diary is full of temperature and weather observations emulating his careful work for the Smithsonian. She followed him into public life, and in that sense again used him as a positive example. However, as a child and young woman she was never certain of his support, especially when she moved into the public sphere. He resisted sending his daughters away to school. He opposed Frances's decision to teach and forbad her studying in Europe with a friend, but he also shepherded her on a trip to New York to find a publisher for her first book and escorted her to every teaching job she had while he was alive. During her childhood Josiah Willard made no secret of his much deeper affection for Frances's younger sister Mary, who died at nineteen, a loss Josiah found almost unbearable.

Willard admired and respected her father and strove for his approval, but she could not look to him for warmth and affection. It was her mother who offered understanding and love and who fully shared her early aspirations and disappointments and her later fame.

Mary Hill Willard was an intelligent, warmhearted woman. She functioned as her daughter's lifelong confidant and companion, and in the process embellished her role as mother to a celebrity with considerable talents. She sang and played the melodeon, and she was a good speaker who could turn a felicitous phrase in her later years when her famous daughter catapulted her into the public arena.

Mary Willard was also a facile writer, as demonstrated by long quotations from her journal cited in *Glimpses of Fifty Years*. Anna Gordon, who lived in the Willard household for many years, commented that her mind was "stored with much of the best English prose and verse" which she frequently recited.[14] She had been a schoolteacher for eleven years before her marriage and remained a teacher throughout her life. She tutored her daughters on the Wisconsin farm and spent her evenings teaching more than one illiterate farmhand to read and write. Later in Evanston she taught her Swedish servants reading, writing, and arithmetic and eventually expanded her little class to include five neighborhood domestics.[15] Mother Willard was an easy taskmaster. She encouraged her daughters to keep journals, an assignment they enjoyed, rather than demanding they write formal essays.[16] She did not force housework on them. She never said, "You must cook, you must sweep, you must sew."[17] The Willard girls were allowed to do what they wished within reason.

Frances Willard never severed her intimate affectional ties with her mother, and she surrounded herself with affectionate admiring women for the rest of her life. Willard's relationships with men were frequently amicable and productive but occasionally stormy. On the whole, she admired and respected men as she had admired and respected her father. But she opened her heart to women and clung to them for comfort and affection as she had clung as a child to her mother. As a young schoolteacher living away from home, she confided in her journal, "I thank God for my Mother as for no other gift of his bestowing. My nature is so woven into hers, that I almost think it would be death to me to have the bonds severed to one so much myself."[18] And Mother Willard found in Frances an outlet for her own aspirations. She later said, "I had many ambitions but I disappeared from the world that I might reappear at some future day in my children."[19]

Willard's early relationships with both her parents contributed to her effectiveness in her public career. Both her mother and father were ambitious, conscious of the outer world, and felt keenly their social responsibilities. Josiah's commitment to politics and public service was lifelong, but Mary Willard was far from a simple homebody. She taught school for many years and attended college as a wife and mother. In her widowhood she was an eager participant in public causes. Like mother, like daughter.

IN 1841 when Willard was two her father sold his substantial farm and business interests in New York State, realizing a sizable capital, and moved the family to Oberlin where Oberlin College had opened its doors eight years before. Eager to make the ministry his profession, Josiah sought the professional training he had been denied in his youth. Oberlin was a pleasant interlude for Mary Willard, who in addition to giving birth to another daughter, Mary, enrolled in the college herself and participated in Lydia Finney's famous "mother's meetings." But in 1846 Josiah Willard abandoned his ministerial studies and moved his family to the Wisconsin frontier. The previous year he had developed the symptoms of tuberculosis that were to plague him the rest of his life, and his doctor prescribed the clear air of the countryside and healthful outdoor life of the farmer as the most likely cure. Frances was to spend the next eleven years on the family farm near Janesville.

The Willards' Wisconsin farm was no tiny clearing in the wilderness, but a substantial enterprise. Originally 360 acres, it grew to a considerable estate of 1,000 acres by the time the Willards left Wisconsin in 1858. It was clear from Frances's journal that most of the time her father functioned as a gentleman farmer, and hired hands performed the physical labor. Although he occasionally put his hand to the plow, Josiah was interested in the entrepreneurial side of farming and in public service.

What kind of child grew to womanhood on the Wisconsin prairies? Looking back many years later, her mother saw Frances as "affectionate, confiding, intuitive, precocious and original" with an "exceeding fondness for books," a marked "bias toward certain studies and pursuits," and believing in "herself and her teachers." Perhaps she believed most in herself, for her mother added, "Even in the privacy of her own room she was often in an ecstacy of aspiration."[20]

In her autobiography Frances Willard considered herself mischievous, irreverent, and possessing a sharp tongue, all characteristics that bespeak self-confidence and independence, in contrast with her sister Mary who was tractable, noble, and good.[21] Mrs. Willard appears to have shared at least part of this assessment because she was quick to see in young Frances traits of her own father, who had a reputation for impatience and impetuosity.[22] In daguerreotypes taken at the time, Frances shows an eagerness and alertness, a sharpness and delicacy of features (chiseled cheekbones already in evidence), and a tilt of the head that resembles her mother. By adolescence she coveted the conventional beauty she saw in others, especially her sister Mary, and wept with discontent at what she saw as her own plainness,[23] although others did not describe her as unattractive.

Josiah Willard believed that "girls and women were to find their sphere in the home."[24] Although Oliver, who was four and a half years older than Frances, was sent to school in Janesville, the Willard daughters studied with their mother for several years. Eventually a neighbor who had been educated in eastern schools taught a class of four in the schoolroom at the Willard home.[25] Two years later a district schoolhouse was built, and a nearby farmer who had trained as an undergraduate at Yale and briefly tutored at Oberlin served as schoolmaster.[26] Still later the family moved to Janesville for part of a winter to permit the Willard girls to attend a private school, and Frances and Mary studied music and French one summer while living in their teacher's home. They also took piano lessons at the school for the blind near Janesville.[27] All of this added up to a spotty if reasonably adequate education. The Willard young ladies received little formal training in mathematics and the sciences, but they were exposed to the books their brother brought home from Beloit College, as well as to the strong intellectual interests of their parents.

Frances resisted housework throughout her life and her childhood was no exception. She did no cooking until she was fourteen and learned to sew and iron at fifteen.[28] Housecleaning was dismissed in her diary as "the scourge of mankind!"[29] But she was a capable carpenter who made carts, sleds, whip handles, and cross guns, while her sister Mary sewed and washed dishes.[30] Her fondness for male pursuits bothered her a little. She wrote, "I fixed my gun. It is queer that a girl

fifteen years old should like a cross gun but I can't help it."[31] Her
involvement with farm chores and agriculture was obvious from her journal. She records the daily work regimens of the four farmhands, comments frequently on the weather in relation to the growing cycle, and describes in vivid prose the process of breaking virgin prairie soil with the plow.[32]

Frances preferred her brother Oliver as a playmate, imitating his games and amusements, spinning tops, walking on stilts, climbing trees, tossing quoits, and shooting cross guns. His games and his ambitions she adopted as her own. Hunting, boating, swimming, and horseback riding were forbidden the girls, but after Mother Willard's intervention Frances was allowed to ride the family horses.[33] Frances Willard later believed that sexual equality was advanced by common activities, that it was "good for boys and girls to know the same things," so that men "shall not feel and act so overwise." A boy whose sister could harness the horse, row a boat, or do gymnastics "will be far more modest, genial and pleasant to have about" as a husband.[34] The free spirited Wisconsin fun indirectly nourished Willard's devotion to the woman question.

While Frances often followed Oliver and imitated his activities, she in turn took the lead with Mary, who was Frances's companion, schoolmate, friend, and confidant. Their relationship was especially close because in the early Wisconsin years they were completely dependent on each other. The nearest neighbors were a mile away, and there could be no school friends when there was no school. Nonetheless, the two children were rivals as well as friends. Mary died at nineteen and was promptly canonized by Frances in a volume called *Nineteen Beautiful Years*,[35] but as a child Frances certainly saw Mary as "her father's favorite beyond all competition."[36] Physically Mary was the beauty. Mary was also the "good" girl who excelled in womanly accomplishments and unquestioningly obeyed authority, parental or otherwise. Although Frances was not above envying Mary's softer feminine charms, she saw her younger sister as someone to love and cherish, not emulate. Oliver set her standards.

Frances Willard spent many childhood hours writing, perfecting a skill that was to be of great importance in her adult life. She composed in her own personal aerie, which she called "the eagle's nest," in the tall black oak standing by the front gate.[37] Her journal was not her only project. At sixteen she got up a small magazine called *The Tyro* and began a novel "Rupert Melville and His Comrades: A Story of Adventure," writing a page or two every day.[38] She wrote poetry that did not always scan but that frequently included vivid imagery, especially of the prairie and woods she knew so well. Already aspiring to publish, she sent many small pieces to local newspapers and farm journals with some success. Her sketches appeared in the *Prairie Farmer* and other rural periodicals. Rejection was hard for her to take but she kept her sense of humor: "What shall I do to the Editor for his stupidity in not being able to know true genius!!!"[39]

Willard may have been intellectually precocious in literature and composition, but she was socially and emotionally young for her age. She recognized this herself. When reviewing her life on her sixteenth birthday she described herself as "small for my age, both mentally and physically."[40] At a time when some girls thought of suitors and marriage, she and her sister were busy framing elaborate rules for a club called "The Artists" with a membership of two and improvising a studio partitioned from their schoolroom by old quilts in which to exhibit their own rough drawings and "a queer collection of pretty stones."[41] The protective isolation of rural life kept them children into adolescence.

Nonetheless, Frances was ambitious. The young woman eventually hailed as queen of temperance once aspired to be "Victoria's maid of honor, next I wanted to be an artist, and next again I wished to be a hunter, but returning from these deviations I've decided to be a music teacher, simply that and nothing more."[42] There were stirrings, however, of a search for wider horizons. She borrowed a women's rights paper and pronounced it "first rate."[43] Sometimes she found the monotony of rural life oppressive: "Was I made for nothing higher? Can I never soar?"[44] Her journal recorded the first time Oliver voted— "Father, Oliver, Mike and Henry gone to assist in saving the country"—but contained no reflections that Frances and her sister envied him that vote and wished to share it, embellishments she added in her autobiography.[45] Her diary also included a much briefer and simpler account than her autobiography of putting up her hair for the first time, calling the process "insipid" and bewailing the waste of time, but hardly implying the traumatic experience recorded in *Glimpses of Fifty Years* where she cried "loud and long," her "head aches miserable," and her spirit was stirred "into a mighty unrest."[46] The adult Willard wanted deeper rebellion in the child than really existed.

Willard had a happy childhood. She always looked back on the Wisconsin years as a joyous season and the best possible environment in which to raise children. She felt the same way as a young girl, writing in her journal, "I went down in the pasture and got up Jack and Grey [two horses]. I rode Grey and went with Oliver. Oh how I did enjoy it! How fast I lived. Grey was inclined to trot and trotted and galloped up hills and through valleys. . . . We didn't get back until almost dark—

such a good time! The memory even is enchanting, and I love to dwell
upon it. So noble with the fresh, free prairie breeze floating 'round
you! The golden sunshine resting on you. The soft dew falling, so
cooling! So beautiful, so pure, without a care, without a fear, without a
grief or pain."[47] Willard's childhood was very different than it would
have been in a more settled region. Isolation had nourished her independence and resourcefulness as well as her dependence on her family.

DURING a brief period, 1857–60, from her seventeenth to her twentieth years, Frances Willard received almost all her formal education. She
was the willing and enthusiastic beneficiary of the young ladies seminary movement that spread rapidly across the Midwest during the middle years of the nineteenth century when this brand of secondary education, often proprietary or church related, became widely available to
middle-class young women.

If the experience of Willard and her sister is at all typical, these young
women received remarkably good literary educations. They were encouraged to write well and copiously, not only in the course of their
formal schoolwork but also in journals and letters. They read widely; in
addition to the sentimental fiction and popular theology of the era,
they explored firsthand the ideas of its serious spokespersons such as
Emerson, Margaret Fuller, and the Beechers. They were exposed at
least superficially to botany, geology, and astronomy and learned a little
history and mathematics. Although their foreign language training was
minimal and they did not receive a thorough classical education, their
training probably compared favorably with the experience provided by
most degree-granting institutions of the time. Willard's diaries confirm
that her preparatory years produced a young woman whose mind had
been stretched by exposure to a great many fertile ideas, and her correspondence with her contemporaries shows that this experience was not
hers alone.

In the spring of 1857, when Frances was seventeen and Mary fourteen, the Willard daughters left home for school. They enrolled at Milwaukee Normal Institute founded six years before by Catharine Beecher, pioneer woman educator. Beecher aimed to provide training for
teachers in the West, and founded several schools of which the Milwaukee Institute (eventually Milwaukee-Downer College) was the only one
to survive.[48] Mary Hill Willard was a devotee of Catharine Beecher.
Beecher's *Domestic Economy* always lay on her bureau and its companion
volume, *Domestic Receipts*, was used in the Willard kitchen.[49] But the
real reason Frances and Mary were permitted to attend Milwaukee

Institute was that Mother Willard's sister had been engaged there as a teacher. Sarah Hill had already made two long visits to Forest Home, the Willards' Wisconsin farm, and contributed her talents to the improvised schoolroom. Now she would act as parental surrogate for nieces eager to join their aunt at college.

Frances Willard was happy in Milwaukee, and her heart ached when she returned home after a single term.[50] She studied geology, history, botany, and composition. She also made lifelong friends. But Josiah vetoed further schooling at Milwaukee. He had not been eager to send his daughters away to school in the first place. He had given in reluctantly to the importuning of the women in the family. Now he had changed his mind again.[51]

After that single term in Milwaukee Frances and Mary remained at home for a year, teaching briefly for a summer term in the local school.[52] Eager for further education, they finally persuaded their father to send them to Evanston where a proprietary women's seminary with Methodist connections had been established three years before. Although the school was eventually absorbed by Northwestern University, the two colleges had no formal ties at this time. However, the institutions were physically contiguous and considerable interaction took place. Despite its name, North Western Female College was at best a good preparatory school that included a self-styled three-year college course.[53] Frances enrolled in the college department, finishing in three terms, but she received no true degree. "Laureatte of science" was inscribed on her diploma, and only two students comprised her graduating class. Most of the school's eighty-one students were in the preparatory department.

Although she had no further schooling, Willard's formal education had been relatively thorough for 1860. She was well prepared in literature and the art of writing. She had a smattering of science and mathematics and some training in languages. She was surprisingly well grounded in philosophy and theology. She had read several provocative books as well as many third-rate productions with strong Methodist overtones. The mid-nineteenth-century ladies seminary had not served her badly, although teaching and travel would do much to expand her view of the world.

The ladies seminary not only provided Frances with formal educational credentials; it also contributed to her socialization and the development of her personal style. She later referred to her first semester in Evanston as her "harem-scarum period."[54] She chose for her special friend a Chicago resident, "the wildest girl in the school." Together they poked fun at the rules, perched themselves on the college steeple during study hours, and generally made mischief for the amusement of their classmates.[55] Nevertheless, the monthly reports to her parents (they have survived intact) show that she received excellent marks in her academic courses—chemistry, philosophy, trigonometry, and algebra.

Perhaps aware of her pranks or simply feeling young women should live at home, the Willard family left tenants on the Wisconsin farm and moved to Evanston in the late summer of 1858 so their daughters could be with them. The Willards were among Evanston's pioneer families.[56] Although Chicago was nearby, the village of Evanston had been laid out and platted only four years before; organized as a town in 1857, it was not to be incorporated until 1863. Northwestern University, which opened its doors in 1855, was the real reason for the town's existence. The Willards bought a house near Lake Michigan, where four Willards lived during the winter of 1858–59. Oliver was finishing his degree at Beloit, but joined them the next year to begin training for the ministry at Garrett Theological Seminary.

Willard asked her sister-in-law, Mary Bannister, a schoolmate at Evanston who later married Oliver Willard, to write a sketch for the chapter in *Glimpses of Fifty Years* that dealt with her North Western College days. Mary Bannister confirmed the madcap first term, that Frances was a leader of what she called "sport," and described her sister Mary as "conquering the hearts of teachers and pupils at once," "but Frances was at first thought proud, haughty, and independent." However, in recitations her "enthusiasm for knowledge and excellence" shone forth, and her schoolmates were impressed by her abilities as well as her nerve. She became the "leader of all the intellectual forces among the students."[57] Willard's diaries for 1858–60 confirm this assessment. She copied out long passages from the books she was reading—Carlyle, Emerson, Margaret Fuller, *Tom Brown's School Days*—and thoughtfully commented on the ideas they presented. She was a madcap schoolgirl, but she was also an intellectually curious young woman.

As a madcap Frances Willard occupied a special niche among the students. Mary Bannister noted that Frances was without a romantic interest among the young men at nearby Northwestern University. She took no "moonlight walks with 'University boys.'" Instead, "she came to be something of a 'beau' herself—a certain dashing recklessness about her having as much fascination for the average school girl as if she had been a senior in the University."[58] Willard had found another outlet for playing the male role she loved so well.

Willard's tomboy qualities were much modified later in her life. Both as a college president and as a temperance worker, she adopted "womanliness" as her trademark. However, this womanly woman appeared on platforms, addressed audiences numbering hundreds, organized, politicked, and played roles normally assigned in her society to men, roles that if played by women were usually assumed by unconventional rebels. Willard played the same male roles, but so effectively garbed herself in the trappings of womanhood that her femininity was not questioned. From a child she found male roles congenial. Eventually she performed them with such skill that she defused antagonism and only her womanliness attracted attention.[59]

At nineteen Frances Willard was bright, ambitious, capable. On the farm she had been allowed the freedom to pursue activities beyond the normal female sphere. She found it difficult if not impossible to become overnight a typical young lady with all the nineteenth-century feminine virtues. She inevitably attracted young women playing a restricted role who envied and admired her audacity. Willard's behavior need not be explained in purely sexual terms.[60] Crushes, best friend syndromes, girls who played the dashing beau have always been part of schoolgirl societies.

Mary Bannister Willard believed Willard's schoolmates saw her as "wild with the girls and doesn't care a fig for the boys."[61] It is true that Frances felt uncomfortable with young men at this time. After a gentleman escorted her to the "grammar party" (the end-of-term social bash), she reported, "I never enjoy 'mixed society.' I was not made, I am not fitted for it. I am, in this one respect, like Charles Lamb. He enjoyed the society of a few persons, his equals, and companions with whom he was well-acquainted and in whom he had entire confidence."[62] Eventually she had a number of male friends, but in late adolescence she was shy. The Wisconsin tomboy had yet to learn the ways of polite society.

While a student at North Western Female College, Willard read the memoirs of Margaret Fuller Ossoli. She identified herself with Fuller. In her journal she copied this extract from Fuller's second volume: "Among this band was the young girl who early taking a solemn view of the duties of life, found it difficult to serve an apprenticeship to its follies. She could not turn her sweetness into 'manner,' nor cultivate love of approbation at the expense of virginity of heart." Commenting on the passage, Frances wrote:

> Now in some respects I'm like that. I've no "sweetness" to lose, 'tis true, but I have some character, some individuality, instead. The last part of the quotation is like me as I would be. Books I

have, nature I have . . . I will learn drawing. Except, oh, I want a
young friend of my own age, nearby, who shall love me, understand me, bear with me! Often and often I have thought I had
such an one, but have found to my bitter regret that I was mis-
taken. The girls say I am fickle; I have always had that reputation
. . . and yet it is not my fault.

Emerson provided her with the answer: "Men cease to interest us,
when we find their limitations."[63] Beneath the madcap adventurer was
a lonely young woman. Independence, intimacy, and understanding are
difficult for all adolescents to achieve. And when Frances tried she was
disappointed. What she got wasn't good enough and she threw it away.

WILLARD's rebellion surfaced in an area more important to nineteenth-century life—religion. The Willards left the Baptists for Congre-
gationalism at Oberlin and became Methodists on the Wisconsin farm.
They were somewhat irregular churchgoers, but the family kept the
sabbath and always professed strong Christian beliefs. Frances at
twenty had not undergone a conversion experience, the mystical feeling
of received grace that the Methodist church taught was essential to
salvation, nor had she been christened, probably a relic of the Willards'
earlier Baptist ties. Her father had been converted at age twenty-nine
after a period of long indifference. Mary Hill Willard was converted as
a girl of twelve.[64] It was usual enough for a young woman of eighteen
to have not yet come to the altar for a lifelong commitment to Christ,
but at North Western Frances began consciously to probe her religious
beliefs. She had doubts when she arrived at school, confessing "I don't
know if I am a Christian or not."[65] She was not shy about announcing
her doubts, and thereby shocked the school community. A school
friend reported, "She won't confess that she knows or believes anything. She says she doesn't know whether there is a God, and she
doesn't know whether the Bible is true;—she is trying to find out."[66]
Willard, who had read William Ellery Channing's defense of Unitarian-
ism, was skeptical of revival enthusiasm: "I'm afraid I will never be
converted. I think I shall never be moved by these meetings."[67] For a
while she absented herself from prayer meetings. Her attitude distressed her teachers, and William P. Jones, president of the Female
College and a man she greatly admired, discussed her aberrations publicly at a college prayer meeting and asked for prayers on her behalf. She
was understandably upset. As she saw it, he called her "an infidel, and I
considered myself to be an inquirer."[68]

Soon after this public rebuke the college was deep in another revival season, a frequent component of the Evanston scene, and Jones urged her to go to the altar. Although she still had doubts, she consented to please him. But her hypocrisy troubled her. When she returned from the meeting that evening she wrote Jones a long letter, a letter he saved and made available to her thirty years later when she was writing her autobiography. Her message to Jones was unequivocal:

> I thank you very much for the interest you manifest in me and at the same time I feel very guilty. I do not think you know how hard my heart is, how far I am from feeling anything. I see I have no excuse to offer for my conduct. Three facts stand out before me as facts, nothing more. . . . I am a great sinner; it is a sin greater than I can comprehend to doubt God. . . . The third fact is that I am as cold as an iceberg, as unconcerned as a stone. I am not proud of it, I am not ashamed of it. I view it simply as a truth. . . . If I were to pray, I should say, if I were candid, "Oh God, if there be a God, save my soul, if I have a soul!" . . . Ought I go to the altar, to kneel before the Christian's God, to hear the Christian's prayer, careless and unconcerned? Soon it will be expected that I speak in church. Congratulations will be numerous, that I have "returned to the fold," and my dark wicked heart alone shall know how far I have wandered, how hypocritical I am. I am willing to attend church, though it interferes very much with my progress in science. I am willing to go, if you think it will do any good, but until I feel differently, I *dare not* go to the altar again. When I do I will go unasked.[69]

Most likely Willard edited that letter very little when it was returned to her, and she published it in 1889. It is an amazing document, honest, candid, and thoughtful, and shows her willingness to take on her mentors and deal with them as equals.

She continued to live with her doubts for a few months more, but eventually she found relief. The experience is described in her autobiography. During a bout with typhoid fever in June 1859, she heard two voices, "One of them saying, 'My child, give me thy heart. . . .' The other said, 'Surely you who are so resolute and strong will not break down now because of physical feebleness.'" But she deferred to the first voice, committing herself: "'If God lets me get well, I'll try to be a Christian girl.' But this resolve did not bring peace. 'You must at once declare this resolution,' said the inward voice. Strange as it seems, and complete as had always been my frankness toward my dear mother, far beyond what is usual even between mother and child, it cost me greater

humbling of my pride to tell her than the resolution had cost of self-
surrender, or than any other utterance of my whole life has involved."[70]

illness, Willard was not keeping a journal at this time. When she resumed her diary that summer she did not mention this incident although she referred to her illness, her graduation in absentia, and her
inability to read her valedictory. Was the experience too sacred to write
about? Or, at fifty, did she embroider on a late adolescent conversion
experience that meant much less to her at the time?

Six months later, in January 1860, Willard formally united with the
Methodist church and prayed earnestly "that I might never falter in the
new life."[71] Willard was not to doubt publicly again. She embraced the
church easily and remained a Methodist in good standing the rest of
her life. She was now able to handle her doubts, but her independence
remained. A few days after her public commitment she made a remarkable entry in her diary:

> I have united with the Methodist church because I like its view of
> the doctrine taught in the Bible, better than those of any other
> branch of God's militant church, because I have been reared in it,
> and for me to attach myself to any other would cause great sor-
> row and dissatisfaction in quarters where I should most desire to
> avoid such consequences. . . . [but] Before I ever declared myself
> determined to live, being helped by God, a Christian life, I re-
> solved to educate myself in an unsectarian spirit. I honestly be-
> lieve that I regard all churches, the branches rather of the one
> Church, with feelings of equal kindness and fellowship.[72]

At twenty she was a free enough spirit to be able to state the ecumenical position toward Christianity she was to articulate publicly in middle
age.

FRANCES Willard also showed her independence by articulating a
growing, if hesitant, feminism. "Feminism," of course, was a term unknown to the mid-nineteenth century. "Woman's rights," "the woman
movement," "the woman question" were the terms used to describe the
growing discontent of women with unequal rights and status.[73] Frances
had been attracted to the woman movement from childhood, and her
tomboy ways, her eagerness to participate in her brother's games and
chores, indicated she would find it difficult to fit the established gender
patterns of the mid-nineteenth century.[74]

At North Western Female College Willard began tentatively to spell out her feelings about sex roles and to suggest that society defined them unjustly. After reading a story in *The Methodist*, a church periodical, she commented in her journal:

> I don't like Harry's ideas about a wife obeying her husband. That I scout wherever I see it. I do not think I am unreasonable; I think I have good grounds for my belief. If I truly believed that the fifth chapter of Ephesians (twenty-second to twenty-fourth verses) was to be understood literally and applied to *me*, if ever I'm any man's wife, I should think the evidence sufficient that God was unjust, unreasonable, a *tyrant*. . . . It may seem wrong to others. It is *my* think and I have a right to it. That right I will maintain.[75]

The delineation of sex roles in marriage certainly concerned her at this time, and she looked for models that fit her beliefs. Such a model was provided by the president of Northwestern University. After attending a party at his home, she reported: "when I see his beautiful home life and home character, when I see him leaving his guests to relieve his wife from the care of a fretful child, when I see him rocking back and forth and murmuring a song to soothe the child to slumber. . . . I have a more exalted opinion of Dr. Foster than of any other living man."[76] Unquestionably the sharing of domestic responsibilities, generally conceded at the time to belong exclusively to women, appealed to her.

Whereas Willard had begun to delineate how she felt about women's position in marriage, she found it more difficult to judge women's position in society. She had doubts about the status quo, but she was still groping for answers: "Men grow learned, and good, and great. . . . They ponder and delve and discover. . . . Women suffer and grow uncomplaining in toil and sacrifice and learn that life's grandest lesson is summed up in four simple words—'Let us be patient'. . . . Public opinion, which is the mouthpiece of society, asks not of any man: 'When did you do this, where did you accomplish it?' but 'What have you done? We do not care for the process, give us the results.'"[77] Although her thoughts were a bit muddy, Willard was reacting to the doctrine of spheres, observing that men could act freely at places and times of their choosing and be judged only by their accomplishments, whereas women had to answer for how, where, and when they made their influence felt rather than being judged by the results of their actions. This hardly added up to a coherent feminist philosophy, but the first faint stirrings were there.

Her concern about spheres was paired with ambition, and she again looked to Margaret Fuller as a model: "Here we see what a woman

achieved for herself. Not so much fame or honor, these are of minor importance, but a whole character, a cultivated intellect, right judgment, self-knowledge, and self-happiness. If she, why not me, by endeavoring."[78] At about the same time Willard prepared her valedictory address where she wrote, "Advancement is directly proportional to effort." She used the analogy of a man standing on a mountain who can see so much more than one standing at its base, "but eminence is not provided for him, he is to reach it by his own efforts." "Discipline, observation, close thought were the blocks, the granite of the mind" with which the edifice was built.[79]

That summer nothing went right. Typhoid kept her from reading her valedictory. Her father was urging her to become a music teacher. Her mother was discouraging her from studying the classics. She did not want to be a genteel lady musician with a few pupils she taught at home, and she wrote, "Have I told you [her journal] I was going away to earn my own living, fight my own battles, and be a felt force in the world?"[80] Frances would escape it all by finding a school where she could teach.

Chapter III  Choices

Approximately fifteen years passed between Frances Willard's graduation from North Western Female College and her professional association with the temperance movement and the WCTU. By 1874 Willard was among the leading woman educators in the United States and head of the women's division of a well-known midwestern college. Her career line seemed clearly delineated, and there was reason to believe she would continue as an educator for the rest of her working life. But at the beginning of this period she saw no such obvious path ahead, and when she looked back later she regarded the first year out of school as "perhaps the most difficult in a young woman's life."[1]

By 1860 Willard had resolved her religious doubts to her own satisfaction and possessed a more than adequate education by the lights of her time. Her father's banking business was prospering, and the family was in comfortable financial circumstances. Nonetheless, she was depressed and uncertain what course she should take. That fall she wrote in an extended journal entry: "I used to think myself smart. I used to plan great things that I would do and be. I meant to be famous, never doubting that I had the power. But it is over. The mist has cleared away and I dream no longer, though I am only twenty-one. . . . I think myself not good, not gifted in any way. I can not see why I should be loved. . . . Never before in all my life have I held myself at so cheap a rate." But her intermittent surges of ambition were not completely absent: "It is a query with me, however, whether really I amount to so little as I think."[2]

She proceeded to catalog her strengths and weaknesses. She was almost eager to admit she was "not beautiful, pretty or even good looking." But also she "was not disagreeable or unpleasant, either in face or figure," her expression "resolute" but guarded. She was moody but "generous, in a spasmodic way" and careful not to wound the feelings of others. She had "a good mind," "quick perceptions," "some

facility as a writer," and "perhaps if you keep your eyes wide open to
your faults, [you] may yet come to be rather good than bad."³ This was
an honest assessment, but it provided no practical pattern for the rest
of her life. Writing at great length in her journal and an occasional
piece for publication in sundry newspapers filled many empty hours.
She read a great deal and took some responsibility for housework. She
was not really idle, but at heart she felt empty and useless.

For the next year, Willard tried to solve her problem by teaching
school, the one occupation other than writing clearly open to young
women. She taught two separate terms at Harlem (now River Forest),
one of rural Cook County's one-room public schools, and a single term
in an academy at Kankakee, Illinois. Her father was not pleased with
her decision to go to work. She commented that he "naturally felt
humiliated."⁴ She thought he feared others would think he could not
support her, although his financial capabilities were certainly not in
question. But her acceptance of his attitude as "natural" shows she
agreed on some level with common attitudes of the day. Frances's devotion to independence and the woman question was still somewhat
tenuous.

In between the two stints at Harlem in the summers of 1860 and 1861,
Frances worked during the fall term of 1860 as an assistant teacher at
Kankakee Academy, which was owned by friends of the Willard family.⁵
To the latter post she brought with her, borrowed from her brother
Oliver, Scott's *Bride of Lammermoor*, D'Aubigne's *History of the Refor-
mation*, and the first volume of Bohn's edition of Plato.⁶ As she was to
teach philosophy, history, grammar, and all the reading classes, her little
library must have proved a godsend.

The Kankakee Academy was a better school than Harlem. Her pupils
were more advanced and she could anticipate the support and companionship of colleagues. Nonetheless, Willard seems to have had misgivings about accepting the post. She felt apprehensive about being separated from her family, and wondered "why I go away to this new work
so soon. I cannot tell. I only know that I have some dim sense that it is
right and best." When her father, who had escorted her to Kankakee,
boarded the train for home, she put on a "broad grin" through "sheer
strength of will" and told herself "to try not to cry once while I am
here, for I am twenty-one."⁷ But of course she did cry, not that day but
later when she wrote her sister Mary, "Remember that I shall never live
with you all at home again," and "will have a sterner life than you will
know about." She would live at home again, but in Kankakee, frightened and brave at the same time, she had to convince herself that she
was "competant to work and work I will."⁸

Nonetheless, Willard stayed only a single term. She did not return after the Christmas holidays "owing to the urgent wishes of my parents."[9] As early as November her mother insisted that she "spend the winter at home and not return here again. I cannot tell, it will be just as I take a fancy, but as I go through the cold and frost and bear many unpleasant things and hear unjust words sometimes, I often wonder that I do not stay at home where they love me and where I am warm and comfortable."[10] She seemed happy enough to leave Kankakee for Evanston at Christmastime ("I am in my own dear little room once more") and doubted "there is a person living who has greater cause for thankfulness than I have."[11]

Young Frances was riddled with conflicts. She did not know if she wanted to laugh or cry, grow up or remain a child, exert her independence or cling to her family.

SHE also wrestled with the question of marriage. Did she want to marry? Was she attractive enough to catch a husband? Could she endure replacing one set of affectional relationships, which held and nurtured her even when she tried to break free, with an affectional bond that would be even more constraining? She was twenty-one and time was passing. Ever since graduation her mother had been urging her to marry, to "settle herself," using Aunt Sarah as an example of single misery.[12] Frances herself worried, "I think I am never to marry. I think I'm to go through the world single handed and alone. I think no man is ever to love me, ever to tell me I'm dearer to him than any other woman."[13] A few months later she lamented that she had "never been in love," had "never shed a tear, or dreamed a dream, or sighed, or had a sleepless hour for love." Instead, she "was too cautious, loved my own peace too well, valued myself too highly."[14]

A young man called frequently during the term at Kankakee. He taught her chess, a game she liked "exceedingly," and she found herself playing it "instead of reading history and the Bible."[15] And "after trivial foolish talk until twelve o'clock went to bed, to sleep, and dreams of dearer, holier things than we had talked of, for every heart knoweth its own sacred things, every heart hath its faces that 'it muses on apart.'"[16] Was she thinking of her chess-playing friend, her family, or something else? In any case, leaving her new friend behind seemed not to diminish her pleasure in going home.

Willard's return to Evanston led to one of the few serious male romantic attachments of her life. At her friends the Bannisters she met Charles Fowler, a fellow divinity student and friend of her brother, and found him "a beautiful talker." They walked home together and she took his arm.[17] They saw each other several times that spring before she

left for Harlem to teach. He bolstered her confidence: "I talk better
with him than with other persons; my knowledge seems more as
though it was held in solution in my mind."[18] In June Fowler accompanied her brother Oliver to Harlem where Frances was teaching and
Oliver was to preach. Fowler proposed on an afternoon walk and was
accepted. It was the "most blessed, beautiful event of all my life. . . . I
never felt so quiet, so perfectly at rest."[19] Willard returned home in July
expecting to marry.

That spring Fowler was graduated from the Theological Institute
(now Garrett Theological Seminary) and became minister of Chicago's
Third Methodist Church. The same year he published his first book,
The Fallacies of Collense. He would later become president of Northwestern University, editor of the *Christian Advocate*, and a Methodist
bishop, a man of no mean talents and a man who could have provided
Willard with security, station, and entry to the public arena as the wife
of a prominent educator, writer, and churchman. Fowler's biographer
described him as a man of keen intellect, flashing wit, and audacious
speech.[20] He was also handsome, brilliant, and strong-minded. Willard's family must have found her choice acceptable as would her
friends, all part of Evanston's Methodist inner circle. But in February
1862 she broke the engagement.

In her autobiography Willard is uncharacteristically reticent about
this aspect of her life.[21] When she wrote her memoirs in 1889, Charles
Fowler was a prominent Methodist leader, married, and father of a
young son. Good taste no doubt impelled her to keep silence about her
feelings, and she simply said that she broke with Fowler because she
was not prepared to abdicate her independence in a way that marriage
would have demanded.

Her relationship with Fowler was indeed troubled by her demand for
independence. Midway through the engagement she wrote, "What it
might be to give oneself up so fearlessly—somewhat as we do to God.
To feel the supremacy of a loftier, stronger nature. Oh! the sweetness of
it, the luxury of it! . . . Yet I do not feel quite sure that it is a possibility
of my nature ever to give myself up."[22]

The termination of Willard's engagement to Fowler is also linked to
the fact that in the late summer of 1861 her brother Oliver became
engaged to Mary Bannister, Frances Willard's intimate friend. This
event triggered severely troubled feelings in Frances, who found herself
insanely jealous of Mary's new relationship. She realized she should be
delighted at the prospect of her best friend joining the family circle, but
instead she was beside herself. Frances felt her troubled feelings meant

she was "wronging Charlie," and "that there is a Fate or Demon over me." She confided to her mother her anxiety about losing her place as Mary Bannister's primary emotional attachment and what this jealousy might mean to her relationship with Charles. Her mother assured her that it was normal and quite right for her and Mary to love each other as before,[23] but such assurances from almost everyone were not enough to put her mind at rest.

Frances had a great need for intimacy that until now she had always met through relationships with girls and women, her mother, sister, and a series of friends. Now she probably asked for the same level of intimacy from Charles Fowler, who may not have been able to commit himself in this way. Willard could not envision marriage or any love relationship without an extraordinary degree of intimacy, and it may well have been this need that doomed her engagement to Fowler. This would explain Willard's inability to come to terms personally with established nineteenth-century patterns of courtship and marriage, which often predicated formal and economic ties rather than strong emotional bonds. One historian has suggested that nineteenth-century courtship often removed intimacy from a relationship, at the same time preserving marriage, "the emotionally trimmed, functional marriage—as the goal."[24] This process made temperamental differences possible and acceptable in the marriage relationship. But Frances could not operate this way.

Whatever the reason, Frances decided she did not really love Fowler, and in February she returned his ring. She felt great relief: "I am just now, thoroughly happy and sufficiently content."[25] She quoted an older friend, "'For a woman to marry a man whom she does not love, is to make one man as good in her sight, as another; hence it is prostitution—more than that it is infernal.' Amen! and if I go alone and hungry to my grave, and spinster is written on my tombstone, I will at least stand before God in the next life, and tell him that I am guiltless of the crime [that] attends a marriage of convenience."[26]

In her autobiography Willard wrote, "How grieved I was over the discovery of my mistake, the journals of that epoch could reveal."[27] And the journals attest that she was indeed grieved if relieved. Willard admired Fowler a great deal and continued to admire him. In 1863 on her way to Pittsburgh she wrote, "went to hear Charlie preach, went to his study to see him in a friendly way. How smart he is, how good, how kind. Among men I have no better friend than he."[28] Nor was Fowler to drop out of Frances Willard's life. They continued to meet as friends in the 1860s, but clashed when both were Northwestern University administrators in the 1870s. A leading Methodist churchman and the leading Methodist laywoman could hardly avoid intermingled, if discordant, interests in the 1880s.

One thing is certain. When Willard broke her engagement with Charles Fowler she did not completely resolve her conflicts about marriage. A month later she wrote, "For a woman, I suppose, to love some man, better than anything else except the God who gave him to her, is the greatest good, if he loves her just as well. . . . I think I have missed this greatest good of a woman's life."[29] Poor Frances, once again the pendulum swayed.

She came close to marriage one more time. A young colleague at the Lima, New York, seminary where she taught in 1866 paid court to her. This relationship was less impetuous and precipitous. Whereas Willard became engaged to Charles Fowler within a month of his taking her arm, she took several months to permit this other relationship to mature. She may have accepted her Lima suitor as a potential husband at one time, but again she could not bring herself to marry,[30] although once more she protested, "He is very much my ideal man."[31]

Willard never relinquished the idea of marriage. Several years later while studying in Paris she wrote her mother, "I wonder whether I shall ever have a quiet home to which to welcome you. . . . I would have had my own nest long ago, but somehow that mate who should have helped me 'to weave it so, and lay the twigs across,' failed to appear."[32] Did that man appear at some later time? In her autobiography, after a brief allusion to her engagement to Fowler, she inserted these enigmatic lines: "Of the real romance in my life, unguessed except by a trio of close friends, these pages may not tell. When I have passed from sight I would be glad to have it known, for I believe it might contribute to a good understanding between good men and women."[33] The identity of this man is still unknown. The enigma persists.

During these crucial years when she attempted to sort out her life, Willard's inner turmoil was interwoven with external crises. Lincoln was elected the fall she was away from home teaching at Kankakee, and the secession crisis was developing at the time she decided to rejoin her family and not return to her post after Christmas. She accepted Fowler's proposal in early June 1861, after Fort Sumter and before the first battle of Bull Run, when patriotic fervor and undiluted optimism were sweeping antislavery circles in the North.

The Willards were Republicans and strongly antislavery. At fifteen Frances reported in her diary that a man was fined $1,000 for helping rescue a slave, commenting, "Shame on my country's laws."[34] Josiah and Oliver voted for Lincoln in 1860, and Frances rejoiced at the election results: "Lincoln is elected President of the United States. Hurrah!"[35] In April 1861, when Frances was back in Evanston, Sumter's evacuation evoked a frenzy of war hysteria in the town.[36] Oliver enlisted for one hundred days in a company formed by the theological students, a company never called up.[37] Quite probably Fowler was a member of the same company. When she accepted his proposal of marriage, Frances may have expected him soon to be under arms fighting for ideals that she shared. Frances herself wanted to volunteer as a nurse, but her father vetoed the idea.[38]

AT the time the Willard family also faced a personal crisis unrelated either to events in the outer world or to Frances's internal struggles and frustrations. Young Mary Willard was dying of consumption. Mary's health had been deteriorating since she suffered an acute illness, diagnosed as typhoid, while Frances was teaching at Kankakee Academy in the fall of 1860. In March 1862, just after the engagement with Charles Fowler was broken, Mary's fatigue and weakness forced her to take to her bed. She died in June.

Frances and Mary had always been close, a closeness fostered by their isolated childhood on the Wisconsin frontier, but a closeness that also reflected the duality of their personalities: Mary, the beautiful, feminine, submissive, always loving daughter; Frances the strong, independent, sharp-witted rebel. Frances both loved and envied Mary. She praised how "sweet and fair and fresh" Mary looked, but added that "I felt hurt when I looked at her."[39] As a young girl Mary was Frances's sweet, soft side, a side that Frances developed in her twenties after Mary's death. Although at first Frances's grief was acute and her life seemed to be falling apart, eventually Mary's death helped mitigate her conflicts. Willard never cut her primary ties to her family. She was particularly close to her mother, who lived almost as long as she did. A dutiful and affectionate daughter, Frances depended on her mother for major emotional sustenance until the very end, but it was a dependence that left her full scope and that she found fulfilling. After Frances became the *only* daughter, she could be herself. Slowly the doubts that had plagued her vanished. Her ambition was freed, and she followed her own star. She wrote later, "I have been called ambitious, and so I am, if to have had from childhood the sense of being born to a fate is an element of ambition. . . . I always wanted to react upon the world about me to my utmost ounce of power; to be widely known, loved, and believed in."[40]

With Mary's death Willard found it possible to pursue her career less hampered by obligations to her family. Eventually she saw ways to meld her career goals with her family's needs. Dependence on family and, in turn, support of home and family were woven into the very fabric of the temperance movement. Willard instinctively became the womanly rebel, the pious iconoclast, the feminine feminist. Her ability to blend the nineteenth century's deep commitment to womanly virtues with the demand for radical change in women's position was the quality that provided the underpinnings for her spectacular success. After Mary's death Frances adopted her sister's feminine virtues, blending them with her own ambitious rebellion. Complete catharsis and resolution came in 1863 when she wrote *Nineteen Beautiful Years*, the story of Mary's life and death.[41]

JOSIAH WILLARD responded to Mary's death by renting out the Willard home in Evanston. Its association with Mary made it impossible for him to live there. That summer he also sold the Wisconsin farm, leaving Frances, as she lamented, "for the first time in my life homeless" as well as "bereft."[42] Oliver, now married and an ordained Methodist minister, was in Denver, Colorado, serving his first church. Mother Willard traveled east to visit her family, and Josiah, tied to Chicago by business, boarded in the city.[43]

Frances solved the problem of her homelessness by returning to North Western Female College, "the scene of my girlish escapades," as the preceptress of natural sciences, "a teacher regularly installed in a ladies school."[44] Although occasionally depressed, she liked her new work, was pleased at her growing influence on her students, and cherished both the affectionate intimacy and intellectual exchange with her colleagues. She learned to "think of Mary dead just as naturally as I used to think of her alive," as Frances pushed "out all by myself into the wide, wide sea."[45] Sometimes the outer world and the war intruded. Lincoln's emancipation proclamation "thrilled me, one that I am thankful transpired in my experience."[46]

At North Western Willard felt challenged and fulfilled. Teaching in a country school had not really satisfied her. At Kankakee Academy she was too conscious of separation from her family to fully savor the experience. At North Western she found meaningful occupation. Her day as preceptress was arduous. Rising at six, she conducted devotions; taught advanced arithmetic, geometry, algebra, and universal history in the morning and elocution, geology, zoology, physiology, and minerals in the afternoon; and "then came upstairs and sat down in my rocking-chair as one who would prefer to rise no more."[47]

But Willard was a good teacher and she enjoyed teaching. She loaned her students books, generously let them absorb her limited free time to unburden themselves of their problems, and used innovative methods

Frontispiece and title page of Willard's *Nineteen Beautiful Years*, which she wrote a year after her sister Mary's death. (Reprinted from *Nineteen Beautiful Years*)

NINETEEN BEAUTIFUL YEARS;

OR,

Sketches·of·a·Girl's·Life.

—

By FRANCES E. WILLARD,

PRESIDENT OF THE NATIONAL WOMAN'S CHRISTIAN TEMPERANCE UNION.

WITH PREFACE
BY
JOHN GREENLEAF WHITTIER,

—

My darling! When thou wast alive with the rest,
I held thee the sweetest, and loved thee the best:
And now thou art dead, shall I not take thy part,
As thy smiles used to do for thyself, gentle Heart?
    —MRS. BROWNING.

—

CHICAGO:
WOMAN'S TEMPERANCE PUBLICATION ASSOCIATION.
1886.

in the classroom, such as having the students pose questions for the teacher to answer rather than the other way around.[48] A colleague described her as "bubbling over with wit and humor" while "at the same time . . . full of pathos and sentiment,"[49] by which she probably meant sympathy and affection.

Willard was twenty-three, independent, earning her own living and successful at her work although she still missed Mary. When a bout of depressive mourning hit in late 1862, an Evanston family friend arranged a position for her at another Methodist school, Pittsburgh Female College, a post she held through the winter of 1863–64. A change of scene was good for her, not that her recurring depressive mourning for Mary ever lasted long. She was too much in love with life for that. But Pittsburgh was different, introducing blackened men around glowing forges, murmuring swift streams, high wooded hills and rocky ledges in contrast to the great blue lake and undulating prairies. "I thank God for life—for life continued on this earth," she wrote.[50]

Ambition still nagged: "Why do you plan to go on teaching ad infinitum, to Pittsburgh it is, then Cincinnati (in your plans) and thence some other where? Why do you content yourself with such a hedged up life. . . . You have abilities for something beyond this. . . . Be determined to write books if you please."[51]

And write she did. The writing came easily during the summer vacation of 1863 when she finished *Nineteen Beautiful Years*. The family was back in the Evanston home, soon to be sold, including its furniture. Josiah needed to erase his memories of Mary completely. The old house was replaced in 1866 by a new Gothic revival structure, later dubbed "Rest Cottage," Willard's home for the rest of her life. But this summer was devoted to the old haunts, the room "where Mary died, darkened and left solitary."[52] No doubt the three Willards, together again, fed each other's grief, but Frances converted her bouts of mourning into positive accomplishment, working "almost constantly" "at Mary's book"[53] and traveling to New York in the early fall to arrange for its publication.[54] Sentimentality marred the volume's literary merit, but it was written in a sentimental age. Willard always wrote well. The words flowed with a sense of rhythm, and her use of her sister's journal entries provided a realistic touch.

In late 1865 and through the summer of 1866, after a brief stint of teaching in Evanston, Willard engaged in her first work for a public cause. She acted as corresponding secretary of the American Methodist Ladies Centenary Association, a national churchwomen's organization that was raising money to build Heck Hall, an addition to Garrett Theological Seminary. As Willard put it, this was her "first introduction

According to Anna Gordon, Willard as preceptress of Genesee Wesleyan Seminary, which would make her age 27. She was probably younger when this was taken (possibly at Kankakee) and the photo misdated by Gordon. (Reprinted from Gordon, *The Beautiful Life of Frances Willard*)

to a really public career."[55] She organized the campaign, produced a voluminous correspondence, "learned much about business and corresponding with dignitaries," and, not least in importance, put her name on all the certificates sent to contributors.[56] These hung on the walls of many of the nation's Methodists and provided her with name recognition that later proved invaluable.

In the fall of 1866 Willard accepted a position as preceptress of Genesee Wesleyan Seminary, the oldest and most prestigious academy sponsored by American Methodists, located at Lima, New York, not far from Churchville where her parents had spent their younger years. Genesee Wesleyan proved Willard's most satisfying teaching experience thus far. The school was coeducational, well established, and "with such history and traditions" as made it "attractive to me."[57] She liked her work and enjoyed her colleagues: "The days glide by, not very hard or easy in their work, . . . never had better occupation, worthier aims than now . . . have no prayers but grateful ones to offer."[58] Nonetheless, she spent a single academic year at Lima. She was eager to move on. This time the prospect of extensive transatlantic travel cut short her stay.

A YOUNG colleague from the Grove Street school where both women had taught in Evanston, Katharine Jackson, joined Willard on the staff of Genesee Wesleyan. The two women had become close friends. Jackson, an accomplished linguist who had taught French in Evanston, came to Genesee largely to be with Willard. Kate Jackson was one of the first of several adult women whom Willard made her intimates.

Willard's relationships with women continued as primary relationships throughout her adult life, although she never quite gave up the alternative of marriage. These women were intellectually and emotionally important to her and the major vehicle through which she expressed affection. Her immediate family was small, consisting of her mother, her brother Oliver, his wife, and eventually his four children. Her brother died when she was thirty-eight. Both her nephews had severe problems with alcohol and proved to be an increasing emotional drain, and her sister-in-law chose to live in Europe with her daughters for many years after Oliver's death. Her mother, of course, never ceased to be of primary importance to Frances. However, she did not have the large, relatively affluent family that the Beechers, for example, could draw on for support. Nor did she have the numerous multigeneration family friends who offered implicit stability for many of her New England contemporaries. Her women friends, in addition to her mother, provided most of her emotional support both in her personal life and in her work.

Willard's affectional ties with women moved through a pattern quite normal for her time—attachment to mother, love between sisters, adolescent crushes, and eventually mature, long lasting emotional attachments to women. Carroll Smith-Rosenberg has called these supportive relationships "homosocial." The security they gave Willard, sometimes including financial security as in the case of Kate Jackson, and always or almost always facilitating her work in the public sphere, contributed much to the achievements of her middle years.[59] Willard and Jackson remained lifelong friends. For several years they followed parallel professional careers. Jackson taught with Willard in Evanston, joined her at Genesee Wesleyan Seminary, took Willard with her to Europe, made her home briefly with the Willards in Evanston, taught at Northwestern's Woman's College when Willard was president and dean, and resided in Evanston for much of the rest of her life.

No doubt there were stresses in the relationship, especially in its early years when Jackson occasionally was jealous of other attachments formed by Willard, but the two friends never ceased caring for each other.[60] When the women first met, Kate was engaged to be married to a young Texan. The engagement was broken in the course of their journey abroad, but the presence or absence of that commitment had no discernible effect on the friendship of Frances and Kate. In Berlin Frances acquired a new friend, a young bride obviously enchanted by Willard. Frances in turn was delighted by the woman's admiration. However, she made conscious efforts to protect Kate from feeling supplanted, which indeed she was not, hiding her new friend's letters from Kate but not from Mother Willard.[61]

From time to time circumstances made one intimate friend more important to Willard than others, but her relationships with women were never exclusive. For example, Kate was not Willard's only intimate female friend at Genesee Wesleyan, for Frances wrote another colleague later, "What different worlds we have drifted into, dear Carrie, since those brief delightful days in Lima, in which we learned to care for one another!"[62]

The complexity of Victorian love relationships has been described as a spectrum of choices and is alien to our contemporary post-Freudian society. Smith-Rosenberg has argued that there was in the nineteenth century a female world, institutionalized by convention, in which intense and loving female relationships were a plausible and socially accepted form of social interaction.[63] Extending Smith-Rosenberg's thesis, Martha Vicinus and Estelle Freedman have observed that, as women took up professional careers in the second half of the nineteenth century, they found themselves torn between old expectations of marriage and children and their new roles and opportunities. A partial solution to this conflict was provided by close and intense friendships with other women.[64] Most Victorian women, married or single, tended to have special women friends, frequently family members, whose intimacy they cherished, and on whom they depended for support in life's crises.[65] The new professional woman also found the support these special relationships provided of crucial importance in carrying out her work. The spectrum of choices meant that in the nineteenth century no one looked askance at the devoted daughter who lavished care and affection on a widowed mother. The young married woman was not so exclusively involved with her husband that she could not cling to the companionship of a special woman friend who had shared the confidences of her youth. The bachelor son who devoted his life to his mother was not seen as an aberration. Victorian society provided many avenues in which supportive emotional relationships could take place. In the course of her life Willard made use of most of them except marriage, and her use of one did not exclude another.

As Smith-Rosenberg has pointed out, these relationships often included physical affection and were frequently passionate, at least as expressed in writing. Perhaps this passion can be accounted for by the nineteenth-century penchant for extravagant language, but there were real differences in the way language was used by the same people in different relationships. For example, Susan B. Anthony used passionate language in her correspondence with Anna Dickinson, nineteenth-century female orator, but never with Willard whom she certainly liked and admired.[66] Willard used passionate language in her letters to Dickinson and Dickinson returned in kind, but Willard talked content, not feeling, in her correspondence with Anthony. Both emoted with Dickinson but never with each other. Willard and Anthony both varied the nature of their relationships with different women.

Some historians have argued that, regardless of the presence or absence of overt sexual practices, "women who love women, who choose women to nurture and support" are lesbians.[67] Other scholars have been much less arbitrary, maintaining that identity—how the woman sees herself—is the crucial factor. Recent scholarship has demonstrated that the participants in these relationships did not regard them as sexual and that society viewed such friendships as "pure and ennobling."[68] If twentieth-century language is used, Smith-Rosenberg's term "homosocial" better describes nineteenth-century practice and how Victorian women viewed their relationships.

Most important in understanding nineteenth-century leaders, however, are women's relationships to each other in carrying out their work.[69] Without each other they could not have done what they did. Not only did the nineteenth century's tolerance of a wide range of affectional relationships enrich Frances Willard's personal life and provide her with emotional ties that substituted at least in part for the absence of husband and children, but this tolerant spectrum also helped her to achieve her public goals and make her influence felt on the world in which she lived.

Willard's experience is a telling illustration of the role of women's friendships in the lives of nineteenth-century women. First of all, Willard was a good user of networks, and her professional relationships were also her friendships. Among her primary attachments, Anna Dickinson alone failed to contribute to the temperance cause. Willard tried hard to get her support, and Anna did make her own unique, if indirect, contribution to Willard's work. But Anna was atypical in not supporting the temperance cause. The WCTU—with its all-female leadership, all-female membership, and almost exclusively female support system—was truly a society of women. Men were allowed to give money to the WCTU, but their contributions were minor in proportion to the total budget. In Evanston, the unofficial headquarters of the WCTU, the all-female household of Frances Willard combined personal, affectional, and professional relationships. Willard gathered under her own roof a coterie of associates who were as primary in running the WCTU as they were in providing an affectional support community for each other, Frances, and her mother. The importance of this female world to the woman movement can scarcely be overestimated.

For at least ten years, from approximately 1864 to 1874, Willard derived her greatest affectional and emotional support from two women, her mother and Kate Jackson. Jackson was the daughter of James Jackson, proprietor of the New Jersey Locomotive Works and a man of considerable wealth. In 1866, while the two were at Genesee Wesleyan, Kate brought Frances home for the Christmas holidays with the expressed intention of convincing her father to send them on a European *Wanderjahr*. James Jackson readily agreed, but the journey was delayed until the spring of 1868. The Willards were opposed to Frances making the trip,[70] and Josiah Willard's long bout with consumption was drawing to a close. In the summer of 1867, he returned to his family home at Churchville, New York, hoping to regain his health, and Frances joined Kate in New Jersey where they continued to plan for their great adventure. As Josiah's illness became terminal, Kate accompanied Frances to Churchville where Josiah died in January 1868.

In her autobiography Frances Willard says little about her feelings concerning her father's death. During his last weeks she was dutiful in her attendance, as was Kate who rented a room across the street from the Willard family home in Churchville. She records that he accepted his fate peacefully after carefully settling his business affairs and making meticulous arrangements for his Evanston burial.[71] But unlike the tranquil last hours of his younger daughter, Josiah Willard's was an agonizing death which left Frances with "images that can never be effaced," and caused her to believe "softening of the brain" had been added to his other infirmities.[72]

Josiah had shown deep tenderness and been able to express his love during Mary's last illness, leaving his Chicago business to be close to her, gently carrying her about the house in a vain effort to make her comfortable. Again he expressed affection for his family during the early stages of his own last illness, his usual severity softened by suffering. Josiah was always punctilious in his paternal concern for Frances. But his solicitude was paired with disapproval. He acquiesced in, but also openly opposed, her insistence on teaching and earning her own living. There was irresolvable tension between them. His death may have provided release from that tension and completed for her the process of growing independence.

WHATEVER emotions Josiah's departure evoked, his death meant Frances could travel abroad with Kate. The two young women, chaperoned only by each other, sailed for Ireland in May 1868. They continued to travel alone for much of their time abroad. They accompanied Henry Bannister, father of Willard's sister-in-law, Mary, and his party on a trip to the Middle East, and toured Russia and the Scandinavian countries in the company of other friends. The rest of the time they were essentially on their own.

Frances had long yearned to travel but until now had seen little of the world other than Wisconsin, the Chicago area, Pittsburgh, New York City and its environs, and upper New York State. She had never been to Washington, D.C., which the two women visited briefly before they sailed. The war was long over, and Andrew Johnson's impeachment trial was underway. As good Republicans they attended one session of the trial, but curiosity impelled them also to call on the beleaguered president at the White House and shake his hand at one of his public receptions. Frances, true to her Republican heritage, referred to him as "an oily, wily individual."[73] Her Republican sentiments did not encourage tolerance.

Frances Willard and Kate Jackson traveled for over two years from the spring of 1868 to the fall of 1870, exploring the British Isles, western Europe, imperial Russia, the Mediterranean basin, Egypt, Palestine, Turkey, and Italy. Their tour was leisurely. They spent six long months in Paris living with a family to improve their French and attending lectures at the Collège de France. Guizot was among their mentors. They divided their three and a half months in Germany between Berlin and Dresden, and spent over four months in Italy. Willard's European

Kate Jackson slightly older than when she and Willard toured Europe and the Middle East. (Reprinted from Gordon, *The Beautiful Life of Frances Willard*)

and Middle Eastern travels were her finishing school and graduate degree program. When this journey ended her education was complete. She returned to the United States fully prepared for her professional career as an educator. She had learned French, some Italian and German, studied classical antiquity firsthand, been exposed to European art and architecture, and observed the workings of monarchial governments. She would never travel so extensively again. She celebrated her thirtieth birthday in Italy, the prairie tomboy and prim Evanston schoolteacher among the sybaritic glories of imperial Rome and the High Renaissance.

James Jackson provided generously for this trip, initially supplying $12,000 in gold, a sum later increased. Willard also furnished some of her own pocket money by writing articles for several newspapers, including the *Independent*, the *Christian Union*, and the *Chicago Republican*. These articles survive in the form of clippings carefully pasted by her mother in a scrapbook.[74] Frances took her writing very seriously and devoted part of almost every day to her manuscripts, although she was unable to create as satisfactory a market for her efforts as she had hoped. Oliver and her mother both assisted in peddling her articles, and Kate sometimes helped with the copying.

Willard and Jackson traveled one hundred miles by carriage through Ireland, guidebooks in hand. Frances described the green island as beautiful with well-built houses—unlike America's Irish communities, those "unsightly suburbs of the town." She wrote about seeing the Killarney lakes, crossing the pass of Keimaneigh, circling the shores of Bantry Bay, and gaping at Magillicuddy's Reeks, the highest peaks in Ireland. Frances and Kate kissed the Blarney stone and, belonging to a nonecological time, took pieces of it away with them.[75] They traveled through London, Scotland, and Yorkshire inspecting churches and cathedrals, then moved on to Frankfurt. In Russia they visited the Tsar's palace in St. Petersburg and ogled the crown jewels—"the largest diamond in the world fitly mounts the scepter of the largest empire"—before touring Moscow and the Kremlin.[76]

In the Middle East Frances and Kate joined a Cook's tour for a thousand-mile journey up the Nile, experiencing "Egyptian fleas" along with "the subtle spirit of the East" for which they had come.[77] They rode along the avenue of sphinxes and thought of the processions of kings and captives that had preceded them; they climbed the pyramid Cheops and by moonlight viewed it from their boat cabin, "a figure often seen before in geometric, geographic illustrations but now standing out in full relief."[78] In March 1870 a Russian steamship brought them to white-walled Jaffa. From there they made their pilgrim's way to Jerusalem, "the most disagreeable, ugly city I have anywhere seen." They entered the city through the Via Dolorosa. Willard expected to approach Christ's tomb with reverence, but her mood was spoiled when she found a museum full of obvious fakes, "bouquets of weed-like flowers, tinsel and tawdry adornings unworthy of a child's dollhouse."[79] The summit of Calvary was equally disappointing. Damascus, Beirut, Constantinople, Athens, and a trip up the Danube to Vienna completed their itinerary. After a month in Paris at the outbreak of the Franco-Prussian War, they sailed on the Cunard Line from Liverpool, reaching New York on 5 September 1870. What Willard called "one of the crowning blessings of my life" was over.[80]

Without her European experience Willard's burning ambition still would have found an outlet and propelled her into a career, but her grand tour provided the sophisticated education that made leadership easier.

JAMES JACKSON died while Frances and Kate were abroad. Kate, who had lost her mother when she was a young child, now returned with Frances to Evanston. There Frances, Kate, and Mother Willard reopened Rest Cottage, which had been closed during the last months of the European journey, and made their home together. Jackson's fortune supplied most of the financial support for their household.

Josiah Willard had always been prosperous and a good provider. He was a successful farmer, businessman, and banker, but his assets, which should have been considerable, had evaporated. Although the Wisconsin farm brought a good price when sold after Mary's death, little was left in Josiah's estate on his death except the Evanston house, and that was in jeopardy. Only the generosity of his friends and the sale of an adjoining lot permitted Frances and her mother to keep the homestead. Josiah wrote a friend that his financial reverses resulted from the war and commercial disasters, and these may have played a role. The real culprit, however, was a $20,000 loan to his son to pay Oliver's debts and to launch him on a new career after he left the ministry in 1863. With all his intellectual promise, Oliver was beset by problems he and his family could not solve. Alcohol was one monkey on his back, but does not explain his need for enormous sums of money. He also may have gambled, or perhaps his gambling took the form of misplaced entrepreneurship. Willard's diaries discuss her brother's need for money and her father's generous response, but are not explicit as to cause.[81] In any case the Willard family was near penury, dependent henceforth on Kate's largesse and what Frances could earn. Frances could hardly stay dependent on Kate forever. In fact, her dependence on Kate rankled on occasion. She wrote, "to be poor and without resource is *biting*."[82]

Undoubtedly Frances Willard would have pursued a professional career whatever her family's financial exigencies, but the need to support herself and her mother lent urgency and point to her search for a meaningful vocation. Such compulsions often encouraged women into the world of work.

Frances came home prepared to embark seriously on a career. A profession, as opposed to marriage, was an option she had toyed with for a long time. Financial necessity now heightened the attractions of a career and laid to rest any earlier objections. Also, her father was dead and could protest no longer. She wrote her mother from Europe that she would try for a teaching position when she returned,[83] although she stated in her autobiography that she decided during the European journey to devote her life to some phase of the woman question.[84] Actually Willard was committed to that principle before she went abroad. On 20 March 1868 she wrote in her diary, "I believe in the woman question more and more. I'm going to give my little help to it in all possible ways."[85]

Willard's European travels markedly sharpened her ideas on women's role. All her experience abroad confirmed her judgment that woman-kind needed a champion. From the veiled drudges of the East to the denizens of the Paris brothels, Frances saw women being exploited, subjugated, denied their just deserts. Sometimes her reactions were naive and untutored, but this only accentuated her experience of con-trasting cultures and customs. In Paris she wondered, "The fate of women *as such*! I have pondered painfully on it today and left off where I began. . . . I find it everywhere. The man best educated, most gifted, liberated from prejudice and this unillumined past, thinks of woman as a human soul placed by a kind Creator on earth to do what she can unfettered by any law or custom so long as our freedom touches on the just rights of no other human soul. And may I be brave enough to speak in a womanly voice my honest word in this behalf."[86]

By the spring of 1871 a career as educator of women had claimed her. Her choice had been made. She wrote a friend of Lima days that she had embarked "upon the wide, wide sea of 'a career' (for such it will be, whether a brilliant one or not)." Her friend had chosen the "sweet and mystical relations of wife and motherhood; I the gentle, fitful friend-ship of a hundred school girls; you into loving service for husband and child; I into earnest, ceaseless work for the baby daughters of a thou-sand homes who shall yet be happier and wiser because of my toil. Who shall say which of us has best fulfilled the will of heaven or served the needy causes of humanity? My cheerful and contented thought is this:—each of us in her natural place."[87]

Willard had been teaching much of the time for over ten years, but she had been practicing a profession rather than pursuing a career. She moved almost willy-nilly from position to position. She lacked consis-tent commitment in terms of personal goals or institutional loyalty. She had struggled with the idea of marriage and abandoned that choice. Part of the time she saw herself as a writer as well as a teacher. Her biography of her sister together with the many articles on the European journey attest to this. But during the winter of 1871 a firm choice was made. She committed herself to the woman movement and to the education of women as the vehicle through which this commitment would be executed.

Chapter IV   Commitment

Three factors moved Frances Willard toward a career as an educator in 1870. The first was her commitment to the woman question; the second, the extent of her training and experience that prepared her for academic life; and the third, the fact that a job of sufficient scope was hers for the taking. A new project was being launched in Evanston.

The founding of Vassar College in 1865 opened new horizons for women. In the early 1860s a dozen or more ambitious seminaries called themselves "ladies colleges," but the Poughkeepsie experiment promised true higher education for women, a chance at training that rivaled that of the best men's colleges, not only in the liberal arts but also in the sciences.

The Midwest was not unaware of this new potential. In the late 1860s a group of Evanston women, aware of the increasing attention paid to higher education for women, developed an interest in establishing a women's college that would offer a more advanced curriculum than the old proprietary North Western Female College. In the fall of 1868, while Frances and Kate were touring in Europe, the Evanston women organized themselves into a formal board and successfully petitioned the city for a donation of land on which to build. Mary Bannister Willard, Oliver's wife and Frances's old friend, was a member of that board. In 1869 the proposed institution, now called the Evanston Ladies College, was granted a charter by the state of Illinois. Almost immediately the trustees of previously all-male Northwestern University, mindful of the new movement, invited women to enroll in Northwestern.

Erastus O. Haven had just been named president of the university. Haven, formerly president of the University of Michigan, was a recent convert to coeducation. Overall, Haven was an innovator. His first act at Northwestern was to merge Chicago Medical College with the university. He also established a department of civil engineering and a

chemical laboratory, enlarged the library by 20,000 volumes, and
strengthened the university's ties with Garrett Theological Seminary. He set out, as he later wrote, "full of hope," to make Northwestern "equal to any university in the country."[1]

As a condition of accepting the presidency, Haven demanded that women be admitted to Northwestern University. But few actually appeared on campus, and Haven believed a women's college within the university, one that offered living accommodations, would swell their ranks appreciably. The board of the new Ladies College was thinking along the same lines. In June 1870 the Ladies College board proposed union with Northwestern, and the proposal was accepted on condition that the Ladies College provide its own building. But what should be done about existing North Western Female College? It was clear from the outset that women students in any numbers would have to come from the Female College ranks, and that without the cooperation of William Jones, its proprietor, the plan could never succeed.[2] The matter was settled in January 1871 when Jones agreed to surrender his charter to the new college, which in turn would rent his building for what proved to be the exorbitant sum of $2,500 a year. The new women's college had now met the conditions of its proposed union with the university. It had acquired a building.

The next step for the Ladies College was to engage a chief administrative officer, and she was close at hand. Frances Willard, home in Evanston since late September, was waiting to be asked. On 14 February 1871 the board named her president of the new college. Her title was a bit pretentious. She could well have been called a dean, but the position of the new women's college within the university was somewhat ambiguous. For the most part, the Ladies College was a separate institution. In that sense Willard was head of a separate college and properly called its president.

Frances was tacking down stair carpets, as her story went, when her across-the-street neighbor, Harriet Kidder, wife of Daniel Parish Kidder, a Garrett theologian, called to suggest that she abandon such domestic pursuits and become more profitably employed as head of the new women's college. She was not surprised. Not only was her sister-in-law on the college board, but also Willard had seen an account of the Ladies College while still in Europe and queried her mother from Switzerland for details. The prospect of a real women's college attached to the university interested her from the beginning. At first she expressed some uncertainty about wanting "a place in your university" (as she wrote her mother from Jerusalem), but Willard undoubtedly was an early candidate for the presidency. Her initial hesitancy was motivated in part by fear that "many others would be preferred."[3] No doubt she was ready and waiting for this call.

There is no way to tell if Frances Willard deliberately used her European journey to prepare for this post, but she could hardly have produced a better plan. She now brought to the presidency her newly acquired skills in foreign languages, art history, and European politics, as well as her experience with French and German universities. Few American women could match the breadth of her experience with the European university system, to say nothing of the informal education she had acquired abroad. She had proved herself as a teacher long before her travels began. She had taught in a number of seminaries and public secondary schools, and her work was respected. Such administrative and promotional skills as she possessed had been obtained through the Garrett Seminary fund-raising campaign, an effort that introduced her to Methodist circles all over the United States. Also, she found a career in women's education ideologically attractive. The press applauded her appointment. The *Chicago Journal* hailed it as "we believe, the first instance on record of a lady being honored with the dignified title of 'president,' but Miss Willard will wear her honors with equal ability and honesty."[4]

In later life Frances Willard was first and foremost an organizer and promoter, and her first job as the new president of Northwestern's Ladies College was to raise money. Renting the building of the old proprietary school was a stopgap. It met the conditions of union with the university and greased the channel for Jones's cooperation, but the women who wished Northwestern to be the major coeducational college in the old Northwest were committed to something more. Already they had convinced the city fathers to provide them with a site, and they intended to build on it. They wanted a fresh start, a new building.

Willard went to work and President Haven supported her. One of the board members, not Willard, conceived the idea of "pre-empting" the Fourth of July, "in the interests of our girls."[5] The author of this elaborate celebration was none other than Jane Blaikie Hoge, Mary Livermore's partner in the spectacular work of the Chicago Sanitary Commission during the Civil War. However, Willard did much of the organizing herself. She prepared a circular for the newspapers and sent out a wide mailing calling for higher education for women as "demanded by the spirit of the age," commending Haven's support of the new college and detailing the program of the celebration at which the cornerstone for the new building would be laid.[6]

When the glorious Fourth arrived, all was ready. The Ellsworth

Zouaves, a local regiment, drilled, baseball was played and the winners received a silver ball for a prize, a regatta sailed on nearby Lake Michigan, a play was performed three times in the university chapel, a United States senator (James Reed Doolittle) spoke, and Evanston women served $3,000 worth of dinners to hungry celebrants, despite the fact that many of those attending picnicked. Dr. Haven, marching at Willard's side from the campus to the site of the cornerstone laying, told her "how deeply he rejoiced in all the on-going movements by which women were coming to their kingdom."[7] This one-day extravaganza added $30,000 to the building fund to which $25,000 had previously been pledged.[8]

For the rest of the summer Willard took to the hustings, presenting the prospectus for the college wherever she could get a hearing. At the same time she planned the curriculum for the fall opening. Three options were open to women students who registered in the new college. By paying the regular university tuition in addition to college fees, they could pursue any university courses they chose. They could confine their studies to the women's college offerings—English, fine arts, modern languages, music, health and home industries; or they could combine college and university courses. Willard was quoted as believing "the true idea of woman's education will include croquet and calculus, tatting and Telemachus, Homer and home."[9] The college was to offer "such special instruction" as women will require "while the regular classes of other departments of the University will be open to its students."[10] Making special curricular provisions for women was a major innovation. Segregating women within a coeducational institution with their own board of trustees, administrative officer, and housing facilities also set Northwestern apart. All Northwestern women were subject to Willard's authority in morals and manners.[11] The affiliate plan developed at Northwestern was used eventually by Radcliffe and Barnard colleges, but they had not yet opened their doors.

When classes began in the fall of 1871, 236 women were enrolled—38 were taking undergraduate courses at the university, 62 were attending Northwestern's preparatory department, and 136 were registered only in the women's college.[12] The new enterprise was a huge success. Women had been admitted to the University of Iowa in 1858, Wisconsin in 1863, and Michigan in 1870, but they had to fend for themselves.[13] No "ladies colleges" were on hand to receive them. There was no special housing, no provision for the nurture of their "morals and manners." Because the Ladies College provided these services, women flocked to Northwestern rather than other midwestern universities.[14] In the beginning only a minority of Northwestern women took advantage of university courses in science, mathematics, or philosophy, but the opportunity was there. Willard and the college adopted a pattern that Willard was to repeat more than once during her life. As she pushed for greater opportunities for women she carefully coddled the nineteenth century's sensitivity to women's special role. Young women were educated in the same classes and in the same disciplines as men, but their special needs as women were not denied, and provision was made for their nurture.

Willard was busy, happy, and challenged. "For the first and only time" in her career she saw herself as a teacher and an educator "free to work my will as an elder sister of girls."[15] She was making a conscious distinction in the way she viewed her work. She was no longer a mere teacher but a molder of women. Her primary contact with students was her Friday afternoon lecture on what she dubbed "moral horticulture." One of her students described these assemblies: "Dear wonderful Miss Willard! What a faculty she had for touching the right chord when talking seriously to her girls! What a teacher she was and what ideals she impressed upon us! Do you remember the devotional exercises she conducted? It seemed at the time as if her prayers took us to the very gates of heaven."[16] Willard visited her students informally in their rooms and led them in evening prayers. According to another student, Willard set the keynote in her first Friday afternoon talk when she related the history of opening Northwestern to women. Coeducation, she said, was still an experiment about which many were doubtful. The success of the experiment would depend on the students, who could make or break their opportunity.[17]

One of Willard's innovations was to replace the odious rules of the old Female College with an honor system. The rules had been "so numerous that nobody could remember them all," and Willard herself had taken particular delight as a schoolgirl in sub-rosa defiance.[18] One of her students reported that the honor system was a complete success, and that Willard, by giving "no specific directions to her girls regarding deportment," inspired "them with a sense of their own individual responsibility."[19] At the Ladies College women students went to church as they pleased, rather than marching together in formal procession as they had in the old college. They were permitted to join the men's literary societies and allowed out in the evenings to attend meetings, despite criticism that their participation "might prevent a young man from having as frequent opportunity to speak as he would have had."[20] President Haven supported Willard's innovations. Commenting on the place of women in the literary societies, he observed: "Here more than

Willard as dean of Woman's College, Northwestern University. (Reprinted from Gordon, *The Life of Frances E. Willard*)

in the recitation room young men will learn that young women are their peers."[21]

THE college had not moved far into its first year, however, when severe troubles arose. The Chicago fire doomed the building program. Chicagoans had been heavy subscribers at the Fourth of July "preemption" and their resources either had been consumed by the flames or were needed for more pressing business. Work on the new building ceased in the spring of 1872 and was not resumed for over a year.

Clearly, only closer union with the university could save the college. At a meeting of Northwestern's trustees in June 1873, at the end of the second year of operation, a new plan of union was presented by Willard and adopted. According to her first condition of union, the Evanston Ladies College was replaced by the Woman's College of Northwestern University. An independent Ladies College board of trustees also ceased to exist. Instead, five women served on the university board and one on its executive committee.[22] Again the Chicago papers heralded a first: Northwestern was the "first institution in the world to inaugurate co-representation of the sexes in the government of colleges."[23] Willard relinquished the title of president and was elected dean of the Woman's College and professor of aesthetics in the university at a salary of $1,800 for the first year.[24] Northwestern took over the college's property and obligations, including completion of the building.[25]

At the trustees' meeting in June, there had been little discussion of this phase of the plan and agreement had been quickly reached. However, the second condition of union, that women continue to exercise all authority within the Woman's College, provoked lengthy debate,[26] although it was finally accepted. Northwestern's board agreed that women attending the university would remain "under the oversight of the faculty of the Ladies' College."[27] Willard had insisted that her authority be preserved. But she welcomed her new rank and duties within the university itself as well as the substantial increase in her salary, previously a precarious $1,000.

The agreement on the governance of women students was not honored. At the same June meeting where the plan of union was adopted, Erastus Haven resigned as president of the university. Willard and Haven had worked closely and well together, and Haven had completely supported Willard's policies and plans. But Haven was no longer in charge at Northwestern. He had regretted his move to the citadel of Methodism. He later wrote that leaving Ann Arbor had been a mistake. He had exchanged a strong institution for a weak one that he felt was little more than "a good preparatory department for the Garrett Bible Institute."[28] The Chicago fire hobbled his expansion plans, which depended on a fund-raising potential that no longer existed—at least for him. Thus, when he was offered the secretaryship of the board of education of the Methodist Episcopal church, he did not hesitate to accept.

If Haven had remained at Northwestern Frances Willard might well have continued her promising career as an educator and lived out her professional life contributing to higher education for women. This also might have been true had Northwestern's trustees picked anyone other than the man they selected to succeed Haven. Their choice was Charles Henry Fowler, whom they had unsuccessfully attempted to interest in the presidency once before, and whose abilities as a speaker and fund-raiser, the qualities they needed most, were widely recognized. Fowler was minister of Centenary Church in downtown Chicago, a church with over a thousand members. He had performed superbly in raising money to rebuild Chicago's Methodist churches after the Chicago fire. That he had once been Willard's fiancé probably did not cross the trustees' minds. In any case, relations between Willard and Fowler were amiable enough. They continued to see each other as friends and in 1871 Willard lectured in his church, where Fowler himself had introduced her, in the words of the *Chicago Tribune*, "in happy style."[29] But Willard must have felt somewhat uneasy about his appointment. Tension, misunderstanding, and a power struggle were possible. There was room for ambiguity in the division of administrative responsibility. In reality, Willard was on the threshold of what she later called "the most painful period of my life."[30]

This potentially awkward relationship was complicated by the fact that Willard was now a professor in the university proper, and Northwestern's male students were the unwilling recipients of her tutelage in composition. Harassment was the order of the day. Willard's blackboard was defiled with belittling sallies; a howling cat was imprisoned in her desk drawer; a dozen gentlemen, one by one, arrived late through a squeaky classroom door after the hour's lesson had begun.[31] No doubt the male faculty sniggered slyly at these ingenious displays of undergraduate wit. Willard herself avoided rising to the bait, controlled her temper, and ignored the assault. But subjection to these daily persecutions could hardly have contributed to her general peace of mind.

A third factor made its inevitable contribution to Willard's deteriorating position. The Woman's College could not support both the new building under construction and pay rent for Jones's building. The lease with Jones had expired, and he refused to negotiate a more favorable contract. Moreover, the new building would not be completed until April. The trustees decided that women would board in town, as the men had done all along, for most of the 1873–74 academic year. In coeducational universities this was normal procedure. University of Michigan women lived and worked under the same rules as men. No measures were taken to provide segregated housing (men and women shared the same boardinghouses) until near the end of the century. But in other universities the women boarding out were clearly university students. Most of the Northwestern women were young adolescents in the preparatory department.

The temporary housing arrangement jeopardized Willard's smoothly working, self-governing honor system to oversee the "manners and morals" of Northwestern women. She replaced it with a system of rules enforced by written self-reports submitted weekly, a variation of the honor system and a procedure that she believed would prove an adequate substitute for the peer pressure she had relied on previously to prevent indiscretions. The women seemed not to mind, "a college full of girls crying for rules like housekeepers for sapolio!"[32] But the Chicago press, supported by male students who saw this as a means of continuing their harassment, got wind of the report system and accused Willard of being a tyrant, even a Bluebeard. Fowler and the faculty, probably dubious in any case of the wisdom of having women within the sacred halls of academia and certainly eager to escape sharing control of these students with a semiautonomous woman administrator, did nothing to help Willard in the face of this attack. The women students signed a resolution supporting Willard and her rules, believing "them to be salutary in their effects."[33] But their support did her no good.

Fowler played an opportunist's game. He painted Willard, the innovator, the opponent of arbitrary rules, as the conservative and himself as the supporter of complete freedom for women university students. They should be allowed to have no connection with the Woman's College and to live where they chose—in short, they should be outside Willard's jurisdiction. Willard correctly argued that the merger agreement stipulated all women were to be under the supervision of the college and its administrator; further, a commitment to this effect was made to parents through the catalog. It seems likely that Fowler's position was based on a desire to undermine Willard's authority through an out-and-out power struggle rather than on a serious commitment to more liberal rules. Indeed, he would find to his liking Ellen Soulé,

Willard's successor as head of the Woman's College, who was much more conservative than Willard in her handling of student social life— segregating the literary societies, for example.[34]

Fowler and the faculty stooped to petty harassment. Although Fowler could not dismiss Willard because she had tenure for life, he could make her position untenable. When the new building was occupied in the spring term of 1874, Willard was denied the privilege of conducting evening prayers, a task now delegated to the college steward, a male clergyman.[35] In April the university faculty assumed full responsibility for decisions on rules for college and university women alike, reducing Willard's position to that of an enforcing officer. She discussed the alternative of resigning with her family and a few friends, all of whom urged her to fight the battle through, confident that her many supporters in Evanston would ensure her ultimate success. Nevertheless, she submitted her resignation to the faculty on 13 June at the close of the academic year. In her letter of resignation she said, "It has slowly become evident that I can never carry into execution my deepest convictions concerning the interests of the Woman's College, under the existing policy of government."[36] Her resignation was accepted first by the committee for the Woman's College and then by the board of Northwestern University.

It had been an agonizing decision, later described with typical Victorian sentimentality:

> This is Professor Jones' college of which he was so fond, and it is my sister Mary's that died and it is mine. With a faculty of women gathered around me that was like a band of sisters, with pupils loving and beloved, with a life position as professor of the branches I like best and know most about, and an adequate income assured, with mother and Rest Cottage only two blocks away. . . . I must go. The world is wide and full of elbow room; this atmosphere is stifling—I must leave it.[37]

In a long letter to the faculty, Willard laid out much more dispassionately the substantive differences between her position and that of Northwestern's faculty and president. Willard chose not to quarrel with Fowler's proposition that women could choose to enter the university on the same basis as men, live where they pleased, meet no "'special' requirements." And she stated that "those parents who desire to entrust their daughters with the responsibilities and prerogatives of self government can certainly make no complaint that this is not practicable in Northwestern University." But she did take issue with the rules drawn up by the faculty for the governance of students living in the college building. She objected "to the fact that a large and estimable class of patrons do not find their wants met by the system of regulations at present prevailing."

Willard cited the example of fifteen-year-olds who were entrusted to her care, but who by the faculty's rules could "receive calls from whomever and when their [the students'] judgment dictates (out of study hours), that they can be attended by gentlemen to nearly all the public exercises of the institution and to all religious meetings without any special permission, . . . [and] leave the ground at all times freely." She found her position vis-à-vis parents untenable. How could she answer their question, " 'What safeguards can you offer to my daughter in her youth and inexperience?' " Her final paragraph suggested to the faculty that they "allow some weight to the womanly judgment of whoever shall succeed me; that the daily devotional exercises at the Women's College be placed under her care; and that upon whatever course you may determine, the policy be clearly stated to the public, especially parents who contemplate sending their daughters to the University."[38] Willard's stand was not unreasonable. She did have "girls of tender years" under her care. But the nub of the matter was Fowler. She could not work with him, nor he with her. The residue of their personal relationship in 1861–62 left too many conflicts, and Willard capitulated in the battle of wills. She gave up, and she gave up a lot. This time Charles Fowler clearly had won.

The trustees accepted Willard's resignation. She lamented, "So it was over, the greatest sacrifice my life had known or ever can know," and she felt a "sense of injustice so overwhelming that no other experience of mine compares with it in poignancy. 'I tried so hard and I meant so well!' "[39] Willard and Fowler were eventually reconciled. The next year she apologized to him for anything she might have done improperly, and he also begged her pardon.[40]

At long last Frances Willard had made a commitment. For years she had vacillated. Was she a teacher? Did she really want a career? With her acceptance of the presidency of the Evanston Ladies College, and later the deanship of the Woman's College, she was committed to her brand of higher education for women at Northwestern. She had created a successful hybrid, an environment where women could combine rebellious innovation and acceptable acquiescence. Women could register in the university and assume the same tasks as men, or they could stay within the protected confines of the college and not enter the broader world of the university. Part innovation, part tradition was a lifelong pattern that Willard followed, a pattern that proved very successful

both for her and for American women generally until the end of the
century.

65
Commitment

IN the summer of 1874 Frances Willard faced the dilemma of shaping her life anew. From her agonizing reappraisal of her life's directions during that bitter last term, Willard's final choice of mission was to come. As she shed angry tears in her lonely room the night after she resigned from the Northwestern faculty, several alternatives were open to her.

Willard could remain an educator, accept a position with another college or preparatory school, and continue with teaching and administration. This course encompassed negative factors that resulted in its ultimate rejection. For one thing, she resisted uprooting her mother and possibly herself from the Evanston milieu, her friends, her brother and his family—the Methodist "heaven," as she affectionately referred to Evanston, that suited all of them so well. Also, the limits that education as a career could place on her autonomy, always dear to her since her Wisconsin childhood, had been clearly demonstrated. She would be at the mercy of boards, administrators, and faculty, to say nothing of students and parents.

Another less conventional course suggested itself to her. The women of the United States were opening new paths outside academia. A militant and vigorous woman's temperance movement was being launched in the churches, streets, and legislative halls of the nation. Willard chose to follow the route these women took and eventually lead them on their journey. Henceforth she dedicated her professional life (with two minor interruptions) to this cause until her death in 1898.

During the winter of 1873–74, when Willard was engaged in her personal armageddon at Northwestern, an amazing number of American women had taken to the streets in a warlike crusade of their own choosing. Disgusted and discouraged by the repudiation of the temperance cause during the Civil War and the rapid growth of the saloon that followed, women spontaneously organized to reverse the patterns they saw consuming American society. In the antebellum period temperance had made substantial gains, a large body of prohibitory legislation had been passed, and an outright decrease in the per capita consumption of spirits was accomplished.[41] But after the war the alcohol consumption curve rose steeply, prohibitory legislation when not repealed was ignored, and the ratio of saloons to adult males in urban working-class areas was as high as one to fifty.

In response the Order of Good Templars, which accepted women on an equal basis with men, already had begun to show significant in-

Crusade women kneeling in the snow during the winter of 1873–74, when women took to the streets to fight alcohol abuse. (Reprinted from Jane Stebbins, *Fifty Years of the Temperance Cause* [Hartford, Conn.: J. P. Fitch, 1876])

creases in membership—from 50,000 in 1859 to 400,000 in 1869. Most of this growth took place after the Civil War. The Ohio branch of the order grew from 3,755 in 1865 to nearly 28,000 in less than three years, and women were playing an increasing role in this movement. By 1872 the Chief Grand Templar of Ohio was a woman, Martha McClelland Brown.[42] The Prohibition party founded in 1868 was also open to women, and thirty women were delegates to its first convention. Although women joined the temperance cause in increasing numbers in the postwar period, their spontaneous mass eruption in the winter of 1873–74 occurred with little warning and bordered on revolutionary action, a "Woman's War" as it was frequently called by the press.

The women's Crusade began in December 1873 when Diocletian Lewis, popular lecturer and advocate of physical exercise programs and more comfortable clothing for women, delivered his usual lecture, "Our Girls," to the Hillsboro, Ohio, lyceum series. The next day was Sunday and Lewis had a free day. In accord with his usual practice, he offered to give Hillsboro a free temperance lecture. Although Lewis had made his temperance appeal many times before with only intermittent and short-lived success, this time his words sparked a rapidly spreading rebellion, an antisaloon Crusade that lasted through much of the next summer and resulted in the organization—in the fall of 1874—of the Woman's Christian Temperance Union to carry on the work.[43]

Women took to the streets in hundreds of towns and cities, attempting to shut down saloons by persuading their owners not to sell or their patrons to pledge abstinence. Women knelt in saloons with their open Bibles on the bar or prayed in the streets outside to ensure divine help for their mission. This "street work" by "praying bands," as the women themselves called it, was widely reported in the press. Mass meetings were held and sermons preached. The whole heartland of the nation was enveloped in a temperance frenzy, a usually nonviolent but none-theless revolutionary confrontation to enforce social reform. And from the first it was a confrontation led by women.

Women had found temperance attractive from the beginning. The first to suffer the full extent of the tragedy brought to the home by a drunken husband or father, they moved eagerly into the moral suasion aspects of temperance in the 1830s and 1840s. But women quickly dis-covered that moral suasion was not enough, that public action, even legislation, would be necessary. Although the doctrine of spheres pre-sumably denied women recourse to public activity, it earmarked home and family as their special area of responsibility. Women did not see participation in the temperance cause as a challenge to prevailing gen-der roles because they were only performing their accepted duties as wives and mothers. Women also had at hand well-developed church networks that they could use in temperance work, further enhancing the movement's respectability and their own position in it.

Evanston, because its temperance proclivities had resulted already in a dry city with no saloons, was not directly involved in the Crusade movement. But the women of Chicago were caught up in the Crusade. After initial organizing meetings using churches as a base, they col-lected over 14,000 signatures and marched through the streets to the council chambers to petition for enforcement of Chicago's Sunday closing ordinance. Their efforts were unsuccessful. Their petition was tabled, the ordinance repealed forthwith, and the petitioners threat-ened with mob violence.[44]

Although Frances Willard was certainly aware of what was going on, she was preoccupied by her own personal struggle and did not partici-pate in this moving drama. Instead, she read the newspaper dispatches and commented, "While we were musing the fire burned."[45] That win-ter and spring she assigned temperance themes to her Northwestern rhetoric and composition classes, and her brother Oliver, then editor of the *Chicago Evening Mail*, "gave favorable and full reports" of the Cru-sade, assuring Willard, "I shall speak just as well of the women as I dare to."[46] Actually the Chicago press covered the local Crusade and the national movement with thoroughness and objectivity if not outright sympathy.[47] Willard's major contribution to the movement was as a speaker at temperance mass meetings held in the spring in several Chicago churches. But once she decided to sever her ties with Northwestern and turned her attention to alternative careers, she saw the woman's temperance movement as a compelling option.

The Willards' devotion to temperance first became evident on the Wisconsin farm. Josiah was an honorary member of the Washingtonians, a pre–Civil War organization founded by reformed drunkards. In 1855 young Frances signed an abstinence pledge, cut from a popular juvenile magazine *Youth's Cabinet*, and pasted it in the family Bible. Willard must have felt this pledge in force for life because, as far as the record shows, she never signed another.[48] In the Methodist circles in which she moved abstinence was accepted social practice. The Methodist church had adopted rules limiting the use of distilled liquor as early as 1790, and went on record to urge total abstinence in 1832. Willard like her friends and colleagues did not use alcoholic beverages as a young woman, and in 1866 she was active in Evanston temperance circles.

On her European trip, however, Willard accepted easily the different practices of the people among whom she lived. She described her departure from abstinence with amazing frankness:

> In Denmark . . . I was suddenly and violently ill with something resembling cholera, and the kind-faced physician in Copenhagen bending above my weakness said in broken French: "Mademoiselle, you must put wine in the water you drink or you will never live to see your home." This prescription I then followed for two years with a gradual tendency so to amend as to make it read, "You may put water in your wine," and a leaning toward the "pure article," especially when some rich friend sent for a costly bottle. . . . But beyond a flushing of the cheek, an unwonted readiness at repartee and an anticipation of the dinner hour, unknown to me before or since, I came under no thralldom.[49]

Upon returning to the accustomed abstinence of her Methodist environment, Willard easily ceased her modest tippling and did not again use intoxicants as a beverage. But this did not mean eschewing their use medicinally. As a Northwestern dean, "When especially 'worn out,' I would take a little of mother's currant wine," and she drank a daily medicinal glass of beer with her dinner during her last traumatic term on campus.[50] Willard freely admitted her former use of alcoholic beverages in her early temperance lectures.[51]

In *Glimpses of Fifty Years* Willard states that she attended only two temperance meetings before 1874, but her diary belies this.[52] She was not, however, one of Chicago's street crusaders or a member of the Templars. Willard's journals show her consistent preoccupation with the woman question from her earliest years, but the temperance question is mentioned only rarely before the 1870s. Temperance, although a congenial cause, had not been high on her list of priorities. Possibly purely personal considerations, her brother Oliver's problems with alcohol, contributed to her growing interest in temperance. However, his problem drinking began before Josiah Willard's death and appears to have been in remission during 1873–74.

More important in stimulating Frances's interest was the fact that during the winter of 1873–74 the women's Crusade transformed the temperance movement into the paramount women's issue of the day. Willard had committed herself to the woman question long before she accepted temperance as her lifework. From adolescence she had railed against sexual inequality, and on her return from Europe she actively pursued this aim both as educator and public lecturer. In her lecture "The New Chivalry," delivered for the first time in 1871 at Charles Fowler's Centenary Church, she argued that her experiences of "real life placed me on the affirmative side of the tremendous 'Woman Question.'"[53] However, in 1871 she came down on that "affirmative side" very gently indeed, seeing her contribution as sending to the oppressed women of other lands America's "dear girls" to bring "streams of healing even to those far off shores."[54]

By championing and pioneering in higher education for women, Willard was contributing to the movement for equal rights, albeit she was timid in overtly expressing her feminist ideology during this period. She blamed her mother for her own failure to join the Evanston equal rights organization, the Pro and Con club organized by Elizabeth Boynton Harbert "in the interests of equal suffrage." Mary Hill Willard was a member but cautioned Frances that it could prove a risky and controversial move for a college administrator.[55] Willard's early journals confirm that she did not exaggerate her level of commitment to equal rights when she assessed that commitment in 1889: "I do not recall the time when my inmost spirit did not perceive the injustice done to woman. . . . and when I did not appreciate to some extent the state's irreparable loss in losing from halls of legislation and courts of justice the woman's judgment and the mother's heart."[56]

FOR Willard, like many other women, temperance and the woman movement had merged by 1874. The public cause that women were joining in the largest numbers, the reform movement that commanded their loyalty in greatest measure, was temperance. Under the banners of the battle against demon rum, women had engaged in both direct action and political lobbying; they now marshaled themselves into permanent organizations. They could not vote, but temperance had drawn them into the political arena. When Willard set forth to find a new career that summer on a trip to the eastern seaboard, she promptly made common cause with the temperance advocates she found there.

Her search for eastern connections also was facilitated by contacts she made among adherents of the woman movement at the National Woman's Congress of 1873. In developing Northwestern Woman's College Willard worked closely with Jane Hoge, Mary Livermore's partner in organizing the work of the Chicago Sanitary Commission during the Civil War. Hoge knew many eastern activists. As Willard became visible as an educator, she moved with Hoge's backing onto the national stage as one of the founders of the Woman's Congress, a major women's organization of the 1870s.

The Woman's Congress was originally a project of Sorosis, a professional club for women writers and journalists, and represented a conservative attempt to bring the nineteenth-century woman movement back within the boundaries of respectable reform. In the late 1860s and early 1870s women's demands for equal rights suffered from unsavory associations that shocked the liberal middle-class world. Victoria Woodhull, who supported short skirts, free love, legalized prostitution, and world government, was linked with the National Woman Suffrage Association led by Elizabeth Cady Stanton and Susan B. Anthony.

The scandal of the age, the Beecher-Tilton marital embroglio, involved three leaders of the more conservative branch of the suffrage movement, Henry Ward Beecher and Elizabeth and Theodore Tilton. Beecher, minister of Brooklyn's famous Plymouth Church and a leading clergyman, was accused of conducting an affair with Elizabeth Tilton, prominent women's rights leader and wife of Theodore Tilton, journalist and social reformer. The Tiltons were members of Beecher's congregation. Elizabeth Tilton first admitted the liaison but later insisted her confession was obtained under duress. Every local newspaper carried stories of Beecher's trial for alienation of affection.[57]

Association with participants in a marital scandal and one of the country's most radical and outspoken proponents of free love did the woman movement no good, and the leaders of Sorosis wished to provide a corrective. Charlotte Wilbour, president of the national society, sent a circular letter "to practical representative women interested in higher education . . . who by voice or pen or practical work have conquered an honorable place in any of the leading reforms of the day," asking for their signatures to a call for a general congress. Approximately a hundred women responded, Frances Willard among them. She was in illustrious company. Sarah Grimké, Isabella Beecher Hooker, Julia Ward Howe, Antoinette Blackwell, Mary Livermore, Stanton, and Lucy Stone also supported the call.[58]

The Woman's Congress convened on 15 October 1873 in the Union League Club of New York and proceeded to organize a new society called the Association for the Advancement of Women. Mary Livermore, journalist, suffragist, and fellow organizer with Willard's friend Jane Hoge of the Chicago Sanitary Commission, was elected first president of the association. The congress was Willard's eastern debut. She offered a paper on "New Departures in Education" in which she described the honor system she had inaugurated at Northwestern.[59] Her name was misspelled as Wilbur in the program, and she was listed as a delegate from the University of Illinois, not Northwestern. Midwestern women luminaries were not yet much recognized in the East. But she was on hand and noticed, and she made friends, among them Mary Livermore, one of the country's most popular lecturers and former editor of the *Woman's Journal*, a major organ of the women's movement. Willard was elected vice-president of the association for Illinois.[60] Through the association she became visible to the eastern leaders of the woman movement, and she made use of these connections in the summer and fall of 1874.

Willard also had temperance connections in the East. She had met William H. Boole, Methodist minister and well-known temperance lecturer, when he appeared in Chicago. She sought out Boole when she arrived in New York and through him met Mary Hartt and Mary C. Johnson, Brooklyn crusaders.[61] In September Willard went with Hartt and other new temperance friends to a temperance camp meeting, a week's ecumenical rally of temperance forces, at Old Orchard Beach, Maine, a popular seaside resort.[62] Here she met Francis Murphy, leader of the reform club movement, an organization of heavy drinkers that used moral suasion techniques similar to those used by Alcoholics Anonymous. The two began a long association with eventual romantic overtones. Murphy wrote Frances love letters in the early 1880s, but she could not have taken them very seriously because they were turned over to her mother for "edification or amusement."[63] At Orchard Beach Willard became acquainted with all the luminaries of the temperance movement, among them Lillian Stevens, who was an associate of Neal Dow, father of the Maine Prohibitory Law; and Dio Lewis, crusade initiator "whose words had been the match that fired the powder mine."[64] Willard was made vice-president of the Temperance Camp Meeting Association.

Soon after this meeting Willard experienced one of her "heavenly gifts." She was caught up in temperance fervor, but concerned about how she could earn her living in the service of temperance. She used an old device to resolve her conflict. While staying at a hotel in Portland, Maine, she opened the hotel Bible to Psalms 37:3, "Trust in the Lord to do good; so shalt thou dwell in the land, and verily thou shalt be fed." God would provide; "here came clinching faith for what was to me a most difficult emergency."[65] Throughout her life Willard's great decisions were influenced by divine revelation, as were the decisions of many of her contemporaries. Looking to the Bible for guidance was a common practice among evangelicals. In just such a manner Willard took her giant steps in support of woman suffrage and in linking the WCTU to the Prohibition party. Nineteenth-century reformers frequently felt themselves part of larger religious patterns that were foreordained and inevitable.

For Willard revelation was always accompanied by calm, common-sense assessment of practical considerations. On this occasion she consulted her mother and her friends, all of whom counseled that if she were financially independent she could afford to be "a philanthropist, but of all work the temperance work pays least, and you cannot afford to take it up." Mary Livermore provided the only voice on the other side.[66] Willard's revelation that God would provide was buttressed in September 1874 by a letter from Louise Rounds of the Chicago woman's temperance organization offering her the presidency of that earnest and committed group. "Here was my 'open door' all unknown and unsought . . . a chance to work for the cause that had in so short a time become so dear to me."[67]

Willard yearned for the excitement and challenge of the temperance crusade, but without some means of livelihood she dared not shut the door on a career in education. The same day the letter arrived from Chicago she was offered the principalship of an "elegant school for young women, adjoining Central Park," with a generous salary attached.[68] Now she could refuse this and other educational offers, stay in Evanston, and embark on a career in public life, an idea that had always attracted her. Perhaps the ease with which Willard was accepted in temperance circles, the readiness with which temperance leaders saw her as a major addition to the movement, unduly influenced her. She may have been seduced by the enthusiastic welcome she received, so different from her recent treatment at Northwestern. For the short term she had chosen a very hard course. For the next few months she worked at a killing pace for practically no financial reward and little recognition.

Anna Gordon, Willard's longtime secretary, friend, and confidant, believed that Willard made her choice with eyes wide open to the import of her action, that from the beginning she "saw the real significance of the WCTU" as the first organization that "could, with proper leadership, be arrayed likewise against every other evil which threatens the home and strikes at our civilization. She saw in it too, a great educational agency for women."[69] There is hindsight in this statement, but also considerable truth. Temperance was the vehicle through which large numbers of women could be organized most effectively during the next two decades. As a temperance leader Willard would maximize her influence both with women and in society at large. For the long run Frances Willard had chosen wisely for herself and the organization she was to lead.

Chapter V  Career

Frances Willard was now launched on the career that would occupy the rest of her life. She was a temperance leader. From time to time she added other roles and occupations to this commitment, but she never permitted other obligations to distract her from her major lifework.

Willard believed that her decision to join the temperance movement revolutionized her life-style: "Instead of peace I was to participate in war; instead of the sweetness of home . . . I was to become a wanderer on the face of the earth; instead of libraries I was to frequent public halls and railway cars; instead of scholarly and cultured men I was to see the dregs of saloon and gambling house and haunts of shame."[1] Academia had not always been peaceful, and Willard continued to associate with many educated and cultured men, but she was to change her life patterns. She became a peripatetic lecturer and organizer and an inveterate traveler, and in her first year with the Chicago WCTU she worked intimately with "the dregs of saloon and gambling house." It was a far cry from playing mother surrogate to Northwestern young women and teaching English and art history.

Her new job was based in Chicago's center city. Willard had spent much of her life in the rural environment typical of American society until the Civil War. She was a child of the prairie farm and American small towns. She now moved into a city that until very recently was itself little more than an overgrown small town but was presently on the verge of becoming a metropolis. This transformation did not take place without traumatic growing pains. The 1870s were a time of tragedy and change in Chicago. The fire of 1871 benumbed the city for awhile, but it also released enormous energy; before the new vitality really got underway, it was aborted by the financial panic of 1873 and the disastrous depression that followed. The great flood of European immigration that resulted by 1890 in one-third of the city's population being of foreign birth had already begun. The stresses and strains of economic upheaval, population growth, and demographic changes

were nowhere more obvious than in the Chicago Loop. Into this mael-
strom the infant temperance movement introduced its plans for solving
the myriad problems of the growing city.

In the early years of the movement the Young Men's Christian Association provided the Chicago Woman's Christian Temperance Union
with an office rent free, and the temperance women regularly met in
the YMCA's Lower Farwell Hall where the Chicago WCTU sponsored
daily gospel temperance prayer meetings for the next ten years. For
several months Willard's life physically revolved around the YMCA,
which meant that she was literally catapulted into the miseries of the
big city. Although Evanston was still home, she more frequently stayed
in Chicago with various friends and fellow workers. She and Kate Jackson continued to be close and boarded together in town that winter
and spring from mid-December on.[2] Willard's excursions out of this
environment were to give temperance speeches and raise money for the
work. She described her life in her notebook: "Came back to the city
from my evening temperance meeting at ———; almost froze getting
from the Lake Shore depot to my office—did freeze indeed. No women
in the streets, everything stark and dead. Found lovely Mrs. F. J. Barnes
and faithful sister Wirt trying to help three poor fellows who had
come in. . . . We have more 'cases,' histories, crises, calamitous distress
revealed to us than could be told in an octavo or helped out by a
millionaire."[3]

That winter the economic depression that followed the panic of 1873
held Chicago in its grip. Willard learned about the hard realities of
urban poverty while she ministered as best she could to the downtrod-
den men who looked for succor to her and the women volunteers who
staffed the office at the downtown YMCA. Frances had a natural sympathy for the oppressed, nourished in her childhood—as was the case
with so many of her generation of reformers including Jane Addams,
Lucy Stone, and Anna Howard Shaw—by her family's strong antislavery convictions.[4] But at this time she had few economic opinions. She
did not envision answers coming from broad social and economic reform programs. No doubt the radical economic views she later espoused owed something to the experiences of this bitter winter, but she
was still groping for solutions, and at least part of the time temperance
combined with strong religious faith appeared to her as sufficient answer to all the problems of the urban poor. But she did attempt to find
practical solutions to distress. On one occasion she called on the head
of the City Relief Committee to propose they sponsor a workhouse
where the unemployed could receive some kind of work relief. She was
rebuffed and disappointed, and fled back to religion: "My strongest

intellectual thirst is to know more of the *Word*. Who is sufficient for these things—these hours when destiny hangs trembling in the uncertain balance of the human will?"[5]

Her greatest satisfactions came from preaching, an art for which she discovered she possessed real talent: "I'd like to go out by myself, looking only to God, and preach the unsearchable riches of Christ! When Bro. —— wrote me that offer to be editor of a New York temperance paper, it didn't stir my soul a bit, but this little Gospel meeting, where wicked men have wept and prayed and said they would see Jesus—it thrills me through and through."[6]

Willard found her ability to play on people's emotions, to inspire them to a level of commitment that might lead them to change their lives, a seductive form of power. She had experienced some of these feelings in teaching, especially when delivering her Friday afternoon homilies to "her girls" at Northwestern, but this was headier stuff. Less than ten years before, a man read the address she had prepared for the meeting at which the Methodist Ladies Centenary Association launched their campaign for funds to build Heck Hall.[7] It had not occurred to her to defy convention and read it herself. Now speaking in public, preaching and exhorting, were her greatest satisfactions.

Much of Willard's preaching that winter was done at the daily Farwell Hall meetings where she frequently led the services. The press reported that attendance was good, enthusiasm "marked." Willard read short extracts of scripture, "explaining and enlarging on each in a lucid manner." The meetings "attract very many whom they are most likely to benefit, young men and boys, strangers in the city, and unemployed, who might otherwise be led to resorts which would end in certain degradation and ruin."[8] She was thirty-five, attractive, and full of zeal. To the young drunkard she offered the sympathy of a mother, to the elderly derelict she played angel of mercy. No doubt she reveled in both roles.

Her identification with the poor was helped by the fact that Willard herself was frequently penniless in the fall of 1874. She began her temperance career with few financial resources. Kate Jackson was traveling in the East until December, and in any case the Willards had not been dependent on her after Frances received her Northwestern appointment. Although certain Kate would gladly have provided her with funds, Frances chose not to ask her for money now.[9] Oliver gave some financial assistance to Mother Willard. But Frances seems to have saved little if any of her quite generous Northwestern salary. Putting money aside never was something Frances Willard did easily, and that fall she went without lunch and walked to save trolley fare because her purse

was literally empty. The little memorandum book for 1874 in which she
kept her accounts showed her nearly $200 in debt by Christmas. She had paid her mother's taxes of $71.55 and spent nearly $60 while attending the state and national WCTU conventions. Her only source of income was the collections taken at meetings where she spoke. For October and November 1874 these totaled $91.60. She spent it all on the movement.[10] When Willard retreated sick and exhausted to Evanston for a fortnight in early December, her mother convinced her she must ask the Chicago women for a salary. Some vague promises of financial support had been made when she was chosen president of the Chicago union. She was now offered $100 a month, but her records show that it was not always forthcoming.[11]

Willard's financial memoranda were sketchy and she was far from meticulous about separating her personal funds—when she had any— from the money she was collecting for the WCTU. A member of the Chicago union eventually suggested she try to be more businesslike, "that when ladies pay you little sums, intended for the Union, as in this bill, that you pass them over to the treasurer or request them to do so as it will save you much bother and perhaps mistakes on both sides which might make hard feelings."[12] Fiscal clarity was unimportant to Willard, and, until the national organization put her on a straight salary in 1886, she always considered money contributed to her personally as subject to any use she saw fit to make of it, including supporting her mother and paying household bills.

Through much of her life Willard talked "poor," although most of the time she lived comfortably enough. Her first months as president of the Chicago union were an exception, and she also experienced lean times when she traveled around the country for the national WCTU in the late 1870s and early 1880s. After that she was paid well for her services, yet she frequently complained of being short of funds. No doubt the shock of her family's sudden penury in the 1860s had shaken her trust in financial security. However, she was never reluctant to beg from all and sundry and accept personal gifts of money, services, or goods from her followers and friends. This help was always given freely and generously acknowledged. Both Willard and her friends believed she was doing the "Lord's work." She conceived of herself as a kind of missionary called to further the temperance cause. She gave generously of her talents and energies. In turn, she found it appropriate that others give to her. And she never profited personally from her writings. She regarded her many books, pamphlets, and articles as contributions to the temperance campaign to which she had dedicated her life, and not as a source of income for herself.

Generous with her own resources, Willard also could accept financial help from others, although she sometimes lamented the position of dependency in which it placed her. Actually during most of her life she was not only self-supporting but also a major source of financial security for her family; moreover, her personal monetary contributions to the movement were not inconsiderable. But gifts from friends made possible luxuries that would otherwise have been denied her. Without Kate's father's generosity she could not have made the journey abroad, although Mr. Jackson felt Frances earned her keep as Kate's companion. Without Lady Henry Somerset's wealth and position, Willard could hardly have presided over the World WCTU from an English country estate with a bevy of secretaries to help her, embarked on her Armenian relief mission in France, or easily shuttled herself, friends, and staff across the Atlantic to cement the Anglo-American women's community of the 1890s. Frances Willard's access to rich friends and her willingness to use them was important in the development of the movement she led.

DESPITE the financial misunderstandings of 1874, the Chicago WCTU was probably the strongest in the nation and proved an excellent base from which Willard moved into the national Union organized that fall. A group of crusaders attending a Sunday school teacher's institute at Chautauqua, New York, issued a call during the summer for a national woman's temperance convention to be held in November 1874 at Cleveland. This convention was preceded by a number of state conventions including one in Illinois. Willard attended as delegate from Chicago and was elected secretary of the Illinois union. She also represented Chicago at the national convention whose delegates were chosen by congressional district. At Cleveland she met a number of well-known temperance women for the first time. Among them were Annie Wittenmyer, probably the leading Methodist laywoman of the 1870s, Martha ("Mattie") McClelland Brown of the Good Templars, J. Ellen Foster, prominent Iowa attorney, and Zerelda Wallace, widow of an Illinois governor and congressman. These women became her close associates for the next few years.

When Willard arrived in Cleveland she was already known to a number of eastern temperance leaders through her activities of the previous summer; in the Midwest, she had gained recognition for her work in Chicago and at the Illinois state convention. Also, just after the Illinois temperance convention the second National Congress of Women met in Chicago. Although Willard did not play a major role at this gathering (the *Chicago Tribune* mentioned her only once), she was elected secretary of the congress.[13] Her address to the assembly was the only temperance speech at the convention, and she thereby staked out her turf as the leading temperance advocate within the broader woman movement.

Although Frances Willard could not yet match Annie Wittenmyer or Mattie McClelland Brown as long-term temperance devotees, she arrived in Cleveland as a fresh, enthusiastic new recruit whose abilities as an organizer and propagandist had been proved and whose platform talents had received modest acclaim in Chicago and in the East. There was some sentiment for nominating her as president, but she withdrew her name, aware that she could hardly compete with temperance stalwarts like Wittenmyer, Brown, and Abbie Fisher Leavitt, all of whom were candidates to preside over the new organization. Wittenmyer was elected president on the second ballot.[14] But Willard was easily elected corresponding secretary on a first ballot, receiving 51 out of 80 votes.[15]

As corresponding secretary Willard held the National Woman's Christian Temperance Union together during its crucial first year. Her organizing efforts, consisting mostly of writing a constant stream of letters to any and all who showed interest in temperance because there was no money for travel, were the primary reason the Union grew in its first year from some 80 delegates from sixteen states to over 200 delegates from twenty-one states and a paid membership of 7,500.

In organizing the National WCTU Willard worked closely with Annie Wittenmyer, twelve years her senior and nationally known for her soldier's relief work during the Civil War, her association with Methodist philanthropic enterprises, and her editorship of the *Christian Woman*, a successful periodical published in Philadelphia. Wittenmyer could tap an enormous circle of churchwomen where her name was a household word. Willard had substantial Methodist connections, but what national prominence she possessed was the product of the last two or three years and not equivalent to that of Wittenmyer. Willard, however, was experienced in planning and making decisions, and she functioned as a leader from the beginning. Her relationship with Wittenmyer was cordial, and she frequently asked her older colleague for both professional and personal advice, for example: "I love you and want you always to deal with me with the utmost plainness. I am trying to be nearer the Master. . . . I know I speak 'rightout' and often it isn't best, but He can make me discreet as well as gentle."[16] The surviving Willard correspondence for the winter of 1874–75 is composed largely of Willard's letters to Wittenmyer. These were hurried notes, almost illegible, that convey a great sense of urgency and frustration. Willard was eager to get on with the work and felt harassed at every turn.

Willard had reason to feel harassed and frustrated. She was adding national organizing to the substantial work load she already shouldered as president of the Chicago union and as secretary of the Illinois WCTU. For the next two years she managed the enormous correspondence of the national Union almost single-handedly, and during that first winter she continued to speak and preach in the Chicago area as well as work directly with distressed men in the Loop. Requests for help came from all over. After the national convention she wrote to Wittenmyer about her plans "to write to each state and territory and stir up women to organize."[17] During the summer of 1875 while presumably on vacation she wrote 160 letters "in six of my resting days." During eighty days that summer she delivered 40 speeches and wrote 2,000 letters.[18] There was no "rest at all," and she was "harried and full of work."[19]

The personal relationship between Willard and Wittenmyer was close and tranquil. Although their differences of opinion were slowly beginning to surface and an outright struggle for power developed later, conflict did not mar their association during the first year. Willard addressed Wittenmyer as "sister" and deferred to her judgment on many occasions. She confided to Wittenmyer that she favored legislative prohibition which the first convention did not endorse and woman suffrage which Wittenmyer strongly opposed. But Willard agreed with Wittenmyer that it would be inexpedient to declare such commitments at this time.[20]

After the 1874 convention Willard and Wittenmyer did not meet until the summer of 1875. Wittenmyer urged Willard to go east in January to attend an executive committee meeting and to accompany her when she presented a petition to Congress supporting a committee to investigate the evils of drink, a major project of the WCTU's first year. But Willard begged off. She did not have the money. Moreover, Chicago needed her and she could "do more good here."[21] By spring Wittenmyer urged Willard to spend part of the summer with her at Sea Cliff, Long Island, a popular temperance watering spot. Willard was eager to join her "if I can go clear of expense and arrange about my mother as I desire to. Especially I want to be with you. I believe we should get along 'first rate.'"[22] At Wittenmyer's suggestion Willard seriously considered leaving Chicago and moving to the eastern seaboard, the seat of WCTU national headquarters and home base for Wittenmyer and Mary Johnson of Brooklyn, the recording secretary. In April she wrote Wittenmyer, "As you say this Chicago is a sterile soil. . . . If I can be more available, I have about concluded I would 'swing loose' from my old moorings. . . . Mother has concluded that where I can do most she prefers to be. This long, cold lonesome winter at Evanston has changed her views materially."[23] However, moving east would create financial problems. Willard now could depend regularly on $100 a month from the Chicago union. Her speaking fees averaged another $100 per month. Salary and fees combined provided a comfortable income at a time when the average postal employee supported a family on less than $1,000 a year and public schoolteachers averaged about $300 per annum.[24] If Willard stayed in Chicago she was assured of a good income. If she moved east she would be dependent solely on the fees from her lectures.

Although Willard did not move east in 1875, she and Kate Jackson traveled in mid-July to Kate's sister's home in Patterson, New Jersey. A few days later Willard joined Annie Wittenmyer at Sea Cliff. Other than their brief encounter at the Cleveland convention, Willard and Wittenmyer had spent no time together. Now they had nearly a month of close association. They discussed tactical and organizational problems, made plans for the fall convention, and conferred on editorial policy for the new WCTU publication, the *Woman's Temperance Union*, a monthly published in Philadelphia by Wittenmyer that they hoped would become the national organ of the woman's temperance movement.[25] They also participated in the National Temperance Camp Meeting, a gathering of workers from the Good Templars, the New York Prohibition party, and the National Temperance Publication Society.[26]

In mid-August Willard attended the temperance rally at Martha's Vineyard. Afterward she traveled in New England, staying with friends, making speeches, and trying to strengthen the state and district unions to ensure a full roster at the national convention to be held in Cincinnati. Willard attended the New York State WCTU convention, visited Buffalo and Canandaigua, and participated in the meetings of the Third Woman's Congress held at Syracuse in mid-October. She was back in Chicago on 25 October.[27]

For over three months Willard was engaged exclusively in work for the national Union, but Chicago continued to pay her salary. She took off again in November for the Cincinnati convention and was gone for nineteen days before Christmas on a speaking tour. The Chicago union was not always pleased with her travel arrangements,[28] but there were advantages for the cause. In effect, the Chicago union subsidized the national union by paying Willard's salary from July 1875 until she resigned as president in 1877. During the WCTU's early years the stronger locals had far greater financial resources than the national Union, and without their help nationwide temperance work would not have been possible.

Willard spent much of the winter of 1875–76 on the road, speaking and organizing for the national WCTU. She led a very different life from the previous winter when she devoted herself to the Chicago union's gospel temperance work with alcoholic men at the downtown mission. Gospel temperance had been a logical extension of the Crusade, using moral suasion to reform drunkards, just as the Crusade attempted to influence both sellers and users to abandon alcoholic beverages. Gospel temperance work proved personally satisfying to Willard and provided her with a great sense of fulfillment. But she turned it aside when she went east that summer and never again regarded preaching to alcoholics as her primary mission. Over time, gospel temperance became less important to Willard as a weapon with which to reform society. As she wrote to Wittenmyer in a memorandum on WCTU goals for the second national convention, they must "pronounce distinctly that our object is not by any means *only* to pull drowning men out of the stream, but . . . to make our influence felt at the fountains of power."[29] Willard was becoming a political animal. A year earlier she had told a large mass meeting in Chicago's First Methodist Church that "she desired to be regarded as a 'doer' rather than a 'sayer.' "[30] The doing to which she aspired had moved her far beyond saving derelicts in Chicago's Loop.

Although Frances Willard chose to earn her living in other professions for short periods during the years she was associated with the WCTU before she became president, she always played an active role in the movement. She continued as president of the Chicago union through 1876, and she served as secretary of the National WCTU until October 1877. She was elected president of the Illinois union in the summer of 1878 and conducted a major suffrage campaign on its behalf. She also made dozens of platform appearances in support of temperance. As long as she was national secretary, she continued her organizing efforts by mail and in person, and worked closely with Annie Wittenmyer in planning for national conventions and the Philadelphia centennial observances. She wrote a column for *Our Union*, the WCTU paper, and performed other editorial duties. At no time did she cease to be a major temperance spokeswoman.

Chapter VI  Interludes

During the winter of 1875–76, Willard changed her goals. Until now she had chosen to exert her influence and make her mark largely through one-to-one relationships with individuals. She had worked as a teacher and administrator. She had functioned as a counselor to derelicts in the Chicago Loop. She had also used her pen to educate and proselytize, though women had long used their skill with the written word to enhance their religious effectiveness or simply to earn money in an acceptable way. Now Willard moved in a quite different direction. Fame tempted her, political influence looked sweet, and the lyceum platform beckoned attractively. Why this turnabout in her priorities?

Perhaps part of the answer can be found in a new friendship that Frances Willard formed in the spring of 1875 with Anna Dickinson, the girl orator of the Civil War lyceum circuit, campaigner for the Republican party cause, and one of the romantic figures of the nineteenth century. Although Dickinson did not attempt to influence Willard's life patterns, she provided her friend with a quite different role model from those to which Willard had previously been exposed. Kate Jackson, for instance, had introduced her to the world of transatlantic travel and life abroad, as well as given her entrée to the eastern monied classes. At a crucial time in Willard's development, Dickinson introduced her to the world of the performer, the spellbinder who could move large audiences. Through her work in the Chicago Loop during 1874–75 Willard had discovered the appeal of pulpit and platform. She developed a taste for performing that teaching and writing could no longer fully satisfy, and she began to experience her extraordinary gift to move large groups of people that had surfaced at the temperance camp meetings of the previous summer. The Farwell Hall noon meetings and the dozens of church temperance meetings she addressed that fall further sharpened her appetite for a mass audience. At just this juncture she met and made friends with Anna Dickinson, an acknowledged celebrity, a powerful speaker, and an entertainer whose gifts had always been used to promote worthy causes, although at this time Dickinson was seriously thinking of using outright drama, the stage, as a vehicle for a career in pure entertainment. Willard's association with Dickinson was her first exposure on a personal level to someone who so clearly functioned as a performer.

Dickinson, the beautiful, innocent young girl with a profound passion for justice and right, had touched the hearts of hundreds of thousands in the decade of the 1860s as she lectured from platforms where women had been unwelcome before. Also Dickinson had mingled with the politically powerful. William Lloyd Garrison had been one of her patrons. She had addressed the House of Representatives in the presence of President Abraham Lincoln, and she had been a stellar attraction at New York's Cooper Union.[1] After the Civil War the fees for her lectures attacking President Andrew Johnson and championing the freedmen brought her an annual income of $20,000 during her most popular years. Dickinson and Willard did not meet until 1875, when Dickinson's fame was already waning, although they had been introduced by mail in 1871 through a mutual friend, Sarah Dolley, and had exchanged a letter or two at that time.[2] But Willard had long been an admirer of Dickinson. While teaching at Pittsburgh Female College she mentioned in her journal reading a sketch of the girl orator, noting that "my heart thrills with the hope of . . . seeing these persons I read about."[3] In 1866 Willard heard Dickinson speak at the Crosby Opera House in Chicago: "went . . . to the Opera House and heard Anna Dickinson on the assassination of Lincoln. [Willard had attended a Frederick Douglass lecture the previous week.] She is a splendid woman and can afford to let people praise or blame her as they listen— but she's too radical."[4] Nonetheless, it was the radical in Dickinson that attracted Frances.

The two women first met in the late winter of 1875 when Willard arranged a lecture for Dickinson in Evanston and entertained her at Rest Cottage. Mother Willard, Anna, and Frances sat up half the night talking. That spring and early summer Dickinson spent several months in Chicago and the friendship flowered. Frances felt as if she had always known her. Anna was easy and spontaneous with people and free to share her emotional intensity. Frances also admired Anna's beauty, the "dark, curly hair flung back from her handsome brow," "her gray eyes," the "poised, elastic tread."[5] Dickinson was about the age Willard's sister Mary would have been had she lived, and Willard may have found some echo in Dickinson of the beautiful sister who had been taken away from her. But unlike Mary, Anna Dickinson was a secularist and a rebel. And although Dickinson shared Willard's goals for women, she did not share Willard's enthusiasm for temperance and evangelical religious commitment.

Willard attempted to enlist Dickinson's services for the temperance cause. She wanted anyone she cared about to share her interests and concerns, and usually she succeeded; but despite herculean efforts she failed this time. Willard was fully aware of Dickinson's potential value to her cause. If Willard had succeeded in recruiting Dickinson for temperance, she would have snared a nineteenth-century popular heroine, the equivalent of Jane Fonda's commitment to peace and social change in the 1970s. Had Dickinson been willing to perform for temperance, she might well have given the cause a great surge of temporary popularity. Willard's first impulse was correct. Anna Dickinson would have helped, at least temporarily. In the long run, however, Dickinson would have hurt temperance by adding a theatrical dimension to the movement. Anna Dickinson was always flamboyant.

For awhile either Dickinson encouraged Willard, or Willard convinced herself that Dickinson would see the light, for she wrote Wittenmyer that "dear Anna Dickinson is coming on bravely in the temperance line. Has promised me to prepare a temperance address for the next campaign—is not going on the stage." At this time Dickinson had appeared only on the lecture platform. Her career as an actress, of which Willard disapproved, did not begin until 1876.[6] Willard had persuaded Dickinson to write a piece on Father Mathew, Irish temperance leader, which, she told Wittenmyer, Dickinson called "a peg to hang the [temperance] speech on." Willard solicited Wittenmyer's support in wooing Anna, a request she was to repeat many times over the next months. She somehow believed that if only Wittenmyer would tackle Dickinson, go to see her after Dickinson returned to her home in Pennsylvania that summer (at about the time Willard and Kate Jackson went east), and invite her to Sea Cliff, Dickinson would be persuaded to join the temperance forces. "I want the temperance women to rally around her. She may yet be all we wish as a Christian and a philanthropist."[7]

But Dickinson did not go to Sea Cliff and she did not join the temperance cause. She wrote Willard, "Dear heart, you are too serious down at that 'Methody' place [Sea Cliff] I am sure." Although she refused to go to the camp meeting, she told Frances, "I read your letter with delight—tho I *don't* agree with you. You must try to love me just as I am, for I do not expect to be otherwise,—& you must love me even if I get worse," for "I love you—in spite of your being so good."[8] A fortnight later Dickinson was still chiding Willard: "If you really care so much for Temperance meetings & religion, let me learn that fact from somebody else. . . . I want you to be interested only in the life, & the things that seem vital to me, & if you are not, I would rather not know the truth."[9] The two women continued to correspond and Willard persisted in trying to interest Wittenmyer in proselytizing for Dickinson's allegiance. Willard and Dickinson met occasionally and remained friends until Willard's death, although after 1876 they ceased to play a central role in each other's lives.[10]

In 1875, however, Anna Dickinson's example may well have propelled Willard irresistibly toward pursuit of the public platform as a major vehicle for furthering her professional life. Of course, she had lectured before. The "New Chivalry" with its mild support of the woman question had been composed for delivery in Chicago in 1871 and repeated several times in midwestern cities as well as the Chicago environs while Willard was at Northwestern. She had written "Everybody's War," her first set temperance piece, in the spring of 1874 and delivered it on many occasions during 1874 and 1875 in churches and at temperance gatherings. She took herself seriously enough as a speaker to arrange for voice lessons from the director of the School of Oratory at Northwestern. She went to his rooms every day for several months and eventually learned to use her voice easily and effectively.[11] But there is no evidence she thought of earning her living as a lecturer until she met Dickinson. Then the prospect of holding thousands in thrall as a spellbinder who commanded substantial fees became compelling. She could never quite match Dickinson's histrionic skills. As one listener wrote, "She [Willard] has not the sauciness, nor the self-assertion of Anna Dickinson, but in persuasive appeal she is far above her."[12]

In the spring and early summer of 1876 Willard lectured frequently, filling engagements in fourteen cities during the month of May alone.[13] That summer she addressed the great Centennial Exposition of 1876 in Philadelphia and the temperance conference at Chautauqua, setting a precedent for women to speak at Chautauqua provided they met the high standards of John Heyl Vincent, founder of the famous New York assembly. Vincent acknowledged that he did not "care for women speakers generally. . . . You [Willard] are one of my magnificent exceptions."[14] In November 1876 she made a formal address at Henry Ward Beecher's world-famed Plymouth Church in Brooklyn, one of the nation's most sought after forums. It was a very high honor indeed.[15]

With such obvious platform success to recommend her, Willard began to look for a commercial agent who could increase her engagements and launch her as part of the top circle of lyceum stars. For assistance she turned to Mary Livermore, who was widely popular

and commanded substantial fees. However, Redpath's lecture bureau,
which managed Livermore and was considered the best in the business, refused to sign on Willard, stating that it would require too much work to promote an "unknown" for the agency's usual ten percent commission. Livermore suggested another agency to Willard and advised her to "get the management of some lecture bureau without delay." She also warned her against going to Boston to give four lectures during Thanksgiving week, when Bostonians were occupied with the holiday.[16]

NOT long afterward Willard acquired her Boston audiences, but once more she changed direction to do it. In January 1877 she joined the staff of the great nineteenth-century evangelist, Dwight Moody. Moody, a successful Chicago businessman who had been born and raised a Unitarian in Massachusetts, had undergone a profound conversion experience as a young man. Already well established in business, he served at the front with the United States Christian Commission during the Civil War, and in 1866 became president of the Chicago YMCA. His work with young men turned him to evangelism, a calling confirmed during his visits to Great Britain in the early 1870s.[17] Moody, with his associate, the organist and singer Ira Sankey, had returned in 1875 from a triumphal evangelical tour of the British Isles where the pair had conducted a series of revival meetings, attended by an estimated 2,530,000 people, that led to an almost unprecedented religious awakening. They returned to the United States with a ready-made audience for their message. Both were superb showmen and spellbinding lay preachers, and thousands of people were eager to find Christ through their ministrations. They preached and sang with tremendous success at great revivals on the eastern seaboard and, during the winter of 1876–77, in Chicago in a large hall seating 8,000 that was built for them on Monroe between Market and Franklin streets.

Frances Willard had first heard of Moody in August 1867 when he returned from his first trip to Europe. However, they did not meet until his crusade of 1876–77 when he asked Willard to lead in prayer a Sunday service attended by 9,000 women. She introduced John B. Gough, temperance orator, at another of Moody's Chicago Tabernacle meetings.[18] Moody obviously was impressed by the Willard charisma. Before leaving Chicago for Boston, he summoned her to his rooms in the Brevoort House where he asked her to join his troupe, first quizzing her about the reasons for her falling out with Charles Fowler at Northwestern. A main base of Moody's support derived from Methodism, and Fowler was a prominent Methodist clergyman. Moody was not looking for trouble. Willard's answer, "Dr. Fowler has the will of a Napoleon, I have the will of a Queen Elizabeth," seemed to satisfy him. They prayed over the decision together. She consulted her mother who counseled her to "enter every open door," advice Willard was likely also to give herself, and in January 1877 she resigned the presidency of the Chicago WCTU.[19]

Willard continued as secretary of the national Union, however. She planned to be useful to the temperance cause, a cause that Moody heartily supported, although his allegiance lay with gospel temperance rather than political solutions like prohibition. But it was the possibility of a career as an evangelist that attracted Willard to Moody. As his colleague she could consistently command an audience of thousands, the press would report her words, the millions of Moody devotees would become her admirers. National fame would be hers at last, for Moody and his movement attracted even more fervent attention and support than did Billy Graham in the twentieth century.

Willard received the fame she coveted in good measure. Six thousand persons were present on a single Sunday afternoon at the Boston Tabernacle to hear Willard preach on "What think ye of Christ," and several hundred converts resulted.[20] She conducted noon meetings, usually called "ladies meetings," every day at the Park Street Church where she would lead the prayers and give a brief informal homily to overflowing audiences. She also presided at Saturday afternoon meetings for young women. These meetings were scheduled in response to requests from teachers and pupils in the public schools and held in churches in different parts of the city.[21] The audiences thrilled her. The power implicit in leading sinners to Christ was ennobling. Here was her métier. At last she had found a course she could follow and feel fulfilled.

But trouble was brewing. Willard seemed prone to financial misunderstandings. Her salary problem with the Chicago union was repeated, because she received no stipend from Moody. Moody was a true philanthropist and never used his enormous religious enterprise for personal gain. Nor as a layman did he ever seek ordination, although he founded the Chicago Bible Institute for religious training. He emphasized the gospel of fatherly love, but he did not pay Willard! She earned her keep by giving temperance lectures in the Boston area in her spare time, an arrangement that may have been part of their agreement from the beginning. However, Moody objected to these lectures. When she explained that her need for funds compelled such a course, a generous check was forthcoming.[22] Moody did not want to share Willard's services, and Willard did not take easily to restrictions on how she saw fit to organize her life. By summer their conflict was open. At temperance meetings Willard shared the platform three times with her friend Mary Livermore, a member of the Unitarian church. Moody felt this association with an unorthodox, if not outright heretical religious movement compromised Willard's work for him. For a time Willard went along with him, and avoided any temperance work of which he would disapprove.

Willard's acquaintance with Unitarians was recent, although there had been Unitarians in her family background. She little understood the central role they played in the New England commonwealth, and she stirred up a real tempest by seconding Moody's proposal that the name of the WCTU be changed to the Woman's Evangelical Christian Temperance Union. The Massachusetts WCTU was aghast. Willard later denied any such intentions, and strongly defended her ecumenicism, writing to Emma Moody, the evangelist's wife, with whom she evidently felt more at ease in rebuttal, "The more I study the subject, the more I fail to see that it is for us to decide who shall work in this cause side by side with us, and who shall not. . . . Whosoever will, may work with me, if only she brings earnest purpose, devout soul, and irreproachable moral character."[23]

Also Willard, the feminist, was offended by Moody's sexist approach to saving souls, whereas Moody no doubt considered himself broadminded in using a woman evangelist. In her letter to Emma Moody, Willard continued, "I cannot think that meetings in which 'the brethern' only are called upon, are one half as effective as those where all are freely invited, and I can but believe that 'women's meetings,' as such, are a relic of an outworn regime."[24] In a way, it was the Fowler struggle all over again. Willard was attracted by the leadership qualities of strong men; however, when they used these qualities to direct the paths she would take, Willard found their interference intolerable.

In fact, Willard had no opportunity to resign from Moody's service. He already had terminated the relationship, although Willard later intimated that it was she who had done so. In August she was informed by Emma Moody, on the evangelist's behalf, that Moody would change his tactics in the fall, that he would work in the smaller New England cities and towns where he would use existing facilities rather than have tabernacles erected. In this more intimate approach, there would be no need for her services.[25] The following month Willard explained her position in a letter to John Heyl Vincent, Chautauqua founder, who also tried to use Frances as an exception to his rule against women lecturers. In the letter, she said she had told Moody, "I cannot give my time and strength and the enthusiasm of my years to bolstering up the old, separatist, oriental idea of her place in the church by conducting his women's meetings!"[26]

Willard later believed she had made great sacrifices for principle when she severed her ties with Dwight Moody. She had dreamed of traveling to England with Moody and carrying the temperance message with her. She felt his prestige would ease the organizing efforts of the WCTU, and his fame would be transferred to women's work for temperance. This would strengthen and unify the movement much sooner than was possible without his support. As she wrote in her autobiography, "It was my dream to do this—to rally under Mr. Moody's direct influence, all the leaders, men and women, of our growing host."[27]

Willard's assessment was wrong. Although the Union's initial successes might have come more quickly had she stayed longer with Moody, such a clear and exclusive tie to orthodox evangelical Christianity would have stunted the WCTU before the century was out. In effect, the WCTU would have been cut off from the mainstream of reform, an association that was to give it broad purpose and flexibility and attract to its banners women of many causes and ideological complexions. Moody was not a simple gospel evangelist. He too was interested in social reform, but he saw social change accomplished only through deep Christian evangelical commitment. The WCTU was able to attract advocates of a broader approach. Willard's instincts in the fall of 1877 were better than her hindsight. She did well to break with evangelism. Moody had given her a great gift. He had made her name something close to a household word in the United States and clearly placed her among the platform personalities of the day. It was a gift she could now use to both further her own career and strengthen the Union. People would come to hear her in greater numbers because of the publicity the Moody connection afforded her. To have prolonged the association would have limited her goals and effectiveness.

MOODY indirectly presented Willard with another great gift. During her Boston revival season Willard met Anna Gordon, a talented young musician from the Boston suburb of Newton who played the organ at Willard's noon meetings. Kate Jackson had not accompanied Willard when she went with Moody to Boston. For the first time in many years Willard was without a confidant, companion, and friend. Jackson had traveled with Willard on her eastern trips in the fall of 1876, and had been with her at the Philadelphia Centennial Exposition in June. But Jackson was not in Boston that winter, and Anna Gordon was able to *"my Little Organist."*

Boston 1877.

Anna A. Gordon. (Reprinted from Willard, *Glimpses of Fifty Years*)

fill the gap caused by her absence. Kate Jackson, though remaining Willard's lifelong friend, did not play the role of companion again.

Photographs taken at the time show Gordon to be a dark-eyed, pensive young woman, not conventionally pretty but with a touch of haunting ethereal beauty. The daughter of a Boston banker who was also treasurer of the American Board of Commissioners for Foreign Missions, Gordon had been brought up in the Congregational church but had already embraced Methodism before she met Willard. Educated at Lasell and Mount Holyoke seminaries, she had recently returned from a year of music study abroad. At twenty-three she volunteered her considerable musical talents to the Moody revival and thereby linked her life for the next twenty-two years to that of Frances Willard, and for the rest of her life Gordon worked for the temperance cause.

Theirs was a happy partnership in every way. To begin with, the performing skills of the two women were complementary, Willard the platform spellbinder, Gordon the facile musician, each with a well-developed sense of theater and an eye for media attention. Over the years Gordon herself developed into a formidable speaker and organizer, specializing in work with young people. Although she loyally supported the older woman's growing allegiance to deep societal change as long as Willard lived, Gordon was at heart an evangelical and a temperance woman, not an advocate of revolutionary social modification. But her devoted service greatly facilitated Willard's ability to pursue the larger social picture.

In Willard's own words, Anna Gordon was her "devoted friend, faithful secretary, and constant travelling companion."[28] Her portrait, which appears in Willard's autobiography, is affectionately titled, "My Little Organist," but Willard did not say much else about their relationship in that prolix volume. A single paragraph sufficed. She described Gordon as "a young woman who has repeatedly convinced ticket-agents that they make mistakes concerning train time; who has a face so honest . . . that she has often got passes for me from entire strangers on her simple say so; who understands travelling as well as Robert Bonner does Maud S.[29] and who hasn't her superior as a business woman on this continent."[30]

Willard's description is correct as far as it goes. Gordon was a superb arranger. No public figure was ever blessed with a more efficient and devoted chief of staff. After the National WCTU began paying her salary in 1886, Gordon's official title was "private secretary to the president." She also held administrative posts within the Union, especially in connection with juvenile work. Her main role, however, was as Willard's personal aide. She relieved Willard of all the petty cares of daily living: "her chief never carries a purse or looks after a bill."[31] She wrote Willard's letters to her mother when they were on the road together, as well as taking care of business correspondence. Her power within the Union also became considerable. For example, she screened all Willard's correspondence, "giving me only those letters that are important for me to read."[32] Gordon was the one person privy to Willard's private machinations and political maneuverings within the increasingly complex organization that Willard led, and she frequently acted as Willard's agent and informant in the internal squabbles that developed over the

years. Willard's work would never have been as effective without efficient, organized Anna Gordon at her side.

But the Gordon-Willard relationship ran much deeper than allegiance and convenience. Gordon was also Willard's confidant, trusted friend, and one of her primary emotional supports. In a way she was also Willard's beloved daughter, the filial paragon of devotion and sacrifice that Willard could not quite force herself to be to her own mother. Gordon made her home with Willard and her mother in Rest Cottage, and also became a surrogate daughter to Mary Hill Willard, as happened with other young associates of Frances over the years and with Kate Jackson earlier. Although several young W C T U workers lived at Rest Cottage as part of the family in the 1880s and early 1890s, serving Frances and her causes and cherishing her mother, Frances's relationship with Anna was primary and Anna's devotion to Frances was total. Gordon's sister was dying in the fall of 1880, yet she spent Thanksgiving with the Willards in Evanston, forgoing with regret the meeting "for the last time on earth" of the quartet of Gordon sisters at Auburndale, Massachusetts.[33] Willard and Gordon became almost two sides of a single coin as their years together unfolded and they pursued their common public and private goals.

After Willard's death, Anna Gordon transferred her loyalty and services to Lillian Stevens, Willard's successor as president of the W C T U. She worked faithfully as Stevens's chief aide, living in her home, relieving her of petty detail, and no doubt influencing W C T U policy until Stevens died in 1914. Only then did Gordon move out in her own right, succeeding Stevens as president of the W C T U, an office she held until 1925. It was Anna Gordon who saw temperance hopes realized in the Eighteenth Amendment.

Much of the success of women's movement into public life in the latter part of the nineteenth century depended on just such supportive emotional relationships between and among women. This world of warm, intense, mutually helpful interaction among women of like interests and goals provided deep satisfaction and fulfillment. When Frances Willard moved away from this supportive circle she confronted disappointment, stress, and hostility—as, for example, in her interactions with Charles Fowler and Dwight Moody. When she clung to other women for aid and succor, her world was relatively safe. Most women reformers of the period, even those who were married, such as Lucy Stone, Mary Livermore, and Elizabeth Cady Stanton, developed such supportive relationships with women. Those who did not, like Emma Goldman, found it hard going.[34]

ANOTHER brief interlude interrupted the course of Frances Willard's total commitment to the temperance cause. On 17 March 1878 Willard's only brother, Oliver, died suddenly, probably of a hemorrhaging intestinal ulcer, at age forty-three. Oliver Willard, educated at Oberlin and Beloit, trained for the ministry at Garrett Theological Seminary, and married to Mary Bannister, daughter of a leading Methodist clergyman, had not had an easy time finding a life course that suited him. Talented and articulate like the rest of the family, Oliver Willard was also plagued with religious doubts and had a drinking problem. After graduation from Garrett in 1861 he spent the next five years as minister of the Methodist church in Denver, Colorado, a post from which his obituary stated he "retired because of ill health." Frances later was convinced that "but for tobacco and alcohol he would become the chief pulpit orator of our church."[35]

Upon retiring from the ministry, Oliver was involved for six years in various businesses and journalistic schemes, with uncertain financial rewards and uncertain success in overcoming his personal problems. In 1872 he became editor of the *Chicago Evening Mail*, a small daily that later became the *Post and Mail*, and still later the *Post*, a struggling enterprise subject to frequent reorganization. At the time of his death, he was editor-in-chief of the *Post* and president of the stock company that owned the paper. Oliver Willard never supported prohibition, but lent his newspaper's support to gospel temperance.

Frances's relationship with her brother, although marred by disappointment and worry, had always been close. He had been on hand with a carriage to escort her from the meeting of Northwestern trustees where she had tendered her resignation. After 1871 he lived in Evanston with his wife and four children and gave family support to Mother Willard when Frances was absent on her many travels. She was lecturing in Saginaw, Michigan, when he died. He had helped assure her an audience in Evanston when she spoke there for the first time after the Moody interlude. He was her "dear, kind brother, life long comrade and friend."[36] She cherished the fact that for a year before his death Oliver had been "punctual to his religious duties," a pillar in the community (he was a member of the Evanston city council), and attentive to his family. Perhaps he had safely settled down at last, but Mother Willard apparently found a modicum of relief in his death. She met the returning Frances, who expected to find her mother shattered and distraught, with the jubilant "Praise Heaven with me—I've grown gray praying for my son—and now to think your brother Oliver is safe with God!"[37]

But there were practical problems. The two Willard ménages lived comfortably, as always, but with few reserves. What assets Oliver had were invested in the *Chicago Post*, in precarious financial condition and once more undergoing reorganization. The paper was losing several hundred dollars a week. When no one else could be found who would undertake to save it, Frances and Mary Bannister Willard decided to make the attempt. They had little to lose. Bankruptcy was the only alternative. Willard assumed the duties of editor, Mary Bannister Willard those of publisher and business manager. The two women directed a staff of sixty men, including a dozen editors and reporters. Faithful Anna Gordon acted as Willard's assistant at the office and also found temperance lecture engagements, their only source of ready income, for Willard.[38]

Despite the financial headaches, Frances Willard enjoyed her role as editor. She brought her devotion to the woman movement and women's superior virtues with her to the *Post*. Short paragraphs in the paper expressed her sentiments—for example, "Some defeats are half-way victories. The ladies who have wrought so industriously to advance the equal suffrage cause in Congress may fairly regard in this light the Senate committee's adverse report given to the public this morning. The report recites the usual arguments against the measure, a thousand times reiterated and as often inadequately met."[39] In announcing the new leadership, she wrote that the *Post* was first of all a newspaper and would remain so. Nevertheless, the two women were determined "to bring with them the amenities and elevating influences which characterize their home life and that can justify women entering circles of influence popularly thought to lie 'beyond their sphere.'" They intended to produce a paper "that the reading thereof will tend to make the world better tomorrow."[40] From some circles their brave venture won mild accolades. A Wisconsin newspaper pointed with pride to the Willards' Wisconsin connections and commented favorably on "women in a new sphere."[41]

Although they refused liquor ads after they assumed management, the financial condition of the *Post* made it impractical for the new editors to cancel existing contracts for such advertisements. The impossible position of a leading temperance spokeswoman flaunting temptation before the public was too much for the abstinent world.[42] Willard was castigated and her unfaithfulness deplored, although the newspaper treated temperance well if one ignored the advertising columns. Essentially the *Post* was a general newspaper, pro–Republican party, propeace, and guilty of the usual American preoccupation with the lives of European royalty.

Women had long practiced journalism in the United States, occasionally taking responsibility for keeping a paper going on the death of a husband in the eighteenth century, and continuing to manage small town newspapers under similar circumstances in the nineteenth.[43] By 1878 women had edited and published a number of suffrage, temperance, and religious journals, but the Willards may have been the first women to assume editorial and business management of a metropolitan daily newspaper. The experiment was brief and traumatic, if optimistic. The mandate of an empty exchequer was inexorable, and in early summer the *Post* was sold at auction to the *Daily News*, owned by Victor E. Lawson and Melville E. Stone.[44] Willard vowed never again to become the responsible head of any journalistic venture, a vow she repudiated at least in part when she became editor of the wctu's organ, the *Union Signal*, in 1892. That position, however, was largely titular and involved no financial responsibility.

Willard's stint with the *Post* was the last time she looked outside the temperance movement for her livelihood. Her interludes with Moody and the *Post* had not distracted her from the temperance cause. Her devotion to the wctu was constant. But from mid-1878 on the wctu came first, and her other interests were intended to further its cause. She never again risked the firm foundation provided her by the Union for status in her own right and ultimate control over what course she would pursue, what stands she would take.

Chapter VII  Victory

Although busy with other professional duties much of the time from 1877 to mid-1878, Willard in no way withdrew from an active role in the temperance movement. She combined her work for Dwight Moody with temperance lecturing and organizing. Economic necessity kept her on the hustings while she attempted to rescue the doomed *Chicago Post*. In fact, during these years Willard cautiously but inexorably acted as leader of a major campaign within the temperance movement, a slow but accelerating battle to commit the Union to woman suffrage.

Like many of her contemporaries, Frances Willard was both a deeply religious woman and an incurable romantic. She was convinced that prayer and a fortuitously discovered Bible passage had propelled her toward temperance in the first place. Another prayer-induced "heavenly gift" persuaded her to adopt suffrage goals. While preparing for a temperance lecture in Columbus, Ohio, in the spring of 1876, Willard remained home on a Sunday morning for Bible study and prayer:

> Upon my knees alone, in the room of my hostess, who was a veteran Crusader, there was borne in upon my mind, as I believe, from loftier regions, the declaration, "You are to speak for woman's ballot as a protection to her home and tempted loved ones from the tyranny of drink," and then for the first and only time in my life, there flashed through my brain a complete line of argument and illustration—the same that I used a few months later before the Woman's Congress, in St. George's Hall, Philadelphia, when I first publicly avowed my faith in the enfranchisement of women.[1]

As a Northwestern administrator, Willard had been afraid to openly express interest in the suffrage movement. Her caution did not disappear when she allied herself with temperance forces. She believed association with the suffrage cause would strain her credibility with the conservative churchgoing Midwesterners attracted to militant temperance during the Crusade winter of 1873–74. However, through her temperance work she developed close associations with suffrage leaders, particularly Mary Livermore, who was an ardent suffragist as well as president of the Massachusetts WCTU. Ideologically, Willard felt no conflict. She was as ardently prosuffrage as Livermore or anyone else. But she also saw that the Union was still weak and financially hard pressed, that it could ill afford to alienate any of its present and potential constituency.

By the spring of 1876, however, Willard's patience had worn thin. She warned Annie Wittenmyer that she could not suppress her suffrage views much longer. Both Willard and Wittenmyer were determined that the WCTU, infant that it was, play a major role at the Philadelphia Centennial Exposition to be held in June. The second WCTU convention sanctioned the Union's participation in the centennial festivities and authorized the calling of an international women's temperance assemblage to coincide with the celebration. Several delegates, including Letitia Yeomans from Canada, Margaret Parker from Scotland, and Margaret Lucas, who was the sister of John Bright, British liberal and free trade advocate, attended the Philadelphia meeting and helped organize an international Union. The new organization was short-lived, however, for the American union was not yet strong enough to give adequate support to such an ambitious undertaking. Willard was tempted to use this international forum to announce publicly her belief in woman suffrage. She asked Wittenmyer's advice, and Wittenmyer unequivocally opposed such a course. Willard somewhat reluctantly agreed that Wittenmyer was right about keeping the suffrage issue out of the international meeting, but added, "its close at home—I don't know how long I can stand it."[2]

Her public commitment to suffrage came later that summer at the Old Orchard Beach temperance camp meeting. Two years earlier Willard had made her eastern debut as a temperance lecturer on those same sandy shores. Again she was well received:

Miss Willard gave another of her masterly and all convincing addresses, at Old Orchard, in the afternoon. In this address she committed herself to "Woman's duty to vote." She had long hesitated, but now that the ballot has been prostituted to undermine the Sabbath, and rob our children of the influence of the Bible in our schools, she thought it time that Woman, who is truest to God and our country by instinct and education, should have a voice at the polls, where the Sabbath and the Bible are now attacked by the infidel foreign population of our country.[3]

The Methodists found her arguments "forcible, her logic almost overwhelming and her elocution captivating."[4] But Willard's blatant appeal in this speech to nativist prejudice was not typical of her approach to social problems. Throughout her life she remained remarkably open to people of all races and religions. She was not a bigot. Nevertheless, her Orchard Beach speech characterized in an important sense the way she worked. She liked to approach problems indirectly. For many years Willard approached the suffrage question obliquely rather than head on. She did not ask for the women's ballot as a matter of natural right, but as an expedient means for achieving what she saw as just social ends.

Willard found less offensive arguments to support the temperance cause, but the evangelical audience at Orchard Beach was not upset by her implicit nativism and patent sabbatarianism. Even Susan Anthony raised no questions about the wisdom of Willard's rationale for supporting the women's vote. Anthony wrote Willard, "I had a most delightful recital of the night of your first public committal. I rejoice that at last you have obliged the 'innerlight' as the Quakers say—the 'divine inspiration' I say, and put under your feet all the timid conservative *human* counsels. I feel sure you will find great peace and strength in your obedience to your *own* highest convictions. Rest assured the *higher & highest truths* never come to us *too soon* for us to give to the world."[5]

Anthony was jubilant. What a catch for the suffrage cause! Willard already was highly visible in Protestant circles. The WCTU, which had only 13,000 dues paying members in the fall of 1876, had nearly doubled its membership during the past year and was much larger and stronger than the National Woman Suffrage Association.

Anthony and Willard had been friends since October 1875, when both were guests of Mary Lattimore, temperance and suffrage activist, during the third national Woman's Congress. On that occasion Anthony heard Willard speak for the first time. Their friendship continued for the rest of Willard's life. Anthony was firmly committed to abstinence and convinced of the necessity for a temperate society although she did not share Willard's faith in legislative prohibition or local option, both of which she believed would only dam the stream temporarily. Rather, she maintained that better born and better educated children, offspring "of cultured, conscientious women," could provide a permanent solution to the alcohol question.[6] Anthony invited Willard to spend a day that summer at Elizabeth Cady Stanton's home in Tenafly, New Jersey, where Anthony and Cady Stanton were working on their *History of Woman Suffrage*, in order "to talk over the whole ground with you."[7] Willard did not join them at this time, returning instead to Illinois for the state convention, but the trio did meet when Willard went east again that fall.

Willard modified her suffrage address significantly before using it at major appearances in the fall of 1876. In doing so, she borrowed a term from Canadian temperance worker Letitia Yeomans, who had also attended the Philadelphia conferences in June and the Orchard Beach camp meetings in August. In a speech at Orchard Beach, Yeomans used the phrase "home protection" in its conventional sense of tariff protection for infant industries.[8] Willard seized on the phrase, recognizing its superb potential as a slogan to concisely express the function of the women's ballot as a natural and proper extension of women's sphere. In October 1876, she changed the title of her temperance lecture of 1874–76 from "Everybody's War" to "Home Protection" and used it early that month when she addressed the fourth Woman's Congress in Philadelphia.[9] Willard's speech was described as "an earnest plea for Woman Suffrage as a temperance instrumentality . . . a fresh breeze, which the great audience cheered with genuine approval."[10] Her message was loud and clear: "We have carried ballots to men year after year, urging them to vote; but we have made up our minds that it is just as easy for us to vote ourselves."[11]

The doctrine of home protection implied careful nurturance, womanly virtue, and love of family—all qualities the nineteenth century found admirable and worthy when practiced by the female sex. The home protection ballot, as advocated by Willard in the 1870s and early 1880s, was also a flexible weapon. A ballot based on natural rights was, by its very nature, total. There was no room for compromise if women had the inalienable right to vote. But there could be levels of home protection. In the early years of the suffrage movement, many WCTU members viewed the home protection ballot as limited to giving women the vote on matters directly related to the liquor traffic, local option, licensing, and prohibition. Home protection soon was expanded to include women's concerns as citizens with a broad continuum of social problems that might directly or indirectly affect the home. Eventually, the home protection argument was little more than rhetoric. Natural rights took its place as the WCTU unequivocally pushed women's demand for the vote in the 1880s.

One of the great strengths of the WCTU was the room for differences in national, state, and local unions. The home protection resolution passed at national conventions could be interpreted in a variety of ways. By 1885 five state unions were committed to full suffrage, and true consensus on a women's ballot was beginning to develop in the North. By 1892 the *Union Signal*, the WCTU's national official publication, stated that men had no more right to disfranchise women than women had to deny men the vote. That year Willard clearly used the natural rights argument rather than home protection in her presidential address. In 1894 consent of the governed replaced home protection as the argument supporting the women's ballot in the resolutions of the national convention.[12]

For Willard personally, progress toward unequivocal support of the women's ballot was swift and sure. Among her papers is a chronology labeled "suffrage," written in her own or Anna Gordon's hand,[13] in which she lists the significant events in her march toward support of woman suffrage. She begins, not with her childhood yearnings but with her Chicago meeting with Anna Dickinson in January 1875. Next she notes her meetings with Anthony the following October and Lucy Stone on 12 February 1876. The notation of Susan Anthony's speech at Evanston on 29 April bears the terse comment, "Conviction." Willard's unsuccessful letter to Annie Wittenmyer asking permission to use the Philadelphia Centennial Exposition as a forum for her public commitment to suffrage is the next item. Meetings with Anthony and Stone in July are noted, but for 29 July, when Willard made her first major address at Chautauqua, she has entered a laconic "refrained." The note of her temperance camp meeting address at Orchard Beach is followed by the phrase "spoke out" in block capitals. Anthony's September letter and her visit to the *Woman's Journal* office are also duly recorded. Certainly this chronology implies that Anna Dickinson started Willard on the suffrage path, that Susan Anthony played a major role in fanning the flames, and that her interaction with Lucy Stone was not unimportant. Though terse, it probably describes her movement toward commitment to the women's ballot more accurately than her romantic accounts in *Glimpses of Fifty Years* and *Woman and Temperance*.

Willard's personal relationships with suffrage leaders were warm and friendly. Lucy Stone, Mary Livermore, Julia Ward Howe, and Susan Anthony were her beloved friends for the rest of her life. The exception was Elizabeth Cady Stanton. Willard's coolness toward Stanton can be traced to an unhappy encounter between the two women in the fall of 1873 when Willard was deep into her losing battle at Northwestern.[14] Eager to exploit the controversy, the *Chicago Tribune* publicized Willard's self-report form for the Woman's College, hoping to stir up conflict over separate rules for men and women. By chance Cady Stanton was in Chicago for lectures. Stanton, who followed the fracas in the newspaper, wrote a letter to the editor in which she praised the *Tribune*'s anti-Willard editorial and scathingly attacked Willard's formulation of women's rules. Willard's students came to her defense in the

Tribune's columns, stating that the paper's account was "unjust, preju-
dicial, and exaggerated," and that the "unkindest cut of all is the attack
by Mrs. Elizabeth Cady Stanton."[15] Willard could never quite forgive
Cady Stanton and felt Stanton had behaved reactively without knowing the facts. The two women worked together but were never personal
friends.

ONCE committed to suffrage, Willard mapped out a campaign to
bring the Union with her and also to cement her connections with the
organized suffrage movement. On their return from the 1876 Maine
camp meetings, Willard and British temperance leader Margaret Parker
called at the offices of the *Woman's Journal*, an organ of the American
Woman Suffrage Association, to officially express "their interest and
sympathy with the cause of Woman Suffrage."[16]

Willard's next step was to introduce a home protection resolution at
the Illinois state WCTU convention at Dixon on 20 September 1876.
She hoped the firm support of Illinois for home protection would
provide ammunition for a similar move at the national convention to
be held the following month. The resolution avoided the word "suffrage" but asked "That by prayer, persuasion, and petition we will seek
to influence those strongholds of power, the national Congress, State
Legislature and Municipal Councils, whence the rum shop derives its
guarantees and safeguards."[17] Jennie Willing, one of the Chautauqua
initiators of the WCTU, immediately saw the suffrage connection, and
another member of the convention moved that the resolution be tabled. But there was also a motion to adopt. Willard defended the proposal in a moving address, stressing that leadership must come from
the West, and the resolution carried unanimously.

With her Illinois victory safely in her pocket, Willard spoke out at the
national convention, which met at Newark in October 1876 right after
the Woman's Congress. This time Willard faced formidable opposition.
Annie Wittenmyer relentlessly opposed both granting women the vote
and injecting the issue into WCTU conclaves, but she could not prevent
Willard from using one of the public evening sessions as a forum for
her suffrage appeal. In the Central Methodist Church, Willard addressed a packed meeting presided over by the president of the New
York WCTU and with Annie Wittenmyer on the platform. She began
by discussing how women's power "may be most effectively exercised,"
proceeding with more caution than plain speaking, and using her argument that women must have "a voice in the decision by which the rum
shop door shall be opened or closed." Then she described the success of
petition campaigns for local prohibition. Women, including lower-class

women, had been more than willing to sign the petitions, "which re- buts the hackneyed assertion that women of the lower class will not be

found on the temperance side, [for] the ignorant, the poor (many of
them wives, mothers, daughters of intemperate men) were among the
most eager to sign the petition, [and] Catholic women would vote with
Protestant women upon this issue for the protection of their homes."[18]
Willard did not use the term "home protection" in the body of this
address, but the idea was clearly delineated.

The reaction of the convention was mixed. Lucy Butler, who chaired
the meeting, dissociated the Union from Willard's discourse: "I wish it
clearly understood that the speaker represents herself and not the
Woman's Christian Temperance Union, for we do not propose to trail
our skirts through the mire of politics." Annie Wittenmyer's bitter
remark, "You might have been a leader, but now you'll only be a scout,"
has been quoted many times.[19] But the applause was stronger than
Willard had hoped for, and the convention passed a mild home protection resolution suggesting that women's wishes on temperance matters
be consulted by petition rather than the ballot. More importantly, Willard had reiterated her personal commitment to woman suffrage and
made it clear that her goal was to win the National WCTU's official
support of the vote for women. This goal would not be achieved until
1881, but her intention to use the temperance movement to further
women's causes including suffrage was now unmistakable.

In taking this step Willard exercised one of her major strengths as a
leader. She was a synthesizer, an accommodator, and an innovator all at
the same time. Willard was able to take cultural values almost universally accepted as being women's special province—for example, the
nurturant home—and transform them into a political arsenal to be used
to advance women's rights and social and economic position.[20] She
performed just this function as she began her campaign to lead the
WCTU into the suffrage camp via home protection. She synthesized
two previously opposite points of view: the women's rights feminism,
best exemplified by Elizabeth Cady Stanton, which was basically egalitarian and antagonistic to the idea of women's separate sphere; and the
idea of a separate women's culture, best exemplified by Catharine Beecher, which emphasized women's special mission in society.[21]

In performing her function as synthesizer, Willard was a consummate and successful manipulator, a talent that greatly facilitated her
success. She was also a canny pragmatist, always willing to compromise
or equivocate. For example, she managed to begin her prosuffrage
campaign within the WCTU without the support, but also without
unduly ruffling the feathers, of Annie Wittenmyer. Until she was strong

enough to win, Willard alternately challenged and deferred to Wittenmyer. She accepted Wittenmyer's veto of using the Philadelphia Centennial as a forum to endorse the women's ballot, but turned around
and used the Orchard Beach temperance rally, over which Wittenmyer
had no control, to acknowledge publicly her interest in the vote for
women. Willard opposed Wittenmyer by suggesting to the WCTU national convention that the home protection ballot was a proper temperance weapon, but the next day renominated Wittenmyer for president
in a respectful and affectionate speech.[22]

Willard was also a planner and a superb tactician. Consciously or not,
she planned years in advance the strategy that would lead to eventual
victory. Five years would elapse before the WCTU officially endorsed
the home protection ballot, but the steps en route were carefully maneuvered by Willard. Her great talent both for words and for compromise served her well as strategist and tactician. As she pursued her final
goal, an unrestricted women's ballot, she stressed minor objectives her
constituency could accept and approve. She carefully charted a course
where small, reasonable, almost universally acceptable demands led in-
sistently and logically to the goal she sought. She did this more than
once as a leader, but the use she made of the doctrine of home protection was crucial to the success of her career. Who could argue that
women did not have a right to protect the home, that citadel of wom-
en's influence? And granting such a premise led inevitably to protecting
the home from demon rum, commonly recognized as a clear and present danger. However, to effectively execute this mission other social
problems—inadequate prisons, unemployment, juvenile delinquency,
the need for kindergartens—needed to be attacked. When confronted
by a frontal assault from the antisuffrage forces, Willard could retreat
into home protection and the turf of general agreement, but as additional problems were accepted, new goals were enunciated and new
instruments required to achieve them. Willard never asked for everything at once. She brought people around.

Willard's creative backing and filling was in direct contrast to the
tactics of Elizabeth Cady Stanton, who most often chose "confrontation and a high moral stance" over political maneuver and compromise.[23] Unlike Willard, Stanton was an enthusiast, not a politician. She
was always forthright in speaking her mind. Willard was an inveterate
dissembler and a clever and effective insinuator. She played the role of
sweet conciliator whereas Cady Stanton assumed the stance of militant
radical. Stanton herself recognized Willard's talent for conciliation.
When in March 1888 Willard appeared before a United States Senate
committee investigating suffrage as a representative of the Interna-

tional Council of Women, Cady Stanton, who was making the arrangements, scheduled Willard as the final speaker, believing she would leave
the committee in a friendly mood. Willard obliged as usual, emphasizing the womanliness of suffrage women and attributing male opposition to women's rights as well meant but misguided chivalry.[24]

AT the same time that Willard began to move the Union toward suffrage support, she began her campaign to achieve another of her goals,
the presidency of the WCTU. Just before the 1877 convention she resigned as corresponding secretary of the national Union. She must have
known her name would be placed in nomination for president that year
and was clearing the decks to avoid embarrassment, although her excuse was "feeling that her Master called her for the present to do more
evangelical work."[25] In fact Willard quietly sought, while openly dis-
avowing, a presidential contest with Annie Wittenmyer. Shortly after
the convention Mary Livermore wrote Lucy Stone, "This letter will tell
you one grievance. Frances Willard wanted to be president of the National Woman's Temperance Union and was defeated."[26] Livermore
had been privy to Willard's plans and ambitions for some time, and the
two had appeared on the same platforms that spring.

Willard's candidacy was placed before the convention by her good
friend, J. Ellen Foster, Iowa attorney, suffragist, and temperance
worker. Foster's nominating speech followed a moment of silent prayer,
and she quoted Jesus speaking to his disciples, "whosoever will be chief
among you, let him be your servant."[27] Although Willard did not see
herself as Jesus, she certainly saw herself as one of his loyal disciples,
and she was not displeased by Foster's encomium. Willard initially
declined the nomination but still received 39 votes to Wittenmyer's 60.
The challenge was clear, if polite and publicly unsolicited. Wittenmyer
had a rival for president of the WCTU.[28]

The convention of 1877 was an appropriate place for Willard to present her first serious challenge to Wittenmyer's leadership. The conclave met in Chicago. Although Willard was no longer president of the
Chicago union, she was in charge of convention arrangements and gave
the welcoming address in an opulent setting she had designed herself.
The stage was draped with festooned banners, vines trailed from pedes-
tals, and flowers and green plants spilled over the podium in lush
profusion.

Willard was on home ground in territory where she was viewed as
the indisputable leader of the Union regardless of who held the presidency, and where support was greatest for her program. Voting for
officers at WCTU conventions was done by secret ballot; therefore, the

record does not show which delegates supported Willard against Wittenmyer, but state unions did publicly commit themselves on issues, and the Midwest clearly supported Willard on suffrage. A reasonable inference can be made that Willard's presidential support was greatest in the Midwest.

By 1877 the differences between Wittenmyer and Willard centered on three issues. First, Wittenmyer believed in a strong, uniform national organization with little program flexibility on the state and local levels. Willard advocated a laissez-faire attitude toward state and local unions with few outright requirements except the payment of national dues. Second, Wittenmyer unequivocally opposed injecting the suffrage issue in any form into the program of the WCTU. Willard openly advocated the home protection ballot and quietly supported full suffrage for women. Third, Wittenmyer supported the existing system of representation in national conventions, a delegate for each congressional district and a system that gave disproportionate strength to the populous East. Willard campaigned for representation based on actual paid membership, a system that would reflect the WCTU's strength in the Midwest and incidentally increase the number of delegates from the states where Willard was most popular.[29] All three differences revolved around the women's ballot and who would ultimately control the Union. Local control permitted prosuffrage state and local unions to pursue Willard's home protection program regardless of national's attitude. A change in the delegate base would strengthen the Willard forces within the Union.

Although the battle lines were solidifying, Willard and Wittenmyer avoided a personal rupture. In discussing their differences, Willard's tone was always conciliatory. Before the 1878 convention she wrote Wittenmyer, "May God bless you dear friend, & may he lead us both, . . . so that we may lay no plans for which we do not feel that He has given us authority. . . . Let us seek to return to the deepest spiritual phase of our work wherein we have departed from it, but let us not judge one another any more if to any it seems religious to mention all the elements of power with which God has invested our cause—even if the ballot be one of them."[30] Couching her point of view in evangelical language came naturally to Willard. She sincerely believed she was furthering God's work, but her piety also served to allay Wittenmyer's fears and avoid open rupture.

Nevertheless, conflict was unavoidable at the 1878 convention. Since the last convention two references to the women's ballot had appeared in *Our Union*, the WCTU national newspaper. Wittenmyer threatened to call a special convention if this happened again. Willard, backed by five state unions, argued that it was unfair to exclude from the national publication news of work done by local unions to promote the home protection ballot. Willard won this round, and the convention agreed that the columns of *Our Union* could be used to promote the home protection ballot, but the debate was long and the issue hard fought by both sides.[31] However, a resolution committing the convention to out-right support of the home protection ballot lost and continued to lose until Willard's method of selecting delegates to the national convention on the basis of paid membership was implemented in 1881.

In 1878 Willard again was nominated for president and lost to Wit-tenmyer by only ten votes. For the first time the convention refused to make Wittenmyer's election unanimous.[32] Victory was within reach. Willard and Wittenmyer continued to correspond, although Willard's salutation changed from an affectionate "Dearie" to "Dear Sister Wit-tenmyer" and she began to sign her letters with a formal "Frances Willard." She continued, however, to urge "kindly thoughts and friendly personal relations toward our sisters who think differently from us."[33] Willard's flexibility and willingness to extend the olive branch never hurt her.

Willard arrived at the Indianapolis convention in 1879 after a trium-phant year spent leading the Illinois union in the first major WCTU campaign for the home protection ballot. Illinois and Willard lost the battle, but in the process had focused spectacular attention on temper-ance. A petition with 180,000 signatures had been presented to the legislature, and a bill placed on the house calendar permitting women to vote on licenses for liquor dealers.[34]

Despite the bill's quiet death, the campaign had been a masterpiece of effective public relations. Willard herself kicked off the petition cam-paign in December and solicited the first signature.[35] She led her forces to the state capitol at Springfield, where they were received in the governor's rooms on 4 March. On the evening of the fifth, a mass meeting was held in the chambers of the house of representatives itself. Women filled the galleries when the bill was introduced and the peti-tion presented to the house on 6 March, and Willard, J. Ellen Foster, and Susan St. John, wife of the Kansas Prohibitionist governor, sat beside the speaker and were allowed to address the house briefly.[36] That spring Willard spent several weeks in Springfield keeping the issue alive. The campaign did not end in legislative action, but it generated impressive publicity and contributed to the success of several hundred local option campaigns in Illinois that year. The whole effort had been Willard's show, and it contributed substantially to her stature as a tem-perance leader.

The commanding leadership Willard exhibited certainly was a factor in her easy defeat of Wittenmyer at the 1879 convention. The vote was 99 to 40 in Willard's favor.

FRANCES WILLARD had just turned forty. Her light brown hair was streaked with gray. The ginger red of her rebellious youth had long since softened. One observer described her as of medium height and slender build, womanly, graceful, with a "sunshiny face."[37] Another commented that she must have been beautiful when young and that she was still uncommonly attractive with a slender, pretty figure, fair complexion, delicate regular features, and a becoming costume, usually a simple well-cut brown or black dress with a sky blue tie at the throat.[38]

Willard had a talent for dressing both appropriately and with an eye to accentuating her best features. She loved blue and looked well in its soft shades, but blue was not a suitable color for business and platform engagements in the nineteenth century. However, her study and bedroom were decorated in shades of blue and when she received women visitors informally in her home or in hotel rooms she frequently wore a blue morning frock or light wrapper, highlighting the bright blue eyes behind the pince-nez spectacles that she always wore.

Willard still lived with her mother and Anna Gordon in Evanston's Rest Cottage, her home of twenty years. She loved Evanston, that "quiet city," which she described as "kissed on one cheek by Lake Michigan's waves, fanned from behind by prairie breezes." Long avenues of trees, widespreading elms and maples and towering oaks, bordered its broad streets and "unfenced velvet lawns."[39] Still a self-contained small midwestern town surrounding the campus of Northwestern University and Garrett Theological Seminary, Evanston was on its way to becoming a major Chicago suburb from which commuter trains carried their daily cargo into the heart of the growing metropolis. Willard took the train regularly to Chicago and the offices of the Chicago WCTU. She also was on the road much of the time, sometimes for weeks on end, lecturing, organizing, and attending meetings and conferences related to her public activities. But Evanston was home and she always saw Rest Cottage as a true haven.

Willard's election as president of the WCTU was more personal triumph than vindication of her support for the women's ballot. A number of elements contributed to her strength. First of all, she had made a major contribution on every level to the WCTU itself. Much of the union's growth during the past five years was attributable to her organizing talents. She had made hundreds of speeches, traveled thousands of miles, and been unstinting in her willingness to attend state and district conventions. While she was corresponding secretary from 1874 through most of 1877, communications from national to local and state unions had gone out over her signature. She was the national officer to whom members wrote for assistance and advice. She had composed much of the practical literature on organization, including *Hints and Helps*, a manual for local officers first published in 1875 and reissued several times. Every member of the Union knew her name, and she had performed some service for almost every active leader including the struggling president of many a small-town WCTU. She was president of one of the strongest state unions at the time of her election and had just led that union with flair and imagination in a major legislative campaign.

Second, in an organization with no dearth of talented and articulate women, Willard stood out with a charisma peculiarly her own. For one thing, she capitalized on her "womanly way" with people. A Boston reporter, watching her in her hotel room before the opening of a convention, described her as a splendid executive, working at all kinds of arrangements, "but never is her manner abrupt or angular"; rather she was gentle and inviting. As people came in she had for each "some special message," a personal greeting. The reporter thought of the power of love as she watched Willard, "responsive, sympathetic, swiftly executive; turning off as much 'business' in five minutes as most women would in five hours; never 'nervous' . . . never at a loss for an instant," always ready with "a clear decision."[40] Her combination of concern, empathy, and affection plus efficient direction was irresistible. Willard's ability to stress womanly techniques for changing society was a major factor in her ability to attract devotion from the forces she led.[41] If her sister Mary's death was responsible for bringing out her softer side, it served her well indeed.

Third, Willard's platform personality contributed in a major way to her ability to inspire personal allegiance. Frances Willard lived in the age of the orator. She faced no competition from radio, television, or even the phonograph. The public platform was the chief form of entertainment rivaled only by the printed word and the stage, and most churchgoers including Willard did not patronize the commercial theater. Willard was among the great platform performers of the late nineteenth century. A Toronto editor who professed to dislike women speakers described Willard's "silver-tongued voice," her "easy flow of choice, poetic language, now rising to a white heat of fervor, and now falling to a tone of melting pathos and appeal," and commented, "her style of address is sharp, incisive and convincing."[42] She often repeated the same speech over and over again, but like a good grass roots campaigner she convinced each audience that her golden words were for it alone. Her home protection address was delivered hundreds of times, but to every new set of hearers it was a fresh effort.

By 1879 Willard was a national figure, another factor that added to her stature within the WCTU. The months with Moody, the gallant try at editing and publishing the *Chicago Post*, and the dramatic home protection campaign in the Illinois legislature had provided Willard with substantial press attention, much of it surprisingly favorable. Church papers were impressed by her popularity and growing fame. Metropolitan dailies admired her womanly decorum. Women watched with growing pride the impressive accomplishments of one of their own sex. All these factors—loyal service to her organization, an aura of womanly charm and concern, platform effectiveness, and a national reputation—played a part in her election as president in 1879. These qualities were more important than any ideological stance she represented.

BUT Willard was not satisfied with personal triumph. Within two years of her election she had brought the Woman's Christian Temperance Union in national convention to accept as part of its program the home protection ballot. In 1880, at the Boston convention, she used her first presidential address to point out that slowly the temperance movement was educating women to the idea that they ought to vote and that they ought to vote against the "grog shops." Women would provide "an army of voters which absenteeism will not decimate and money cannot buy," and, she optimistically continued, "When we desire this 'home protection' weapon, American manhood will place it in our hands." Of course, she mentioned the carrot she always proffered with the stick, that changes would not come suddenly and old values would be preserved. Men "must be convinced that womanliness can never be legislated out of being."[43] Although Annie Wittenmyer was no mean speaker, Willard's address was quite the most eloquent presidential message yet delivered to a national convention. The president's address was a better vehicle for eloquence than the mundane facts and figures of the corresponding secretary's report, and Willard took full advantage of the opportunity. Not only was it the most eloquent, but it was also the longest presidential speech thus far. The previous year Annie Wittenmyer had filled a mere seven pages in the minutes. Willard went on for sixteen.[44] The fact that Wittenmyer herself presided at this session of the convention must have sweetened Willard's triumph, although no resolution for the home protection ballot was passed in Boston.

The next convention brought victory. Meeting in Washington, D.C.,

in October 1881, the delegates went on record for "Home Protection
where Home Protection is the strongest rallying cry; Equal Franchise,
where the votes of women joined to those of men can alone give stability to temperance legislation."[45] The resolution was passed without a
dissenting voice. What is more, the resolution was implemented by a
Committee on Franchise charged with the duty "to furnish advice,
instruction and assistance to States that so desire, in inaugurating measures for securing and using the woman's ballot in the interest of
temperance."[46]

The convention had been a triumphant occasion. Willard's mother
was with her to share the accolades, and Frances was received at the
White House by President Arthur. The majority of delegates supporting her reelection had been overwhelming. She wrote Anna Gordon,
forced to be in Boston because of illness, "Convention has gone splen-
didly!"[47] Woman suffrage, cloaked in womanliness and linked to temperance, had become acceptable to thousands of mainstream American
women, and Frances Willard had articulated this change of view.

Chapter VIII  Celebrity

In the course of the 1880s Frances Willard became America's best known woman, a position she would occupy until her death. Her phenomenal personal success and the wide scope of her professional activities were closely intertwined. During this period she engaged in a strenuous organizing campaign to expand the membership of the Woman's Christian Temperance Union; wrote several books and innumerable small pieces; perfected a life-style centered in Evanston and Chicago that revolved around her mother, Anna Gordon, and several close women associates; and coped with two severely alcoholic nephews whose problems could have proved a substantial embarrassment to her career as a temperance leader. At the same time, she played a major role in the Chicago circle of reform women. She expanded her political base nationally, and slowly developed a cohesive and radical social and economic philosophy. She was visible in religious circles and found herself by the end of the decade the leading lay spokeswoman not only for Methodism but also for Protestant Christianity.

Willard's organizing campaign to spur the WCTU's growth was a triumph in itself. During the eighties the Union grew from 27,000 to nearly 200,000 members, and Willard could take credit for much of this remarkable expansion. For many years she was at home in Evanston for only a few weeks out of fifty-two. She visited a thousand American towns and cities at least once and averaged a meeting a day for a ten-year stint. Willard was on the road not only to organize the Union but also to earn her living, for she received no salary from the WCTU until 1886. Her mother, Anna Gordon, and Frances all were financially dependent on the fees she could command as a platform speaker.

After Willard's brief experiment with a lecture bureau in 1879, she made her own arrangements, which essentially meant that Anna Gordon made them for her.[1] Gordon became adept at wheedling passes from the railroads, arranging transportation at odd hours to out-of-the-way places, even if it meant riding the caboose car on a slow freight train, and shared the hardships and kudos of Willard's transcontinental lecture-organizing tours.

In the early 1880s Willard's most ambitious organizing tours were in the South. This was virgin territory for women's organizations. Aside from their churches and affiliated missionary societies, southern women had little experience with voluntary organizations and no real involvement in the political process. Since early in the nineteenth century, they had shared no common ground with other American women. Willard changed all this by bringing white middle-class southern women into the women's temperance movement. She also put northern women in touch with their southern sisters.

Willard was able to convince southern women that a common cause would soften northern antagonism. At the same time she convinced antislavery northerners that white southerners not only were eager to join this crusade that northern women held dear but also were willing to enlist blacks in the temperance cause. In her autobiography Willard makes much of conciliatory sentiment in the South. Southern temperance women showed sincere reconstructionist attitudes toward the war. They urged Willard to speak to Negroes and recruit them for temperance. They were willing to advocate education for blacks.[2] The diary she kept at the time was less sanguine. When she visited her first large rice plantation near Savannah, she commented, "They are all glad slavery is over—but think the means unjust. Look upon it so differently from our view—think we began the war and must answer for it."[3]

How Willard herself felt about black Americans is difficult to ascertain. She came from an antislavery background, and as a young girl in Evanston had shown true but distant compassion for Chicago's small black population. She was generally sympathetic to the freedmen, but she may never have met a Negro socially until this first southern tour. Over the years, Willard acquired close friends among non-Caucasian and Indian peoples. Pundita Ramabai of India was one of her intimates. Whenever she was in Oklahoma she visited Jane Stapler, daughter of a Cherokee chief. Although she never traveled to the Far East, she had several Japanese friends who visited her in the United States. But there is no evidence that she was intimate with any American black women. She worked with them in the WCTU, and she spoke warmly of the Booker T. Washingtons when she visited Tuskegee. Nevertheless, she does not seem to have courted the society of blacks as friend, house guest, or intimate, as she did other people of color.

Willard returned to the South time after time. Her last southern tour was in 1896. Something about the South attracted her. Her closest southern friend was Sallie Chapin of South Carolina, and this friendship deepened over the years. As early as 1881, when Willard and Anna Gordon were staying with Chapin in Charleston, Gordon wrote Mother Willard on Frances's behalf, "all that is said of southern hospitality is true." Chapin regaled them with "incidents of the war. She was a thorough rebel, but her kindness to us could not be exceeded." Gordon added, "Mrs. Chapin had the floor, and Frank for once in her life keeps relatively quiet."[4]

But the southern charms of Sallie Chapin and others were not enough to explain Willard's affinity for southern work. Heading into alien territory and conquering it seemed to meet some deep-seated need. Frances Willard always had been insecure about being accepted. As a young girl she was never sure where she stood. Did young gentlemen like her? Did her father approve of her? Even her brother, although she modeled herself after him, was never seen as surely in her corner. Like her father he needed to be wooed, probably unsuccessfully. In the South Frances Willard wooed a reluctant lover. Her cause was apt, but her person was suspect. Temperance was congenial to southerners, but an activist woman challenged the South's deepest prejudices. Willard took on this challenge and won.

Also, Willard went to the South at a propitious moment. Reconstruction was over. White upper-class southerners had regained control of the political process. At the same time, their reaction to Populist fervor had not yet frightened them into believing the black man must be stripped of his civil rights. The result was that Willard could move easily from white to black audiences, organize black locals, speak on the campuses of black schools. She always extended an outstretched hand to the black South. As late as 1896 on her last southern tour, she was still speaking to many, as she called them, "colored" groups.[5]

For a woman to speak on public platforms was an arresting new departure below the Mason-Dixon line. Willard attracted large audiences, partly from curiosity, partly because her cause was seen as worthy and respectable and she was sponsored by churchmen and judges. But once assembled, her audiences listened not just with respect but with reverence. Here was "a graceful beautiful woman, simply yet tastefully dressed," speaking in "soft, sweet tones," a womanly woman.[6] The South Carolina *Baptist Courier* described her speech to an audience of 500 in Charleston, few of whom had ever heard a woman speak in public before, noting that she wore a tasteful black suit and bonnet, and that she did not posture, used almost no gestures, and produced an address that was a "literary gem."[7]

On Willard's first excursion to the Southland, Anna Gordon became ill and was sent home to recover. Her place as companion-arranger was taken by Georgia Hulse McLeod of Baltimore and Sallie Chapin of Charleston. One result of this separation was that Willard wrote frequent and vivid letters to Gordon describing her reception. From Mobile she informed Anna that she had spoken nine times in the last three days, once at a temperance rally of 1,500 at the Opera House, as well as receiving calls from individuals and groups.[8]

Traveling and living expenses were usually paid by Willard's hosts, but as a gesture of goodwill she collected no fees on her first southern trips. This made for a very empty exchequer in Evanston. On later journeys Willard visited the boondocks as well as the major cities, and travel conditions were often primitive: "I was never in such a dog kennel as this caboose—cold, dark, 'orrid—and 5½ hours coming 36 miles. So tired, hungry, and dolorous."[9]

Overall, however, her southern travels proved triumphant journeys. Not only was she well received, but also a warm, cordial, almost adulatory welcome awaited her everywhere she went, an enthusiastic response to her person and her message far beyond what anyone would have projected for a northern woman. Willard felt the experience changed her. Of one tour, she wrote in her autobiography: "That trip was the most unique of all my history. It 'reconstructed' me."[10] And she reassured the WCTU convention, "I have seen their [the South's] acceptance in good faith of the issues of the war."[11] She had been present when Gulf state legislatures voted funds for Negro education, and she had been encouraged by southern whites to address black audiences.[12]

THE southern trips were only a part of Willard's busy lecturing and organizing schedule in the 1880s. Except for a week at Christmas, she traveled constantly during the fall and winter of 1881–82. After speaking for two weeks in New York City in November, she went to Delaware for a week after Thanksgiving, then to Pennsylvania before spending the holiday in Evanston; afterward, she returned to the South.[13] Between January and May she visited sixty-six cities in fourteen states. In 1883–84, the decennial year of the women's temperance Crusade, Willard and Gordon traveled to every state in the union in what they called their "Crusade roundup." The previous spring and summer they made a major organizing excursion into the Far West, where they held 116 meetings in 105 days and organized the WCTU in six western states.

This relentless pace took its toll. In March 1884, the Crusade trip completed, Willard announced that after ten years on the road she intended to spend more time with her eighty-year-old mother in Evanston, that her time could be better spent working and planning from

the *Union Signal* offices in Chicago.[14] This vow was honored largely in
the breach. Willard traveled South again before the year was out. She
attended all the state conventions in 1885, and by March was complain-
ing, "What a whirl it has been! meetings—people until I hardly knew if
I was a responsible being or not. Seldom asleep till midnight. I feel 450
years old at a moderate estimate."[15] After the 1886 convention gave
Willard a salary of $1,000 a year, the financial need for this peripatetic
pace disappeared, but she continued to spend much of her time on the
road.

In the 1880s Willard not only traveled and spoke constantly, but she
also wrote prodigiously—four books as well as dozens of shorter
pieces, pamphlets, newspaper columns, and speeches. Her most important book length work was her autobiography, *Glimpses of Fifty Years*, an
impressive if somewhat diffuse chronicle, published in 1889 to mark her
half-century birthday. Seven hundred pages of reminiscences, social
philosophy, Christian testimony, and long excerpts from her diaries
were produced in six frantic weeks. Editing to eliminate repetition and
provide cohesive organization would no doubt have improved this volume; nonetheless, it was an amazing achievement.

On Christmas day of 1888 Willard sequestered herself at a family
hotel in Chicago to write *Glimpses*. Until its completion she saw no one
except a stenographer and the business manager of the *Union Signal*
(who acted as courier) and had her meals served in her room. She
wrote Anna Gordon several times a day, but apparently the two did not
see each other. Willard arranged seven tables in the room, corresponding to seven periods in her life, and tossed the material on the table that
pertained to its period. She "then went to each table in turn," took up
the material item by item, "and dictated to the stenographer the
thoughts that it suggested to her mind," ending up with hundreds of
unconnected pages that she had to weave together.[16] This process was
not always successful, as the organization of *Glimpses* is certainly flawed.
But Willard was a splendid stylist with a true flair for words, a talent
she had cultivated since childhood. *Glimpses* sold well, and the first
printing of 50,000 was exhausted in a few months.[17]

Woman and Temperance, published in 1883, was a somewhat less ambitious project. Largely a compilation of sketches of temperance
women and activities written by various leaders of the WCTU, it also
includes a good deal of material for which Willard was the primary
author. Mary Lathbury, who wrote the sketch of Willard appearing in
the volume, assisted with the editing.[18] Willard was never reluctant to
use the research and editorial services of others for her publications.

In 1886 she brought out a new edition of *Nineteen Beautiful Years*,
then out of print, with an introduction by John Greenleaf Whittier. The same year she published *How to Win: A Book for Girls*, an inspirational piece urging young women to "cultivate your specialty," earn their own livings, be independent, and marry men who shared their interests. The feminist tone of this little volume is clear.

Woman in the Pulpit, a strong plea for the ordination of women, which would permit them to perform all pastoral duties, and for their full acceptance into the governance of the church, was published in 1888.[19] Willard wrote this well-researched and tightly reasoned little volume in response to the hostility of the Methodist General Conference to the participation of women in church affairs. From the point of view of scholarship, *Woman in the Pulpit* shows considerable mastery of church history and biblical texts; it was Willard's most ambitious work. It has been asserted that in this volume Willard viewed women in the ministry as an extension of the motherly role.[20] I find Willard's argument tied more closely to womanliness than to motherhood, as well as constantly emphasizing egalitarian principles. It was Willard's skillful use of womanliness that made her plea for equality so effective throughout her life.

Willard continued to publish in the 1890s. *Evanston: A Classic Town*, a memoir of the city where she lived so many years and spent so little time, was published in 1891. With Mary Livermore, Willard edited *A Woman of the Century*, a major biographical dictionary containing sketches and photographs of 1,400 prominent nineteenth-century women; it is still a valuable source book. *A Great Mother*, a sentimental and effusive tribute to Mary Hill Willard that appealed to the mother idealization propensities of WCTU members, was published in 1894 after the death of Willard's mother; it was written with considerable assistance from her cousin, Minerva Bruce Norton.[21] *A Wheel within a Wheel*, Willard's last book but one, describes with wit and enthusiasm her adoption in her fifties of the bicycle as a source of exercise and transportation. Shortly before her death she published *Occupations for Women*, an impressive contribution to the literature on female careers and an early attempt to provide useful vocational guidance and identify suitable careers other than teaching for the rapidly increasing number of college-trained women in the United States. Again Willard did not work without assistance, but she oversaw the project and lent it her formidable prestige.[22]

The works of Frances Willard were widely read in the late nineteenth century. In this sense she fully realized one of her most intensely felt childhood ambitions. Her books found a place on thousands of parlor tables on both sides of the Atlantic. However, she was hardly a literary figure of even minor import. She wrote well, easily, and prolifically, but she was always in a hurry, eager to be on to the next task, the next conference, the next city. She had no time to edit and perfect. In mid-life she saw herself not as a literary figure but as a propagandist, expediter, mover and shaker, and the quality of her literary craftsmanship was of small importance to her and to the people who read her works. Nonetheless, Willard could use words with rare precision and vividness. All those childhood journals, poems, and little stories in farm publications bore fruit. Willard had literary talent that could have been honed to true artistry with discipline and care. Instead, she joined the ranks of the practitioners of what has been called clerical-feminine history.[23] Willard wrote intimate biographies and memoirs of basically obscure people, her sister, her mother, her friend Julia Ames. She wrote her anecdotal and affectionate history of Evanston, and she did her bit toward popularizing the bicycle. No one could have the slightest interest in reading her books today except as they provide insights into Willard herself and her times.

IN 1885 the WCTU moved its national headquarters from New York to Chicago, combining under one roof the offices of the Union and its primary organ, the *Union Signal*. Although Willard had never spent much time working out of the New York office, her ostensible goal in urging this change was to be able to spend more time with her mother in Evanston. In the immediate future Willard's schedule retained its previously frantic pace, but the move resulted in Rest Cottage being transformed into an auxiliary headquarters of the WCTU until 1892 when Mother Willard's death and Frances's long stays in England disrupted the pattern.

After Oliver Willard's death, Rest Cottage was remodeled to provide two separate domiciles for the Willard family under one roof. One wing was occupied by Mary Bannister Willard and her four children, Mary, Katherine, Robert, and Frank. Frances, her mother, Anna Gordon, and usually one or more young women who acted as secretaries, friends, and companions, occupied the other half of the house. This arrangement ensured that Mother Willard would have family close at hand during Frances's long absences. However, in 1885 when Mary Bannister Willard, who served for several years as editor of the *Illinois Signal* and later the *Union Signal*, left Evanston to make her home in Berlin, the wing of Rest Cottage occupied by her and her family was converted to offices of the WCTU.

By 1886 the Willard household had eight members, including several

Union employees. Willard and the other WCTU workers at Evanston
were connected to the Chicago headquarters by telephone and seventy commuter trains a day.[24] Communication was easy, and although Willard was still without much leisure she tried to spend more time at home.

In Evanston, Willard's life-style was gracious and unhurried. It is described for us by a New Orleans reporter, who visited her home on a hot August day in 1886. The reporter was met at the train by Willard herself and taken to Rest Cottage, one of a long row of attractive if modest suburban residences only a block from Lake Michigan. The parlor was full of books, with light summer curtains at the windows, wicker armchairs, a red sofa, Mother Willard's spinning wheel, and the organ played by Anna Gordon. The visitor (probably Caroline Merrick, a Louisiana WCTU stalwart) and the family partook of a simple tea served at twilight by the single servant. She also describes Willard's study, facing east to get the morning sun, a back room with book-lined walls, a heavy oak writing desk, unframed photographs of philanthropist friends, an easy chair, and a window opening onto a porch overlooking the lawn and flower beds.[25] Willard's den, as she called it, was refurbished in the summer of 1890. Apparently this renovation was the gift of a friend, to whom she wrote in the cozy style she sometimes used with intimates, "We had a dedication of the new 'sky parlor' (they won't call it 'den' anymore) on Saturday eve with 'speeches and cream.' We spoke of thee and thine and the good fairies generally. How I wish you'd been there. Send me the best name for this beautiful and lovesome place you have bestowed on Frances."[26]

When Willard was at home she rose at seven, breakfasted at eight, then worked from nine to twelve and from one to six in her study writing speeches and articles and attending to her voluminous correspondence. She retired early, usually by 9:30 P.M., unless she had an evening engagement. She made it a practice to walk for at least half an hour daily, and enjoyed a carriage ride when she had time.[27] She always kept a horse.

But even at Evanston the pace was sometimes frantic. Willard kept a slate by her bed where she could make notes in the dark if awakened at night. She could not escape her mail wherever she was, as in England when she made these comments:

> Sat in my pretty, quiet den and read my mail—now grown so large—from all parts of Christendom. All through my public life this wall has come between me and the speeches, articles, stories, poems that I have felt it in my bones I could write.

A reformer must keep in touch with his cohorts in temperance, labor and the woman question. To have helped them onward a little, is greater than to have written what would probably have made haste to die.[28]

She was probably right, but the mail was always a burden, despite the assistance of Anna Gordon and sometimes a battery of stenographers, and she attended to it conscientiously.

Willard worked long and hard all her life. According to her mother, however, "she strongly repelled occupations not to her taste, but was eager to grapple with principles, philosophies, and philanthropies, and was unwearingly industrious along her favorite lines."[29] This was an accurate assessment. Willard appreciated a well-run household, for example, but admitted that it would have to be made "wholesome and delightful by other hands than mine."[30] At the same time she could keep several secretaries busy. This was the case when she visited the Beauchamp family in Lexington, Kentucky, for three weeks of ostensible "rest" before undertaking her southern tour in 1895. Arriving with Anna Gordon and a secretary, she promptly proceeded to hire two or three additional typists. She wrote forty to sixty letters a day plus articles and news stories, but went about this with such efficiency that she still had time for drives and strolls around the city.[31] Another observer saw her as absentminded and forgetful alongside Anna Gordon, who was a model of promptness and capability.[32] Willard's efficiency may well have been the direct result of Gordon's organizational skills.

As an employer Willard inspired intense loyalty. Anna Gordon and the other young women who lived over the years at Rest Cottage were devoted friends as well as members of her staff. But Willard also rated well with casual employees. In 1889 she employed a young man, a student at Northwestern, as one of her typists. He too saw her as an exemplary employer who "always put one at ease," who "gave me to understand at the beginning that she did not wish the pressure of her work to encroach upon my powers for sleep," and who rarely met him "when she did not speak some encouraging word about my studies or my purposes in life."[33]

Prone to food fads, Willard ate more and more simply as she grew older. By the late 1880s she had given up tea and coffee, which she had always used sparingly; and the steak she once relished for breakfast was no longer on the menu.[34] In fact, by the mid-1890s Willard came close to being a vegetarian. She dined on whole wheat bread, vegetables, fruit, fish, and a little meat, and used milk as her chief beverage.[35] In an interview published in *Our Day*, she was reported to believe that flesh

Mary Hill Willard (*seated at left*), her daughter Frances (*standing*), and Anna Gordon in the 1880s. (Reprinted from Gordon, *The Beautiful Life of Frances Willard*)

Winter at Rest Cottage. (Courtesy of the Bentley Historical Library, University of Michigan, Ann Arbor)

eating was "savagery" and belonged to "the lower animals," that Americans ate too much, and that "the enlightened mortals of the twentieth century will surely be vegetarians."[36] No doubt her close association with the John Harvey Kelloggs of Battle Creek, Michigan health food adherents, contributed to the change in her eating habits. Ella Kellogg was one of the leaders of the WCTU. But the rich meat and fat laden diet of Americans was under general attack as unhealthy by late nineteenth-century reformers.

Frances Willard also embraced dress reform as part of her plan for the emancipation of American women. As a schoolteacher Willard had asked, "Why don't clothes *grow* on to people," and insisted she concerned herself with clothes "only of necessity."[37] Later in life, however, her ideological commitment to simpler and more comfortable clothing was tempered by her real interest in looking her best. She instinctively chose a becoming setting in which to present herself publicly. Willard was too much the performer, too conscious of the impression she made in public and in private to forsake what her world saw as womanly style for reform conviction. During her early years on the platform she had little money for clothes and frequently was forced to improvise. Anna Gordon's family seamstress, for example, made over a dress for the Boston convention in 1882.[38] But by the nineties Willard could and did indulge her taste for pretty clothes. In Caroline Merrick's New Orleans drawing room she wore a gray silk gown with frills of yellow lace; in a

The den at Rest Cottage before it was remodeled. (Reprinted from Gordon, *The Beautiful Life of Frances Willard*)

local pulpit the next day she wore an "appropriate gown of dark hued simplicity."[39] At the same time, Willard publicly complained against corsets and trailing skirts, even calling for legislation to regulate the dress of women. Again, most nineteenth-century reformers shared her views. They railed against pinched waists and dust-catching hems, although contemporary photographs show they practiced no startling deviations from the fashions of the day.

THE fact that Willard did not marry relieved her from many domestic responsibilities, but she, like other single women of her time, was not free of family obligations. Probably her mother provided every bit as much support for Willard's strenuous professional life as she took from her daughter in emotional demands and calls upon her time. The extended family, based in upper New York with a few cousins in other midwestern states, was visited regularly and written to conscientiously. Although its members occasionally asked for money, their claims on Willard were not conspicuously onerous. On the other hand, her brother Oliver's two sons proved to be an almost overwhelming burden, and one for which she assumed primary responsibility after Mary Bannister Willard left the United States. It was a burden she shared with Anna Gordon and her mother, and one that could have proved a

The office at Rest Cottage from which Willard directed the WCTU in the 1880s and 1890s. (Reprinted from Willard, *Glimpses of Fifty Years*)

public embarrassment if widely known. Although a number of people were privy to the problems of the Willard nephews, no hint of their difficulties appeared in the press.

As youths and young men, both sons of Oliver Willard, (Josiah) Frank and (Oliver) Robert, had severe problems with alcohol. Robert's addiction surfaced before his mother left for Europe; in fact, Frances had already taken responsibility for finding suitable eastern boarding schools and counselors to protect him from the temptations of his Evanston companions.[40] With infinite patience the family tried for years to find the proper environment to effect a cure. In the spring of 1883 Willard wrote to her mother from California that she hoped "Rob" would make a new beginning.[41] Six years later she was still hoping. Robert had just been sent to a home for intemperate men for a four-week stay, but left after four days.[42] There were other episodes between these two. In 1887 Frank Willard was committed to reform school in Pennsylvania for horse stealing and compounded his difficulties by breaking parole the next year.[43]

Although Willard bemoaned her nephews' fate, pitied them, and suggested to her mother they make a will to leave nothing to the

A letter to "Alice" in 1890 shows the elliptical style and almost undecipherable handwriting Willard typically used in the dozens of letters she wrote each day. (Courtesy of the Bentley Historical Library, University of Michigan, Ann Arbor) nephews,[44] she also expressed love and sympathy, helped them continually, and was constantly hopeful that they were at last conquering their problems. Her optimism was justified in the case of Frank who, under the pen name Josiah Flint, eventually became a popular writer and by the 1890s was an accepted and appreciated member of the Willard family. However, Robert was never able to conquer his drinking for long.[45]

Mary and Oliver Willard's daughters were affectionate admirers of their famous aunt. Frances, in turn, enjoyed her nieces and was close to them. Katherine, a talented singer, was a Wells College classmate of Frances Folsom, the wife of President Grover Cleveland, and a frequent houseguest at the White House during Cleveland's first administration. She married William Woodward Baldwin, Cleveland's assistant secretary of state. Mary, her mother's namesake, who studied Pestalozzi kindergarten methods in Europe, ran a small kindergarten for the Cleveland children in the White House and in the 1890s was chairman of kindergarten work for the National WCTU.[46]

Willard was probably less conflicted about her life-style than many of her contemporaries. She compromised by making many of her concessions to true womanhood largely rhetorical. But like other women professionals, she found surrogate children in her nieces and nephews. Throughout her life she felt one of her identities, if not her salient identity, was that of loving daughter to her adored mother.[47]

DURING the 1880s Willard's major device for influencing American public opinion was her presidential address at the WCTU's annual national convention, and she prepared it with great care. Willard wrote her 1880 address while staying with affluent friends near the Canadian border at Derby Line, Vermont, in what she called "this castle of a house, in a room looking out on the mountains," a haven that offered "quiet, peace, plenty of hired help," and "a carriage ride every afternoon."[48] Over the years the preparation of presidential addresses became a ritual. They were composed in seclusion, usually at some opulent retreat provided by a friend but occasionally on the premises of a cause-serving organization, as in 1888 when she sequestered herself at a North Carolina industrial school for girls. However, Anna Gordon was frequently about, and she joined Willard in Vermont before the 1880 interval was complete.

By today's standards, Frances Willard's presidential addresses were both eloquent (if florid) and disorganized. Although subject headings were distributed throughout, one wonders how this device was handled orally. Probably it was ignored. Frequently the topics addressed had no logical sequence. Organizational matters quite properly took over large sections of her messages. She was, after all, leader of the largest women's movement in the United States, and it was her job both to inspire the Union to do efficient work and to show how this could be accomplished. Interwoven with internal concerns were temperance questions, social issues, and, in the early years, impassioned pleas for evangelical Christianity.

Willard's presidential addresses were committed to memory before they were delivered. Willard cherished what she called her "liberty," a word often used by evangelical preachers to describe the spontaneity that they associated with being divinely inspired.[49] She was a spellbinder, and she worked at perfecting that talent. Although her speeches were very long, frequenty running to fifty printed pages, the delegates eagerly listened to every word, and visitors filled every vacant seat. She was the nation's leading woman orator after Anna Dickinson forsook the lecture circuit for the stage, and the public platform was the major instrument through which she projected her social ideas.

Willard's greatest personal triumph during the eighties may well have been the WCTU convention of 1888. The Union convened on 19 October at the sparkling new Metropolitan Opera House in New York City. That day 4,000 visitors joined 400 delegates to hear Willard's presidential address.[50] The New York press reported the convention's every move. Willard and Anna Gordon stayed with Ellen and William Jennings Demorest, fashion magnates and philanthropists, in their town house on Fifty-Seventh Street. As her carriage took her to the second day's session, Willard wrote in a hurried note to her mother, "Elegant throngs *turned away* from that great Opera House. A magnificent success, press full of it. *Graphic* gives full page illustration."[51] Clinton Fisk, Prohibition party candidate for president in 1888, also wrote to Mother Willard, "Tier on tier of boxes [are] crowded with the best representatives of the best social life in this great metropolis, and noble men and noble women from the chief centers of the Republic grace the occasion."[52]

Willard's mother had accompanied the Illinois delegation when the annual meeting was held in Washington in 1881, stayed at Senator Henry Blair's home along with Frances, and enjoyed the sights of the capital city.[53] But Mother Willard was left at home in 1888. Her daughter's eventual triumph was by no means a foregone conclusion, and Frances needed to focus her full attention on her presidential tasks without the distractions of family responsibility.

That autumn Willard came to New York with understandable trepidation. First of all, New York City was not a major stronghold of temperance forces. The press might well prove hostile, popular response could be lukewarm, and she could expect to face enemies as well as friends among the public. Second, the WCTU had chosen for its deliberations a secular hall, not a church, and one of the five largest audience rooms in the world. If its sessions did not attract sympathetic lay followers, their absence would be conspicuous indeed. What is more, the cost of staging the convention at the Metropolitan was sizable and had to be met by the sale of boxes and seats to interested onlookers. Also, convention delegates, as was the Union's custom, had to depend on hospitality in private homes for sleeping accommodations, which was not a typical New York City practice.[54] Third, the conflict over WCTU endorsement of the Prohibition party was on the agenda. Prohibition party endorsement, a major WCTU issue of the 1880s, received the full and unlimited debate it had been denied at the last two conventions. The Union's internal squabbling was on view from a national platform for all the world to see.

It was not an easy time for Willard, but she managed herself and the convention with consummate finesse. She won easily on the vote to support the Prohibition party, and, equally important to her and her reputation, the press believed she handled insurrection well and deserved victory.[55] Moreover, the hall was packed, many potential observers had to be turned away, and the audiences were enthusiastic. The battle for public approbation was over.[56] The New York convention was a resounding success. All obstacles had been conquered. Frances Willard was on the crest of the wave. Her organization was solidly behind her. She was also America's heroine, known to millions, her attention from the press unequaled by any other American woman of the time.

Chapter IX  Reformer

To understand the depth of Frances Willard's prestige and fame by the 1890s, it is necessary to examine the evolution of her social, political, and religious ideas and roles during the decade when her national fame matured. By the mid-1890s Willard was not only a major celebrity. She also had embraced Fabian socialism; was allied closely with the labor movement, especially Terence Powderly and the Knights of Labor; and had imaginatively sponsored a national political reform coalition that included the Populist party. She interpreted with literal thoroughness that pithy slogan, "Do Everything," which she invented for the Woman's Christian Temperance Union, and she treated temperance reform as part of a complex of related social issues that should be dealt with simultaneously.

However, the base from which she approached her comprehensive reform ideology was relatively narrow. Willard moved into national prominence in the late 1870s with a position on very few social questions. Publicly her support was limited to two issues. She endorsed federal constitutional prohibition as the most effective way to deal with alcohol abuse, and she supported the temperance ballot for women (which she called the "Home Protection Ballot") as the surest way to achieve prohibition. Privately she was also committed to full, unlimited franchise and equal rights for women under the law.

Willard's first presidential address was a relatively narrow document concerned chiefly with problems and patterns of Union organization, temperance education in Sunday schools and public schools, the temperance ballot, and "what women are doing for the temperance cause."[1] She recognized that as yet support for a mild temperance ballot for women was not unanimous within the Union, and she attempted to ward off conflict by suggesting that "to disagree with gentleness is a far higher triumph of Christian grace than to be gentle just because we happen to agree." But she discussed briefly what she called "philanthropic work," the importance of organized societies of associated charities which would found industrial homes and reformatories for delinquent girls, or agitate for public fountains, baths, and gymnasiums.[2] In the summer of 1879 she spoke at the new women's prison in Framingham, Massachusetts. She probably had paid a visit to Zebulon Brockway and his model reformatory for boys the previous year, for she agreed to write an article on the Elmira (New York) reformatory early in 1879.[3] Prison reform early engaged Willard's interest as it did the organization she led. Women's organizations were quick to develop a special affinity for work with women prisoners and delinquents.[4]

The number of issues Willard and the Union were willing to address did not expand rapidly in the first two years of her presidency. But by 1890 she and the Union accepted no limits on the range of the WCTU's program. When Frances Willard first used the term "Do Everything" in her 1881 presidential address, she was referring to tactics rather than goals, to methods rather than program content. She envisioned the WCTU using every possible technique to achieve its aims—lobbying, the petition, moral suasion, gospel temperance, work with children, and publications. But she did not mean "Do Everything" in the sense of taking on every problem, promoting every reform.[5] The shift in emphasis was gradual over the next eight or nine years, and of course she never gave up her belief in multiple roads to the multiplicity of goals she began to seek. The impetus for this broadening of goals came both from Willard's own experience and from the membership.

One departure from strictly temperance issues was Willard's plea for WCTU cooperation with the American Social Science Association (ASSA) and the Commission on Charities and Corrections.[6] Founded in 1865, the ASSA had become a strong reform voice in the United States by 1880, and stressed the new role of the expert in problem solving. The association attracted literary, academic, and professional men and women who were aware of the new dimensions that urbanization and industrialization had brought to American society. The social thinkers who joined its ranks recognized that the old value systems emphasizing self-reliance were inadequate to cope with the new interdependent social fabric. They attempted to bring the insights of the budding social sciences to shed objective light on the tangle of abuse and inadequacy that was consuming American cities.[7] By the mid-1880s Willard was active in the association, appearing on its program in 1887 with an address on the temperance question. The Commission on Charities and Corrections was one of many organizational offshoots of the ASSA, and included members of lay governing boards as well as professional administrators working in the charities and corrections field.

By endorsing the goals of these two organizations, Willard showed her awareness of problems far beyond the ken of simple personal morality on the one hand, and equal rights for women on the other. She was beginning to identify herself with broader causes. In 1883 she endorsed the free kindergarten movement, already supported by WCTU women. In her presidential address she praised the Chicago Free Kindergarten Association with its "1700 little children" and "forty teachers under training," as well as the San Francisco kindergarten, both of which were essentially the creations of WCTU locals. However, her formal recommendations to the 1883 convention were limited to temperance except for renewing an earlier call to suppress the *Police Gazette*, a sensational and suggestive popular magazine that catered to male readers and that women generally found "corrupting."[8]

In 1883 Willard also took on some purely feminist issues—for example, women's release from domestic drudgery. She foresaw meals sent from central kitchens "by pneumatic tubes, and the debris thereof returned to a general clearing-up establishment," as well as houses heated from central gas works and "supplied with water from general reservoirs."[9] Women produced schemes for easing the onerous demands of housekeeping at a rapid rate in the 1870s and 1880s. Dr. Mary Jane Stafford developed a plan for building family homes around a common service area. Earlier Melissina Fry had advocated cooperative housekeeping.[10] Although Willard promoted the use of labor-saving devices and the release of women from household chores, she was careful to keep the domestic revolution she supported within the sphere of womanliness, because it "is not what woman does, but what she is." Women "came into the college and humanized it, into literature and hallowed it, into the business world and ennobled it." While she preached revolution in role, she emphasized women's traditional qualities, although she saw these combined with "the growing individuality, independence and prestige of the gentler sex."[11]

Willard had been committed to the woman question for a long time, but her commitment to other aspects of social reform came more slowly. Frequently, the WCTU membership stretched the Union's goals faster than Willard and was more eager than she to carry out her admonition to do everything. In 1883 the WCTU added to its work plan the "Social Evil Reform," which advocated raising the age of consent laws, holding men equally guilty with women in prostitution offenses as a way of stamping out the brothel, and strengthening and enforcing laws against rape. The WCTU was attacking very real evils. Prostitution in the lumber camps was literally white slavery, and, when the Union began its campaign to change such legislation, the age of consent was set at a mere 10 in twenty states and only 7 in one state.[12]

The Union as an organization was also ahead of Willard on the social purity issue. A Committee of Work with Fallen Women had been organized as early as 1877, and the Iowa and Maine unions had long been active in this area.[13] Willard did not include social purity in her own agenda until the Philadelphia convention of 1885, when she devoted a major portion of her presidential address to the problem.[14] She was almost forced to make the cause her own after shocking disclosures a few weeks earlier by the *Pall Mall Gazette* of forced prostitution in England, and after Elizabeth Blackwell's assertion that similar conditions existed in American cities.[15]

William T. Stead, notable British reform journalist, published his exposé on British white slavery in 1885 at the plea of Josephine Butler and several prominent British feminists.[16] At first Stead's articles created an enormous outcry, not against prostitution and white slavery but against Stead himself. However, public opinion eventually turned in his favor. The British made procurance a criminal offense, and the age of consent was raised to sixteen. In 1885 Willard probably knew about the British campaign only through the public press, but by the next year she was corresponding directly with friends of Stead.[17] Once the problem of prostitution was added to Willard's catalog of evils, she devoted herself to the question with vigor and counseled her constituency:

> It is not by the vain attempt to re-introduce the exploded harem method of excluding women that they are to be saved. It is rather by holding men to the same standard of morality . . . that society shall rise to higher levels, and by punishing with extreme penalties such men as inflict upon women atrocities compared with which death would be infinitely welcome. . . . When we reflect— that in Massachusetts and Vermont it is a greater crime to steal a cow than to abduct and ruin a girl, and that in Illinois seduction is not recognized as a crime, it is a marvel not to be explained, that we go the even tenor of our way, too delicate, too refined, too prudish to make any allusion to these awful facts, much less to take up arms against these awful crimes. We have been the victims of conventional cowardice too long.[18]

In many ways Willard's position in this speech was similar to the attitude of the woman movement toward sexual crimes a century later.

By seduction Willard meant rape and asked that it be recognized as a
heinous felony. She also asked that the sexual crimes of men no longer
go unpunished, and that the man who patronized the prostitute be
treated under the law as equally guilty with the woman who served
him. Finally, she asked women to lead the fight for justice in the courts
and for effective legislation. One historian has viewed Willard's position on social purity as antagonism to a masculine culture, that Willard
believed women were subjugated by too great an emphasis on sex in
the relations between men and women.[19] Willard felt society discriminated against women, but she did not believe that the basic ills of
society all stemmed from sexual subjugation, and she held very positive
views toward marriage except possibly for herself.[20]

Nonetheless, in adopting the social purity campaign as one of her
goals Willard fell victim to the age of progress. She failed to understand
that good intentions would not obviate the fact that the social purity
campaign, if successful, would by its very nature separate the prostitute
from her community and limit her chances of returning to it. Social
purity reform argued for the single standard and equal punishment of
prostitutes and their patrons, but, in its attempt to rehabilitate and
protect the fallen woman, it reduced rather than increased her options
for survival.[21] Overall, the nineteenth-century women's movement concentrated on women's sexual powerlessness and the dangers to which
women were subject, seeking to devise ways to protect them within this
framework.[22] By focusing on danger, nineteenth-century reformers ignored the prostitute's economic advantage or women's potential for
sexual enjoyment. But Willard did understand that sexual equality and
autonomy—for example, divorce or control of childbearing—could
not be separated from political and economic power. And on both sides
of the Atlantic the social purity movement proved to be the nineteenth
century's chief defender of children against child abuse.[23]

As late as 1885 the WCTU was still ahead of its president in adopting
positions on social issues. Frances Willard was essentially a political
animal. She arrived at goals when she believed they were acceptable to
her constituency (which she never envisioned solely as the WCTU),
although she might prod a little and when necessary take a step backward. Significant numbers of middle-class nineteenth-century women
were able to identify with the outcast and subjugated, although they
themselves were protected from experiencing the ravages of poverty
through the economic security provided by their husbands and families, because they dealt personally with servants who put them in touch
with another world. When they moved out as volunteers, attempting
to convert the impoverished class to a Christian life, temperance, or

chastity, middle-class women began to see ways of ameliorating social evils. In the early 1880s Willard tapped into women's social concerns rather than leading the way. In 1885 the WCTU adopted as part of its "plan of work" relief of the "worthy poor," day nurseries for the children of working women, federal aid to education as a way of compelling southern states to provide schooling for blacks, and a department of hygiene to study municipal sanitation and urge cities to establish boards of health to fight epidemics.[24] Willard did not disagree with this program, but she did not initiate it. However, she was ahead of her constituency in her support of the labor movement and Christian Socialism.

ALTHOUGH social questions other than temperance and women's rights only gradually engaged Willard in the 1880s, political influence and power became one of her major concerns soon after her position as undisputed leader of the WCTU was confirmed by her nearly unanimous reelection in 1880. When asked to the Prohibition party's national convention that year, she stuck by her Republican sympathies and refused the invitation. She attended James Garfield's inauguration in March 1881 and visited the White House four days later to present— on behalf of the WCTU—Lucy Hayes's portrait, a tribute to Mrs. Hayes's strong temperance convictions. But by summer Willard had doubts about ignoring the Prohibition party. Whereas the GOP would never favor Willard with a voice in its higher councils, her friends in the Prohibition party were eager for her support and willing to take seriously what influence she could lend to their cause.

For the next few years "influence" became an important word in Willard's political vocabulary. It was incorporated into presidential addresses, it was a key phrase in convention resolutions, and it was a slogan for the columns of the WCTU newspaper, the *Union Signal*. "To lend their influence to that political party" most clearly sharing the goals of the Union and Willard provided the avenue down which Willard led the WCTU to accept outright party endorsement before the presidential election of 1884. Influence was a womanly word. Almost any woman could accept the idea that she had influence. The whole doctrine of spheres revolved around woman's influence in the home. Women were expected to influence their husbands and sons through moral suasion. It was a small leap to lend their influence to a political party and Willard knew it.[25]

In the summer of 1881, the National Temperance Society met in Saratoga, New York, its 337 delegates representing several church bodies as well as temperance organizations. The temperance movement of the

1880s was composed of a variety of organizations and points of view. Its chief political vehicle was the Prohibition party, which ran its first presidential slate in 1872 and was the major third-party contender from 1884 to 1892 when it was eclipsed by the People's party. The Prohibition party not only supported a prohibition amendment to the federal constitution but also advocated direct election of senators, the income tax, and the vote for women. Both the party and the Good Templars, a fraternal order, admitted women to membership and leadership roles, and active Templars were among the founders of the WCTU. Although the Washingtonians, a society of reformed drunkards, had reached maximum strength much earlier, moral suasion was still attractive to those who wished to treat alcohol abuse as a personal rather than a political reform. Moral suasion continued to be an important point of view in many church circles including Roman Catholic groups.

Frances Willard was present at the 1881 assembly in Saratoga that brought together the whole spectrum of temperance advocates. There she met for the first time James G. Birney, son of the abolitionist, and James Black, Prohibition party candidate in 1872, as well as renewing her ties with an old friend and temperance colleague, John B. Gough. Later that summer Willard attended the temperance convocation held annually at Lake Bluff on the shores of Lake Michigan. Colonel George Bain and John B. Finch were present to talk about the Prohibition party and no doubt to suggest that combining the woman power of the WCTU with temperance organizations and third-party reform political groups would result in gains for everyone. All were urging Willard to use her influence.

Where to throw her "influence" was not a simple decision for Willard. First, her long attachment to the Republican party predisposed her against Prohibition party ties. Her family had been Republican since 1856. A Republican president had received her in the White House and wished her godspeed on her organizing tour of the South the previous winter. That same president now lay dying, the victim of an assassin, and presidential assassinations were as likely to provoke intense loyalty and support and subsequent canonization in the nineteenth century as in the twentieth. Garfield had been an effective president for only four months, hardly the inaugurator of important policy. What is more, he disappointed his temperance supporters by turning lukewarm to their cause. But now he was a martyr and martyrs enlist sympathy.[26]

Second, Willard gauged correctly that the Union membership, aside from a few recent southern converts, was almost solidly Republican in its traditions. The WCTU, like Willard, had strong antislavery antecedents, and this emotional tie to the Republican party was difficult to sever. In the South, affection for the Democratic party was equally strong. Only in a few western states like Kansas, where a strong third-party tradition was linked to temperance, could the WCTU be expected to move easily toward Prohibition party endorsement.

Willard did not give up. Instead, she perfected her strategy. She began to organize home protection clubs, independent of the WCTU but obviously composed of WCTU members and their male relatives. This canny move served two purposes: it developed organized support within the Union for Prohibition party affiliation, and it provided a strong constituency that Willard could use to bargain for influence within the Prohibition party at its next convention. When the Prohibition party met in Chicago in August 1882, Willard and her clubs won major concessions from the old party leadership. The name of the party was changed to the Prohibition Home Protection party, and Willard was made a member of its central committee,[27] thereby securing political influence for herself. But, as she was well aware, these successes did not guarantee that she could bring the WCTU as an organization into the Prohibition party.

Willard's personal political preference was now clear. In her 1882 presidential address she made her first strong plea for Union endorsement of the Prohibition party, warning that individual southerners, no matter what their temperance sympathies, could never support a Republican candidate nor could antislavery Republicans support a Democrat. Sectional unity, one of her strong attachments since her southern tours, as well as temperance, could best be served by Southern Democrats and Northern Republicans uniting in the Prohibition Home Protection party.[28] What was more, the Prohibition party supported the vote for women.

The WCTU was not moved by her arguments, and outright endorsement was not forthcoming. However, Willard could always find authorization somewhere for the direction she wished to take. Although the convention could not be persuaded to endorse the Prohibition party by name, it did accept what it saw as a nonpartisan principle. It resolved "to influence the best men in all communities to commit themselves to that party, *by whatever name called* [italics mine], that shall give to them the best embodiment of Prohibition principles, and will most surely protect their homes."[29] From this innocuous statement Willard slowly moved the Union toward outright endorsement.

To implement the nonpartisan principle, nonpartisan prohibition conventions were to be held in every state to apply pressure on the major parties. The year 1884 was a presidential year and Willard was

determined to marshal her womanly legions behind Prohibition party
candidate John St. John, former governor of Kansas. Although the
WCTU had failed to endorse the Prohibition party by name until 1885,
Willard reasoned that only the Prohibition party on the national level
supported prohibition in the campaign of 1884. Therefore, the national
WCTU and the national officers must endorse St. John. The columns of
the *Union Signal* were filled with campaign propaganda urging the
Union rank and file to support the Prohibition party. Despite the vocal
opposition to her tactics in the national convention, which preceded
the presidential election by a few days, Willard easily defeated her opponents by a vote of 182 to 52. A minority in the WCTU continued to
oppose party endorsement until 1889 when J. Ellen Foster, Iowa WCTU
leader and longtime friend of Willard, led a small group of dissenters
out of the Union and formed the Non-partisan Woman's Christian
Temperance Union.[30]

Willard's successful campaign to associate the WCTU with the Prohibition party clearly broadened her political base. She was a member of
the party's executive committee from 1882 until 1891. In 1888 she campaigned actively and prominently for its presidential candidate, thereby
gaining another national forum in which to exercise her influence. For
example, that year she attended the party's national convention with
Anna Gordon and Anna Howard Shaw and served on its platform
committee. Her address at its great Decoration Day mass meeting received a tumultuous ovation.[31] Political recognition was important to
her. Willard was ambitious and coveted power. Moreover, she was a
consummate practitioner of the skills needed to both acquire and make
use of political forces.

ALTHOUGH Willard's motives are less clear, she also may have attempted to widen her influence and broaden her power in her next
outreach beyond the WCTU. However, in this maneuver she ran
greater risks and could easily have lost a large part of her constituency
within the Union itself. In May 1886, at Willard's urging, the general
officers of the WCTU sent a delegation bearing greetings to the national convention of the Knights of Labor. WCTU conventions had
authorized similar delegations to church bodies and temperance organizations, but this was further afield. The Knights of Labor was America's first mass labor organization. It had its beginnings in 1869 in a
secret society of Philadelphia artisans. By 1880 the Knights of Labor
had a wide base among skilled workers who belonged to its hundreds
of local and district assemblies. It supported a broad program of social
reform including cooperatives for industrial enterprise. In specific in-

Display of state banners at a WCTU national convention in the 1890s.
(Reprinted from Willard, *Glimpses of Fifty Years*)

dustries and plants, however, it also functioned as a labor union, working for better wages, hours, and working conditions.[32] The Knights were surprised but pleased by the WCTU's friendly gesture, and Terence Powderly, president of the labor union, wrote that it was the first time a representative of another organization had been admitted to their convention.[33]

The WCTU's outreach came at an interesting time. In early May of that year the Haymarket Massacre occurred in Chicago. A bomb exploded killing a policeman and wounding six others at a demonstration against police brutality called by anarchists and revolutionary groups. Although the Knights had nothing to do with the demonstration or the bombing, they were associated with the wave of strikes that swept the nation the same year, and the accompanying violence smeared the labor movement as a whole despite Powderly's reluctance to encourage strikes and his consistent support of mediation and conciliation.[34] Instead of creating sympathy for the labor movement, the Haymarket affair repelled and frightened the middle classes.

Why did Willard choose this particular time to make her overture to the Knights? The Knights had always been friendly to the temperance cause. Powderly himself was a temperate man and the order barred from membership anyone associated with the liquor traffic, although total abstinence was not a condition of joining. The Knights also were consistent champions of women's rights. In their first constitution (1878) they supported equal pay for equal work regardless of sex. Women were admitted to the order in 1882, sixty-four women's locals had been organized by 1885, and over 50,000 women were members by the next year.[35] However, if the Knights' sympathy for women's rights and temperance was the factor that led Willard to reach out a fraternal hand, why had she not done so earlier?

It seems unlikely that her gesture can be explained by her friendship with Henry Demarest Lloyd, a Chicago journalist, who became one of the few champions of the foreign-born radicals arrested and convicted of the bombing. Lloyd believed his whole life changed direction because of what he saw as a gross miscarriage of justice in this case. He and Willard had known each other since 1876, when he had attempted to buy her brother's newspaper, the *Chicago Post*, and lost out to Victor Lawson. However, at the time of the Haymarket incident Lloyd was in Europe and did not return until August, long after Willard had dispatched her delegation to the Knights' convention.[36]

Although the Haymarket riot cooled popular and press support for labor, its political strength was still rising. Hundreds of district and local assemblies moved into politics on the local level, and labor candi-

dates did surprisingly well in local elections in major cities that fall.[37]
Frances Willard may have sensed this upsurge in the political vitality of
the labor movement.

Such was the climate in which she decided to send a WCTU delegation to the Knights of Labor convention. It could not have been an
easy decision. Willard had not yet met Powderly so personal loyalties
did not enter the picture. Certainly there was no outcry from the
WCTU rank and file urging support for the labor movement although
they did endorse shorter hours. Willard herself had yet to advocate
basic reform of the social and economic fabric of American society.
Why did she embrace this controversial ally? Was her gesture to the
Knights an act of courage or misguided opportunism? Did she fully
realize that the labor movement including the Knights, for whom support had previously been relatively widespread, was about to lose public sympathy, and was she reaching out a hand to show that middle-
class disapproval was not universal? If so, she performed an act of rare
courage. She risked a great deal in terms of her own constituency. If she
wanted to broaden her base by associating herself and her movement
with the rapidly growing strength of the Knights of Labor, which in
the twelve months before the Haymarket affair had experienced phenomenal growth, her motives were self-serving. She had seized a
chance to expand her influence.

During this period Willard also reached out to Chicago women who
were prominent in labor circles. In August 1886 Elizabeth Rodgers,
active in the Chicago Knights of Labor, was appointed Master Work-
man of District Assembly 24, the central organization of all Knights of
Labor assemblies in Chicago. She was the first woman to hold such a
post. Willard, describing herself as "always desirous of meeting remarkable women," was quick to request an interview with her. The following year Willard wrote a sympathetic article about Rodgers for the
Christian Union; the piece probably formed the basis for the sketch of
Rodgers in *Glimpses of Fifty Years*. The two women became friends and
later cooperated in the Chicago Woman's League and the Illinois
Woman's Alliance.[38]

Not until several months after Willard sent WCTU delegates to the
Knights of Labor convention did she actually address the WCTU membership on the labor question. In her presidential message of 1886 she
suggested that the WCTU could "do much to ameliorate the deepening
battle between capital and labor." Pointing out that unemployment
stood at over one million, she urged adoption of the eight-hour day to
make jobs for idle workers. She went on to say, "The labor movement
has my warmest sympathy, so far as it is carried forward by the peaceful

methods of arbitration, cooperation and the all powerful ballot box," and concluded with a prophecy that heaven would "bless all lawful efforts of the toiling millions to better their condition. We will stand by them. Their triumph is our own."[39] She sweetened these radical sentiments for the membership by tying economic reform to temperance. The WCTU could teach the Knights that the central question of labor reform was not "how to get higher wages," but "how to turn present wages to better account," that giving up beer and tobacco and learning the rules of hygiene and nutrition would keep workers from poverty.[40] The membership authorized Willard to address labor on behalf of the WCTU to suggest a plan for cooperation between them.[41]

Willard's resulting message, which she circulated in December 1886, was addressed "To all Working Men and Women—Brothers and Sisters of a Common Hope." It stated, in part:

> We come to you naturally as to our friends and allies. With such of your methods as involve cooperation, arbitration and the ballot box, we are in hearty sympathy. Measures which involve compulsion of labor, the destruction of property or harm to life and limb, we profoundly deplore. . . . We rejoice in your broad platform of mutual help, which recognizes neither sex, race nor creed. Especially do we appreciate the tendency of your great movement to elevate women industrially to their rightful place, by claiming that they have equal pay for equal work; recognizing them as officers and members of your societies, and advocating the ballot in their hands as their rightful weapon of self help in our representative government.[42]

The statement went on to commend the Knights for the order's hostile attitude toward the saloon and for the pledge of total abstinence taken by its newly elected officers, then asked for their support of prohibition, temperance education in the schools, sabbatarianism which was linked to the shorter work week, and the WCTU's social purity program. Powderly was pleased with the message and published it in the Knights' official newspaper.[43] He also supported political issues advocated by the WCTU. He distributed 95,000 petitions for the protection of women to his membership, successfully encouraged the Knights to adopt a resolution supporting the Blair federal aid to education bill, and invited Willard to address a mass meeting of the Knights in February 1887.[44]

Willard and Powderly did not meet until early 1887 when she called on him in his Philadelphia offices to present her request for help in the petition campaign. She described him as a man with a "noble head," "handsome brow," "clear cut profile and magisterial nose," and as "thoughtful, quiet, and steady-eyed."[45] Willard asked him for his photograph which he sent her; she kept it on her desk for the rest of her life along with pictures of Elizabeth Fry, Josephine Butler, Mrs. Cleveland, and Pundita Ramabai. Earhart suggests that Powderly may have been the unfulfilled romantic attachment to which Willard alludes in her autobiography.[46] The papers of Willard and Powderly both contain letters exchanged between them. This correspondence is warm but thoroughly businesslike. They met seldom, and, although they obviously admired each other, their relationship appears to have been entirely professional.

Willard did not escape opposition within the WCTU for her attempts to associate the Knights of Labor and the Union, and several of her colleagues were unhappy with this new affiliation. Her mother warned her to be careful. Frances replied, "I will do as you say in respect to being careful about the K of L, but I will not have the matter put aside all together, nor do I think you desire to have me."[47] Lucy Stone berated her and watched her overtures "with fear and trembling." Stone viewed the Knights as disruptive to business and looked with horror at their strikes.[48]

By convention time opposition had surfaced among the WCTU rank and file. Willard countered that the Knights of Labor was a truly temperate organization as well as totally committed to women's issues, equal franchise, and equal pay for equal work. She applauded Powderly's growing influence and asserted that the Knights were revolutionizing the outlook of the working man. Some WCTU criticism centered on the fact that the Knights of Labor was a secret society. But Willard reminded the membership that so was the Order of Good Templars, which the WCTU had always found acceptable, declaring that, although she normally opposed secret fraternal orders, she could not oppose these two. With her usual talent for reducing the import of practices that did not conform to her overall view, she suggested that the Knights were only minimally secret and would soon abandon the practice.[49] She emphasized the Knights' technical disavowal of strikes and violence as weapons. The strike, although frequently used by the Knights especially in 1886, was to become an acceptable weapon in labor disputes only through the influence of Samuel Gompers and the American Federation of Labor a good deal later.

Willard actually joined the Knights in 1887, and she continued to be criticized for her labor ties into the 1890s. The columns of the *Union Signal* carried letters opposing endorsement, fearing it would alienate the WCTU's more conservative friends, as well as protesting that the

Knights of Labor was a secret society.[50] Willard remained loyal to both the Knights and Powderly. This loyalty did not prevent her from attempting to establish contact with Samuel Gompers in the mid-1890s when he began to challenge Powderly and the Knights. She wrote Henry Demarest Lloyd to put her "in friendly relations with Samuel Gompers."[51] Because of Gompers's narrower view of labor's position, however, he and Willard never shared the communality of interest she had with Powderly. In any case, Willard soon lost her paramount position among women reformers.

The reasons that propelled Willard toward affiliation with labor were no doubt complex. Her genuine concern with economic distress and injustice was of primary importance. She had not forgotten her center city experience of the mid-seventies and seems to have been further radicalized by the combination of unemployment, economic distress, and labor unrest that characterized the 1880s. To urge temperance and philanthropic aid no longer seemed enough to solve the economic and social problems she saw all around her. She was not keeping a journal at this time and the sources that exist for her views are largely public, but her letters to her mother confirm this conjecture. Perhaps her motives are insignificant.

Willard allied temperance women with the labor movement at a critical juncture in the history of American labor and worked closely with Powderly for ten years. She saw labor as a counterforce to the new aggressive corporate capitalism. But her need—for both public and private reasons—to make her power base as wide as possible cannot be ignored. Willard promoted the temperance cause by broad affiliation. As a woman who knew the shape the good society should assume, she thought it her Christian duty to play her full part in American political and economic life and guide her followers on the proper path.

GERMANE to the very idea of temperance was belief in the efficacy of prevention. When Willard allied herself with the temperance movement she embraced preventive reform as a major tenet of her social philosophy, an emphasis that was central to mainstream nineteenth-century American reform thought. Preventive reform was crucial to the way Americans approached social and economic change at least from the early nineteenth century, and preventive reform was to remain a favorite solution for "society savers" until well into the last half of the twentieth century.

For example, advocates of the moral reform movement of the pre–Civil War period first believed that conversion to Christianity would prevent prostitution and crime; they later believed social evils could be cured by private charity and improved economic conditions.[52] During the Jacksonian era the childsavers espoused the asylum as a way to prevent contamination of society by the unfit or the criminal.[53] The temperance movement in all its phases was designed to prevent crime, poverty, child and wife abuse, and family dissolution by controlling the abuse of alcohol in one way or another. The social programs of the New Deal period were designed to prevent the ravages of poverty, unemployment, and economic dislocation through compulsory, state-managed insurance programs. This list can be expanded indefinitely to include antitrust laws, immigration restriction, eugenics movements, the cooperative movement, utility regulation, and so forth.

The preventive reformers believed society could be made rational and its problems solved. Despite their failures, which they saw as merely temporary, they were congenital optimists. Only in the 1970s and 1980s did American social analysts begin to wonder if the prevention of problems was a realistic way of looking at the world, if problems actually were solvable.[54] In the last quarter of the nineteenth century social critics felt preventive reform was realizable through everything from personal hygiene and public sanitation to industrial schools and the eight-hour day. The free kindergarten, scientific temperance education in the public schools, cheap lodging houses for working girls, even cremation found a place under this capacious umbrella. By 1888 Frances Willard had embraced the whole reform cornucopia.

The American Social Science Association adopted preventive reform's optimistic tenets much earlier. Franklin Sanborn, one of the leaders of the ASSA, wrote in 1880 that "We felt ourselves [in 1865] to be literally 'heirs of all the ages' . . . and there was little we did not fancy ourselves capable of achieving."[55] Sanborn believed in the "Science of Society," and as a reformer was convinced that the era when the unsystematic, ameliorative philanthropic efforts of individuals or religious groups could make a difference had come to an end. Like his contemporaries, Sanborn had committed himself to centralized reform, which inevitably led to dependence on the state for implementation. Only the state, the centralized state in the last analysis, could accomplish preventive reform. Government, very big government, was seen as the answer.[56]

This point of view spread through women's reform groups in the 1880s. It found its ultimate popular expression in Edward Bellamy's *Looking Backward*, published in 1887. Bellamy laid out a whole new logical and conformist society that eliminated all the economic and social evils of the nineteenth century through total control of the economy by a benevolent egalitarian state. Here was preventive reform pushed to its absolute limits.

Willard had long showed an affinity for utopian solutions. Even as a child she and her sister envisioned a model community where justice prevailed, jails were unnecessary, and the saloon did not exist.[57] But Bellamy put it all together both for her and for some of her closest cohorts in the temperance movement, as he did for many leading reformers. Willard must have read Bellamy's book soon after it was published because in late 1887 and early 1888 she was corresponding with him about a "manifesto" of Nationalism to be published in the *Union Signal*.[58] In tracing the evolution of Willard's ideas, the importance of *Looking Backward* cannot be exaggerated. Once Bellamy engaged her, she was truly committed to "do everything."

In her presidential address of 1888, Frances Willard urged the WCTU to read Bellamy to "see how the tyranny of 'Trusts' may perhaps be yet transformed into the boon of brotherhood, if only 'We, Us & Company,' can agree to organize one great 'trust' in our own interest, whose dividend will be declared, and whose combinations concentrated for the greatest numbers' greatest good."[59] She went on to talk about the delicate transition from the old to the new social order. Bellamy promised peaceful change in which class conflict was eliminated and unnecessary, thus solving one of Willard's great dilemmas, her inability to support violence as a desirable means, although she deeply believed that the working classes were cruelly exploited and that drastic modification in the conditions under which they lived and worked was both necessary and inevitable. Bellamy advocated an orderly and gradual transition from industrial warfare and cutthroat competition to a society rationally organized to provide for the general good. This appeal was very real to American women and one of Nationalism's great attractions.

At the same time these women faced a dilemma that they did not always understand or of which they were not always consciously aware. Statism might produce egalitarianism, but simultaneously it endangered the very democratic-egalitarian core of feminism.[60] Most nineteenth-century feminists placed less emphasis on individualism than did their twentieth-century sisters. Feminists of Willard's ilk—among them Julia Ward Howe, Mary Livermore, Charlotte Perkins Gilman, Zerelda Wallace, and Lucy Stone—were attracted to statist ideologies such as Bellamy's Nationalism because they satisfied their quest for equality and justice. Bellamy's all-powerful state promised to better the condition of women and provide them with equal status. This was enough for an impressive roster of leaders of the woman movement who identified with Nationalism. Few feminists withstood Bellamy's blandishments; the exceptions were anarchists like Emma Goldman and suffragists like Matilda Joslyn Gage and Elizabeth Cady Stanton who feared an all-powerful state as the source of female emancipation.[61]

Bellamy also was party to substantial downgrading of the Puritan ethic and absolute morality. He glorified consumerism and leisure. His Utopia was very free with its bread and circuses. Bellamy's version of Orwell's *1984* was benign, but nonetheless it describes a society that no post-Hitlerian can accept with ease. Forced labor service, limited suffrage, an elitist ruling class were linked with the happy consumption of an abundant economy. There was no room for dissent or self-conscious individualism. But with a few notable exceptions like Elizabeth Cady Stanton, the feminist reformers saw none of the evils of statism, only Utopia. Frances Willard was seduced like the rest by the solutions Bellamy proposed. The means—however coercive, provided they were nonviolent—did not concern her.

An interesting related question is why Willard and reform women in general were so attracted to Bellamy compared to Henry George, who was advancing his single-tax ideas at the same time. Willard gave passing endorsement to George in the 1890s when she was eager to unite all reform political positions, compatible or not. But she never shared George's antipathy to the all-powerful state, his belief in the transcendent good of its withering away. To her the state was quite capable, if not always so motivated, of being the instrument of the good society. She was essentially a planner and a meddler, and Bellamy's comprehensive and detailed diagram for his Utopia appealed to her. Both, of course, would have triggered her optimism, and both fit with her millenarianism, a millenarianism that had wide appeal in a society experiencing the drastic adjustments caused by rapid social change and dislocation.

Temperance women, entranced by Bellamy's beautifully ordered society, scrambled for a bit, but not over the inherent dangers of the superstate. Their misgivings centered around the fact that Bellamy was not committed to total abstinence; his characters indulged in wine and cigars. Eventually Willard and several other temperance leaders, finding in Bellamy's model society so much that pleased them, were able to overlook this flaw. For example, Zerelda Wallace wrote Willard that prohibition would be unnecessary once Bellamy's commonwealth was installed, for there would be no need for anyone to benumb himself with alcohol.[62]

No doubt women also liked Bellamy's solutions to the problems of domestic drudgery—goods delivered by vacuum tube, meals prepared in communal kitchens, the availability of centralized maintenance services—all of which Willard had advocated earlier. Another attraction of *Looking Backward* may have been Bellamy's plan that the whole society adopt what women viewed as their special affinity for cooperation. Women believed they were already capable of working cooperatively together. Their talent for mutual aid and sisterly sharing of responsibility and rewards would now become universal. Actually Willard misunderstood Bellamy, thinking he proposed a cooperative commonwealth, an interpretation that Bellamy refuted. His model society was not composed of cooperatives with varying compensations, each owned by its own trade; rather, his was a plan of social reform in which "the nation is one and indivisible," in which "all citizens own all the capital, conduct all the businesses and employ all the people for the benefit of all."[63]

Bellamy and his followers, calling their utopian vision "Nationalism," went on to organize a semipolitical arm of the movement, the Nationalist clubs. Although Willard participated in this development, she did not abandon her other political commitments. She continued to be active in the Prohibition party as well as maintaining her association with Terence Powderly and the Knights of Labor. All these allegiances played a role when she made her major move to create a united reform coalition in 1892.[64]

Willard was quite capable of allying herself with a variety of causes simultaneously. In her presidential address of 1889 she attacked "enormous accumulations of capital," sweatshop labor, and technological unemployment. She also made a plea for Christian Socialism: "the land and all resources of the earth to be held under some system as the gift of God equally to his children," the "capital and all means of industry to be held and controlled in some way by the community as a whole." Specifically, she advocated work relief for the unemployed, the eight-hour day, the forty-five-hour week, free technical education, free school lunches, and gradually nationalized or municipalized utilities and transportation facilities.[65] In the same address she praised the Nationalists and urged WCTU members to join Nationalist clubs, discussed the "labor question," lauded Powderly and the Knights of Labor, had kind words for the single taxers, endorsed the Pan American Commission, and appealed to the Czarina "against slow martyrdom in the snows of Siberia."[66]

Frances Willard was never tied to a single creed. She could embrace Nationalism, Christian Socialism, prohibition, and woman suffrage, each as individual causes; at the same time, she could find no reason

One of the hundreds of water fountains built or subsidized by the WCTU at the turn of the century. This one is in Churchville, N.Y., Willard's birthplace, and has a new, sanitary, late-twentieth-century spigot. (Photo by author)

why they should not join forces, a development that to her would make ultimate sense.

WILLARD'S Chicago environment and her friends and associates also affected the etiology of her social and economic philosophy. In the eighties Chicago was a center of intellectual and political ferment and artistic innovation. The women of the city were carving new niches for themselves in the labor movement, civic enterprises, and political reform. Although Willard was much away, Chicago was home base, and she was an integral part of its struggles to solve the problems of the emerging metropolis.

In the 1880s Chicago was the center of a new flowering of culture and reform that burst into full bloom in the 1890s. Not only was the city hog butcher to the world, stacker of wheat, and the railroad hub of the continent, but also Louis Sullivan, Daniel Burnham, William Le Baron Jenney, and others were creating America's great architectural revolution in Chicago's Loop on the shores of Lake Michigan. By the end of the decade the University of Chicago opened its doors to both men and women. The Art Institute and Sullivan's magnificent new auditorium provided settings for a great surge of artistic and cultural achievement.[67]

Chicago's reform activity was stimulated at least in part by the brutal industrialization the city symbolized and despite, or perhaps because of, its hopelessly corrupt, boss-laden municipal government. It was the headquarters of the WCTU, with all its burgeoning social programs; the home of Hull House, leading star in the growing settlement house movement, which would begin its work in 1889; and a center of militant labor union activity. The role of women was central in this "flowering of Chicago," especially as it related to municipal reform. In paying tribute to Jane Hoge, who had been a critical force in the development of Chicago's powerful and omnipresent women's network, Frances Willard called Chicago a "paradise of exceptional women."[68] Willard was both an influential member of the women's group that led the exceptionally broad and well-integrated reform effort and a beneficiary of the stimulation and aid it afforded.[69]

The Chicago women's network had its origins during the Civil War when Mary Livermore and Jane Hoge worked together in the city's Sanitary Commission. Their mammoth bazaar, modeled after the old-fashioned church fair, set the pattern for effective money raising events held by women across the nation. Several of the women who participated in their patriotic fund-raising moved with them into the equal rights campaign after the war. A measure of their energy and influence was their success in persuading the legislature to pass a married woman's property act for Illinois in 1869. Chicago's first women's club was founded by this same nucleus of Sanitary Commission workers, although *the* Chicago Woman's Club did not appear until 1876. Jane Hoge was also involved in the work of the Presbyterian women's foreign missionary society and shared churchwomen's growing concern with education for women.

Education for women brought Frances Willard within Jane Hoge's

orbit when the two worked together to establish the Evanston Ladies
College as part of Northwestern University.[70] After 1871 Willard's place
as an integral part of the Chicago network's leadership was clear, although for several years her academic responsibilities restricted the
breadth of her participation. She added substantially to the network's
scope and power in 1885 when she brought to Chicago the national
headquarters of the WCTU, the largest women's organization in the
United States.

At the same time Chicago women pioneered in the labor movement.
Women were admitted to membership in the Chicago Typographical
Union as early as 1870, and women organized their own union in 1878
when the city's Council of Trades and Labor Unions made a concerted
effort to organize women.[71] Alzina Stevens, Elizabeth Rodgers, and
Elizabeth Morgan were working-class women who became leading
Chicago trade unionists and later moved onto the national stage. The
fact that Rodgers headed the citywide assembly of Knights of Labor in
the eighties underlines the importance of women in the Chicago trade
union movement.[72]

Chicago's trade unionists and middle-class reformers did not operate
in separate worlds. In the 1880s the Chicago Woman's Club included
philanthropic social denizens like Bertha Palmer and Ellen Henrotin as
well as many middle-class reformers like Frances Willard. It also was
the motivating force behind several philanthropies that functioned in
working-class areas such as the Protective Agency for Women and Children, a legal aid service for the poor, and the Industrial Art Association,
which provided Saturday vocational classes for working-class boys.[73]
These organizations antedated Hull House and Jane Addams's arrival
in 1889 by several years. Actually Addams and Ellen Starr joined the
Woman's Club before they opened Hull House and while they were
making their initial survey of Chicago's receptivity to the settlement
idea.[74] The Woman's Club and the WCTU also had links to women
trade unionists—for example, Frances Willard's friendship with Elizabeth Rodgers. Corinne Brown, another member of the Woman's Club,
was born into a trade union family and eventually married a prominent
Chicago banker.[75]

How the network functioned and Willard's germinal role within it
are best illustrated by tracing the steps in the organization of the Illinois Woman's Alliance (IWA). A forerunner of the alliance, the Chicago Woman's League, was organized in June 1888 when representatives of fifty-six Chicago women's organizations met to share with each
other the rich variety of activities in which they were engaged. This
heterogeneous group included such unlikely partners as the women's

missionary societies, the Ladies Federal Labor Union (sometimes referred to as the Woman's Federal Labor Union), female assemblies of
the Knights of Labor, the suffragists, and a wide range of philanthropic
societies. Women with both narrow and broad interests attended the
meeting. As one of its founders commented, the Woman's Alliance
brought together women doing "good, earnest work in narrow
grooves" with "women who have rolled away the stone from the sepul-
chre."[76] In one sense the Chicago Woman's League developed as a
"spontaneous growth" arising "from organized womanhood," as the
WCTU newspaper described it.[77] However, it was also a direct out-
growth on the local level of the great International Council of Women
held in March 1888 under the auspices of the National Woman Suffrage
Association to commemorate the fortieth anniversary of the Seneca
Falls declaration. Willard and other WCTU women played a prominent
role at the council meeting, and Willard chaired the committee that
created a permanent organization on both the national and international levels.

Willard was elected president of the National Council of Women, the
permanent organization that resulted from the 1888 meeting. Forty national women's organizations sent delegates to the first triennial meeting in 1891. But immediately after the 1888 congress Willard saw the
need for local implementation to give force to the national movement.
She envisioned local councils that would act as effective lobbying devices and that would unify and inform women's various but related
efforts in their own localities.[78] She was willing to give her own time
and energy to that end. In the summer of 1888 Willard was frantically
busy. She faced the aftermath of a tumultuous row generated by her
election as a delegate to the General Conference of the Methodist
church, and she was preparing for one of the most challenging WCTU
conventions of her career.[79] Nonetheless, she agreed to serve as president of the local Chicago Woman's League in the interest of unifying
women's efforts.

That summer the *Chicago Times* ran a series of articles exposing the
disgraceful conditions under which women and children worked in the
city. These stories inspired the Ladies Federal Labor Union to urge
the Chicago Trades Assembly to initiate a committee to cooperate
with various women's organizations in investigating the conditions of
women and children in workshops, stores, and factories.[80] Trade union
women were also moving toward the broad cooperation and unity
envisioned by the National Council of Women. The Chicago Woman's
League was the result.

The first meeting of the league was held on Tuesday, 4 October 1888, in the Woman's Club rooms at the Art Institute. Frances Willard delivered her inaugural address as president, and several organizations reported on their work. Willard also invited Knights of Labor leader Elizabeth Rodgers to discuss the *Times* exposé and answer questions about working conditions of women and children.[81] Two days later club women and labor women joined to organize the Illinois Woman's Alliance (IWA) for the specific purpose of enforcing the city's factory ordinance and the compulsory education act of the state of Illinois.[82]

The alliance performed these tasks well. In its six years of life it successfully investigated the sweating system, forced the legislature to tighten school attendance laws, and obtained greater representation of women on the Chicago school board.[83] Frances Willard was peripheral to these accomplishments, but in the IWA's germinal phase she was central, making use of the well-developed Chicago women's network which so often acted as a pacesetter for the national scene.

Both the Illinois Woman's Alliance on the local level and the National Council of Women illustrate general trends in the women's movement at this time. Women were involved in multiple single-issue organizations promoting a hundred causes, but they were also unifying their separate efforts in broad-based coalitions of these same organizations. Through their clubs and societies they were eagerly pursuing personal interests that most attracted them as individuals and joining together to maximize the results of their efforts in the political and economic spheres.[84] The framework for cooperation of women's organizations was formalized in the National Council of Women headed by Willard. She found this pattern congenial as well as helpful in consolidating her own leadership. Willard described the council's work and spirit as "Orthodox and heterodox, Republican, Democrat, and Prohibitionist, native and foreign, we agreed . . . by a tacit understanding, that while loyal each to her own belief, we had met to counsel for the further advancement of Woman's sacred cause."[85] The Illinois Woman's Alliance epitomized this coming together of womanhood. In few communities was the new spirit of unity as successfully implemented as in Chicago.

ALTHOUGH Chicago was an important arena for Willard's growing influence, her national reputation was equally formidable by the end of the eighties. She formally led all organized American women through the National Council of Women, and she was the leader of America's largest women's organization, the WCTU. She was in touch with everyone who represented innovative social thinking in this country and some from abroad. By the mid-1870s Willard was a correspondent of

Susan Anthony and by 1881 of Clara Barton. By 1880 she corresponded with most of the suffrage leadership, including Lucy Stone, Julia Ward Howe, Henry Blackwell, and Mary Livermore. Terence Powderly entered her circle in 1886, whereas she had known Henry Demarest Lloyd since 1878. Dwight Moody had been an early influence as had Anna Dickinson. Harriet Beecher Stowe and the James Russell Lowells were her very good friends. By the mid- to late 1880s Willard knew and corresponded with the economist Richard Ely, woman educators Alice Freeman Palmer and M. Carey Thomas, single taxer Henry George, social workers Grace Dodge and Jane Addams, novelist Mary Terhune, and sculptor Loredo Taft.

Willard's leadership and her reputation as a major force for reform were well established in the East. Her position was illustrated by the fact that in 1889, when Florence Kelley, consumer advocate and feminist, looked for a place to advance the causes that interested her and also earn her living, she went to Chicago and the La Salle Street headquarters of the WCTU to ask for a job. No paid position was available, and Kelley went to Hull House to cast her lot with Jane Addams.[86]

In 1880 Willard had been committed only to temperance, the women's movement, and Protestant Christianity. In 1889 she was ready to change an entire society. By 1890 the eastern reform establishment to which she was unknown in 1870 needed her perhaps more than she needed it. The number of followers whose allegiance she could claim was far greater than that of her reform contemporaries. Only the farmers' alliance movement could show a constituency that matched the size of the woman's temperance movement. And through Willard's efforts, the WCTU would attempt to establish a bridge between the eastern reformers with their relatively small constituency and the masses of angry farmers organizing in the South and West. By the end of the 1880s Willard knew everyone who counted in reform circles, and almost everyone in the United States knew of Willard. Daughter of the Wisconsin prairies, preceptress of a struggling midwestern girls' academy, leader of a movement with midwestern roots, Frances Willard was a household word by 1889 and her reputation spanned the continent. Of equal importance, she had moved from a social philosophy that revolved around temperance and the woman question to support of the labor movement and acceptance of Christian Socialism.

Chapter X  Christian

Throughout her life Frances Willard was a loyal, devoted member of the Methodist Episcopal church, and for most of the last two decades of the nineteenth century she was that denomination's most prominent laywoman. Her affection for the Methodist church was both deep and genuine. She gloried in its uninhibited plea for emotional commitment. She loved the gospel hymns, the exhortatory sermons. She was herself a practiced evangelist. Although her causes varied, her style was Methodist to the core. The enthusiasm of enthusiastic religion and John Wesley's method and rule as applied to social concerns were at the very heart of the way she worked. She was not unaware that Methodists were the largest Protestant denomination in the United States, and that as a Methodist the causes she espoused would attract sympathetic attention from the faithful. But her attachment to Methodism antedated her national prominence, and stood on its own as one of the great commitments of her life. However, the Methodist establishment was not always kind to Willard, and by the 1890s her personal religious convictions had moved far beyond Methodism.

Willard had experimented with free thinking and religious rebellion as an adolescent. But after her conversion in 1860, her religious convictions troubled her only occasionally, and for a number of years she was comfortable with the conventional practices of a conformist.[1] Her sister Mary's death in 1862 accentuated her religious feelings. She needed condolence, and her belief in a conventional heaven became very real. She wrote her schoolgirl chum who had also lost a sister that she liked to think their two sisters "speak sometimes of you and me. I like to think that were our vision clearer we might catch the gleam of their shining wings, and hear those wondrous voices calling to us: 'Come up hither!' "[2] This is a child's vision of heaven, angels with shining wings, the persistence of earthly relationships after death, but it was written by a woman of twenty-five. *Nineteen Beautiful Years*, Willard's memoir of her sister published the same year, is replete with similar conventional Victorian religious conviction and sentiment.

By the late 1860s Willard's religious faith seemed both orthodox and secure. Nonetheless, during the winter of 1866 she became involved in the holiness movement, a pietistic sect that began within Methodism but also attracted adherents from other denominations. Its practitioners preached freedom from sin through the present availability of God's perfect love and urged unsanctified but converted sinners to consecrate themselves to God to obtain complete sanctification. Walter and Phoebe Palmer became holiness's major advocates in the mid-nineteenth century, and during the winter of 1866 the Palmers conducted meetings in Evanston. The whole Willard family attended these meetings. Frances's diaries reveal that she read seriously the books Mrs. Palmer suggested, but she also confessed she did not "fully comprehend this doctrine of holiness," although she felt "no opposition to it and wish to know and feel more of it." She reported her mother's "going to the altar" but not her own, and by late March 1866 her religious enthusiasm seemed far from central to her life.[3] In fact, throughout that winter she was more occupied with mundane concerns such as her work and living arrangements.

In a later testimonial she believed she had been much moved by these meetings.[4] As with her conversion, Willard looked back and saw more spiritual wrestling than she experienced at the time. To understand Willard's true religious feelings, one must read her writings juxtaposed against her diary. Religion was important to Willard. She took its challenges and its ordeals with great seriousness. But she always remained her own self. Her questioning mind counteracted her emotional soul. Because she lived at a time when evangelical enthusiasm was popular culture, she wrote articles and memoirs that fitted that mold. But underneath she knew even in 1866 that she could not be part of the holiness movement.[5]

A few years later, when Willard first began working for temperance in Chicago's inner city, she admitted that her greatest personal satisfaction came from preaching and conducting services for the "fallen men" of the Chicago Loop.[6] She loved to bring people to Christ although she was never certain that was her mission. In 1876 she eagerly joined Dwight Moody's staff as one of his principal evangelists, and as late as 1888 she stated that she would have liked to be an ordained minister.

Willard never quite gave up her belief in the happy heavenly reunions she had wanted so much as a young woman. Writing to her mother in 1882, she commented that it was twenty years since Mary's

death and that "More and more I see our life as one, here and beyond.
Let us try in the strength of divine grace to make it so."[7]

Willard's curiosity about heaven was part of her interest in psychic phenomena. While still a student she went with her Aunt Sarah to hear a woman preach on spiritualism but was not impressed: "Verdict. Fine thoughts, that's all."[8] In 1862 a friend introduced her to Swedenborgian writings. She was somewhat attracted, confiding in her journal, "The Swedenborgian demon pleased me quite. It is new and curious, of course, yet its spirit seems sweet and kind. . . . I love and cherish the general idea that the material universe is made for our spiritual enlightenment and instruction,"[9] but she continued to find true solace in her old faith: "Oh, Christ! All my quietness is through my belief in thee."[10]

Willard's real interest in psychic phenomena dates from the late 1880s. As early as 1888 she was corresponding with Elliot Cones of the Society for Psychical Research.[11] In the 1890s she became interested in theosophy and an admirer of Annie Besant, English social reformer, agnostic, and early advocate of birth control who in 1889 embraced theosophy,[12] a philosophical system akin to mysticism that claimed knowledge of God through direct experience. Willard found this emphasis on experientialism congenial. From colonial times American women frequently found religious fulfillment in the occult, a well-established tradition of female piety.[13] Willard was part of this tradition. She truly believed in an unseen world, a world of the spirit in touch with the everyday world and a very real heaven where she would again live happily with those she had lost on earth. Theosophy appealed to Willard because it promised a oneness between the world of the spirit and earthly reality.

Willard was not alone in these beliefs. Her Nationalist cohorts also were prone to theosophy, and Annie Besant was herself a Fabian socialist. Victoria Woodhull, radical suffragist, contemporary of Willard, and sometime protégé of Elizabeth Cady Stanton and Susan B. Anthony, also dabbled in the occult, as did many reformers in the Gilded Age including Mary Livermore. Times of rapid social change inevitably nourish a feeling of loss of control and a misplaced faith in simple solutions. Theosophy, Nationalism, and Fabianism were all part of the search for easy answers to the myriad problems posed by industrialization and urbanization.

Willard shared with Bellamyites and theosophists the conviction that the reform of human nature was a precondition for the spiritual and material uplift of society and the establishment of a just state. In this she and her contemporaries were more prone than twentieth-century reformers to hold the individual accountable. Reform of the individual could be achieved in more than one way. Willard, perhaps more than others, never let her pursuit of spiritualism distract her from her dedication to attaining change in the here and now. But she did see women's spirituality as a vehicle for successful social reform. In this she joined the tradition of Elizabeth Seton, Dorothea Dix, and Catharine Beecher.[14] Willard was not a true mystic. Her approach to psychic experience had the aura of late nineteenth-century scientific rationalism; it was more in the nature of Conan Doyle's search for contact with another world. And her use of the vocabulary of feminine spirituality, Christian virtue, female moral superiority, the religious virtues inherent in social and economic reform, was designed to translate Christian idealism into a rational and just social and economic system.

In the late 1870s Willard began to doubt the necessity for a literal interpretation of the Bible. After reading Alexander Winchell's *The Reconciliation of Science and Religion*, published in 1877,[15] she wrote to Winchell about the Genesis story of the rib and its use as justification for the subjugation of women. Winchell, who was not only a scientist but also a prominent Methodist, replied that he did not take the "rib business literally," but thought it referred to the "close psychical and physical union between man and woman," that man and woman together "constitute one complete individual."[16] Willard was reassured that her reservations were not heretical.

The rhetoric of Willard's autobiography, *Glimpses of Fifty Years*, written for her half-century birthday, reveals a woman deeply committed to Christianity, but questioning the validity of Christianity's claim to be the only true faith, and a woman who no longer accepted evangelical Protestantism as the only way that faith could be realized. By 1889 Willard had embraced ecumenicism. She found the same ethical principles espoused by Jew and gentile, Catholic and Protestant, as well as in the classics of many cultures. She wrote:

> I am a strictly loyal and orthodox Methodist, but I find great good in all religions and in the writings of those lofty and beautiful moralists who are building better than they know. . . . No word of faith in God or love toward man is alien to my sympathy. . . . I am eclectic in religious feeling, friendship and inspiration. . . . But like the bee that gathers from many fragrant gardens, but flies home with his varied gains to the same friendly and familiar hive, so I fly home to the sweetness and sanctity of the old faith that has been my shelter and solace so long.[17]

Thus she continued to acknowledge her affectional ties to the Methodist church.

By 1893 Willard explicitly included the Oriental religions as part of
her ecumenical stance and urged that westerners going to the East
accept eastern teachings as far as their convictions could be stretched
rather than engage in relentless proselytizing. She linked missionary
activity to capitalism, warning that Americans should not forget that
"It is the Christian nations that illustrate the wage slavery carried to its
extreme conclusion of sin and misery, the reign of capital, and the
enforced serfdom of labor." In the same speech, she observed: "God
has spoken to us not once but at *sundry* times, not in one but in *divers*
manners. . . . His is a continuous revelation . . . and when once this
view of the subject, simple and reasonable as it is, has been understood
and accepted, theological controversies will be practically nil, and what
a rest and comfort that will be to all the world."[18]

Willard continued to preach Christian Socialism at the same time she
embraced religious eclecticism. Her idea of Christian Socialism embodied an idea she had no doubt cherished in her childhood, the simple
precept "God is love." In 1893, when she addressed her first great English meeting at Exeter Hall in London, she observed:

> Nothing less [than love] will ever fuse the hearts of men in those
> reforms by which the Gospel of Christ becomes regnant in the
> world. If we had love, the slums of London would not last an-
> other day. . . . The time will come when the human heart will be
> so much alive that no one could sleep in any given community; if
> any of that group of human beings were cold, hungry, or miser-
> able. . . . Some day the great world-mind, tutored and untaught,
> will lend its mighty force to each child of humanity.[19]

It was all there: her Methodist oneness with Christ, the pervasive optimism of late nineteenth-century reformers, the socialism she had accepted after reading Bellamy's *Looking Backward* in 1887, and her little
girl faith in a personal God, a God who under her aegis had grown to
encompass by this time all the world's religions. But when she talked to
him or of him, he was still the God of Methodism, the denomination in
which she had been reared.

Willard never gave up her hope of spreading the idea of "God is love,
Christian love" throughout the world. During her last illness, lying on
her bed in a New York City hotel room, she said to Anna Gordon, "I
want our women to have a new concept of religion! The religion of the
world is a religion of love; it is a home religion; it is a religion of

peace."[20] For the last time she put into words both her commitment to Methodism and her commitment to what to her was the life-giving force of the world, concern for people.

ALTHOUGH always a religious woman, Willard was also a church-woman, and she put her religious convictions into practice in very practical ways. She had every intention of playing an active role within the Methodist church. Here she met some of her greatest disappoint-ments and most aggravating frustrations. She was dealt several severe blows by organized Methodism, delivered by a hierarchy that admired her gifts and supported many of her causes, but that could not accept her demands for an equal role for women in the church. It is a truism of American religious history that women have always outnumbered men in church membership, but men have exercised authority in the churches.[21] Possibly the increasing bureaucratization of America's orga-nized churches (along with other voluntary organizations) in the late nineteenth century led to tightening hierarchical authority and further restricted the role played by women in church governance. But the overall pattern had been in place since the early days of the Massachu-setts Bay Colony.[22]

At its sixth national convention in 1879, the year Willard was elected president, the WCTU decided to send fraternal delegates to the national convocations of various Protestant churches during the following year. Willard herself was delegated to attend two, the Presbyterian General Assembly and the General Conference of her own beloved Methodist Episcopal church. The Union expected to use these occasions to publi-cize its work and to foster an exchange of fraternal delegates with various church bodies. The scheme was hatched innocently enough, no one expecting the confrontation that ensued.

On 14 May 1880 Willard and Jennie Duty, another WCTU leader and prominent Methodist laywoman, presented their written credentials to the Methodist Conference officials assembled in Cincinnati, Ohio. The document was returned forthwith by Conference officials with a state-ment that only ecclesiastical visitors would be recognized. Willard was shocked but accepted this rebuff. However, several delegates to the Conference did not. When a resolution was introduced that Willard be invited to speak to the assembly, a battle erupted that shook the Con-ference and the Methodist community generally and forced Willard to recognize how deep was the feeling of the Methodist hierarchy against the participation of women in the governance of the church.[23]

Her chief opponent was James M. Buckley, a prominent Brooklyn clergyman who succeeded Charles Fowler as editor of the *Christian*

Advocate, the Methodists' national newspaper. Buckley argued that letting Willard speak would create a dangerous precedent and suggested an inappropriate analogy. If Frances Willard could talk for ten minutes today, Robert Ingersoll, the celebrated agnostic, could demand ten minutes tomorrow. John Heyl Vincent, who had given the WCTU his early blessing at its first organizing meeting at Chautauqua, joined Buckley in opposing the resolution. As the acrimonious debate dragged on, it became clear that the General Conference was really addressing itself to the "Woman Question." It was certainly thus perceived at the time, both by the commercial newspapers and the women's press.[24] Buckley countered arguments that women were left unrepresented in church councils despite their work in education, their contributions to church literature and missions, and their substantive efforts in local churches by pointing to "the magnificent privilege they have of presenting memorials and petitions to this body,"[25] hardly a convincing argument to the friends of women who were present! Willard sat in the gallery watching the proceedings. When the vote was taken, it went 238 to 138 in favor of permitting her to speak. Buckley was so angry at the result that he secured an adjournment of the assembly for the rest of the day.

In a brief statement composed with the advice of her supporters at the Conference, Willard declined the privilege so reluctantly proffered. She explained that she had "no idea of the strong opposition that would be manifested," stated that her intention had been only to bring greetings from her national organization, and pointed to the fact that she frequently had been invited to speak to ecclesiastical bodies.[26] According to the daily secular press, she had the last laugh and gave better than she got. But in her autobiography she stated that her friends were weakening under the pressures of her opponents. They suggested that Buckley would continue his obstructionist tactics and urged Willard to refuse the right to a hearing which was now hers. She preferred to continue the fight, but bowed to their wishes.[27]

Willard's next encounter as a fraternal delegate to the Presbyterian General Assembly in Madison, Wisconsin, went no better. Dr. John Vine Hall, minister of the New York City Fifth Avenue Presbyterian Church, requested an interview with Willard in the morning before the assembly session convened. Anna Gordon was present and described the occasion to Willard's mother. Hall asked Willard *"if she were a member of the church*! Furthermore he told her that it was his opinion . . . that she ought to speak only to those of *her own sex*." Tears rushed to Willard's eyes and for a moment she was speechless. But "then she argued her case grandly," and the delegation left after graciously inviting the Presbyterians to the WCTU's annual meeting in Boston. Gordon was irate about the whole affair and described it as a "terrible blow to Frank." The three women, including Elizabeth Grier Hibben, a prominent Presbyterian laywoman, had handed in their credentials anyway, but of course they were not received.[28] The matter was of such little importance to the Presbyterians that the question never went to the floor.[29]

Willard was deeply distressed by her peremptory treatment from the very churchmen who had welcomed her to church halls and auditoriums as a popular lecturer and who had professed great admiration for the work she was doing as a temperance advocate. John Heyl Vincent, who opposed her at Cincinnati, was always eager to engage her as a Chautauqua lecturer. After all, her drawing power was considerable. James Buckley solicited her articles for the *Christian Advocate* and was willing to pay for them.[30] But she was not welcome as a visitor to their all-male church conclaves.

Willard's immediate response was subdued, although she made clear the depth of her pique and frustration in her presidential address to the 1880 convention, commenting that the WCTU had viewed its overtures to the Presbyterian and Methodist convocations as part of the Union's educational work. Instead, the Union had been taught to understand that "women are not received as fraternal delegates in ministerial assemblies!"[31] Her immediate response was to withdraw the unmeant challenge. She suggested that in the future any resolutions the WCTU wished introduced in such bodies be entrusted to a male friend who was already eligible to speak.

Protestant churchmen had been eager to make use of Willard's great gifts as an orator and organizer, but consistently resisted any exercise on her part of independence or power. Charles Fowler denied her administrative authority over Northwestern's women. Dwight Moody wished her to serve only as his talented handmaiden and helper. James Buckley was angered that she even presumed to address informally the ultimate seat of power in the Methodist church. John Vine Hall and the Presbyterian clerics felt no differently.

This demeaning treatment of women by Protestant religious leaders and ecclesiastical governing bodies led Willard to examine critically and aggressively the overall position of women in the Protestant church. *Woman in the Pulpit* was the result of this examination.[32] Willard began her book by citing example upon example of biblical strictures that were not applied literally by Protestant Christianity because to do so would be inconvenient. Churchmen refused to cite scripture to condemn Martin Luther or George Washington for rebelling against con-

stituted authority as suggested in Romans 13. Nor had northern clergymen condoned Paul's words, "be obedient to them that are your
masters" (Ephesians 6.5), to uphold slavery. Nonetheless, these same
churchmen did take literally Paul's admonition that women keep silence
in the churches, using this passage to justify excluding women from
preaching or church governance. She conducted her own exegesis to
compare passages that restricted the participation of women with those
that encouraged them to play an active role, as well as citing contemporary biblical scholarship to show the probable corruption of some of
the unfavorable texts.[33]

Willard found the explanation for the attitude of male churchmen in
what she called the "world-old motto of men," the "white male dynas-
ty['s]" need to reign undisputed over the earth, "lording it over every
heritage, and constituting the only unquestioned 'apostolic succession.'"[34] These were strong words for a prominent Protestant church-
woman to use in the nineteenth century.

In this volume Willard also cataloged in detail the qualifications of
women for pulpit and hierarchy and countered the argument that wife-
hood and motherhood could not be reconciled with the duties of holding ministerial office, citing the testimony of an impressive body of
women ministers and sympathetic male preachers to support her views.
This little exercise in biblical exegesis and clerical testimony, designed
to rebut the male Methodist hierarchy, was in process but not yet
published as a book when the relationship of women to Methodism
was put to another challenging test. (Earlier, however, Willard had
written an article embodying some of this material for *The Homiletic
Monthly*.)

IN October 1887, Frances Willard was elected by her diocese in Illinois,
the Rock River Conference, as a delegate to the Methodist General
Conference scheduled to meet in New York City in April 1888. Although by far the most eminent, she was only one of five women
elected delegates that year. Mary Ninde of Minnesota, president of the
Methodist Women's Foreign Missionary Society and WCTU leader,
Amanda C. Rippey, head of the Kansas Conference delegation, Angie
Newman of Nebraska, and Lizzie Van Kirk of Pittsburgh were the
others. Although seventy-six women had been chosen as alternate delegates to previous conferences, women had never appeared on the roll of
seated delegates.

Willard received the news of her election while attending the New
York WCTU state convention at Binghamton. She was both deeply
pleased and moved. Anna Gordon wrote Mother Willard, "I wish you

could have heard her praise of those noble men who were the means of her election, and seen her delight when the news came. We were at the breakfast table. When she tried to tell her hostess she could hardly speak for tears."[35]

Although Willard later protested that it did not occur to her that women, who "constitute at least two-thirds of the church membership, bear more than one-half its burdens, and have patiently conceded to the brethern, during all generations, its emoluments and honors," would prove unacceptable as delegates,[36] she actually was much less naive. She knew full well that the Conference would not accept her and her fellow women delegates easily. She began to plan her strategy in the early spring.

It was clear that James Buckley, still editor of the *Christian Advocate*, would continue as her adversary and that he would not be without enthusiastic cohorts. She corresponded with John M. Hamilton, founder of the People's Church in Boston whom she must have known at least since her work with Moody in 1877 and who was to lead the prowoman forces on the Conference floor. Hamilton assured her that the women's names would appear on the official roll; that, if objections were raised, he would object to the objections on a point of order; and that only a delegate's constituency could object, not the Conference as a whole.[37]

As the meeting approached, the Methodist establishment divided on the question of woman delegates. *Zion's Herald*, a Chicago publication representing the progressive West, believed women certainly could be delegates, pointing to the long tradition of their participation in the electoral conferences where they helped choose General Conference delegates. The *Christian Advocate* and the *Methodist Review* both opposed the admission of women, although the *Western Christian Advocate* lined up on the other side, and at least some part of the Methodist press was convinced that not a single male member of the Conference would dare challenge Frances Willard's right to be there.[38]

On 1 May 1888 the twenty-fifth General Conference was called to order in the Metropolitan Opera House. As the national legislative body of the Methodist church, the Conference assembled for a month every four years. The very length of time between conferences ensured a heavy order of business. Society and the churches had not stood still in the interim, and the twenty-fifth General Conference was faced with several problems considered of great import: extension of the three-year term for pastors, election of the presiding elders of the Conference rather than having them appointed by the bishops, addition of laymen as delegates to the 103 regional annual conferences that were now entirely ministerial, election of new bishops (one of the candidates was Willard's enemy, Buckley), endorsement of legislative prohibition, and the question of the eligibility of women. The woman question would come first to the floor, and the *New York Times* saw this issue as the most important decision the Conference would make in 1888.[39] Change was in the wind. That women intended to play a role was indicated by the unprecedented election of five women from five separate conferences.

The annual conferences of the church had dispatched some five hundred delegates to New York for the conclave, the majority of them clergymen, one minister for each forty-five members of each conference, a ratio that guaranteed that almost all full-time ordained pastors could serve. Each conference also was permitted two lay delegates, and it was in this capacity that Frances Willard had been elected. The *Times* commented that "elderly men with bald heads and white hair are to be seen all over the auditorium."[40] But at least two women, Mary Ninde and Angie Newman, were in their seats on the floor when the presiding bishop's gavel opened the first session.

Frances Willard, however, was not at the opera house. When she arrived in New York her mother had been ill for over a fortnight. The day before the meetings convened a telegram from home suggested Anna Gordon return to Evanston to be at Mary Willard's bedside. Frances knew such a summons meant her mother's condition was serious and decided she herself must go. Mary Willard had pneumonia and was the sickest she had been in her life.

Willard's disappointment must have been acute. Gordon arrived in New York by the time the General Conference formally convened, and Willard attempted to use her as surrogate. Anna received a barrage of messages from Frances. She was told to use Clinton Fisk as a speaker on behalf of the women, to keep careful account of the votes, and to urge "the women to sit it out and never withdraw until forced to it."[41] By the end of the week the battle was lost for all practical purposes, but Willard still suggested new tactics: substitute motions, second amendments, another phraseology, and a reminder to male lay delegates that it was women's votes that had brought them their seats in the Conference.[42] Laymen had been seated as delegates for the first time in 1882, although the movement for lay delegates first reached the Conference floor in 1878, when several laymen were elected—with female support—in the Electoral Conference where women had voted for sixteen years.

Willard's absence from the convention was a severe blow to the cause of the women delegates and the damage was irreparable.[43] The *Times* regarded the strongest argument of the prowoman forces as, "They can't think of putting Miss Willard out, can they?"[44] The editor envisioned Willard sitting on the floor, and "the issue of whether women shall be admitted will be contested with the charm of her presence in their favor."[45] But Willard was not sitting on the floor and her absence may well have been fatal to the cause, although prowoman adherents among the bishops were never in a majority. The *Times* described the fight as a "battle royal," which "brought such an audience to the Metropolitan Opera House as is seldom drawn to it by the profane attractions which are usually there presented," and emphasized that ladies were in the majority.[46]

But by Monday, 7 May, when the vote was finally taken, interest had begun to lag. Both sides reiterated the same old arguments the delegates had heard a half dozen times before. A resolution by the National Woman Suffrage Association, which met concurrently with the Conference, calling for Methodist women to withdraw from the church if the delegates were not seated, did not help the women's cause. Placing women's rights above denominational loyalty was not acceptable to good Methodists. The delaying tactics of the opposition also had an adverse effect. The press believed that had the vote come at the beginning of the Conference the women might well have won.[47] In the end, the resolution to seat women was defeated in both lay and ministerial votes. The bishops were delighted; Charles Fowler, Willard's old suitor and adversary, was reported by the *Times* as jubilant.[48] James Buckley was not elected bishop, but he continued to be a consistent foe of women's rights. In 1909 he published a book entitled *The Wrong and Peril of Woman Suffrage.*[49]

Willard, as was her practice, addressed the question in her annual message to the WCTU at its fall meeting in the same New York hall where her cause had been rejected in May. She urged her sympathetic and disappointed followers to work in the church for a "voice in all its circles of power." She saw this year of "unprecedented discussion relative to woman's church relations" as a positive gain. Women had experienced a national forum to air their views and present their case and had won considerable support. In closing, Willard reaffirmed her devotion to Methodism: "I love my mother church so well and recognize so thoroughly that the base and body of the great pyramid she forms is broader than its apex, that I would fain give her a little time in which to deal justly by the great household of her loving, loyal, and devoted daughters."[50]

Although Willard loved the Methodist church, she did not neglect her strategy. The next General Conference would meet in 1892, and the WCTU planned its campaign long before the 1891 election of delegates.

The *Union Signal* advised women to inform their hometown ministers
of the arguments for admitting women to the Conference,[51] and *Woman in the Pulpit* was available to give them ammunition. The church press countered by accusing Willard of consorting with doctrinal heretics. For example, at the February 1891 meetings of the National Council of Women, of which she was president, she shared the council's platform with unbelievers and Unitarians. Such natural fellowship in the woman movement was used by the Methodist anti-women forces to prejudice the newly elected delegates to the General Conference.[52]

Willard was also falsely accused of being a candidate for bishop, and rumors flourished that the move for admission of women delegates was a political strategy inspired by the Prohibition party and the WCTU.[53] Although Willard was active politically at this time, she had not had political schemes in her head in 1888 and had certainly not maneuvered her election as a Conference delegate.

The *Christian Advocate*, edited by Buckley, suggested that male lay delegates had been admitted only because their business and legal abilities were needed by the Conference. Because the *Advocate*'s editor did not credit women with such qualifications, he saw this as a telling argument. His final point was, "what high-minded man would permit himself to be nominated against a woman?"[54] However, the opponents of women delegates were not uniformly successful. By October 1891 nearly half the delegates elected to attend the May assembly favored women as lay delegates. Opposition was strongest among the German Methodists, who also fought seating women in 1888.[55] Women won the lay vote in 1892 but the ministerial vote was negative. Victory was finally achieved in 1896 when the full Conference voted to accept women as delegates to the 1904 assembly where they took their seats long after Willard's death.

During the last forty years of the nineteenth century the Methodist Episcopal church simultaneously constricted and expanded the role of women within the denomination.[56] Women were channeled into a separate sphere—for example, female missionary societies and Sunday school work—but denied the right to preach, be ordained, or have a voice in church governing councils. This clear definition of place assured strong, autonomous female societies through which women could exert their influence and exercise leadership, and through which they could play a considerable role within the church as a whole. However, Willard was not satisfied with anything less than true equality. Although she was quite capable of using the doctrine of spheres to move women toward equality and independence, she refused to accept a separate role in the church, the long acknowledged proper if limited sphere of women. She called on the special virtues of womanliness to buttress her arguments for full power, but in the last analysis she held fast for equal treatment. She used the doctrine of spheres but refused to abide by its strictures. In this ambivalent stance she found her strength and realized her leadership.

Although Willard lost her personal battle with the Methodist church, the very fact that she was part of the fight publicized the issue of women's role in church governance in a way that no one else could. Willard could hardly be displaced as the United States' best-known Methodist, and she made clear that she remained a loyal and devoted daughter of her church. But the rejection she had experienced at its hands was not accepted lightly by American women.

WILLARD reached out to the Roman Catholic community and again encountered controversy. This time the controversy occurred not in the larger community but within the Woman's Christian Temperance Union itself. From the early days of her WCTU presidency, Willard was eager to join hands with her Catholic temperance cohorts, but her strongly Protestant colleagues were not always willing to cooperate, despite several overtures towards Catholics made by temperance women during the great temperance Crusade of 1874.[57] As a child Willard herself shared the typical American Protestant prejudices against Catholics. Her 1855 journal told of reading a copy of *The Tablet*, a Catholic publication: "Oh, how I hate it!" she wrote.[58] As late as 1876 she used Protestant temperance prejudice against immigrant Catholics to urge the vote for women.[59] But a few years later she welcomed cooperation with Catholics for temperance goals.

Willard first attempted to cooperate with Catholics in 1881. That year she wrote a note to the Catholic Total Abstinence Society expressing thanks for its recent resolution favoring women's temperance work. After receiving a polite response, she suggested to her constituency that the WCTU now seek counsel from Catholic leaders on the most expeditious way to pursue this spirit of fraternity.[60] Little was done, although Willard always insisted that the Union welcomed as members both Catholics and Jews. In February 1887, when she visited Philadelphia, Willard attended the regular Sunday afternoon meeting in Cathedral Hall of the local Catholic Total Abstinence Society which boasted 13,000 members, 2,000 of whom were women. She sat on the platform with Mrs. Willis Barnes, superintendent of the Young Women's branch of the Union, and was asked to address the gathering.[61]

This outreach was bound to attract hostility among Willard's Protestant cohorts. Irish Catholics were becoming a force in the corrupt machines of eastern cities where the New Immigration was depositing more and more foreign-born of non-Protestant background. Mary Livermore, liberal feminist and Unitarian, suggested that only good could result from the anti-Catholic agitation then rampant: "I do not object to Catholics on religious grounds—but I am intensely opposed to it [the Catholic church], as a political organization, and hope it [the anti-Catholic agitation] will continue."[62] Livermore was only one of many in the middle-class liberal establishment who feared the growing power of Catholics in America. Willard was paddling against the current.

Her next major effort to bridge the Catholic temperance forces and the WCTU took place in 1891. In August Willard and Julia Ames, a young editor of the *Union Signal*, attended the national meetings of the Catholic Total Abstinence Society. They were joined part of the time by Sallie Chapin, southern WCTU leader. The convention met in the Lincoln Music Hall in Washington, D.C., and daily masses were held at St. Patrick's Church. Willard was there as a duly appointed fraternal delegate of the WCTU, authorized by the Atlanta convention the previous fall.[63] On the train to Washington Willard and Ames met two of the delegates, both Catholic priests, "had a pleasant talk at breakfast," and learned that women were "members of their society on equal terms with men."[64] All in all, Willard had a smashingly good time at the conference. As she said, they were "beautifully received." Both Willard and Ames were greeted with cheers and invited to speak and to sit on the platform. They met Cardinal James Gibbons and Bishop John J. Keane, rector of Catholic University. They attended high mass and were impressed by the "heavenly music."[65] The priests were "charming."[66]

Willard obviously was delighted to explore this new forum, and the Catholic community appears to have felt equally favored. The *Irish Catholic Benevolent Journal* reported, "The most pleasing incident of the convention was the presence of Miss Frances Willard, president of the Woman's Christian Temperance Union, [and] Miss Ames, editor of the *Union Signal*."[67] However, the Methodists were irate. The *Free Methodist* bemoaned "Rome's bloody record," its "persistent efforts to demolish our free schools," as preface to observing that "it is indeed strange that Protestants will bow and scrape to the Pope and his subjects as much as they do." The writer added a final admonition, "Such taffy in order to curry favor with the Church of Rome ought to be rebuked by every local WCTU woman in the land."[68] Charles Parkhurst,

Presbyterian clergyman and opponent of Tammany Hall, shared Willard's views, but warned her that it would be difficult to convince Methodism to support their opinions.[69]

Willard defended her actions to the WCTU after the fact. Two weeks after the meetings, she reported through the *Union Signal* that she had suddenly realized the WCTU had established fraternal relations with all other national temperance groups except the Catholic Total Abstinence Society, and that this omission called for action.[70] Subsequent issues of the *Signal* reported at length on the work of the Catholic temperance society and the importance of fraternal relations.[71] These efforts to counteract criticism were at least partially successful. Catholic fraternal delegates, a priest and a woman, attended the 1891 WCTU convention and presented greetings "at some length."[72] And Willard devoted a portion of her presidential address to a glowing account of her Washington experience.[73]

Substantial overt opposition to cooperation with Catholic groups did not develop in the Union until later. One factor that fed the growing discontent may have been that Catholic priests played a more prominent role at the religious exercises of the WCTU's Baltimore convention in 1895.[74] Also important was the fact that during the 1890s anti-Catholic sentiment in the United States was again on the rise. At the same time, Willard was pushing harder than ever for ecumenical cooperation and outreach. She was victorious at the 1895 convention, obtaining passage of a resolution inviting Catholic and Hebrew women to join the WCTU.[75] But not everyone was happy. Some were shocked when the benediction at one evening meeting was pronounced by a Catholic priest.[76] Moreover, rancor and disaffection survived the convention. In an open letter to the press, Boston women protested "the inroads which Romanists are making in our ranks, preventing freedom of speech and action."[77] Willard did not apologize, and the bad feelings on the part of some Union members continued at least into 1896.[78]

Overall, Willard's efforts to provide bridges between the American Protestant and Catholic communities, coming at the time they did, were impressive, and they did not go unrecognized. The *Chicago Tribune* commented in an editorial at the time of her death, three years after the 1895 fracas, that one of Willard's major accomplishments had been "winning into heartiest fellowship and drawing into enthusiastic cooperation along the main lines of Christian and humanitarian effort, persons of all grades of culture and religionists of every name, Protestant or Catholic."[79]

WILLARD'S central position within organized Christianity and her liberal ecumenical and theological ideas take on an added dimension when placed in the context of the importance in which the Protestant church was held in late nineteenth-century society. The Gilded Age, for all its blatant materialism, pursuit of industrial know-how and abundance, exploitation of labor, and disregard by much of its establishment of earlier rural agricultural values, was not truly a secular age. The new entrepreneurial class and the new immigrant proletariat composed an upper and under class that as yet had small input into the pervading moral ethos. The tone of American society was still overwhelmingly Protestant. The attention paid to the activities of the various denominations by the newspapers bears witness to this fact. The secular press, both in small towns and major cities, reported the Sunday sermons delivered from local pulpits in impressive detail. The politics of Protestantism—the machinations of its ecclesiastical bodies, the quarrels among the luminaries who composed its hierarchies, its doctrinal disputes within and between denominations—found full, amazingly objective, and sometimes witty coverage in the public press, to say nothing of the fact that dozens of weekly and monthly church periodicals were read in America's parlors. The reading public was deluged with church-related news that nearly rivaled politics and much outdistanced sports in the competition for the public's attention.

Frances Willard was very much part of an American theological tradition that may well have remained with us until quite recently, remnants of which are present today. William McLoughlin has suggested that America has never been as materialistic as some social critics would like to think, that the constant denunciation by reformist commentators of American materialism in itself bears witness to American society's basic religious commitment.[80] McLoughlin sees even our dreams of success and our continual evaluation of the pursuit of happiness in terms of higher standards of living as "better described as a variant upon the search for a new Eden or the coming of the Kingdom of God on earth as we think it is in heaven."[81] Certainly this view of the world is exemplified by how Willard saw the relationship between her religious beliefs and her visions of the new society.

Her influence within this overall framework cannot be minimized. The nation's foremost Methodist laywoman was inevitably a loud voice in the land. When Frances Willard was elected to the General Conference, a large public—not just Methodists, not just women, not just temperance advocates—was following her fate. When she urged cooperation with the Catholic and Jewish communities, she exposed a huge audience to the idea of fundamental Judeo-Christian unity, an idea in

sharp contrast to the antisemitism and anti-Catholic bigotry being ped-
dled by others, including some reformers, in the 1890s. Willard epitomized American Protestant Christianity. She was so much a part of it,
so close to its very center, so psychologically in tune with its rhetoric,
so unwilling to transfer her basic affections to some other cause, that
she did not alienate the group from which she sprang. Her constituents
contested her when she pushed them too hard in directions they found
uncongenial, but few of them hated her and none dared denounce her.
She could never be identified with the anti-Christ no matter where her
social, economic, and religious beliefs led her.

AN example of Frances Willard's unwillingness to cut herself off from
the mainstream of Christianity was her reaction to Elizabeth Cady
Stanton's project for *The Woman's Bible*. Stanton's motivation for com-
piling *The Woman's Bible* was much the same as Willard's motivation
for writing *Woman in the Pulpit*. Both women were distressed by clerics
and churchmen who cited scripture to justify a society in which women
were prevented from exercising full political and social rights. Both
hoped that their writings would spark genuine debate of the biblical
position on the status of women. Both used scriptural exegesis as a
principal means to prove their points.

At first Willard was attracted to Stanton's project. She thought it was
designed to corroborate her own position that scripture was misused to
defend an inferior position for women within the church and justify
denial of equal political rights to women. Willard agreed to serve on the
committee of prominent women that Stanton assembled in 1895 to give
legitimacy to her work.[82] However, Willard made this commitment
before she had seen any of Stanton's commentary which appeared in
the *Woman's Tribune* of Washington, D.C., and which stimulated much
adverse comment.

Although Stanton had originally intended her Bible to be a new
feminist translation, similar in format to the Revised Version published
in 1881, she was unable to command the resources for such an ambitious
project. Instead, *The Woman's Bible* was essentially a series of polemical
commentaries in the form of scriptural exegesis, ignoring ninety percent of scriptural texts and concentrating on passages that dealt with
women. But Stanton did not stop there. Whereas Willard had stuck to
scripture and cited scripture to prove her points in *Woman in the Pulpit*,
Stanton not only reiterated and reemphasized feminist arguments that
she had used many times in the past but also criticized biblical women's
subjection to men, denied the divinity of Christ and virginity of Mary,

and was particularly adamant in her assertion that the Old Testament was little more than a collection of Jewish mythology.

Stanton would always be anticlerical and antichurch. Willard could fight with the church hierarchy and eschew a literal interpretation of the Bible, but in the last analysis her basic affections lay with the church. She believed with other adherents of the Social Gospel that Christianity overall had been a force for good in the world and was a continuing inspiration for social reform. Stanton believed religion was a major instrument of woman's oppression, a fetter used by men to keep her in bondage.[83] Emotionally, Willard and Stanton were worlds apart.

The Protestant hierarchy was hardly pleased by *Woman in the Pulpit*. It was aghast at *The Woman's Bible*. The WCTU was quick to deny any endorsement,[84] and Willard withdrew her first tentative approval. *The Woman's Bible* was not her way to fight. Stanton was disappointed and angry, but eventually some kind of peace was patched up between them. Willard wrote Stanton, "You have shown us your large heartedness in appreciating the difficulty of our position," adding that "it is better that we do not try to work together on that one subject." Holding out her own olive branch, she stated that she would always publicly acknowledge the affection and regard she felt for Stanton "as a mighty pioneer in the work of uplift for one-half the human race."[85]

THE doctrine of spheres and submission to Christ carried for women a strong symbolic attraction. From antebellum days trust in one's husband and devotion to the Master were unconsciously linked and somehow made the doctrine of spheres more palatable. But the linkage of Christian submission and the acceptance of spheres could work in two ways.[86] Christian submission also spawned the circumvention of spheres. Religion can have myriad uses. In the antebellum period middle-class women were deeply attracted to philanthropy. They urged society (in small but insistent voices) to change its ways and be just and compassionate; they used all their skills to provide relief for the disadvantaged. But during the Gilded Age this emphasis on Christianity to explain existing social forces shifted to an emphasis on the state as the vehicle for translating Christ's teachings to ensure social justice. Personal philanthropy was still desirable, but government became the major instrument for social change, and the Social Gospel movement was born.

The Social Gospel, combined with the idea of progress, made for profound ferment and change in Protestant churches in the late nineteenth century. It could be argued that Willard's ideas reflected this change. But in many other ways she was in the forefront, a leader rather than a follower. Washington Gladden, who was the most influential leader of the Social Gospel movement, did not publish his *Applied Christianity* until 1886 and Walter Rauschenbusch's *Christianity and the Social Crisis* did not appear until 1907. Charles Sheldon's novel, *In His Steps*, the most popular expression of Social Gospel ideology, was first published in 1896.[87] Although women had long used religion to justify social reform, Frances Willard clearly stressed the social, pragmatic, and political implications of Christian ethics. She called for both private charity and state-sponsored social reform. In this sense she was part of the Social Gospel's first wave.

Willard was regarded by her followers as the "Social gospel theologian of the age."[88] One historian has suggested that her great contribution was her ability to reconcile "the Enlightenment idealism of the first women's rights advocates with the missionary mentality of rural Protestant women."[89] Willard's firm attachment to orthodox Protestantism and her consistent use of its rhetoric enabled her to effect this reconciliation. Christian culture was so pervasive in the late nineteenth century that Christian terminology was commonly used, at least on the popular level, to express most social, economic, and political ideas. Herbert Gutman, who has pointed to its use by trade unionists, sees this as an essential part of legitimatizing labor's demands.[90] Radical criticism and labor discontent found sanction through appeal to the Christian tradition and the use of Christian rhetoric. Early women socialists used Christian phraseology to express their economic radicalism.[91] Willard, of course, was among the most articulate. Prison reformers also were constant users of Christian rhetoric both to justify and to implement their methods and correctional philosophy. At its meetings in the 1880s the American Prison Association attended church in a body and opened its sessions with a sermon. But the most fluent expression of reform ideology in Christian terms came from the lips and pen of Frances Willard, and this was a primary strength of her message and appeal.

Chapter XI Politician

Frances Willard entered the decade of the 1890s at the height of her political influence. Although they did not have the vote, the WCTU women she led had authored and successfully supported an impressive body of legislation. They had sponsored and shepherded through the legislative process dozens of local option and age of consent laws. Because of their systematic prodding, scientific temperance education had been mandated for the public schools in all states except Georgia. Laws had been passed in a number of states requiring special institutions for the treatment of handicapped and delinquent females, again with WCTU support. Union women were expert in the use of the petition. They had developed and perfected a variety of lobbying skills that special interest groups have imitated ever since, including hiring professional lobbyists to work in Washington.

As the leader of the largest women's organization in the United States, Willard had been using the WCTU and her position within it for political purposes for over a decade. She had mounted her first major political campaign in 1879 when, as president of the Illinois WCTU, she staged her intensive and unsuccessful lobbying effort to obtain a home protection ballot. She had developed flexible manipulative skills that made her highly effective at operating within the existing system. Hers was a pragmatic approach to political questions accompanied by an almost instinctive ordering of priorities, an ability to make use of each developing situation to maximize her influence and promote the social interests she thought important. She also had a decade's experience at broadening her political base by allying herself with other organizations—the Prohibition party, Bellamy's Nationalists, and the Knights of Labor. However, the economic and social upheavals of the late 1880s and early 1890s resulted in political changes that threatened the power of the Prohibition party and the Knights, thereby jeopardizing the carefully forged foundation on which Willard's political influence rested.

Two reform movements—the farmers' alliances and the WCTU—were spectacularly successful in creating mass organizations in the 1880s. Both had their beginnings in transappalachia rather than the eastern seaboard. Both organized segments of the population that felt American society treated them unfairly, farmers and women. Both were radical and conservative at the same time. And both strove for fundamental changes in American society.

The farmers' alliances were the product of the economic problems of rural America, tight credit, deflation, hopelessness. The WCTU had its origins in a social or individual problem, alcohol abuse, but a problem women felt was directly related to their lack of political clout. Both groups were responding to what they saw as their helplessness. The two movements were also alike in mobilizing their supporters on the basis of reform issues rather than sectional rivalries. Unlike the old parties, they had no interest in waving the bloody shirt the Civil War had made so dear. They pioneered in other ways. Both accepted black members, and both were aggressive organizers. By 1891 the farmers' alliances were fully in place in forty-three states and territories. The WCTU's organizing efforts of the 1880s reached every state and territory, and by 1890 its paid membership totaled nearly 200,000.

In the 1880s the discontented farmers of the alliances, like the temperance forces early in the century, professed to be nonpolitical. They soon realized, however, that only through political action could they effect change. The alliances entered the political arena in the 1890 elections and experienced considerable success. In the South working through the Democratic party they elected four governors, and a number of legislators, congressmen, and senators pledged to support their demands. In the West, where sentiment for a new reform party was strongest, they worked through independent third parties to win similar electoral victories.

Conversely, by 1890 the Prohibition party had lost what promise it once had of capturing broad political support. Despite the fact that prohibition as an issue could still pull a substantial vote, the party's national appeal was eroding.[1] The growing strength of the farmers' movement sapped the party's electoral strength in many areas, and the Prohibitionists were clearly in danger of losing their place as the largest reform party. By 1892 the farmers' movement had replaced the Prohibitionists as the major source of third-party strength. Although Willard was sympathetic to the alliances she was not among the early leaders of

The Temple office building, Chicago, headquarters of the WCTU, was both the union's downfall and its glory. While seriously overextending the WCTU's financial resources, this structure uplifted American womanhood by its sheer grandeur and power. (Reprinted from Gordon, *The Beautiful Life of Frances Willard*)

that movement, and she knew by 1890 that through the impending political realignment she could lose much of the political influence she had so carefully achieved.

As the farmers' movement began to crystallize after 1890 into the People's party, some attempt to merge these two reform movements—Populism and temperance—with their vast and frequently overlapping constituencies was inevitable.[2] The alliances did not begin as a single organization. They had their own factions, rivalries, and sectional biases, but good progress was made toward union among the various branches of their own organizations as a result of the St. Louis Congress of reform organizations in 1889. A common platform was adopted by the several groups represented, although they were not yet ready to merge their separate identities in a single organization.

In May 1891 a congress called by Kansas alliance members, eager for speedy formation of a new party, convened in Cincinnati. All reform groups present at the St. Louis meetings of 1889 were invited, including Bellamy's Nationalists and Henry George's single taxers. The Prohibition party had a number of representatives. Although Willard was not among them, Helen Gougar, one of the party's prominent women leaders, and John St. John, its presidential candidate in 1884, were on hand.[3] Ignatius Donnelly, Minnesota alliance leader, novelist, and publicist, led the pro-third-party forces and chaired the resolutions committee. However, a brewer was chairman of local arrangements at Cincinnati, and the Prohibitionists were howled down when they attempted to get a temperance plank in the platform. Most of the party's delegates withdrew from the meeting to protest the treatment they had received.[4]

AFTER Cincinnati a new third party was no longer a matter for discussion but a reality, and the breadth of its support was evident at the St. Louis Industrial Conference convened in February 1892. Willard was eager to merge the new party with the Prohibition party. She had everything to gain from such an alliance. The new party clearly would preempt what previous claim the Prohibition party had possessed to influence either elections or the major party platforms. Also, if the influence Willard exercised in the Prohibition party could be transferred intact to the new party, her position in American politics would be enhanced; if she was unsuccessful, she would lose much of the influence she had been able to exert on the body politic. If she could maneuver the new party to accept woman suffrage and prohibition even in modified form as part of its program, the two goals to which she was most firmly committed would receive a substantial boost. Although Prohibition party influence had been declining since 1884, Willard could not abandon that party outright no matter how attractive a new People's party might prove. She had too long commended it to her WCTU constituents. To maintain her political position her only hope was to get the two together somehow, despite the bad feeling created at Cincinnati. Fusion was the only satisfactory answer.

Willard used tactics typical of her approach to political questions. She took a private, womanly stance. She wrote personal letters to a number of reform leaders suggesting a private conference in January at Chicago's Sherman House to "carefully consider the planks for the platform of 1892 on which we could agree," "not only concerning principles but men, in the hope that such agreement may foreshadow the platform and ticket of the 'malcontents' of this country in 1892."[5]

The response Willard received to these letters is a measure of her position as a major force in American reform politics. Her personal invitation to a patently unofficial gathering brought a galaxy of leaders—twenty-eight in all (twenty-two men and six women)—to Chicago. Among the Populists were James B. Weaver, the People's party's first candidate for president; Ignatius Donnelly; Herbert Taubeneck, of Illinois, who had been elected temporary chairman of the new party in Cincinnati; Annie Diggs of Kansas; and George Washburn, prominent Nationalist and later a member of the executive committee of the People's party. Henry Demarest Lloyd was among the independent reformers who accepted. Prohibitionist forces were represented by Willard and several other WCTU leaders; Samuel Dickie, Prohibition party chairman; and Edward J. Wheeler, editor of *Voice*, the Prohibition party organ.[6] Some of this enthusiastic response to Willard's call can be attributed to the fact that Willard struck a sympathetic chord. She was not alone in wanting a united reform front in 1892. But the initiative for this meeting was hers, and she planned its strategy. The Sherman House conference represented the peak of Willard's influence in reform political circles in the United States. The conference also probably brought fusion closer to success (although it did not come very close) than at any other time in the period 1890–96 when reform forces were considering union.

Willard hoped to achieve some kind of consensus at Chicago. She called this consensus an "address," a position paper to which all conferees could subscribe and that could be presented to the St. Louis Industrial Conference and used as the basis for its platform, while also providing a common, agreed upon agenda for the platforms of the People's and Prohibition parties when their conventions met that summer. A committee of six including Donnelly, Wheeler, and Willard prepared the address. Donnelly, who presented it to the conference, protested that he did not feel the liquor plank stressing the saloon as an instrument of social destruction would be acceptable to all Populists and therefore should be modified.[7] In the final document nothing was said about either prohibition or Bellamy's recent proposal for reform of alcohol abuse via nationalization of the liquor trade. Only condemnation of the saloon appeared in the address.[8]

As for woman suffrage, the Populists, afraid of southern displeasure, accepted only municipal suffrage for women with an educational qualification. Planks advocating cheap money, condemning land speculation, and asking for limitations on the amount of land that could be owned by any corporation or individual were adopted. The reform leaders also agreed on government control rather than ownership of public transportation and communication.[9]

At best, the address was a fragile compromise in which Willard had done most of the giving. The Prohibitionists were unlikely to accept it, especially as they already felt rebuffed and overridden at Cincinnati. Nor was the mild antiliquor plank acceptable to German farmers or the mild suffrage statement likely to be endorsed by southern Populists. Even at the little Sherman House meeting, endorsement was not unanimous. Taubeneck and Washburn refused to sign the liquor plank, and Dickie signed nothing. Willard and Wheeler put their signatures to the document for the Prohibitionists, and Donnelly and Weaver for the Populists; the others simply agreed. The first round of Willard's fight for joined goals did not augur well for the impending St. Louis confrontation where she could depend neither on the full support of the Prohibitionists nor the recognition by the Populists of any real need to compromise in order to woo temperance support. Both groups were well endowed with members for whom expediency could never replace principle.

On the other hand, Willard could always take the expedient road, partly because she had an eye for the larger rewards that trade-offs could bring her, but also because she was confident that eventually she could bring her associates along to where she wished them to be. This approach had proved effective with her WCTU constituency. Expediency was the tactic she had used to achieve WCTU acceptance of a woman suffrage plank, endorsement of the Prohibition party, and Union cooperation with the Knights of Labor. It was quite in character for Willard to compromise radically her own position in order to keep the options open, but the compromise this time was of an order that many of her Prohibitionist colleagues would find unacceptable. They could hardly abandon their primary goal, prohibition, for some vague reform ideology. Willard did not have time to persuade them. The St. Louis Industrial Conference convened in less than a month.

WILLARD did not go to St. Louis alone. She was accompanied by Lady Henry Somerset, president of the British Woman's Temperance Association (BWTA), who was visiting in the United States. Lady Henry had come to attend the first World WCTU convention in Boston in November 1891, study the organizational methods of the United States WCTU, and possibly attend a couple of state conventions.[10] Her welcome was so warm and her friendship with Frances Willard so immediately rewarding that she stayed in the United States, living and traveling with Willard and Anna Gordon until the following spring.

Lady Henry Somerset was born in 1851, the first child of the third Earl of Somer, John Somers Cocks. As a young woman she was a great beauty who was presented at court at nineteen and married at twenty-two to Lord Henry Somerset, second son of the Duke of Beaufort. The marriage was arranged. Isabel Cocks was heiress to estates, manor houses, and lucrative London property.[11] Somerset as second son was essentially penniless. The marriage was not a success, and by the time she and Willard met, Isabel Somerset had already shown a large capacity for independence. She was separated from her husband, who allegedly abused her. She had left the Church of England and attached herself in 1885 to the Methodists, hardly a British upper-class sect. And she had become president of the British Woman's Temperance Association in 1890. Her biographer attributed her substantial sympathy with scapegoats and outcasts to her ostracism from society after the deterioration of her marriage.[12]

By 1891 Lady Henry had found a congenial home in British reform circles. She had endowed philanthropic enterprises, among them a "home for friendless children, many of whom she has rescued from the slums of London."[13] She also had a strong political bent, which she found she could exercise in the United States more easily than in England, especially as she followed Willard around. She was present at the Sherman House meetings and at all the maneuverings of the St. Louis conference. She was not viewed by reform politicians as an outsider. The Americans accepted her. She provided a desirable upper-class patina to the goals Willard championed. As Neal Dow put it in a letter to Willard shortly after Lady Henry departed for England in the spring of 1892, "Lady Somerset's visit to this country will be of great value I think to the W.C.T.U. Tho' very little is thought of it and nothing said about it—there is lingering in this country yet—something of the old feeling—that temperance work 'is well enough for the vulgar!' The visit of Lady S. with her active participation in it will go far to dissipate that."[14] Not only did Isabel Somerset lend chic to temperance; she also added luster to Populist politics.

The story may be apocryphal, but Lady Henry purportedly first became aware of Willard when she saw a little blue book, *Nineteen Beautiful Years*, on her housekeeper's table.[15] The two women were corresponding by January 1891. The human connecting link was Hannah Whitall Smith, popular religious writer and WCTU leader. Smith and Willard were close friends, and Willard often rested at Smith's home near Philadelphia to recover from the strain imposed by national conventions. Smith, now an expatriate American living in England, had been instrumental in having Lady Henry succeed Margaret Bright Lucas as president of the BWTA.

Lady Henry had begun her public career as a philanthropist, an acceptable and challenging outlet that helped mend her broken life after the collapse of her marriage. Philanthropy led her into sympathy with reform causes. Her drift to the temperance movement came later and may have been partly motivated by self-interest, a way of promoting herself as a leader within the British reform milieu. Her personal commitment to abstinence was always questioned by her detractors, who were quick to point out that among her vast holdings were numerous British pubs, and that she took a last glass of port at a railroad restaurant before signing the pledge so she could assume leadership of the BWTA. The press and some WCTU members were always eager to suspect that any clear liquid in a glass that Frances Willard and Lady Henry were sipping was wine. For both of them temperance may have been as much a vehicle as a cause, but by the 1890s there was no doubt about their commitment to temperance and broad reform goals, as well as their active interest in obtaining the greatest possible political influence.

WILLARD arrived at the St. Louis Industrial Conference with her prestigious English friend, her fragile compromise, and less than enthusiastic support from the Prohibition party. Helen Gougar and John St. John, remembering the affront of Cincinnati and probably resenting Willard's leadership gambit in calling the Chicago meetings, were ready to do battle. Quite naturally they felt Willard had tried to take over leadership of the party and point the direction it would take.

The Prohibitionists were not sympathetic to Willard, but in this case Lady Henry proved an asset for Willard's campaign. She inevitably attracted attention at the convention, both from the press and the rank and file. As she was constantly at Willard's side, she no doubt assisted

Willard in obtaining public notice for her proposals and the principle of fusion, although notice would not be enough.

Willard and the executive committee of the Prohibition party met in St. Louis the morning of 22 February 1892 before the industrial conference convened at noon. Gougar and St. John made clear that they were aghast at what Willard and Edward J. Wheeler had proposed in Chicago. The leaders of the Prohibition party felt Willard and Wheeler were selling out on the liquor plank and equivocating on suffrage, and in many ways this was a realistic assessment. Willard and Wheeler denied the sellout and won the first round. A resolution placed before the executive committee repudiating the Sherman House compromises on the liquor and suffrage planks was defeated 28 to 13.[16] But the party caucus adopted a resolution stating that the Prohibition party would not deal with "any party not committed 'to the principle and policy of Prohibition,' and therefore would talk about union only when the farmer's movement shall have placed itself in open hostility to the liquor traffic."[17] The upshot of this pronouncement was that the Prohibition party withdrew from the St. Louis conference and closed the door to compromise with the Populists. Willard told the press, and tried to convince herself, that the party's resolution did not interfere "with efforts being put forth so earnestly by herself and other prohibitionists as individuals" to lead the industrial conference to embrace "united action among labor reformers and temperance reformers,"[18] but she was whistling in the dark.

Both the industrial conference and the Populists proved equally unyielding. In his opening remarks the temporary chairman of the conference suggested that the convention stick to economic issues and abandon "moral reform" until they had more time. Willard was seated on the platform, and, as he spoke, "her features [were] shaded by a frown."[19] Another door had been shut on compromise. However, the Populists felt they had enough trouble holding their own group together. There was no room for extending olive branches elsewhere. Only a prohibition plank would satisfy the Prohibitionists. The price was too high.[20] Because the Prohibition party had withdrawn from the conference, Willard now was without official status at St. Louis, but Ignatius Donnelly proposed that she be made a delegate of the WCTU which was not officially represented at the meeting. Willard acceded and continued to play a leading role at the conference. She was made a member of the platform committee, chosen one of the vice-presidents, and delivered a major speech.

In the platform committee Willard fought hard for an antisaloon plank. She was willing to compromise to the same extent that she had in Chicago, but the Populists felt too strongly that an antisaloon stance would cost them support. As the press saw it, the Populists clearly "slammed the doors in the face of a national party claiming 1,000,000 voters."[21] Unsuccessful in the platform committee after an all-night session, Willard brought the universal suffrage and antisaloon planks to the floor of the conference as a minority report and lost again. The battle was convoluted and the tactics were not always honorable. In the end, the suffrage and antisaloon planks were rejected by a vote of 352 to 238.[22]

Willard was bitter and some of her bitterness was revealed to the press. She commented that the "means employed to scuttle these planks were most dishonorable. Crooked methods were resorted to and disgraceful work done." She blamed convention defeat of the antisaloon plank on what she called the "liquor element," which, according to her, was represented by Robert Schilling, former Greenbacker and Milwaukee Knights of Labor organizer of German extraction. She attributed the defeat of the suffrage plank to the fears of southern alliance leaders. She minimized the fact that not all Prohibitionists favored cooperation.[23] But she also professed to feel that all was not yet lost. If the two parties meeting in their separate conventions in June and July could agree on a common platform, cooperation if not union might still occur.[24] Edward J. Wheeler was personally assuring: "we have set the ferment to working in *both* parties"; success would come later, after the election, when both groups would recognize that victory could result only through fusion.[25]

Willard was not yet prepared to abandon the fusion fight. In a mid-June editorial in the *Union Signal*, she suggested that, if the People's party nominated a presidential candidate who supported prohibition and suffrage, the Prohibition party should make him their candidate and thereby "mass" the reform vote.[26]

THAT year the Prohibition party convention was held in Cincinnati. Willard, though chastened, was still battling for union. She abandoned the term "fusionist" because it aroused the ire of Helen Gougar and John St. John. But she drafted a resolution urging steps be taken toward union after the election of 1892. She adopted Wheeler's tactic of delay in the interest of eventual success. She also made a firm commitment to "total suppression of the liquor traffic" and "the enfranchisement of women" as a condition of union.[27] Once more Willard tried her old gambit: accept the opposition's position—in this case, no fusion—but use words equivocally in such a way as to essentially accept the position being denied. The gambit would fail. This was not a WCTU convention.

The convention nominated not James B. Weaver, who would be the People's party candidate, but two obscure Prohibitionists, John Bidwell of California for president and a southern Baptist minister from Texas for vice-president. Moreover, fusion commanded no support at Cincinnati. Willard reported that she sat all day waiting to present her resolution, which was never brought to the floor.[28] She had hoped that the Prohibition party would nominate a dummy candidate who would withdraw after Weaver's nomination by the Populist party in July, but this did not happen. Again she was opposed by Gougar and St. John. Although she was careful not to place blame in her accounts of the convention, she took no part in the presidential campaign that year.

When the WCTU convention met in the fall, Willard's influence was seen in a resolution adopted by the delegates stating that "because we are positive rather than negative . . . we express earnest hope that the Prohibition party, will, in the near future adopt a name that is as broad as its purpose toward humanity."[29] As late as November Willard was still preaching union. When interviewed at her New York hotel before sailing for England that fall, she emphasized, "There must be a new party continuing the reform elements for the interest of humanity. The Democrats and Republicans are like boulders in the path; the Prohibition and People's parties must combine."[30] But for all practical purposes Willard had abandoned the fight for unity during the summer of 1892, although she continued to go through the motions.

In August of that year Willard's mother died after a few weeks of rapidly deteriorating health. Willard grieved deeply on her mother's death. Several years later her mother's chair was still in its place in Frances's den; her mother's picture had become a little shrine with fresh flowers always placed before it.[31] Lady Henry described her mourning: "I have never known a human soul feel sorrow so acutely as did this daughter. . . . It was like the grieving of a little child who holds out its hands in the dark and feels in vain for the accustomed clasp that sent it happily to sleep."[32] Long ago at Kankakee Academy Willard had written in her diary that of the four, Oliver, Mary, mother, and father, her mother was most important to her.[33]

Frances abandoned her politicking in the summer of 1892 to spend several weeks easing her mother's final days, and this devotion was both explainable and expected. As she said in 1894, "Mother's influence on me was always calming. . . . When folks got after me and tore me to pieces with false accusations and political trickery, etc., she would say,

'Keep quiet child; we were not born to reign but to wrestle.'" Frances worried that no one was left to "smooth her down."[34] Also, her mother had never lagged in support of Willard's activism. Mary Willard had been forced to forfeit her own ambitions and goals, but in Frances she had achieved them all in good measure.

Willard's mourning on her mother's death contained an element of symbolism for the grief she felt at losing her political fight that summer. She saw her influence slipping away along with the last member of her immediate family. Never again would she entertain such high hopes of bringing off a coup that would place her near the center of American political life. Willard continued to work for a union of reform parties through 1896. But during these years she was more frequently in England than in the United States, and she was handicapped by being dependent on the mails for most of her machinations. Willard spent more and more time abroad, partly to ease her bereavement and also because her own health was deteriorating. Equally important to her feeling of loss was her failure as political arbiter and expediter of a new unified reform party, the most ambitious scheme of her career. Her disappointment was profound and explains to some extent why she found England and her growing fame abroad so attractive.

WILLARD made her major attempt to bring about political fusion in 1891–92. Had the Populists been able to enlist the nationwide grass roots organizational machines of the WCTU and the Prohibition party for the elections of 1892, they might well have found a larger measure of electoral success. Would that success have kept them independent in 1896? Members of the WCTU could not vote, but their organizational network was broad and capable. The Prohibition party claimed over one million adherents, and it too possessed strong local organizational networks. Fusion could have helped. A permanent new party might have emerged.

Despite the failure of Willard's efforts to achieve compromise, the role she played, especially in January and February 1892, embodied a personal triumph. No American woman before her had demonstrated such influence in controlling the direction of an important political movement.

Why was Frances Willard able to do this? She represented a substantial constituency numbering in the hundreds of thousands, but that constituency was also disfranchised, and there is no reason to believe that women universally controlled the votes of their male relatives. Women contributed a great deal of volunteer time to political issues, and their work was important to third parties. This no doubt is part of

A Woman in Politics.

"AS ONCE HE SAT OVER AGAINST THE TREASURY, SO NOW
CHRIST SITS OVER AGAINST THE BALLOT BOX TO SEE WHAT
HIS DISCIPLES CAST THEREIN."

—*Mary Allen West.*

This drawing, used to introduce the chapter on Willard's political role in her autobiography, is a symbolic portrayal of Willard's mission as she saw it—the white rose of the Prohibition party, the olive branch for peace, the flag of the United States, and the shield foremost, both protecting women and leading them forward—epitomize Willard and the movement Willard led. (Reprinted from Willard, *Glimpses of Fifty Years*)

One of the hundreds of appeals used by the temperance movement to save children from alcohol abuse. (Courtesy of the Bentley Historical Library, University of Michigan, Ann Arbor)

the answer. Nonetheless, paradoxical as it may seem, American devo- tion to the cult of domesticity may best explain women's political influence in the nineteenth century. American society embraced with conviction the idea of women's moral superiority, and as women moved into the public sphere they carried with them that aura of uncorrupted righteousness bestowed on them to justify the importance of their role as guardians of the home and nurturers of children. When the political issue was a moral one, the position taken on it by women could not be ignored, especially by men of reform principles who were cloaking their own causes in moral righteousness. The pedestal moved with women into the public sphere and for a brief season elevated their influence in that arena.

Willard certainly hoped women in politics would be seen this way. In an editorial in the 1892 *Union Signal*, she cited women's recent political activities—among them, women's agitation for the vote in England, Susan B. Anthony's testimony for suffrage before the Republican and Democratic conventions of 1892, women's participation as delegates, officers, and leaders in the Prohibition and People's parties—and asked, "What shall we do? Just what we have so long done in home, church and school—be an influence for gentle strength, intelligent patience and wise, heroic counsel. Woman . . . must possess her soul in quietness; she must avoid personalities and push principles to the front."[35]

The WCTU had been exerting its political influence ever since the temperance Crusade attempted to secure local ordinances regulating the sale of alcoholic beverages and the infant WCTU offered its first petition to the United States Congress. Frances Willard had been leading women in their public role since the 1870s, and the sum of what she and her cohorts had accomplished was impressive. Eventually temperance women would play a major part in the passage of the Eighteenth and Nineteenth amendments to the United States Constitution, but these were single issue victories. Willard's hope of changing the whole society failed its critical test in the summer of 1892. She did not narrow the breadth of her vision, but never again did she come close to realizing her dream.

Chapter XII · Expatriate

AFTER Mother Willard's death in the summer of 1892, Frances Willard and Anna Gordon sailed for England to join Lady Henry Somerset at Eastnor Castle. This visit, labeled as private in the press, was brief and devoted to rest and respite. Willard returned to the United States in ample time for the WCTU's fall convention. Nonetheless, the English visit marked a major change in her way of life. From 1892 until late 1896 she was to make her real home in England, not in Evanston. The dateline on her letters was Reigate Manor or Eastnor Castle, rather than Rest Cottage. Willard used her residence in England as an embarkation point to consolidate her position as a world leader; at the same time, her British sojourn met personal needs unassociated with her international position.

No doubt Willard would have found some way to extend her outreach whether or not her life's path had crossed that of Lady Henry Somerset. Willard first expressed interest in organizing an international temperance movement in 1875 in a short piece she wrote for *Our Union*, an early national organ of the WCTU. The following year an attempt was made to initiate an international society at the temperance conclave convened in connection with the Philadelphia Centennial Exposition of 1876, but the effort proved abortive. However, Willard continued to pursue the idea of world outreach using another approach, the WCTU world missionary, actually an international organizer sponsored by the American WCTU. As she explained it, "But for the intervention of the sea, the shores of China and the Far East would be part and parcel of our land. We are *one world* of tempted humanity. . . . We must no longer be hedged about by the artificial boundaries of states and nations," and we must declare "the whole world is my parish and to do good my religion."[1] The WCTU's world missionary efforts were spectacularly successful. Organizers traveled to over forty countries, and unions were formed in many of them.

The Orient in particular attracted Willard, as it did many late nineteenth-century women.[2] The great Orientalists of the period fascinated the Western world with treasures of ancient civilizations, and the East exerted an almost mesmeric attraction in Occidental societies. Frances Willard's excursion into Asia Minor clearly provided the high point of excitement during her years abroad. But the nineteenth-century woman balanced the fascination and excitement aroused by the East with her revulsion at the harem or seraglio and her conviction that Asian women experienced the ultimate degradation of womanhood. To American women the message was clear. Their privileged position of protection and respect must be used to save the world's oppressed women. This message was first transmitted by thousands of Protestant missionary society members before and after the Civil War; by the 1880s it went out to tens of thousands of WCTU members.

In large part the interest American women manifested in the Orient reflected their unquestioning acceptance of Christian values. Through Christianity they wished to save their oppressed sisters and bring to them the values of what they saw as a superior ethical system. But other factors played a role. The imperial impulse and the will to govern also were important. For American women this attraction was in part an extension of the old feeling of Manifest Destiny, the notion that the United States had moved naturally toward the Pacific, its obvious boundary, and now should spread its influence to the other side of the great sea that separated it from the East. Mary Clement Leavitt, the first WCTU world organizer, made her way around the world from East to West, as did most of the WCTU emissaries who followed her. Mary Allen West, another Union organizer, lost her life while proselytizing in Japan. Willard herself was captivated by Pundita Ramabai, an Indian woman educated in England, who worked to alleviate the degraded status of widows in her native land. When Ramabai came to the United States in 1886 on a money raising tour, she and Willard became fast friends; they corresponded for the rest of Willard's life. Although Willard never traveled to the Far East, Asia loomed large and important in her view of the world. Christian duty provided the primary motivation for a global movement, but the women who set out to change the world took an inevitable westward course that smacked of earlier patterns of expansionism.

In 1884 Willard introduced the polyglot petition, an astonishing document calling on the world's rulers to inaugurate total prohibition in their countries. WCTU world missionaries collected signatures wherever they went, and women all over the world put their names to resolutions that eventually took the form of a huge canvas roll on which were pasted the signatures of nearly a million women from fifty nations asking for an end to the trade in alcohol.

Willard's interest in other forms of world outreach did not cause her to abandon her scheme for an international organization. As early as 1886 she was trying to interest the officers of the British Woman's Temperance Association (BWTA)—who in the early phases were less enthusiastic about her plan than their American counterparts—in a World WCTU.[3] Eventually she succeeded, for in November 1891 delegates from every continent except South America (nineteen from other countries and seven from the United States) gathered in Boston, organized themselves, elected Frances Willard world president, and adopted a declaration of principles and a plan of work.[4] The call to meeting had been signed by Willard and Mary Clement Leavitt.

AT the time that Willard first met Isabel Somerset and the World WCTU was organized, both the British woman's movement and the role of temperance forces within it were changing. The women's rights movement in Britain dated from the 1860s, some two decades after the British movement for women's schools and colleges got underway. Both the impetus provided by the English political radicals of the 1850s and 1860s and the increased interest in philanthropy that dates from the same period helped contribute the leaven from which the British woman's movement sprang. In England as in America, philanthropy, because it was considered an acceptable and respectable form of public activity, proved a liberating force for women, and the English *Woman's Journal*, founded in 1857, provided reform women with an effective outlet for proselytizing their burgeoning causes.

For two decades at mid-century British women concentrated on equal rights and suffrage, but in the 1880s their movement changed its focus. By the 1870s British women had made substantial legal and educational gains. The married woman's property act had become law, women's right to equal elementary education had been accepted, the first women's colleges had been founded, and women rate payers could vote in municipal elections and were eligible to serve on school boards.[5] By 1884 virtually all males were enfranchised, but the Liberal party had failed to support woman suffrage, and women could no longer expect much help from the Liberal party in their quest for the vote.[6] Because of this shift away from suffrage as an immediate and achievable goal, the British women's movement turned to other issues. Rather than legislative action leading to suffrage and equal rights, the movement began to concern itself with the quality of life, including broad social

The polyglot petition—it contained seven million signatures. (Reprinted from Gordon, *The Beautiful Life of Frances Willard*)

issues such as temperance, prostitution, personal purity, and venereal disease as well as the overriding problems of poverty and public health. Women did not totally give up legislative solutions to problems. They continued to ask Parliament and municipal councils to implement the reforms they pushed—for example, closing hours and local option. And the Contagious Diseases Acts (for the licensing and inspection of prostitutes to control venereal disease) were to be a major women's issue in the last two decades of the century. But the focus shifted from immediate concern with woman suffrage and equal rights to largely social issues.

The British temperance movement had been underway for over half a century when Frances Willard convened the 1891 international convention. In the British Isles, as in the United States, the temperance cause first attracted a substantial following in the 1820s and 1830s, and may well have had its origins in the United States, making use of links established by antislavery reformers. In Britain temperance began with the grass roots rather than the social elite, in provincial cities rather than in London, and among nonconformist dissenters rather than adherents of the established church.[7] These characteristics did not set it apart from the American temperance movement, although in the United States the temperance cause represented dominant social groups by mid-century, a development that did not occur in England until somewhat later. By 1870 temperance was endorsed by members of the upper classes, and by 1890 it had acquired real support within the Liberal party and the Anglican church.[8]

The British Woman's Temperance Association was organized in April 1876, a year and one-half after the WCTU. From its beginnings the BWTA had ties to the American WCTU. A delegate was sent from its first convention to the temperance congress at the Philadelphia Centennial Exposition of 1876, and the same year Eliza Stewart, American temperance leader, was induced to go to England where she spent five months lecturing and assisting in the early organizational efforts of the BWTA and attending a world convention of the Good Templars.[9]

Hannah Whitall Smith, the American Quaker preacher and religious writer who introduced Lady Henry to Willard, also played an important role in strengthening the Anglo-American women's temperance connection. Smith was in England visiting her daughter when news of the woman's crusade of 1873–74 first reached her. On her return to the United States she joined the WCTU, playing an active role in the Pennsylvania union and serving as one of the national WCTU departmental superintendents. However, Smith and her husband Robert Pearsall Smith spent increasingly large blocks of time in England during the 1880s, making Britain their permanent home in 1888. Hannah Smith then turned her energies to the BWTA. She served as a member of its executive committee, as recording secretary, and as vice-president, continuing as an officer of that organization until her seventieth birthday in 1903.[10]

Smith easily moved back and forth between reform circles in the United States and Great Britain. Frances Willard was her intimate friend, as was Isabel Somerset. Her British salon included playwright George Bernard Shaw, her son-in-law, philosopher Bertrand Russell, Oliver and Lytton Strachey, and art critic Bernard Berenson, second husband of her other daughter. In the United States she and her husband were related to Philadelphia's old Quaker families, knew well most of Boston's intellectual establishment, and supported handsomely their interest in religion and reform from the prosperous bottle manufactory left them by her father. The Smiths were equally at home in both worlds, and Hannah Smith was a substantial force in uniting the temperance movements of the two countries.

The transatlantic reform community was, of course, much broader than temperance. Dating at least from the mid-nineteenth century, it comprised a small but influential group of British and Americans who looked for liberal solutions to social questions, often held unorthodox

Lady Henry Somerset in 1890. (Reprinted from Gordon, *The Beautiful Life of Frances Willard*)

religious views, and expected leadership in the reforms they supported to come from a moral and intellectual elite.[11] Before the Civil War, the problem of slavery and the propagation of liberal religion were the major foci of this Anglo-American attention, but temperance and the woman question had also begun to attract notice. Women played a larger role in the Atlantic reform community after the Civil War, although they also participated in the earlier period. Elizabeth Blackwell had brought the revolutionary idea of women physicians to England when she lectured there in 1859.[12] And Elizabeth Cady Stanton's primary focus was changed, at least in part, from slavery to the woman question as a result of her trip to the London antislavery meetings in 1840.[13]

During the Gilded Age the transatlantic community of like-minded women came into its own, and the base from which it sprang became much broader. Frances Willard and Lady Henry Somerset symbolized the postwar popularization of the earlier elitist movement. The number of reform activists shuttling across the Atlantic in the 1890s is impressive. They addressed each other's meetings, wrote for each other's publications, and participated in each other's quarrels. Willard and Somerset helped to enlarge the emphasis of the women's transatlantic reform community to include the woman question as well as legislation on temperance. Although these women continued to look for solutions to alcohol abuse, they also campaigned against what they saw as women's sexual degradation and addressed the labor question. They did not abandon the idea of an elitist, moral, almost specially ordained leadership, but the relationship of reform to religion changed. For most women religion became the very core of their ideological commitment, the nurturant broth that fed the other reforms they championed. The British dissenting sects that had supported temperance from the beginning continued to be important in that movement, but there also was room for Anglicans. In the United States, the Methodists and other Protestant sects predominated; however, in the American milieu this was hardly an expression of dissent, and all groups could be found within the fold. Particularly toward the end of the Victorian Era, influence flowed in both directions across the Atlantic, and what we think of as Victorian culture in both societies was characterized by its identification with bourgeois evangelicalism.[14] Although they accepted it with great affection rather than burning zeal, Willard and Lady Henry felt comfortable with evangelical religion, but like other women reformers they could not live with establishment politics.

Not only were Willard and Lady Henry part of a merged Atlantic community, but also they were seen as such by others. C. H. Grant, a

Boston friend, wrote Willard that Mother Willard, in encouraging the
friendship between her daughter and Lady Henry, "doubtless saw what
a blessing it would be to the women of both countries when you united
your forces."[15] Caroline Merrick, the prominent Louisiana White Rib-
boner and friend of Willard, Somerset, and Anna Gordon, wrote of
Willard and Lady Henry, "these two historic women are chief figures in
the records of their sex, and while they were needful to each other, their
united labor was more important for the world's reforms."[16] When
Lady Henry was in the United States, she did not feel she was in a
foreign place. She served on the board of directors of the Temple,
WCTU headquarters, and was a corresponding editor of the *Union
Signal*. Willard, who frequently referred to England as the mother
country, was a corresponding editor of the British *Woman's Signal* and
served as a vice-president of the BWTA. When Lady Henry came to the
United States, she was feted and honored; even the People's party
accepted her into its councils. Willard, in turn, was feted and honored
in Britain.

AT the end of October 1891, soon after they arrived in the United
States, Hannah Smith and Lady Henry traveled to Chicago where
Frances Willard and her English counterpart were to meet for the first
time. Smith described herself as "trembling in her shoes."[17] Obviously
she believed this meeting was of high importance. Because most of her
time had been spent in England, she had not seen Willard for four or
five years, and she feared Willard might have changed, that Lady Henry
would not find her as attractive as Smith remembered her being.[18] Her
fears were groundless. True, Lady Henry was not impressed with Chicago. She wrote to her mother that it was a "detestable city, black and
horrible," but evangelist Dwight Moody's school was "perfectly delightful." When Somerset met Willard, who presided when Lady
Henry spoke to an audience of four thousand at Chicago's concert hall,
Lady Henry was enchanted: "I cannot say how delightful Miss Willard
is, she is quite unique, so refined, winning and gentle."[19] So began the
friendship that kept Willard in England for much of the rest of her life.
   In the fall Willard and Lady Henry went on to the Boston conventions together. There Lady Henry was the "social lioness." Everyone
wanted to shake her hand; on one occasion she was nearly torn to
pieces making her way through the crowd.[20] She was both beautiful
and giving, and the addition of a title was for the Americans literally
the crowning touch. Hannah Smith wrote of this first visit that she had

to physically guard Somerset or she would have been crushed by "kisses, handshakes, and birthday books. Every form of adulation possible."[21]

When Willard went to England the next fall, the adulation was repeated. She was welcomed at a great meeting at Exeter Hall in London as had been "no other philanthropist in our time." Lady Henry described the gathering as "the most representative that has ever assembled in that historic building."[22] Members of Parliament, dignitaries of the Anglican church, temperance leaders, commanders of the Salvation Army, leaders of the labor movement, delegates from the English Methodists, Baptists, Congregationalists, and Society of Friends all gathered to pay Willard homage. The *Woman's Herald* described her as "a woman in a thousand, a woman born to be a leader of women," and the *Review of Reviews* (U.K.) saw her as "a personality worth studying," the "most conspicuous representative of the Emancipation of Women," and went on to compare her to Queen Victoria. William T. Stead called her the uncrowned "Queen of American Democracy."[23] The time she spent in England that fall was a triumphal procession.

The relationship of Frances Willard and Lady Henry differs from that of many other well known pairs of nineteenth-century women because it was a partnership of equals. Neither played the dominant role. Both were distinguished public figures. Each was a leader in her own land. Now each was hailed as a veritable queen in the land of the other. They seemed not to envy the attention and adulation each received, but took real joy in each other's successes. Isabel Somerset later described Willard as "the greatest woman philanthropist of our generation," as well as "the most beautiful friendship of my life."[24] She saw in Willard a "rare combination of power and perfect gentleness, of playful humor and tender pathos." "She [Willard] was inspired by a love . . . that gave of the treasure that had been poured into her life as freely as the sunshine ripens and blesses the world."[25] Willard's admiration for Somerset, although only expressed privately, was equally great. Willard did not have the opportunity to eulogize her friend, but wrote in her diary, "I never knew a squarer head than Cossie carries on her shoulders or a braver leadership."[26] (Cosimo, often contracted to Cossie or Cozzie, was Willard's private name for Lady Henry.) On another occasion Willard referred to her as "the woman with the head of a statesman and the heart of a child."[27] At still another time, thinking of Mother Willard's death, Frances wrote, "You [her mother] knew that I was to be sheltered and comforted, companioned and consoled by one whom God had given me."[28] To be apart from Isabel was distressing, although separation occurred often. On the memorandum page at the end of one

of her diaries, Frances wrote, "Why must Isabel and I be separated?
Because we put our work before our love."[29] Admiration, respect, and
the love nineteenth-century women often gave to each other were the
elements in their equation.

The friendship of Frances Willard and Isabel Somerset significantly
affected the women's movement of the transatlantic community. The
kind of intimate and supportive cooperation they henceforth brought
to their leadership both strengthened and weakened their causes on
both sides of the Atlantic. The fact that they were most comfortable
working side by side resulted in long absences from their home territories, and the subsequent leadership vacuums occurred at critical junc-
tures in both the WCTU and the BWTA. At the same time, Willard and
Somerset bolstered each other's prestige and effectiveness by providing
new and exciting personalities for public platforms. They also gave to
each other a warm and nurturant intimacy, a shelter from the inevitable
buffetings that come with national and world leadership of a militant
and controversial cause. Also Lady Henry had money, and her largesse
cushioned Willard's experience with the mid-1890s' financial crisis in
the United States and perhaps made her less perceptive of the ways this
crisis threatened a number of WCTU goals. Lady Henry in turn became
a victim of Willard's weaknesses, such as her equivocation on lynching.
Both paid large prices for their partnership, and both reaped large
rewards. In a sense the American and British women's movements were
merged by the joining of these two lives as they played their roles in an
inevitable counterpoint of achievement and disappointment.

Willard's attachment to Lady Henry was, of course, not the first
important friendship in her life. Mary Bannister Willard, Kate Jackson,
Anna Dickinson, and her youthful crushes all preceded Lady Henry,
but Isabel Somerset, along with Anna Gordon, was Frances's most
important emotional support after her mother's death in 1892. Anna
Gordon was not displaced. Anna's role continued as loving daughter,
caring friend, and efficient expediter, but now to both women. A small
file of the Somerset correspondence in the WCTU's Evanston library
contains many affectionate letters from Lady Henry to Anna Gordon.
Anna added Lady Henry to the panoply of women (earlier including
Willard's mother) she served so well. Anna wrote in Frances's diaries,
which she took over when Willard found keeping up the daily entries
too onerous, that "Lady Henry carries enormous burdens. I wish I
could help her,"[30] which of course she did. Anna went on to say, "It is
heartbreaking that they must part [for the United States WCTU con-
vention]. It puts a shadow over everything, but Frances says she must
go."[31]

In 1893, as she saw Isabel leave for the United States to join Anna who was already there (Somerset substituted for Willard that year), Frances wrote, "[I] thought of little Nan and her heroic spirit and behavior, and thanked God who had given me two such inner heart comrades."[32] Ten days later she added, "Why should two such rare women as Lady Henry and Anna Gordon be supremely devoted to poor old 'sissy' whose 'dress ached' even when she was little but whose hurt heart has been healed by help from Heaven and Humanity."[33] When Anna and Frances were apart, Frances was bereft. When Lady Henry was absent she was equally deprived.

In many ways Willard and Lady Henry complemented each other and brought different strengths to their joint work. Lady Henry was not a Prohibitionist and hoped that the day would come when wine drinking would once again be safe.[34] She tended to support local option and strict licensing schemes. Willard had been a convinced Prohibitionist since the 1870s. Although in the 1890s she accepted moderate consumption of alcohol as possible and safe for some people, she believed that society as a whole could not afford to risk anything less than total prohibition. Lady Henry was a fearful, if accomplished, public speaker who suffered from stage fright. Willard was never more at home than on a public platform, and over the years Lady Henry began to conquer her fears under Willard's tutelage. Lady Henry also learned much from Willard about the practical details of organization, and Willard no doubt learned much from the English lady about the amenities of upper-class living. Life in Evanston was far from the sumptuous scale to which she now became accustomed. Willard, in turn, may have been influential in converting Somerset to socialism. By 1890 Willard was firmly committed to major social and economic change, to the Edward Bellamy brand of the socialist state. But it was not until she met Frances Willard that Lady Henry joined the Fabian Society, to which she certainly had been exposed for some time.[35]

FRANCES WILLARD and Anna Gordon sailed for England as Lady Henry's guests on 27 August 1892, three weeks after Mother Willard's death. This trip was intended to ease Frances's grief. They returned to the United States in time for the WCTU convention in Denver. Lady Henry accompanied them, and the three sailed back across the Atlantic soon after the meetings were over. They spent only a week in Evanston, just long enough to attend the formal dedication of Willard Hall in the Temple, the new WCTU headquarters building in Chicago, and to arrange for the rental of the north side of Rest Cottage to a former pupil of Willard. Frances Willard never again lived in Rest Cottage for more than a week or two, although Anna Gordon spent several weeks there with her own mother in the fall of 1893.[36] Henceforth Willard's American residence was to be a rustic cottage at Twilight Park in the Catskills that she dubbed the Eagle's Nest, which was built for her in the spring of 1892. But this retreat was rarely used because of her long absences in England and her increasing ill health. Her longest sojourns in the United States were spent at Dr. Cordelia Greene's sanatorium, a famous spot for feminists, in Castile, New York, where Willard, Anna Gordon, and whoever was with them shared "Daily Cottage," on top of its hill "and under its ice and snow."[37]

Willard performed one other ceremonial function while in the Chicago area in the fall of 1892, when she participated with Lady Henry in the dedication of the World's Columbian Exposition. The great fair was far from finished and would not be opened formally until the following May, a year later than originally planned. Willard herself did not see its wonders during the exposition year. However, she was a member of the Board of Lady Managers and had participated actively in the planning.

The Columbian Exposition on the Chicago lakeshore both symbolized and fostered the growing central role of Chicago in late nineteenth-century American culture. Its planning and execution proved a major forum for the Chicago women's network. It was also in a very real sense a celebration of women. As Bertha Palmer, chairman of the planning committee for the women's building, observed at the inaugural ceremonies, "Columbus discovered a new world, but the Columbian Exposition has discovered woman."[38] Willard had pressed hard and successfully for an exhibition on the working conditions of women in industry.[39] The WCTU also sponsored an exhibit that included the polyglot petition in all its bulk and myriad languages. But other than her brief appearance at the dedicatory festivities where she did not even speak, Willard was not in Chicago to aid, abet, or profit from the fair's celebration of the accomplishments of the new woman.

When the fair opened its doors, Willard was undoubtedly the best known American woman. Had she been in Chicago to participate in the fair's many ceremonies, she may well have rivaled Susan B. Anthony as the heroine of the exposition, because the fair was to provide Anthony with the popular recognition so long denied her. But Willard was not present and she had to be content with second-hand accounts of its glories. Illness kept her in England. Lady Henry, who went in her place in the fall of 1893, brought Willard the news that "by scores and companies people have come out to Rest Cottage from Chicago all summer. It is touching beyond words."[40] Women had journeyed from around the world with the expressed intention of meeting Frances Willard, but she was not there to receive them.

Willard's withdrawal from the American scene in 1892 was so abrupt and seemingly final that rumors were rampant that she had left the United States for good. She denied such rumors emphatically—"The talk about my making England my home is, of course, absurd"—and she announced she would return in April.[41] She excused her long sojourn abroad by explaining that she and Lady Henry planned to collaborate on a new history of the temperance movement and that she also expected to write a biography of her mother. (The second goal was accomplished with considerable help from a cousin.) She further reported that Anna Gordon would spend the winter organizing children's work in England. As president of the World WCTU, Willard could justify the need to spend part of her time overseas. However, the American Union paid her salary, and not everyone was happy with these new arrangements. Her long absence was difficult for her American followers to understand.

Lady Henry Somerset also paid a price for not being at home. Although her personal popularity was never in doubt, and she easily won reelection as president of the BWTA, she returned from the United States in 1892 to dissension in the British temperance ranks, dissension that increased over the next several months. She found that an anti-American conservative majority on her executive committee violently opposed the prosuffrage resolution she supported, did not favor a World WCTU, and generally distrusted the innovations she imported from the United States. The conservatives in the BWTA supported a single goal, total abstinence won by moral suasion, and felt that Lady Henry was adopting American ideas when she advocated a broader program.[42] Many members of the BWTA had distrusted Lady Henry from the beginning. They wanted their president to be titled; at the same time, they hoped the office would be treated as an honorary post. It was not.

These difficulties were compounded by Isabel Somerset's long stay in the United States, although the split certainly antedated Willard's arrival in England in the fall of 1892. Its origins, at least, cannot be attributed to Willard's growing influence. The nub of the question was, should the British association continue as a single issue movement, or should it become, as had the American union, a women's society with temperance at its core but embracing all branches of social reform including woman suffrage, the labor movement, peace, and social purity?[43]

Much of Lady Henry's campaign was fought with Frances Willard at her side, a circumstance that both exacerbated the grievances of her opponents and increased her popularity with her supporters. In the winter and spring of 1893 Lady Henry, who had been associated with the British Liberal party since the mid-1880s, and Willard spent several weeks addressing meetings of the Woman's Liberal Federation, an auxiliary of Gladstone's party, as well as temperance groups. Their winter tour began in London's East End where both women spoke "to an enthusiastic, hearty, working class audience of 4000 in Cherrington's famous hall."[44] For the next month they traveled constantly, pushing north to Leeds, Liverpool, and Manchester where "the great free trade hall was packed to its limits."[45] Midway they returned to London for a large meeting at the New Court Congregational Church, and then moved on to Scotland where they addressed huge crowds. After making their way back to London and Reigate via York, Willard complained, "At it, always at it. How I wish for time to read and study, to meet the fittest survivals among woman and man. But it is a wider world that Lady Henry has opened to me like an oyster."[46] It was a wider world, but still a world of endless travel and speeches. In May the two women as delegates, and Anna Gordon and Hannah Smith as visitors, attended the Woman's Liberal Federation meetings in London. There Willard again spoke and helped to carry the day for endorsement of "social purity."[47]

One of the attractions that drew crowds to these meetings was Frances Willard. She was the American woman with a mass following. She spoke to British working-class audiences with a fresh accent and a becoming boldness. She addressed temperance crowds with an evangelical fervor that came straight from the heartland of enthusiastic religion, and the dissenting sects in England were eager for her message. The British press interviewed her at length. Everyone wanted to lure this American paragon to speak at a meeting.[48]

As an oddity and a celebrity Frances Willard was helpful to Isabel Somerset in her fight to broaden the BWTA. But the presence of an American adviser also rankled some British temperance leaders. Should Lady Henry be attending so closely to someone who knew so little about the English scene? A strong minority in British temperance circles said no.[49] In 1893 Lady Henry was again able to win reelection, but only by a majority of 69 in a total vote of 455. The defeated minority "left the convention [and the BWTA] in indignation, declaring the introduction of politics into the association's work would split the organization and ruin the temperance cause."[50]

BOTH by her actions and her absence Willard at the same time was in trouble with her own constituency. She may have believed that in England she expanded her horizons and helped the movement, but she also left room at home for those who either disagreed with her or found her leadership stifling to their own ambitions. On her return from the long lecture tour, Willard received disquieting news: "Miserable cablegrams from the Temple [WCTU Chicago headquarters] showing the stirring up of strife. Why is there such a rising all on a sudden."[51] Two crises, each on its own side of the Atlantic, needed attention.

Frances Willard had survived crises before. Only a few years earlier she had successfully brought her movement through the disruptive secession of J. Ellen Foster and her cohorts over the WCTU's endorsement of the Prohibition party. However, the current crisis was not over principle. It revolved around personalities and money, and that made for stickier business. The panic of 1893 hit the American WCTU hard. Its credit was already overextended by an ambitious headquarters building for which it had indirect financial responsibility and to which Willard was deeply committed. The Temple, an office tower that housed WCTU headquarters and the temperance publishing association, as well as providing considerable choice rental office space, was an independent corporation financed largely by borrowed money. It should have proved self-liquidating. But the panic of 1893 ensured that much of its rental space stood vacant. The bonds came due nonetheless, and for several years the WCTU attempted to keep the project afloat at the price of disastrous dissension within the Union itself and with a budget that was far out of balance.

But long before the panic hit in June, several officers of the Union were jockeying for position in the leadership void created by Willard's absence. The Temple project, which had been under fire for some time, was now used by the challengers as part of their power play.[52] Most of the conflict revolved around personalities. Two factions had developed at WCTU headquarters, one that supported Willard, another that looked for ways to scuttle the building scheme and undermine Willard's friends among its supporters. The differences were not ideological but simply jealous antagonism. The panic brought everything to a head. Although Willard commented in her diary, "I'm like a cat—when struck, I strike back,"[53] she did not return to the United States and attempt personally to resolve the Union's problems. Anna Gordon went instead, because, in Willard's words, "There is such a crisis here that I can't leave. Alas for poor humans."[54] The crisis to which she alluded was, of course, the conflict over policy in the BWTA. This was a strange and atypical ordering of priorities for Willard to make. In fact, her diary for these months deals more with developments in the BWTA than with what was happening in America.[55] Willard was not unconcerned and waited eagerly for news from Gordon, but why did she not feel that she herself was needed to spread oil on the troubled waters?

The national officers who supported Willard believed her place was in Chicago. Helen Barker, one of the headquarters staff, wrote Lillian Stevens, who would become Willard's heir apparent, that there "never was a time in the history of our organization when she was needed as now. I really think she should come home at once."[56] In March, when the British trouble was reaching a climax, the Duke of Bedford, whose wife was Isabel's sister, died. This meant that Isabel was in mourning, unable to address meetings and public functions, and Frances substituted for her on several occasions. However, that event was hardly foreseen when the American crisis broke in February and Anna Gordon was dispatched to the United States. Willard herself became ill later in the spring, but she was in good health in February and had just completed an ambitious tour.

The diaries are not much help in explaining her attitude. Considering the seriousness of the crisis, she mentioned the problems in Chicago briefly and infrequently. After Gordon returned to England in April and took over the diary writing for awhile, she said nothing about her mission to the United States. This strange silence probably indicates that Willard underestimated the seriousness of the dissension in America and overestimated her usefulness in Lady Henry's campaign to retain control of the British movement. Undoubtedly, Isabel Somerset's leadership was in jeopardy. Her opponents even used J. Ellen Foster, whose earlier challenge to Willard's leadership in the United States had been unsuccessful, to provide ammunition for their fight to keep the BWTA a single issue organization.[57] But the presence of Willard and her obvious influence over Lady Henry only inflamed the latter's opponents the more. Somerset's cause was not always strengthened by her use of "foreign" strategies, and Willard was needed at home to protect her own interests, a realization to which she came much too late. For once Willard had deluded herself into believing that her personal preferences and needs coincided with her professional goals and duties. In the process she risked her American eminence. Although she continued to be worshiped by the Union rank and file and was personally popular in the United States, her leadership of American women was never again as secure as it had been in 1892.

The situation remained precarious, especially as the summer's worsening economic conditions also threatened financial stability of the

WCTU and its enterprises. Nevertheless, the insurrection was quelled. Plans were made to replace the rebellious officers at the 1893 convention, and Lillian Stevens was designated to exert executive authority in the absence of Willard and Gordon. Stevens, who succeeded Willard as WCTU president, was a kind and tactful woman of many talents not least of which was the ability to heal wounded feelings, and she did the best she could to strengthen Willard's position in the state unions. Had Willard come home she would have mended her fences with her usual expert grace, but by summer she was unable to make the Atlantic crossing.

IN 1893 Willard was fifty-four. Although she had driven herself mercilessly for the last twenty-five years, her health generally had been good, and she should have been able to look forward to another decade or two of active work. In the spring of 1893, however, she began to suffer severely from the illness responsible for her death five years later. She first mentions her symptoms in her diary of April 1893, reporting that she was not well, and that the red spots on her tongue and throat had reappeared. She wondered what they portended and remembered her mother was plagued by similar symptoms for several years before her death.[58] Months earlier, in September 1892, Hannah Smith had reported that the least effort tired Willard and prevented her from making public appearances.[59] Willard had a heavy speaking schedule for April 1893—nine engagements between 13 and 26 April, for example— and she was not able to fill them all. Lady Henry and Hannah Smith both substituted for her.[60]

By this time rumors of Willard's illness had reached Chicago. When Anna Gordon arrived in Southampton on her return from the United States during the third week in April, the reports she received were ominous. The diagnosis was pernicious anemia. The condition of Willard's mouth and tongue made it difficult for her to eat, she had skin lesions on her legs and ankles, and she was so severely fatigued that she lost her desire to go to meetings or participate in public gatherings.[61] By June she had a bad cold that developed into pleurisy, and her physician forbad any active work. For the whole month of June she was a very sick woman. She had to be carried downstairs, could do no work including dictation, and had to be read to.[62] Isabel Somerset was also unwell, suffering frequently the severe migraine headaches that plagued most of her adult life. That spring even the weather contributed to the feeling of stress and malaise, for England was experiencing its worst drought in eighty years. No rain fell for eight solid weeks, and then only enough to break partially the cycle of uninterrupted dry days.

Willard was ailing, Lady Henry was ailing, the English countryside was parched and unwell. The British association was rebellious, insurrection was brewing in Chicago, and the American economy was in distress.

Triumphs were still possible, however, and fame and adoration from both Willard's immediate circle and the wider society were still very much a part of the rhythm and tenor of her life. But her diary shows how much she contemplated death, both her mother's and her own, and how often her thoughts turned not to the next task, but to some other world. In a sense the last new territory Willard saw herself exploring was the hereafter.

Willard had always speculated about life after death and believed in another world, a real heaven. This interest and concern in a future life received new impetus with her mother's death. She relived that event in great detail on its one-year anniversary, and her diary shows not only how frequently her mother was in her thoughts, but also how often she speculated about her mother's whereabouts and possible presence, what knowledge her mother might have of Frances's present life, activities, and feelings. "My thoughts are greatly on the future life," she wrote,[63] and a few days later, "I feel that she is surely with God and those she loved best—only if I could but know!"[64]

These thoughts about her mother were often coupled with her interest in spiritualism: "Some day a telegraph will reach ships on the sea and sojourners in paradise."[65] In many ways Willard's concern with the hereafter was not so much a morbid preoccupation with death as it was an extension of her lifelong curiosity about psychic transmission, and she speculated about and explored the afterlife in much the same way that she explored other ideas—Spencerian thought, Darwinian theory, the single tax, or Bellamy's nationalism. But after the marked deterioration of her health in 1893 she began on occasion to look less with curiosity and more welcomingly toward the hereafter as a new and effortless world: "So soon I shall [die] and Isabel and Nan and all the rest and great peace will be upon us here, and, as I truly feel, [we will be] uplifted to other planets, other work and worth."[66]

Willard's welcoming attitude toward death was counterbalanced by a strong and willful urge to regain her physical strength and thus extend and broaden the scope of the work to which she had dedicated her life. She loved work. When denied its pleasures, she wrote, "Somehow I seem to myself like a dog that has lost its bone. Work was my bone and a meaty one it has been."[67] Not working was difficult for Willard. In this sense her ill health fed her interest in the afterlife where ambition was stilled and work no longer compelling. That summer, while resting and fighting for her health in Switzerland, she dreamed of a "novel I might write in which a woman becomes president of the United States after a complete revolution which she leads."[68] Willard would have been quite happy to have chewed at more than one bone. Like A. Conan Doyle she would have relished an occasional excursion into the hereafter to see what it was like and keep track of her mother, her sister Mary, and others whom she had been forced to relinquish to its unknown regions. She would also have liked being president of the United States and leader of a "complete revolution," much the same way as she enjoyed going to England, where she had a new existence as a celebrity and world leader.

The heroic efforts Willard took to restore her health testify to her will to live. Bicycling was the craze of the 1890s,[69] and Willard embraced it. Actually, like most reformers of her generation, she saw exercise and a healthy diet as part and parcel of the good cause. She had long ridden a tricycle, and in the summer of 1892 she tried tricycling again. But Willard was not one to let a new "craze" go uninvestigated, and in the fall of 1893, on the recommendation of her physician, she took up bicycling as a way to regain her health and strength.[70] It was not easy. She often fell and needed the support of several of her friends. The exercise was not to mend her broken body, but she kept at it until 1896. By that time she was bicycling fair distances when she was least unwell.[71] Her devotion to the bicycle attracted attention. The *New York World* reported that her cycling costume was "a navy blue blazer, a shirt waist and a skirt, 5½ inches from the floor, alpine hat and bicycle boots."[72] Her book, *A Wheel within a Wheel*, was a best seller and probably encouraged many a sedentary woman to take up the cycle.

Willard also became a devotee of calisthenics, and a small gym and an exercise teacher were provided at Reigate.[73] She also tried health diets and substituted frequent small light meals for normal eating patterns, presumably to help build up her strength and wasting body. The trip to Switzerland in the summer of 1893 was also seen as a "cure." Lady Henry and Frances took as much exercise as her strength would permit, "walking for two hours in this valley—a goblet filled with the breath of God and the wine of rehabilitation."[74] But frequently they could do little but lie on a balcony hoping for sun, and Willard's bouts of fever and diarrhea recurred as did Lady Henry's migraines.

Although broken health and the attempts to mend it were constant preoccupations in 1893, there also were brighter facets to Willard's new life as an expatriate. In early April her nieces and her sister-in-law Mary arrived from Berlin for an extended visit. After Lady Henry entertained them at Reigate for two weeks, they were introduced to the splendors

of Eastnor Castle later that month. Mary's son Frank joined the family
gathering in mid-April. He was now twenty-three, his youthful indiscretions behind him. He had contributed pieces to the *Century* and *Contemporary Review*, and was soon to graduate from the University of Berlin. His aunt described him as a "thoughtful intellectual young fellow."[75]

The same month Willard "met Sidney Webb the 'scientific socialist' and his wife Beatrice Potter," as well as Herbert Spencer.[76] Ever wider intellectual horizons were opening for Willard. British reformers, like their American counterparts, embraced temperance as an integral part of their overall philosophy. Richard Pankhurst was a temperance advocate before he joined the labor movement. Sidney Webb was converted to temperance by his early work in the slums of London.[77] Not only did Willard find the ideas of the British socialists congenial with her own commitment to Bellamy's Nationalist state, but also the Fabians shared her enthusiasm for temperance.

In 1893 Frances Willard identified closely with the Fabians but Lady Henry had to be converted. Before leaving for their Swiss holiday in July 1893 they agreed to investigate socialism together. Although frequently indisposed and burdened with the onerous task of answering mail, they pursued their plan to study socialism that summer, and both joined the Fabian Society while at Grundenwald.[78] As they read their "socialistic" books, however, they declared that they detested the socialists' disbelief in immortality: "Isabel and I are Christian socialists, not pagan."[79]

Also Willard, who always enjoyed comfortable living, had never before lived so well. As the American financial crisis deepened, her salary from the United States was seldom forthcoming and reduced temporarily by the action of the 1893 WCTU convention to a very modest $600. Lady Henry was a generous friend, and both her purse and her social connections were open to Willard. In Switzerland they stayed in quarters originally fitted up for the German emperor.[80] At Reigate "a little new iron house" was built for the use of secretaries and helpers, who frequently numbered three or four and whose salaries were paid by Isabel Somerset.[81] When Willard was well enough to participate in London life, she received noble treatment. In May 1893 she attended the opening of the Royal Institute alongside the Queen, the Prince of Wales, Mrs. Gladstone, and a host of other notables and members of the royal family: "Gay was no word for the wonderful display of uniforms and equipages."[82] The long English residence had its tangible rewards.

As fall 1893 arrived, the great question facing the inhabitants of Reigate focused on the 1893 WCTU convention. Would Willard be well enough to attend the meetings and preside over the annual conclave?[83] In fact, as early as June this question had been debated on both sides of the Atlantic. Her physician forbad any public work for a year, but in July Willard was still hoping that somehow she could make the convention: "Shall I be able to go home? Will Isabel? It now looks as if I shall. . . . The whole subject is open at both ends waiting developments."[84] The developments were not propitious. Willard's health grew worse again, and by the end of August the doctor delivered a clear fiat that she was not to go. But she worried that "the women at home do not appreciate the fact that I can't stand the racket of a convention."[85] Nonetheless, she was trying to write a presidential address, a task she eventually accomplished with difficulty: "Have no pith to put in it"; she felt "worthless," and always referred to it as "my poor speech."[86]

Although Lady Henry actually read the speech, it was to be one of Willard's most memorable addresses. One section, called "Gospel Socialism," contained her strongest plea thus far for a new ordering of society to ensure economic justice. The address as a whole was entitled "The Do Everything Policy." She began by reiterating the old theme she had made acceptable many years before, that "a one-sided movement makes for one-sided advocates. Virtues, like hounds, hunt in packs." But she also attempted to state her Fabian ideas in such a way as to make them understandable and palatable to the WCTU membership. She made use of the Union's devotion to Christianity as she wrote, "In every Christian there exists a socialist, and in every socialist a Christian." She pointed to "two kinds of socialism; one gives and the other takes; one says all thine is mine; the other says 'all mine is thine.'" She pleaded for the country to develop a "corporate" conscience and "conceive of society as a unity which has such relations to every faction thereof that there could be no rest while any lacked food, clothing or shelter or while any were so shackled by the grim circumstances of life that they were unable to develop the best that was in them in body and mind."[87]

Both the 1893 World WCTU convention and the American convention were to be held in Chicago in October. Willard was president of both organizations. In late August Anna Gordon left for the United States to make arrangements, mend fences, and do what she could to prepare for the meetings, including executing the suggestions and answering the queries that Frances Willard sent in a steady stream across the Atlantic. By early September, they decided that Lady Henry would also attend. The fact that her son was in New York and urging her to visit made her appearance in Chicago plausible enough.[88] When Frances saw Lady Henry off at Southampton, Isabel told her on the boat train that she went in her stead, because if Frances went "sick or well, they would never let you come back; and I go for the Cause [the women's movement] and to see my boy,"[89] a very mixed message. Isabel Somerset wanted her dear friend Frances at her side, but she also cared deeply about the outcome of the conventions, which she felt were crucial to the "Cause." Willard truly wanted to go to the meetings, reestablish her constituency, and convert it to exciting new vistas. The easy way out for both women would have been for Willard to resign the American presidency, lead the world movement from England close to her friend, and enjoy some of the ease and leisure she had always denied herself. But Willard and Lady Henry were too committed to reform to take the easier path.

To regain complete control of the American movement would not be simple. Everyone who was in Willard's corner in the WCTU was fully aware of the difficulties. Willard would be both target and expediter if she appeared in Chicago. Heads were scheduled to roll, several officers were to be retired, and the messy financial picture of the Temple office building would have to be explained. Some of Willard's supporters thought these matters could be handled more expeditiously in the absence of the president. But under the bylaws, if Willard was not present, Caroline Buell, one of the Chicago dissenting clique, would preside as corresponding secretary of the national Union.[90]

Willard stayed with Hannah and Robert Smith for the three weeks that Lady Henry was away. Another guest of the Smiths was Bessie Gordon, Anna's sister, who had come from Boston to be with Frances. No doubt everyone feared that developments at the Chicago convention could upset Willard and further threaten her precarious health. Every effort was made to provide her with adequate support.

There was real apprehension in the Smith household. By 20 October, the WCTU delegates assembled at the convention had sent five telegrams citing biblical texts, as was their wont,

> but no news! Hannah says in view of this *she* is going to send one, "fewer texts—more information" . . . I do wish I knew the outcome of world's [convention] and fate of Mrs. R[astall] in stockholder's meeting but never a word. I told Carsie [Matilda Carse, president of the Temple corporation] and Nan that they would miss my guess if there wasn't a falling away from me this year and if the opposition to the Temple and Carsie didn't take definite form in the retention of certain [officers], whom [the] leaders

have proposed to oust for "the good of the order." Almost while I write came another cable "Temple Victorious" which means much in view of this year's unequalled complications at the Temple. . . . I feel grieved over it all and I do not pretend to understand it.[91]

Neither Willard nor Anna Gordon felt any personal glee over besting their opponents. As the displaced officers were leaving headquarters after the convention, Gordon wrote Willard, "'Tis forlorn to see Esther [Pugh], Callie [Caroline Buell] and Alice G. packing up and off."[92] Frances Willard had assigned herself two mottoes for 1893, "Forget thyself," and "Believe others are trying to do right,"[93] and she faithfully executed them at this time of trial. The day after the announcement of Temple support a cable arrived announcing Willard's reelection with only ten votes against her: "the only wonder is that there were not more."[94] Ten days later the letters and newspapers arrived confirming Willard's personal victory and that of the issues she had supported. Lady Henry sailed for home almost immediately after the convention. Anna Gordon stayed on in Chicago until the new officers and staff were settled in their jobs.

The Woman's Christian Temperance Union convention of 1893 could have been consumed by an acrimonious assessment of Willard's weaknesses and strengths and provided the stage on which bitter personal feuds were played out. The very real conflict over the wisdom of the Temple project could have split the organization wide open. The leadership crisis for which Willard herself was responsible because of her long absence could have proved fatal. But instead Lady Henry, with considerable help from Anna Gordon and others, had transformed this potential disaster into a convention that committed itself to the Temple headquarters of the WCTU as a physical monument to women's increasing strength and power, and a convention that acclaimed Willard as the adored, if somewhat inactive, St. Frances of the American temperance movement.

Lady Henry's role at the convention emphasized the strengths of the Anglo-American connection. She had presided as Willard's substitute at the World WCTU convention, and she had been made a member almost automatically of the executive committee of the American WCTU and a delegate-at-large of the national convention.[95] There was grumbling about her growing influence on Willard, but it did not prove serious. Community of interest prevailed. Meanwhile, most of the delegates were captivated by Lady Henry's beauty and charm. Willard could not have made a better choice of surrogate. Lady Henry was both regal and simple, composed and caring. Willard rejoiced, "It is so good to think of them in harmony now at the Temple Beautiful."[96]

AFTER the convention Willard expended much of her energy on her partially successful campaign to regain her health. She also did considerable writing for both British and American publications, completed *A Great Mother* and probably began work on *A Wheel within a Wheel*. *Glimpses of Fifty Years* was published in England in 1894 as *My Happy Half Century*, and *Do Everything* came out in an English edition in 1895. In addition, she actively pursued the polyglot petition project and tried to arrange a great world tour on which she and Lady Henry, accompanied by other prominent women, would personally take the petition's impressive mass of signatures to heads of state to commend temperance to their attention. She went so far as to investigate chartering a steamer for the trip,[97] and, had she completely regained her health, she probably would have accomplished this mission. Although Lady Henry found Willard's devotion to the polyglot petition naive and was less than enthusiastic,[98] Willard's faith in its propaganda value was real.

As the spring of 1894 approached, Frances Willard prepared to go home. Her longest residence in England was drawing to a close. She was at Lady Henry's side during the BWTA annual meetings in early May, where a farewell testimonial to Willard occupied one of the sessions.[99] She then made a week's visit to Ireland, speaking in Cork and Dublin, before she sailed from Liverpool on the *Teutonic* on 13 June. She would go to Evanston briefly and then to her cottage in the Catskills.[100] Willard knew she could no longer escape her American responsibilities.

Chapter XIII   Homecoming

Frances Willard was welcomed by a jubilant if apprehensive crowd of friends and well-wishers when she landed at New York harbor in June 1894. She had been away from the United States for nearly two years. She was noticeably frail. The *Chicago Tribune* reported she had "lost none of her unparalleled brilliancy as a conversationalist or her gentleness as a woman," but added sadly "the bloom of health has fled from Miss Willard's cheeks."[1] At a "welcome home" gathering in New York's Calvary Baptist Church, Terence Powderly of the Knights of Labor, Maud Ballington Booth of the Salvation Army, and Lillie Devereux Blake of the New York suffrage society joined the WCTU in paying her homage. But homage would not solve Willard's problems.

Some of Willard's troubles were initiated and aggravated by her health. Others stemmed from politics within and without the WCTU. Neither category was easily solved. Also, Willard could not live abroad with her primary role that of an international leader and continue to act as the queenpin of American womanhood. American women were pleased to see her back, but they expected her to repay with hard work and much attention their patience during her long absence.

A month of heavy traveling lay ahead. Willard first went north to Montreal via Boston and Portland to address Canadian temperance women. She then spent nearly two weeks in Evanston and the Chicago area seeing old friends and tending to WCTU business. By 25 July she and Anna Gordon were at Eagle's Nest in the Catskills where they were to spend much of their time until the November convention.[2] Willard was not well enough to resume her old pace. The invitations poured in and had to be refused with the attendant disappointments and misunderstandings. Willard could no longer drive herself to carry on, but she could not let go. For the next three years her life was a precarious balance between her obligations and her physical limitations.

Among the problems Willard faced was the proper political role of the WCTU. She returned to the United States to find growing controversy over party allegiance within the Union. As early as January 1893, WCTU members complained that Willard had forsaken the Prohibition party and thrown her support to the Knights of Labor. A letter she had written to Terence Powderly saying "she would be glad to see them [the Knights] in power" was widely quoted to prove this charge. From England she had replied via the *Union Signal* that she had meant only that she "would be glad to see labor in its place of power, side by side with capital and did not refer to any political movement," although she admitted believing the Prohibition party would eventually be the nucleus of a party that would include the Knights. Moreover, the *Union Signal*, whose editorial policy she controlled, continued to push for the fusion of reform groups and parties. An editorial, possibly written by Willard in November 1893, had suggested, "The most hopeful feature of the political situation today is the gathering of reform forces. . . . Soon the exigencies of the hour will unite them under one banner which shall not be Republican or Democratic, Populist or Prohibition, but a consolidation of the best in all."[3] Willard's insistence that the WCTU play a political role, in fact a radical political role, added to her problems with her constituency in the 1890s. Many WCTU women were disinclined to agitate for fundamental change in American society.

Less fundamental issues also played a part. Petty jealousies and controversies flourished in the Union to which Willard returned in the summer of 1894. That year marked the twentieth anniversary of the founding of the WCTU and the crusade that gave it birth, and successful mature organizations are seldom without factions. The Union was rife with bickering over who the founding mothers really were. Eliza Stewart and the Washington Court House group challenged the generally accepted claims of Mother Eliza Thompson of Hillsboro fame, but there were also advocates for the prior if abortive efforts of the women of Fredonia, New York. Prestige and position were not taken lightly in that anniversary year, and with good reason, for the WCTU was the largest women's organization the world had yet known. But poor Willard had to be friend to all and partisan toward none, keeping everyone's place in the sun intact.

The opposition that had focused around the Temple office building would not go away no matter how many defeats it suffered. It surfaced again at the 1894 convention. Simultaneously Mary Clement Leavitt, Willard's old friend and the WCTU's aging but beloved first world missionary, continued to fault Willard in public and accuse her in private of disloyalty and deviousness. Willard's homecoming was not marked by harmony and goodwill!

Also facing Willard was the need to consolidate the gains made at the

1893 convention to ensure her control over the leadership of the WCTU. She decided that a constitutionally authorized second-in-command, who could assume presidential prerogatives if necessary and preside in her absence, would meet this need. She had a candidate in mind, her loyal friend, Lillian Stevens of Maine, but she could not expect to dictate a surrogate without some opposition. The appointment of an executive vice-president would require an amendment to the WCTU constitution. Notice of intent to amend had been given at last year's convention, paving the way for action. Now the battle to implement this plan would have to be fought and won.

The lynching issue, however, proved the thorniest problem and the most persistent cause of trouble. The 1890s was a decade of intensified racial repression in the South. Jim Crow laws, segregation, lynching, and exacerbated bitterness between the races were increasing rapidly. White vigilantes were on the rampage, and in 1892 the number of lynchings of Negro men peaked after rising for several years. Willard was aware of accelerating tensions even from her English haven, and she could hardly avoid taking a position although it meant confronting political dynamite. At her request the WCTU passed an antilynching resolution in 1893, and she commented in her presidential address, "Our duty to the colored people have [sic] never impressed me so solemnly as this year when the antagonism between them and the white race have [sic] seemed to be more vivid than at any previous time, and lurid vengeance has devoured the devourers of women and children."[4] Her language was both obscure and flamboyant, but it was also equivocal and paralleled the dilemma in which she found herself. She referred sympathetically to the worsening racial situation in the South for blacks, but she also accepted the rallying cry of the lynchers who used the excuse of protecting white womanhood from assault and rape to justify their crimes. She condemned lynching but took as fact the assertion that lynching resulted from the rape of white women by blacks. She was responding to liberal northern civil rights champions and her southern white colleagues at the same time.

In 1892, the year that lynching peaked, Ida Wells, a young black teacher and journalist who edited a small newspaper, the Memphis *Free Speech*, began a valiant and eloquent crusade in defense of black manhood and against lynching. As a result, Wells herself experienced vigilante treatment. Her newspaper office was destroyed and she was forced to flee Memphis. However, Wells continued her antilynching campaign with even greater vigor, forcing white liberals to take notice of her and her cause and declare themselves in ways that proved embarrassing to Willard. It is a measure of Ida Wells's considerable abilities that, despite Frances Willard's enormous prestige as a reformer and champion of worthy causes in the 1890s, she could challenge Willard's integrity and make her scramble for ground on which to defend herself. Willard did not survive the battle unscathed. Wells also succeeded in changing the statistics. Lynchings began to decrease in numbers as the white liberal community made clear its horror at vigilante action.

The main thrust of Wells's campaign was to arouse antilynching sentiment in defense of innocent black victims. She argued against the double standard that ignored sexual abuse of black women by white men while calling rape if black men and white women cohabited. In her little book *Southern Horrors*, she described the case of a white woman who had seduced a black man and later charged him with rape. Wells went on to say, "There are thousands of such cases throughout the South."[5] This was a shocking charge, an attack on womanhood, especially southern white womanhood, that left the ladies of the WCTU reeling and upset. Although Willard was unequivocal in her denunciation of lynching as a barbarous betrayal of justice, she joined the WCTU in being unable to accept the idea that white women might willingly acquiesce in sexual congress between the races. Wells had touched a raw nerve, and Willard was forced to reconcile her lifelong support of black causes with the repugnance Wells's accusation aroused. Willard managed after a fashion but without the unquestioning conviction reformers must emanate or lose their moral force.

Wells became a popular lecturer who soon attracted a following and considerable press attention. She highly criticized the dual nature of Willard's and the WCTU's position that condemned both lynching and "the unspeakable outrages which have so often provoked such lawlessness."[6] In 1895 she was invited to England where she was lionized in British reform circles and where she continued to be critical of Willard. She also denied having stated that white women had taken "the initiative in nameless acts between the races,"[7] and accused Willard of misrepresenting her. In this instance Wells was wrong. She had used such language, no doubt with ample justification, but used it nonetheless. However, Wells was an able and aggressive critic, and Willard could not escape being compromised by her attacks. To many militant reformers, especially in Britain, Willard seemed to equivocate on racial issues. In February 1895 Frederick Douglass, William Lloyd Garrison, and Julia Ward Howe among others published an open letter to Willard defending her against Wells's charges and affirming her lifelong support of black causes.[8] But the lynching issue continued to reverberate in England where it was used by Lady Henry's opponents to embarrass her.

Willard and the WCTU were doubly vulnerable when race relations were at issue. The Union was ahead of its time in organizing black locals, seating blacks at national conventions, and appointing blacks among the superintendents of its departments. Black and white were members of the same national Union, met together in a common convention, and shared the columns of the *Union Signal*. The WCTU had been organized in the South just after Reconstruction and before the Populist revolt of the 1890s sent Jim Crow off on its more violent rampages. The timing had been right. Furthermore, the WCTU was never an exclusively white organization in North or South, as were most late nineteenth-century women's organizations, but it was by and large segregated. The prejudices of its large numbers of southern white members were accommodated in many ways. The WCTU could not satisfy equal rights protagonists and keep happy its southern white adherents, and, as the decade wore on, inevitably WCTU policies on race were strongly attacked by equal rights protagonists in the United States and Great Britain. Because the Union was seen as a force for radical change, it was expected to keep its reform skirts clean. At the same time, the WCTU, which was overwhelmingly an organization of middle-class white women, was especially prone to overreact to the possibility of interracial rape with white women as victims.[9]

THE historic twentieth anniversary of the founding of the WCTU was celebrated in Cleveland, where the first WCTU convention had been held in 1874. The convention was widely and sympathetically reported by the press. The WCTU of the 1890s was a major force in American life, an important vehicle for decision making in American society. The newspaper reports generated by the Cleveland conclave were not unlike those of a national political convention. Press clippings in the Willard scrapbooks from all major American newspapers—including personal sketches of prominent delegates, press interviews with Willard and other national officers, and discussion of the Union's stand on national issues—attest to the serious attention paid the convention by the mass media. The WCTU prepared for the convention accordingly. The leadership hoped its careful and elaborate plans would not be put at risk by a few jealous women promoting their personal goals through internal squabbles.

Political allegiance proved a stormy issue at the 1894 WCTU convention. Debate over the wisdom of outright endorsement of the Prohibition party was heated and divisive. Willard was "forced to expend almost the limit of her strength wielding the gavel," and once sat down, saying, "I have done all I can to make you keep order. The rest must be done by yourselves."[10] The 1894 convention again endorsed the Prohibition party, but such an endorsement by itself was not enough to

further Willard's hope for a broad-based reform coalition. She did not
relinquish her larger goals. She urged the Union to create a department
of politics that would marshal every local in the country to bring together Prohibition party and Populist party members in equal numbers. She called this device a "Home Protection Union," returning to
her earlier reliance on the guardianship of the home as a rallying cry.
And as in her earlier suffrage campaign within the Union when Wittenmyer would not join her, she looked to the grass roots for support.
Because her attempt to unite the leaders of reform movements had
failed, she now felt such a goal could be achieved only when the rank
and file demanded common action. She was ready to make a start for
the 1896 election.[11] She asked in her New Year's message to the membership, as she had done in 1882 when she founded the home protec-
tionist clubs, for local action to bring Populists and Prohibitionists
together. She affirmed with conviction that this "request lies nearer my
heart than any other."[12]

Willard's continued support of a fusion reform party was not universally acclaimed by either the WCTU or the Prohibitionists. Sentiment to
convert the temperance movement into a single issue cause unattached
to broad reform questions and stressing personal morality was already
strong. One West Virginia Prohibitionist chided Willard for treating
other issues as of equal importance to "the obliteration of a national
sin."[13] Colonel George Bain, prominent Prohibitionist leader and lecturer, complained to her that the prohibition cause was being wounded
in the house of its friends by some of its leaders "running off after free
silver and making the dominant issue other than temperance."[14] Dissent against broad political commitment also was growing within the
WCTU. Not everyone shared Willard's larger vision. The president of
the Illinois union, Louise Rounds, used her presidential address at the
state convention to comment that the strength of the WCTU was being
sadly sapped: "what our society [the WCTU] needs today in my judgment is to cut off without hesitancy and without regret every scheme
which has no legitimate claim upon us, and which does not directly
advance on the two great lines which form the basis of our work, viz.
total abstinence for the individual and prohibition for the state."
Rounds was an old friend and colleague of Willard, but that did not
prevent her from adding, "This might overturn some huge ambitions,
but would also end much strife and bitterness."[15] Even in her home
town, the *Evanston Index* joined the chorus: Willard "has rushed into
an endorsement of the free silver craze without giving herself time to
think about it," and this is "only one of several follies which she has

commended to the women who wish to reform humanity."[16] The single issue faction that had surfaced in both the WCTU and the Prohibition party would be ascendent in both organizations by the presidential election of 1896.

Willard was more successful in controlling the succession problem. A constitutional amendment had been proposed to authorize the president to appoint a deputy. Debate was lively. The opposition feared that Matilda Carse, the controversial promoter of the Temple office building and president of the Union's publishing association, would be Willard's anointed. But Willard skillfully defused the opposition by announcing that the new executive vice-president would be chosen from among the state presidents, and Carse was not one of them. There was no real fight over the change, and the amendment passed easily.

Overall, the convention was a personal triumph for Willard. Her long absence abroad had not irreparably loosened the reins. The press responded favorably to her leadership. The *New York World* reported, "Although the majority of Americans regard Miss Willard's views with respect to the suppression of the liquor traffic as impracticable, she is everywhere looked upon with genuine respect."[17] A Florida delegate wrote that Willard's "sweetness and light, her wisdom and gentleness, were all pervasive and genial as sunshine." She was "there to straighten out the ranks, and soothe and reassure the impatient, and to be, in very truth as she is in name, the head."[18]

Somehow Willard's health hung together for the duration of the convention, and she found the necessary stamina to perform well. After the meetings she was almost constantly ill. Bronchitis laid her low in Boston. She could not attend the funeral of her old colleague, Mary Woodbridge. One engagement after another was canceled at the last moment. Isabel Somerset did much of Frances's traveling for her in January and February 1895. In March Willard, Somerset, and Anna Gordon returned to England to prepare for the world meetings a month earlier than they had planned so Frances could rest.

Two matters received much of Willard's attention in the period from the convention until her return to the British Isles. First, the time had come to present the polyglot petition to President Cleveland in Washington, and she wished to secure a large audience and maximum publicity for the occasion. Second, the triennial meeting of the National Council of Women was to be held in Washington in February 1895. Willard was on the executive committee and scheduled to address the sessions.

Willard had helped to found the National Council of Women, and the WCTU had been among its major supporters since its beginnings in 1888. Willard had been its first president and she now wished to combine presentation of the polyglot petition to the Congress and the president with the council's meetings when most of the leading women of the United States would be present in the capital.[19]

The polyglot petition, affectionately referred to in personal correspondence as "the pet," was brought in all its bulk to Washington by Katherine Stevenson, WCTU national corresponding secretary. Two days of celebratory meetings preceded its presentation to Cleveland. As usual Willard was ill, as was Lady Henry on this occasion, and the launching ceremony had to be managed without their help. Anna Gordon read Willard's address to the gathering of four thousand in a hall where center stage was occupied by the petition itself, as it hung in great festoons from the girders.[20] Both Lady Henry and Willard managed to recover sufficiently to be present for the presidential presentation, along with the general officers of the World and American WCTUs. Cleveland accepted this colorful and colossal plea for world prohibition with his usual caution and grace. However, his equivocation did not deceive the delegation, which viewed his reply as "altogether friendly and eminently safe."[21]

FRANCES WILLARD, Anna Gordon, and Isabel Somerset sailed for England in March 1895 and stayed in Great Britain only until September. In mid-June the BWTA meetings convened in London. This great gathering of British temperance women represented a membership of 100,000 from 500 British locals. Oddly enough, the most controversial issue facing the convention was the antilynching resolution. There was no real need for the BWTA to concern itself with lynching. It was not a British issue. But the focus on lynching was an indirect way for Lady Henry's enemies to call attention to her close connection with Frances Willard and embarrass both women by suggesting that Willard was less than straightforward on the question of Negro rights.

At the time Ida Wells was in England and working closely with Lady Henry's enemies. Letters to the editor, for and against the WCTU's position on lynching, appeared in the British newspapers as early as February 1895. The campaign picked up speed as the BWTA and world conventions approached. Much to Lady Henry's distress, a salaried member of the English *Woman's Signal* staff, Florence Balgarnie, led the attack on Willard and the WCTU lynching position. Internal squabbles within the BWTA certainly fueled the flames. Lady Henry was able to carry her organization, and the British and World's conventions adopted resolutions very similar to the American one. Somerset and

Willard believed that the resolutions unequivocally condemned lynching. But the reform press was not satisfied. The *Christian World* (U.K.) wrote, "It is pitiable beyond measure that there should be apologists of lynching within the rank of the World's Women's [sic] Christian Temperance Union. It is a calamity that these apologists should be numerous enough to control the Union in America, and to make the *Woman's Signal* the organ of their views."[22] Another editorial condemned Willard as "a temporizer when it comes to questions relating to Afro-Americans and southern whites. In plain words she tries to convince both that she is 'with them' if not 'of them.'"[23] There was some truth in that observation. Willard tried to assure both Negro rights advocates and southern women that they had her support. William Lloyd Garrison, Frederick Douglass, Julia Ward Howe, and others came to Willard's defense, affirming that she was "devoted to the cause of the colored people" and that no color line was drawn in either the World WCTU or the National WCTU. Lady Henry ultimately issued a private statement on the matter for members of the BWTA; included with her statement were the supportive letters of American civil rights leaders. Lady Henry's correspondence with Florence Balgarnie contained strong evidence that the real issue was a power struggle in the BWTA, an interpretation confirmed by Hannah Smith's correspondence.[24] Eventually the fracas died down, but the attendant acrimony had not been conducive to rest and relaxation during the summer holiday of 1895.

Although Willard's summer in England had been far from peaceful, she happily welcomed the American delegates who arrived in a chartered steamer for the world convention. They were treated to excursions to Windsor and Eastnor castles and a lavish reception at Reigate Manor.[25] Willard presided over the world meeting before returning to the United States in the fall to meet her own convention in Baltimore's music hall. Looking hearty and happy, she delivered her usual "magnetic address when all were thrilled with the dignity and inspiration of the noble occasion." As one of her southern supporters saw the scene, "It means much to be part of and to help bring about such a sense of enthusiasm for the defense of the home and the elevation of womanhood."[26]

Soon after the convention Willard embarked on her last southern tour, another formidable undertaking for a woman of uncertain health. In most ways this excursion was simply a repetition of earlier triumphs, but no longer was Willard required to hustle for southern audiences or face the prejudice a bold woman called forth simply by daring to address public meetings. At Jackson, Mississippi, there were "carriages at the station and a committee of men and women—white ribboners all about—Governor's wife on committee—kindest words in press—so different from reception in 1881, when Judge Watson brot [sic] me over at his own expense and there was a pig in the parlor of the hotel."[27] The *Chattanooga Times* reported that "society belle and satin begowned matron sat beside the shop girl and seamstress. The shoemaker and the clerk jostled the banker and lawyer. The front row of the balcony on the right as one entered was interspersed with a number of small Negro children, who slept during the lecture."[28] Blacks still were members of the audiences she addressed, and among her other pilgrimages she included a journey to Tuskegee where Booker T. Washington escorted her on a tour of the school and where she spoke to the students in chapel: "I talked the best I could and shook hands with all."[29] Willard worried about the fate of educated blacks in American society. After she and Anna Gordon had spoken to Negro children at another school, she confided in her diary, "They are a pathetic people when educated [Willard meant that sorrow was bound to be their lot]. Life must seem grievous. If I were in their place I'd make a beeline to Africa."[30] She had no understanding of what a sterile solution African immigration would prove for American blacks.

Susan B. Anthony also caused Willard anxiety. Anthony feared that the next national WCTU convention, scheduled to be held in San Francisco in the fall of 1896 at about the time the state would be voting on woman suffrage, would frighten the "wet" vote and adversely affect suffrage chances. Willard, in turn, regarded the WCTU as a positive force in the suffrage election, "but Susan is 'set', and I think for good feelings sake we would better change,"[31] and she so convinced the other general officers. The California WCTU tried hard to cooperate and not be conspicuous in the suffrage campaign. As it happened, the WCTU annual meeting that year was held not in California but in St. Louis, far away from the California battle. Willard's dissatisfactions at this time also touched her WCTU constituency. She tossed out a rare complaint in observing, "I wish White Ribbon women were keener minded than they are. But then women have brooded so long!"[32]

Frances Willard's problems with her followers, colleagues, and allies in the mid-1890s were not unusual for a national political leader attempting to hold an uneasy coalition together. In no way could she avoid controversy while operating on so wide a stage. She equivocated on more than one occasion. She maneuvered and she schemed. She cut her losses, and she sometimes protected herself at the expense of the weak to retain personal and political power. But she did not lose sight of her long-range goals, and she did not compromise seriously her basic positions. Like every ethical politician, she clung to power for the influence it could bring her to further the causes she believed in. She could have left the American WCTU to its own battles, but she chose to fight.

On a dreary day in late February, Willard listed her "tribulations" in her diary. They ranged from problems with her black constituents to dealing with the Temple's opponents as well as a half dozen other thorns in her side, including the WCTU's familial row over founding honors. But she ended the entry, "Never mind. Keep the peace as best we can and keep the tenor of our way."[33]

Before Willard and Anna Gordon sailed for Great Britain in April 1896 the general officers of the WCTU conferred in Chicago, made final plans for the fall meetings, and mapped out the Union's work for the rest of the year. Willard also visited old friends. She spent a nostalgic Sunday reminiscing with Kate Jackson at her Evanston home "so close by the great blue lake" and the Northwestern campus. Kate also was ill, suffering with bad legs, but unlike Frances she was thoroughly preoccupied with and depressed by her physical problems. Frances also saw Ada Brigham, one of her girlhood friends, whom she found "soft yet brave, mild, accomplished, cosmopolitan."[34] She was touching all her old bases. When she left the Chicago area she visited relatives in Churchville, New York, before going on to Washington, D.C., where she stayed with her niece, Kate Baldwin, and managed to make a couple of speeches. She was to repeat these pilgrimages the next summer and fall, touching once more those who had been near and dear to her at various times in her life. England beckoned, but clearly the United States again was home and she was satisfied to have it so.

Chapter XIV  Passages

After a bon voyage extravaganza at Chickering Hall in New York, Frances Willard and Anna Gordon sailed for England on 22 April 1896 on the S.S. *Paris*.[1] Intertwined English and American flags, flowers, and fifteen speeches "each nicer than the last," delivered to a packed hall with many standing, combined to produce in Willard a strong feeling that her American popularity was still intact.[2] At the same time, she was apprehensive about returning to England after seven months away from Isabel Somerset. She had speculated earlier that spring, "And Cossie—dearest and most adequate companion of them all who are cherished in my heart's heart. Will she be with me—will we still be two cherries on a single stem? I pray for it."[3] Relationships, not causes, were uppermost in her mind as she made this passage.

When Frances Willard and Anna Gordon first arrived in England, all seemed to go well, just as it had for all the months apart when cables, letters, and requests for support crossed the Atlantic in a steady stream. Isabel Somerset was on the docks at Southampton to greet them, along with Hannah Whitall Smith and other friends. Their first night was spent at Lady Henry's new London town house and Willard wrote, "it seemed as natural to be here as to breathe."[4] The next day they made their way to Reigate Manor.

At Reigate, where they had spent so many months in 1892–95, the domestic arrangements had been changed. No longer did Frances and Isabel reside under the same roof, although they were much together. Lady Henry's son had married the previous winter, and the Priory, the major residence at Reigate, had been remodeled to accommodate the young couple. Lady Henry kept quarters for herself at the Priory, but Willard, Gordon, and their entourage now lived at the Cottage, the second Reigate residence. Isabel came to the Cottage for breakfast or tea, and Frances was frequently invited (but did not always go) to grander social affairs at the Priory. Frances and Isabel now occupied separate houses.

Joining forces once more may have been less glorious than Willard thought it would be. Underneath the joy of reunion ran a small note of disappointment. Lady Henry was so busy, harried, and preoccupied with her many philanthropic ventures and her organizational duties that Willard, again fighting illness, saw much less of her than if she physically had been able to be always at her friend's side. Also Lady Henry's religious sympathies had undergone a change. The admonitions of Canon Albert Orme Wilberforce, prominent British temperance leader, led Isabel Somerset to return to the Anglicanism of her youth. During Willard's absence she had arranged for the construction of an oratory off her bedroom, and prayers were conducted in this chapel every morning.[5]

Willard always had trouble accepting the ceremonies of the Anglican church. "How uncongenial to me is every form of ritualism," she confided in her diary at an earlier time.[6] She was uncomfortable with the "mumbo jumbo," as she called it, of high church England, and Isabel's regression was unsettling. It rankled the Methodist in her.[7]

Another facet of the Willard-Somerset relationship underwent real change. By 1896 Lady Henry was less dependent on Willard than Willard was on Lady Henry. The relationship between them had been reversed. Willard was never much bothered by being beholden to others for money and financial support, but Lady Henry was essentially her sole source of funds from 1893, when the worsening panic and subsequent depression seriously cut into the American WCTU's budget. Henceforth what money Willard received was needed for the intervals she and Gordon spent in the United States. However, Willard's financial dependence on Lady Henry had existed almost from the beginning of their relationship, and Willard was accustomed to her limited budget being supplemented by the largesse of wealthy friends.

On the other hand, formerly Willard had been cast in the role of tutor and Lady Henry as pupil. When Willard first went to England in 1892, not only was she a fresh new face, but also for the less developed English temperance movement she provided an inexhaustible fund of techniques, gimmicks, even principles that the British women's temperance movement needed and for which it was grateful. Training methods, organizational patterns, even a name for the British publication, the *Woman's Signal*, mimicked American counterparts. But Willard was less essential to her friend by 1896 than she had been earlier. The balance of their relationship had changed if ever so subtly. This may have been difficult for Willard to accept.

Willard's deteriorating health also influenced their relationship. During her first English trip, she was an enormous success on the popular

Willard in 1895 in the drawing room of the Cottage, Reigate Manor.
(Reprinted from Gordon, *The Beautiful Life of Frances Willard*)

platform, as Dwight Moody and to some extent the Quaker Pearsall Smiths had been before her. If Americans had an insatiable penchant for adulation of British aristocracy, the British in the nineteenth century had an equal penchant for admiring American knowhow, ingenuity, and democratic forthrightness. In a sense, Americans were the British alter ego. Americans may have separated themselves from Britain, but no other society had accepted in as uncompromising a fashion as the United States what British middle-class intellectuals thought was a fundamental tenet of their own belief system: a secure place in society for the common man. The British were as enamored of the Americans as the Americans were of them. Until her health failed, Willard had swept England. Now she was forced to play a more private role.

The Anglo-American connection still functioned well, and Frances Willard and Hannah Whitall Smith, both vice-presidents of the BWTA, continued to be important in the councils of the British Woman's Temperance Association. But Lady Henry was no longer the uncertain, timorous leader of earlier years. After watching Isabel preside over the BWTA's annual convention in June 1896, Willard commented, "Dear Cossie has grown up admirably under the duties of presiding. How she has grown since '94 when I sat beside her and prompted, at her request. [Willard was forgetting Lady Henry's triumphs at the American and world conventions in 1893.] And how she steps out strong and firm in her parliamentary knowledge and leads her host. They love her better every year—she has them in her hand for love."[8] Isabel Somerset was clearly the star on her own turf.

Willard's sojourn in the United States from 1894 to 1896 had been for her in many ways a triumph, despite the fact that at the time she frequently and truly believed she would rather be in England. She performed her American duties gallantly and with enthusiasm. She fully enjoyed her 1896 tour of the South. In the United States Willard knew exactly who she was and understood intuitively the moods of her constituencies. Usually they were adulatory, but if they were not she was well prepared to handle them. Willard was American queen of temperance and of the women's movement, and her rivals had never lasted for long. In England her position was not as secure.

IN 1895 Frances Willard and Isabel Somerset adopted a new cause. In late 1894 and early 1895 reports coming largely through the Middle Eastern missionary community indicated that wholesale massacres of Armenian Christians had taken place in eastern Turkey near the western end of Lake Van. Armenia was the oldest Christian state, and the Armenians as a nation had adopted Christianity in the late third century. But by the sixteenth century most of Armenia had fallen to the Ottoman Turks in whose empire they became merchants and financiers with a vital economic role to play, although they were intermittently persecuted and always discriminated against as Christians in a Muslim society. Their peril increased, however, in 1894 when Sultan Abd al-Hamid II embarked on a plan of systematic extermination in response to growing Armenian nationalist activity.[9] Estimates of the number of Armenians killed varied from 25,000 to 300,000 out of a population of two and one-half million. Many more Armenians would be killed in the 1915 massacres during World War I, but the 1894 massacres were the first attempt in modern times to systematically eradicate whole villages and practice genocide as such. The sheer brutality with which the massacres were carried out added to the horror and revulsion felt by the Western world.

By the spring of 1895 Frances Willard was active in the popular movement sweeping the United States and Great Britain to spur the United States and British governments to take official action (via economic sanctions or gunboats) to stop the slaughter. In May she and Lady Henry Somerset participated in the great mass meeting on the Armenian question at London's St. James Hall where both sat on the platform and Lady Henry was the only woman speaker.[10] In June an Armenian woman, Rebecca Krikorian, was on hand for the World WCTU

meeting in London, having been advised to attend by an American
missionary in Turkey. Willard invited her to participate in the American
WCTU annual convention that fall, and Krikorian stayed on in the
United States for a year, lecturing and raising money for Armenian
relief.[11]

The Armenian question and relief for Armenian refugees were of
consuming interest to American women. The very thought of Christian
women being driven from their homes by infidel Kurds and Turks and
left unprotected and defenseless, subject to slaughter and rape, played
on both women's religious prejudices and their devotion to the bonds
of sisterhood.[12] Good Christian women expected the good Christian
state to intervene on behalf of Armenian women and children.

By the 1890s women had perfected their political skills. Once more
they were prepared to use their "influence" in a cause that engaged
them. Human rights issues had a special appeal to women, and women
formed the heart of the rapidly forming lobby that advocated punitive
action against the Turks and relief for the Armenians. During the decade American women were concerned with political issues worldwide.
Although the polyglot petition may in many ways have been a naive
gesture, it was also a firm step by women toward demanding influence
in the world's councils. In 1887 the WCTU had authorized a Department of Peace and Arbitration. Now women took their place as champions of human rights.

Churchwomen were loud in their calls for action on the Armenian
question and so were temperance women. In January 1896 the American WCTU petitioned Congress for an appropriation for Armenian
relief.[13] Six thousand people attended a Sunday afternoon meeting, the
largest session of the 1896 national WCTU convention, dedicated to the
Armenian question.[14] Willard encouraged their concern from both
sides of the Atlantic. In addition to her speeches she wrote the introduction to Edwin Bliss's *Turkey and the Armenian Atrocities*, and she
had been one of twenty prominent Americans who vouched for the
authenticity of the accounts of the massacre in Frederick Greene's little
book on the Armenian crisis. By February 1896 Willard was asking,
"How Lord Salisbury can go to church I cannot imagine,"[15] and in July
Willard Howard, a reporter just returned from Persia, Armenia, and
Turkey, was entertained as a luncheon guest at Reigate Manor. Frances
reported, "We are greatly stirred by his book of horrors," and she
promptly adopted his suggestion that temperance women help raise
money for Armenian relief.[16]

In the late summer of 1896, Willard and Lady Henry embarked for
France where they expected to vacation on a bicycle tour of Normandy.

But the inhospitable weather made bicycling impossible, and the two women returned to Paris where they learned of the increasing numbers of Armenian refugees arriving in Marseilles by ship from the eastern Mediterranean and of the lack of facilities for their care. The French government was providing only minimal shelter and a small dole for food. Willard and Lady Henry decided to attempt a personal rescue effort of their own.[17] Using Lady Henry's money, they were able to obtain from the French authorities an abandoned hospital dating from the time of Louis XV where they set up a kitchen and provided shelter for 300 refugees. The two ministering angels, with a large dose of noblesse oblige, personally handed out lengths of cloth to the refugees to make shirts and other garments.[18] They enlisted the help of the Salvation Army and turned over the operation to that organization later in the fall of 1896 when they both returned to London. Meanwhile, they had organized a functioning hospice and found homes on the continent, in England, and in the United States for approximately 500 refugees. At one point, over 20 Armenians were staying at Reigate Manor and being nursed by Lady Henry and her staff.[19] Later that fall, Laura Orme Chant, a leading figure in the British Woman's Temperance Association, was sent to Bulgaria where she organized under World WCTU auspices another shelter that housed 800 refugees as well as providing food, clothing, and medical attention for large numbers of displaced Armenians. The polyglot petition was an early attempt by temperance women to exert concrete influence on the international scene. The Armenian question provided them with a specific opportunity and obligation.

In many ways the Marseilles venture was closer to Lady Henry's style of activism than Frances Willard's. Lady Henry always assumed a direct approach to the alleviation of social problems. She personally managed and financed a philanthropic refuge for delinquent women on her estate near Reigate. As part of the English aristocracy, philanthropy was her natural milieu. Willard's approach was much less personal. She had no bounty of her own to dispense. She looked for legislative solutions, political action, or WCTU sponsorship of charitable institutions.

Although the United States experienced a great outpouring of sympathy for the Armenians, many American newspapers expressed the usual nativist alarm at making the country a "dumping ground" for Armenian unfortunates.[20] The *Chicago Observer* commented, "If Frances Willard will head her bicycle this way, she will find as much squalid misery as she has ever seen among the exiled Armenians in Marseilles."[21] There also were threats in the British and American press that refugees destined for the United States would be sent back. It was not

until the end of October that the Armenians' Reigate champions knew
those sent to the United States had actually been admitted, and that
their efforts—despite considerable opposition—had been successful.[22]

For Willard and for many other reform women in the United States
and England, the Armenian crisis was a symbolic cause. In the late
nineteenth century American women believed they occupied a particularly safe and favored place among the world's women. A generation of
support for foreign missionary activity had taught them to view with
horror what they saw as the degradation and sexual exploitation of
women in much of the non-Christian world.[23] Like many other American women, Willard had early expressed her belief that American
women were especially blessed by the favored position in which their
society held them. She first had been impressed by their good treatment when she toured Europe and the Mideast in 1869–71, and she had
never seen anything to change her mind. What was happening in Turkey fit her cosmology well. When addressing the World WCTU at its
London meetings in 1895, Willard stated, "The atrocities committed
upon women in Armenia are the natural outcome of the sex-worship of
themselves by men, and of the giving over to them of women, as
polygamous wives and concubines."[24] When she spoke extemporane-
ously to the 1896 convention of the American WCTU (her Armenian
relief efforts had prevented her from preparing a formal address that
year), she credited the Armenians with standing for her ideas, "the
White Ribbon ideas; the sanctity of home life, the faithful loyalty of
one man to one woman; and they have illustrated this like no other
nation on the face of the earth; they lived it centuries before Moham-
med had ever conceived his vile religion which degrades manhood,
puts lust instead of love, and makes woman a bond-slave of man in the
harem to which he has consigned her."[25] No longer did Islam receive
her sympathetic tolerance. No longer did she emphasize that "God had
spoken to us not once but at *sundry* times, not in one but in *divers*
manners."[26] For as she wrote in her diary earlier in 1896, before the
Marseilles experience, "Nothing in all my life—not even our Civil War
has outraged my spirit like the fate of that martyr nation."[27] By 1896
her concern with outraged womanhood had eclipsed her concern for
ecumenicism.

WILLARD was happy abroad and found meaningful causes to espouse,
but she could not abandon her American causes. The way in which she
continued to function as promoter of a political reform coalition is a
case in point. In 1896 she still hoped for a strong third party, but her
ability to manipulate support for her political aims was severely handi-

Armenian refugees from the Constantinople massacre. (Reprinted from Gordon, *The Beautiful Life of Frances Willard*)

capped both by her increasing frailty and by her absence from the United States. In letters that crossed the Atlantic with impressive frequency she attempted to shape the political stance of the WCTU, but she could hardly exert much influence on Prohibition party councils or on the larger reform coalition movement in absentia.

The Prohibition party continued to be recalcitrant. Meeting in Chicago in December 1895, its executive committee took no action on a WCTU memorial proposing to change the party's name to the Home Protection party. Willard's great idea of the early 1880s, to merge protection of the home—women's cherished and acceptable sphere—with political action, no longer carried much weight. The Prohibitionists were steadily moving toward the single issue politics that eventually brought them victory in 1918, and Willard fought a losing battle.

By 1896 the Prohibition party itself was irreconcilably split. The single issue faction was pushing hard for confining the party to support of prohibition, blaming the broader reform platform of the 1880s and early 1890s for the party's lack of success. Although Willard's sympathies were naturally with the broad gauge approach, she neither liked nor trusted Helen Gougar, who, with John St. John, led that faction. The single issue group won at the Prohibition party convention, and several hundred broad gauge members withdrew and formed what they dubbed the National party. In an obvious ploy to capture Willard and the WCTU, this group adopted "Home Protection" as its motto.[28]

Willard faced a dilemma but she did not hesitate on what course to follow. She wrote Lillian Stevens, her close friend and WCTU vice-president, that she "would as soon follow a boomerang or a distempered canine" as have anything to do with the women leaders of the new party. Years ago, she observed, Susan B. Anthony had told her that Gougar wrecked everything she touched.[29] But Willard could not make these kinds of statements in public, and the WCTU's *Union Signal* editorialized, "for the present at least each one must decide for herself which party 'furnishes the best embodiment of prohibition principles and will most surely protect our homes.'"[30]

This was a dangerous course and Willard knew it. State and local unions would take sides, attaching themselves to either the Nationalists or the single issue Prohibition party, and in no time the WCTU could be split wide open. Willard was prepared to abandon the larger prohibition movement to keep her own organization intact. She understood the real source of her power and influence. Her leadership of temperance women provided the base for her position in American public life. But it was not that simple. The state unions were already taking sides. Quick action was necessary, and word went out to all state presidents urging a neutral attitude toward the two parties representing the Prohibitionists. WCTU women were warned that they had comrades on both sides, and that no resolution, official utterance, or other action favoring either party should be made until after the national convention at St. Louis.[31] Willard was a superb politician in her dealings with the WCTU. She rarely made a mistake. Even from a distance and a sick bed, the old touch was there.

At the WCTU convention in the fall of 1896, Willard would be on hand to guide the WCTU's thinking; also, the election would be over and endorsement a hollow issue. Meanwhile a variety of fusion, although not the kind Frances Willard had worked for, had taken place. The Populists had joined the Democrats in supporting the candidacy of William Jennings Bryan. Essentially the farmers' movement had joined the mainstream of American politics, and the battle among the Prohibitionists was nothing but a minor skirmish. In her presidential address Willard had kind things to say about both Bryan and William McKinley, that year's presidential contenders, and pledged to the new president-elect "my truest loyalty and good will."[32]

None of these developments prevented a floor fight over party endorsement at the WCTU convention in St. Louis. The two Prohibition parties still had many firm partisans in the WCTU, and only the strong nonendorsement stand of Willard prevented a split. In 1897, the last convention over which Willard presided, she reaffirmed that position. Willard was eager to see women play an active political role, but she would not risk the basic unity of her constituency in the process.

WHEN Frances Willard and Lady Henry returned from Marseilles in the fall of 1896, Frances was put to bed in Reigate Priory's dome room with its handsome yellow satin hangings. The Armenian relief effort obviously had been too much for her, though she had not been really fit since she arrived in England in April. Part of the time she was "well enough to be out on her bike, in the gymnasium and dictating letters,"[33] but her "poor throat and tongue are like a flame," and she complained, "How long have I had this misery, and how weary and spiritless it makes one."[34] She attempted speaking engagements from time to time but was forced to cancel most appearances and in July vowed to make no more such promises.[35]

There were public events that summer that would have brought Willard great satisfaction. In July 1896 the International Socialist and Labor Conference convened in London. Charlotte Gilman was among the Americans participating, rubbing elbows with Fabians and European socialists.[36] Willard would have wished to play a similar role at the conclave. Although she and Anna Gordon were able to attend as spectators the great London peace demonstration and march that preceded the conference, that small excursion so exhausted her that she was unable to write in her diary for a week afterward.[37] The BWTA national meetings had laid her low in early June. Full participation in the London conference would have been an impossible strain.

An exhausted rather than a refreshed Frances Willard disembarked in New York on 7 November in time for the 1896 WCTU convention to be held in St. Louis a few days later. Willard was always seasick, even on the channel boat. This had been a bad crossing. The nurse Isabel had insisted on sending with Frances and Anna lay incapacitated in her cabin for most of the journey. But the two women went on to St. Louis and Willard presided with vigor over a volatile convention that successfully skirted the explosive issue of partisan endorsement, enthusiastically applauded Willard's Armenian commitment, and again ratified with reservations the Temple office building project. The convention over, Willard collapsed at Dr. Cordelia Greene's sanatorium in Castile, New York, where she remained through the spring of 1897 and where she was to spend much of the rest of her life.

Anna Gordon was constantly at Willard's side at Castile or elsewhere

when she thought a change of scene might improve her health. In April
Frances spent three weeks in Atlantic City where Kate Jackson joined her briefly, and in May she visited for a few days with the Demorests in New York.[38] She managed two major addresses in New York City and New Jersey and then went on to stay with Cambridge friends and at Anna's home near Boston before moving to New England resorts to escape the summer heat and write her presidential address. Often her tongue was so sore that she could not speak, and she vomited frequently. She ate seven meals a day in a vain effort to keep up her strength. Although frequent small meals may have helped to avoid overtaxing Willard's heart, her vegetarian practices probably aggravated her anemia. When iron supplements and massive doses of vitamin B_{12} were unavailable, anemia was treated by eating liver and red meat, and these were not part of her regimen.

Lady Henry was in England, also too sick to travel. In January 1897 she had suffered a carriage accident in Westminster and in February had undergone surgery for an abscess in her side. She was also diagnosed as suffering from heart trouble.[39] Isabel still hoped to come to the United States for the World WCTU convention in Toronto and the Buffalo meetings of the American WCTU, but by September she wrote Lillian Stevens from Eastnor Castle that she was too sick to make the trip although she had not yet broken the news to Frances.[40] From the point of view of Willard's relationship to a sizable group in the WCTU leadership, Isabel's absence may have proved an advantage. Lady Henry was no longer in favor, and Willard had enough trouble keeping the Union on a course that she approved.

Willard spent the year between the conventions of 1896 and 1897 conscientiously following Dr. Greene's regimen of rest, diet, and carefully controlled exercise, and traveling from spa to spa looking for some new elixir of sea or mountain air, new faces, and old friends that would put her right again. Always the business required by her position followed her. Editorials and articles flowed from her pen. A spate of letters dealt with the Temple office building affair. The Nashville meetings of the National Council of Women had their share of attention. Willard would not be able to attend because of a conflict with the World WCTU meetings in Canada and the American WCTU convention in Buffalo,[41] and she resisted losing Anna Howard Shaw, prominent suffrage and temperance leader, to the council meetings because she felt she needed her at the Toronto and Buffalo conventions to present the council's point of view to temperance women.[42] As always, the public and private Willard are intertwined in her correspondence of that year.

Her mind and pen were busy with a variety of public projects while her poor body, except for those rare occasions when her will overcame her infirmities, struggled through an invalid's life.

A NOTHER battle royal spilled over the Atlantic to the United States during that difficult summer of 1897. By the late nineties Frances Willard and Lady Henry had expanded their spheres of influence to encompass both sides of the Atlantic, only to discover that their spheres of vulnerability had expanded to the same borders. The Contagious Diseases Acts for the regulation of venereal disease among British troops were again at issue in the United Kingdom. First passed in 1864, these laws were designed to control venereal infections among enlisted men in garrison towns and ports in Great Britain itself. The legislation met little opposition until the 1870s, when Josephine Butler led an organized women's crusade against them based on women's horror at the licensing of prostitution. Because their implicit sanction of prostition via regulation and inspection was anathema to British reformers, the acts were repealed in 1886, before Frances Willard's residence in England.

The principle of regulation had now been revived to protect British troops stationed in India from contagion, and, as Lady Henry saw it, to protect British women who might otherwise be infected by returning soldiers. But the militant wing of the British women's movement saw the legislation (now called the Cantonment Acts) quite differently. To these women the acts provided the sanctity of law to a practice, selling their own bodies, that epitomized the degradation of womanhood.[43] In 1897 Lady Henry publicly announced her position favoring regulation in an address before the executive committee of the BWTA.[44] Association members eventually agreed to differ among themselves on this issue. Many disagreed with Lady Henry but, according to Hannah Whitall Smith, were willing to give her the same freedom they asked for themselves.[45]

Lady Henry's support of the Contagious Diseases Acts provided a convenient handle on which her American enemies could fasten. Their jealous discomfit with Frances Willard's attention to Lady Henry and the British scene now found an outlet in a legitimate issue that they could rally round. The Atlantic connection worked more than one way. Willard was saddled with the opprobrium the women's movement attached to the Contagious Diseases Acts, and it has been suggested that the Americans were among the loudest detractors of Lady Henry on this issue.[46] On the other hand, Lady Henry had been forced to involve herself in the American quarrel over the wording of antilynching reso-

lutions, and her enemies had fastened on that issue to embarrass her.
The Atlantic was a very small lake when controversies involving the Passages
reform community or the woman question were concerned.

Willard was forced to concede that Lady Henry's position on the
Contagious Diseases Acts had been a mistake, if inspired by understandable motives, that she did not agree with it, and that she would
have argued against it had the two been together.[47] One result of the
controversy was bad feeling in the United States over the election of
Lady Henry as president of the World WCTU at the Toronto convention. This was the last world meeting at which Frances Willard presided. She retired from the presidency that year. Lady Henry was to
succeed her, but a campaign to stop the Somerset candidacy and condemning Lady Henry's stand on the Contagious Diseases Acts was
launched during the summer.[48] Willard met the issue head-on in her
presidential address, sympathetically explaining Isabel Somerset's position but labeling it "a grievous mistake."[49] Open conflict did not erupt
at the meetings themselves, and Somerset was easily elected.

Willard's disagreement with Lady Henry on this issue was genuine.
As early as June, Willard wrote Elizabeth Blackwell, then in England,
urging that she visit Lady Henry and remonstrate with her to change
her mind. "She [Isabel Somerset] has not been as long in the reform
work as you and I, and when Florence Nightengale 'goes over' and
other ladies to whose opinion she is apt to look, and no end of men
whom she reveres, it is not much wonder that she should have taken
the position that cannot but be a sorrow to the veteran reformers."[50]
Lady Henry did eventually withdraw her support in January 1898.
Her biographer attributes this change of heart to her fear that open
conflict would shorten Willard's life, rather than to a reversal in her
convictions.[51]

I F the world convention over which Willard presided in October 1897
was not easy, the Buffalo convention of the American WCTU, which
followed, was a veritable donnybrook. Once more the fate of the Temple office building provided the focus for searing disagreement, and
only Willard's personal pledge to raise money outside the Union itself
prevented the Temple project from being abandoned outright. Willard
was in no position to fulfill this promise, but a promise was a promise,
and her loyalty to her old friend Matilda Carse, the Temple's primary
sponsor, was unshaken. She was eager to return to England, but first
she must try her hand at enlisting the support of well-off New York
friends on behalf of the Temple cause.

Frances Willard and Anna Gordon spent December in Chicago, tying up loose ends of WCTU business after the convention and preparing for a long English sojourn. But New York and the money raising effort had to come first. In early January 1898 they installed themselves in a sunny suite of rooms on the first floor of New York's Empire Hotel as guests of the proprietor. Their proximity to Riverside Drive and Central Park made possible pleasant afternoon drives as far north as Grant's Tomb. Friends dropped by for social visits, but no fund-raising was attempted. Frances complained of "great weariness and unnatural languor."⁵² She had confessed to Lillian Stevens at Christmastime that she was "far from strong" and "keeping pretty quiet,"⁵³ and now she began to complain of great fatigue, although she kept at her work regularly.

Before the month was out, Willard took to her bed and on 5 February she sat up and dictated a business letter for the last time. Anna Gordon said that from the onset of this spell of acute illness Frances did not expect to recover. This conviction must have inspired Willard to make a last effort at setting the record straight. About a week before she died a *New York Tribune* reporter, who was also a friend, was summoned for an interview. In the account of her visit, the reporter noted that Willard was eager for her arrival, impatient at an unavoidable day's delay, up and sitting in a sunny bay window wearing a robin's-egg blue negligee trimmed with lace. She chided the reporter for being so long getting there and, naming no names, talked about people who had tried to injure her in the past, behavior that had previously made her unhappy, but "lately all the ache and ugly sensations have gone. . . . The force of love has flooded out of sight all those individual pettinesses." In another reference to unkind gossip about her she asked the reporter to "speak out when the time comes, won't you. . . . I have so much to say to you—so much before it is too late."⁵⁴ Obviously Willard was dying and wished her side of any controversy recorded. Willard, the clever politician, the public woman, was making a last attempt to ensure for herself her proper place in the world's annals.

Willard also needed to return to her beginnings. Her success depended on never leaving her roots behind. New England's discipline and intellectual rigor, Methodism's concentration on behavior and spirit had all tempered the unfolding of her life. She found in her beginnings the strength to manage her end. Thus she gathered family and friends for her "passing." Willard's niece, Katherine Willard Baldwin, who lived in New York City, was a frequent visitor and Lillian Stevens, her chosen successor, was summoned by Anna Gordon to her bedside. Other WCTU officials and friends were present from time to time. Until the very last, Frances was true to her unfailing appetite for

The platform of Willard Hall, Temple office building, as it was decorated for Willard's funeral, 23 February 1898. (Reprinted from Gordon, *The Beautiful Life of Frances Willard*)

sentiment. She asked to be alone with Anna and repeated the little ritual she had practiced regularly with her sister Mary, including the night that Mary died: "I want to say what Mary and I used to say to each other away back in the old days on the farm when we were going to sleep. I would say to Mary, 'I ask your pardon and I thank you,' and she would say, 'I freely forgive you and welcome,' and then we would change about with the same sweet words of forgiveness and gratitude."[55] On her last day, she told Clara Hoffman, the secretary of the National WCTU, "I've crept in with mother, and it's the same beautiful world and the same people." She stayed awake a little longer for a last cable from Isabel. After falling asleep she roused only once to murmur, "How beautiful to be with God."[56] She died, or as she would have said, was translated, at midnight on 17 February 1898.

AT her death Willard was faithful to her unique ability to bridge Victorian morality with the modern world. She died as she lived, true to friendship, family, and God, the moral virtues of her girlhood, despite her crusades to change the world. Willard had anchored her push for societal change in two conservative bulwarks of the age in which she lived, the home and the church, and used the interest of women as acknowledged custodians of the home and the interest of the evangelical church in temperance as her bases from which to move. She thereby made many of her radical ideas palatable to middle-class America. For this she was loved, and in time forgotten.

Frances Willard understood the nineteenth century and was able to use for her own ends its addiction to both progress and sentiment. She subscribed to the goals of the Victorian reformer—the perfectly ordered society, the celebration of intellect and education, the promotion of peaceful and just relations between individuals and nations; and she understood the importance to her time of lubricating the promotion of its cherished reforms with a large dose of sentiment. She died as she had lived, a womanly woman, beyond woman's sphere as a public figure but thoroughly comfortable with its professed values.

Notes

PREFACE

1. Original materials are in the Woman's Christian Temperance Union Papers, Willard Memorial Library, which is the national headquarters of the WCTU. The bulk of these materials is available in the *Temperance and Prohibition Papers*, microfilm ed. See Jimerson, Blouin, and Isetts, *Guide to the Microfilm Edition of the Temperance and Prohibition Papers*, for a description of the papers. The supplement to the microfilm edition, WCTU series, was prepared by the Michigan Historical Collections of the Bentley Historical Library, University of Michigan, Ann Arbor. Unless otherwise noted, the microfilm edition rather than the originals was used throughout this volume.

2. The Hannah Whitall Smith Papers are in the possession of her great-granddaughter, Barbara Strachey Halpern, of Oxford, England, who graciously permits their use by scholars.

3. Rachel Strachey, *Frances Willard*.

4. Willard, *Glimpses of Fifty Years*.

5. Anna A. Gordon, *The Beautiful Life of Frances Willard* and *The Life of Frances E. Willard*.

6. Earhart, *Frances Willard*.

7. Lee, "Evangelical Domesticity"; Bordin, *Woman and Temperance*.

8. Anselm Strauss in his introduction to Wiener, *Politics of Alcoholism*.

9. Hannah Smith to Olive [Schreiner], 28 March 1898, Hannah Whitall Smith Papers.

CHAPTER I

1. Anna A. Gordon, *The Life of Frances E. Willard*, 281–82 (hereafter cited as Gordon, *Willard*).

2. *Union Signal*, 24 February 1898, 2.

3. Quoted in Gordon, *Willard*, 287. This description of Willard's funeral is largely based on Gordon's account and reports of the *Chicago Tribune* and *New York Times* in February 1898.

4. Quoted in Gordon, *Willard*, 278.

5. Clipped in the *Temperance and Prohibition Papers*, microfilm ed., WCTU series, reel 27, frame 108 (hereafter cited as WCTU series).

6. Poem, 1899, by Mrs. V. G. Ramsey, WCTU series, reel 27, frame 76.

7. Editorial, *California Christian Advocate*, 1898, clipped in WCTU series, reel 27, folder 114, frame 110. These folders of Willard's papers include a comprehensive collection of press clippings on her death.

8. The most recent biography of Willard is Earhart's *Frances Willard: From Prayers to Politics*. Several dissertations have discussed the WCTU and incidentally Willard from the temperance point of view. Early examples are Mezvinsky, "The White Ribbon Reform," and Unger, "History of the National Woman's Christian Temperance Union." Giele's "Social Change in the Feminine Role" was a seminal study of the WCTU's place in the woman movement, and Gusfield's "Social Structure and Moral Reform" was another landmark sociological study. Recent studies in which Willard herself figured began with DuBois, "Radicalism of the Woman Suffrage Movement." Blocker, *Retreat from Reform*, analyzed Willard's personality and leadership (pp. 29–32), especially her role in the Prohibition party (pp. 51–61). Buhle, *Women and American Socialism*, assessed the importance of Willard's leadership in reform causes. Epstein, *Politics of Domesticity*, explored the movement of the WCTU under Willard's leadership into the suffrage movement and reform politics. Willard's leadership is also analyzed in Bordin, *Woman and Temperance*. Two recent dissertations dealing with Willard are Miller, "Frances Elizabeth Willard"; Lee, "Evangelical Domesticity."

9. Beveridge's speech is reproduced in Gordon, *Willard*, 309.

10. Quoted in the *Union Signal*, 22 August 1889, 3.

11. From a speech of 23 July 1879, quoted in Powderly's autobiography, *The Path I Trod*, 344.

12. Quoted in Harrison, *Drink and the Victorians*, 395–96.

13. See Teichman, *Alice Roosevelt Longworth*, 5, 114–15.

14. Buhle, *Women and American Socialism*, 64.

15. Earhart, *Frances Willard*.

16. Grant, "Domestic Experience and Feminist Theory," 221.

17. By now the doctrine of domesticity has been explored by many historians of women. The seminal article was, of course, Welter's "The Cult of True Womanhood."

18. Sicherman's "American History" was among the first statements of this point of view. A more recent analysis can be found in Sweet, *The Minister's Wife*, chap. 2.

19. See, among others, Smith-Rosenberg, *Religion and the Rise of the American City*; Berg, *Remembered Gate*; Cott, *Bonds of Womanhood*; Ryan, *Cradle of the Middle Class*.

20. Mari Jo Buhle agrees that Frances Willard popularized the idea that from the home "woman could reach out to purify all aspects of the human condition," including "reforming government and ending wars." *Women and American Socialism*, 117.

21. These quotations are from the *Brooklyn Eagle*, the *Chatham, Ontario, Evening Banner*, the *Living Church* (Protestant Episcopal), and the *Evangelical Messenger* as excerpted in the *Literary Digest*, 26 February 1898 (p. 248), 19 March 1898 (p. 355), 12 March 1898 (pp. 319–20).

22. Presidential address, 1882 convention, *Minutes of the National Woman's*

Christian Temperance Union, 67, WCTU series, reel 1 (hereafter cited as *Minutes*).

23. Hill, *Charlotte Perkins Gilman*, 3.

24. DuBois, "Radicalism of the Woman Suffrage Movement," 63–71.

25. Epstein, *Politics of Domesticity*, 132–33, 147.

26. Buhle, *Women and American Socialism*, 117.

27. See Harding, "Family Reform Movements." Harding sees two distinct strategies for organizing families in the contemporary scene: the feminist strategy of reducing the role of the family "in defining a woman's life and identity," and the antifeminist strategy of protecting and celebrating "the role of the family in defining a woman's life and identity." Somehow Willard was able to combine these seemingly incompatible goals.

28. See Bordin, *Woman and Temperance*, 120–21.

29. Resolution presented to Illinois WCTU convention, 1876, quoted in Earhart, *Frances Willard*, 153. The address is quoted with slightly different wording in Anna A. Gordon, *The Beautiful Life of Frances Willard*, 119.

30. Willard, *Woman in the Pulpit*, 65. See also Hardesty, "Minister as Prophet? Or as Mother?," 1:88–101. I disagree with Hardesty that woman as mother was Willard's goal. She used the language of womanliness to push women forward instead.

31. *Cincinnati Commercial*, 25 October 1882, clipped in scrapbook 11, WCTU series, reel 31, frame 237.

32. Testimony of Richard L. Douglass, reported in *Ann Arbor News*, 27 February 1979, A–11. See also Weiner, *Politics of Alcoholism*.

33. Norman Clark's *Deliver Us from Evil*, was the first general work in the new temperance scholarship. See also Blocker, *Retreat from Reform* and *Alcohol, Reform, and Society*; Engelmans, *Intemperance*; Rorabaugh, *The Alcoholic Republic*; Tyrrell, *Sobering Up*. Lender and Martin's *Drinking in America* is the most recent general history of temperance and the alcohol problem. An interdisciplinary international conference on the social history of alcohol was held in January 1984 at the University of California, Berkeley. The *Alcohol and Temperance History Group Newsletter* has been published for several years to facilitate communication within the rapidly growing group of temperance historians. The entire issue of *American Psychologist* 38 (October 1983) was devoted to alcohol-related problems and contemporary research on alcoholism. *Time* magazine (20 May 1985) devoted its cover and major article to America's new and abstemious drinking habits.

34. Rossi, "A Biosocial Perspective on Parenting," is generally credited with beginning this new examination of women's role by feminists.

35. Stacey, "The New Conservative Feminism." Stacey is not sympathetic to this new feminism. She sees today's feminist movement afflicted by "a crisis of confidence," faced by a "backlash that poses a serious challenge to the women's movement" (p. 59).

36. The phrase "maternal struggle" was used by Senator Henry William Blair to describe women's leadership of the temperance movement, but it also referred to all women's reform activities in the public sphere. See Blair, *The Temperance Movement*, 504. Friedan describes the "feminine mode" in *The Second Stage*, 243.

37. *The Second Stage*, 164. In 1985 Friedan continues to urge that women "must not surrender family values and religious principles to the far right," and "affirm the differences between men and women." See Betty Friedan, "How to Get the Women's Movement Moving Again," *New York Times Magazine*, 3 November 1985.

38. Presidential address, 1894 convention, *Minutes*, 177, WCTU series, reel 4.

CHAPTER II

1. Willard, *Glimpses of Fifty Years*, opposite p. xvi (hereafter cited as *Glimpses*).

2. Ibid., 1–2.

3. Ibid., 9–10. Frank was a common nickname for Frances, just as Ray was invariably used for Rachel.

4. Anna A. Gordon, *The Beautiful Life of Frances Willard*, 18–20 (hereafter cited as Gordon, *Beautiful Life*).

5. Material on Frances Willard's ancestry can be found in *Glimpses*, 2–5; *Temperance and Prohibition Papers*, microfilm ed., WCTU series, reel 26, folder 113, frame 450ff. (hereafter cited as WCTU series); Earhart, *Frances Willard*, 12–23.

6. *Glimpses*, 666.

7. Anna A. Gordon, *The Life of Frances E. Willard* (hereafter cited as Gordon, *Willard*).

8. See *Glimpses*, 666.

9. Diary of Frances Willard, 24 January 1856 (hereafter cited as Diary). I referred to the original journals and diaries, and my citations are made to the originals rather than to the supplement to the *Temperance and Prohibition Papers*, microfilm ed.

10. Typed note by Willard, WCTU series, reel 26, folder 113, frame 640.

11. Willard questioned her mother during her last illness about her father's extreme reserve and his avoidance of paternal affection, and her mother excused him, saying he was nervous and unwell and this "accounted for much." Willard note, WCTU series, reel 26, folder 113, frame 640.

12. *Glimpses*, 4.

13. For example, see Diary, 8 March 1863.

14. Gordon, *Beautiful Life*, 180.

15. *Glimpses*, 73, 180, 660–61.

16. These journals, which are now available for inspection, confirm Mother Willard's pedagogical techniques.

17. *Glimpses*, 25.

18. Diary, 25 October 1860, p. 64.

19. Quoted in Gordon, *Willard*, 10.

20. Quoted in ibid., 9.

21. See *Glimpses*, sections I, II, III.

22. M. R. R. to Anna Gordon, 14 March 1898, WCTU series, reel 27, frame 83; *Glimpses*, 12; Gordon, *Willard*, 42.

23. Gordon, *Willard*, 42.

24. *Glimpses*, 54.

25. Ibid., 75–77.

26. Diary, 1855.

27. *Glimpses*, 84–88.

28. Diary, 7 January 1855.

29. Ibid., 1 March 1855.

30. Ibid., 22 March, 19 July, 25 October 1855; see also *Glimpses*, 25.

31. Diary, 22 March 1855.

32. See especially the journals for 1855 which are rich in agricultural observations and show her keen interest in all the farm's activities.

33. *Glimpses*, 42.

34. Ibid., 43.

35. See below, pp. 38–42.

36. *Glimpses*, 54.

37. Ibid., 41.

38. Diary, Fall 1855. *The Tyro* was dubbed the *Tribune* in *Glimpses*.

39. Diary, 21 February 1855.

40. Diary, 28 September 1855.

41. *Glimpses*, 51–52.

42. Diary, 1 January 1855.

43. Ibid., 27 June 1855.

44. Ibid., 31 October 1855.

45. Ibid., 6 November 1855; *Glimpses*, 69–70.

46. Ibid., 4 December 1855; see also *Glimpses*, 69.

47. Diary, 6 August 1855.

48. See Sklar, *Catharine Beecher*, for a discussion of Beecher's schemes for endowing nondenominational women's teachers' colleges to provide a corps of trained teachers for the western states.

49. *Glimpses*, 659.

50. Diary, 22–23 July 1857.

51. Ibid., 27 April 1857.

52. *Glimpses*, 97.

53. A more detailed discussion of North Western Female College appears in Earhart, *Frances Willard*, 41–45.

54. *Glimpses*, 116. Some of these episodes are mentioned in Mary Willard's diary, 19, 30 April 1858.

55. Maggie Hawley was Frances's special friend; they remained close for many years.

56. See Willard, *Evanston: A Classic Town*, 48, 68–69.

57. Mary Bannister Willard, quoted in *Glimpses*, 99–100. No diary for most of Frances's first term at North Western is available.

58. Mary Bannister Willard, quoted in ibid., 100. Northwestern University was not coeducational at this time.

59. O'Brien, in "Tomboyism and Adolescent Conflict," 350–72, believes that, as a schoolgirl, Willard combined the qualities of womanliness with assertiveness that would later characterize her role as leader of the WCTU, where she both sanctified the home and defied male authority without seeming unwomanly. I agree that Willard was relatively free of personal conflict in her expansion of the female role, and that Mary Hill Willard was instrumental in encouraging her to reach out.

60. See Chapter IV for a discussion of Willard and the problem of sexuality.

Helen Horowitz discusses the student crush at length in *Alma Mater*, 65–68, 166–67, 191–93.

61. Mary Bannister Willard, quoted in *Glimpses*, 100.

62. Diary, 29 May 1859.

63. Ibid., 10, 12 June 1859.

64. The Willards' worship patterns emerge clearly from the diaries. Willard may have exaggerated the family's piety somewhat in *Glimpses*, 621–25, 629, but there was no doubt about their devotion to Methodism by the time they arrived in Evanston.

65. Diary, 28 March 1858.

66. Reminiscences of Willard by North Western's president, William Jones, quoted in *Glimpses*, 121.

67. Diary, 4 April 1859.

68. *Glimpses*, 112.

69. Reproduced in ibid., 112–13.

70. Ibid., 622–23.

71. Diary, 17 January 1860.

72. Ibid., 20 January 1860.

73. In this volume I use the term "feminism" in the dictionary sense of advocating legal and social changes to establish political, social, and economic equality of the sexes.

74. In the nineteenth-century doctrine of spheres, the wife was seen as the nurturer of the family and children but the husband had legal authority, owning his wife's wages and sometimes her inherited property; he frequently had sole legal custody of children, sometimes before they were born. The husband was considered the head of the household and represented the family in the public sphere. Although both men and women were citizens, only males voted, held office, and were able to participate in public affairs.

75. Diary, 26 May 1859.

76. Ibid., 1 June 1859.

77. Diary, quoted in Mary Bannister Willard's sketch in *Glimpses*, 104. I have not been able to identify this passage in the diaries themselves. It was undoubtedly written in 1859, which is not fully covered in the two volumes extant. However, I believe it likely that it is an accurate quote because Willard would not have tampered with her sister-in-law's account.

78. Diary, 26 May 1859.

79. Manuscript in Willard's handwriting, June 1859, WCTU series, reel 26, folder 112, frame 250.

80. Diary, 9 August 1859.

CHAPTER III

1. Willard, *Glimpses of Fifty Years*, 124 (hereafter cited as *Glimpses*).

2. Diary of Frances Willard, 17 February 1861 (hereafter cited as Diary).

3. Ibid.

4. *Glimpses*, 134.

5. Ibid., 146; Diary, Fall 1860. The school's principal was former superinten-

dent of the Wisconsin Institute for the Blind at Janesville, where Josiah Willard once served on the Board of Overseers.

6. Diary, 28 September 1860.

7. Ibid., 27 September 1860.

8. Ibid., 8 October 1860. The account in *Glimpses*, 148–49, 151, parallels this entry, although it is much cut.

9. *Glimpses*, 146.

10. Diary, 21 November 1860; see also *Glimpses*, 157.

11. Diary, 26 December 1860.

12. Ibid., 1859–60.

13. Ibid., 30 April 1859.

14. Ibid., 8 October 1860.

15. Ibid., Fall 1860. When Willard died in 1898, this same man wrote of the Frances he had known forty years before that her complexion was lovely, "her magnificent hair of a beautiful bronze color, a slender willowy form graceful in every movement, not a studied grace for it was nature's own." Frank Nichols to Mrs. Grow, *Temperance and Prohibition Papers*, microfilm ed., WCTU series, reel 27, folder 114, frame 274 (hereafter cited as WCTU series).

16. Diary, 5 December 1860.

17. Ibid., 11 May 1861.

18. Ibid., 18 May 1861.

19. Ibid., 5 June 1861.

20. James R. Joy in Johnson and Malone, *Dictionary of American Biography*, 526.

21. *Glimpses*, 162.

22. Diary, 17 December 1862.

23. Ibid., 4 September 1861.

24. See Stowe, "The Thing Not Its Vision."

25. Diary, 21 February 1862.

26. Ibid., 27 February 1862.

27. *Glimpses*, 645.

28. Diary, 23 January 1863.

29. Ibid., 31 March 1862.

30. This courtship is traced in diaries for October 1866 and April, May, June 1867.

31. Diary, 9 June 1867.

32. Willard to M. H. Willard, 3 March 1869, WCTU series supplement, reel 5.

33. *Glimpses*, 645.

34. Diary, 24 January 1855.

35. Ibid., 7 November 1860.

36. Frances Willard describes these events in a chapter of her *Evanston: A Classic Town*, 176–79.

37. *Glimpses*, 131–32.

38. Ibid., 163, 688.

39. Diary, 26 April 1862.

40. *Glimpses*, 687–88.

41. See below, p. 42. See also Diary, 20 April 1862; *Glimpses*, 163–64; Willard, *Evanston: A Classic Town*, 74.

42. *Glimpses*, 169.

43. Ibid., 171.

44. Diary, 2 September 1862; *Glimpses*, 169.

45. Diary, 14, 18 September 1862.

46. Ibid., 1 January 1863.

47. Interview with Willard in *Review of Reviews* (U.K.), 15 October 1892, clipped in scrapbook 57, WCTU series, reel 39, frame 302.

48. *Glimpses*, 186–87. Solomon, in *In the Company of Educated Women*, chaps. 2, 3, discusses with understanding and intelligence the seminary's contribution to the education of women.

49. Quoted in Anna A. Gordon, *The Life of Frances E. Willard*, 53.

50. Diary, 1 January 1863.

51. Ibid., 3 January 1863.

52. Ibid., 9 July 1863.

53. Ibid., 24 July 1863.

54. For an account of this journey, see ibid., 29 September–24 October 1863, and *Glimpses*, 508ff.

55. *Glimpses*, 188.

56. Diary, January–August 1866; *Glimpses*, 188. See also circular letter of Willard to the American Methodist Ladies Centenary Association, 1866, WCTU series, reel 11, frame 187.

57. *Glimpses*, 190.

58. Diary, 16 October 1866.

59. Smith-Rosenberg, in "The Female World of Love and Ritual," her seminal study of thirty-five literate middle-class nineteenth-century families, found the pattern displayed by Willard as typical of the society in which she lived. The most recent comprehensive account of women's friendships appears in Faderman, *Surpassing the Love of Men*.

60. Evidence of Kate Jackson's jealousy can be found in the diaries for these years and in Willard's letters to her mother (Special WCTU Correspondence File, Willard Memorial Library—hereafter cited as Special WCTU File). Kate was also jealous of Frances's Lima suitor.

61. Willard to Mary Hill Willard, November–December 1868, 20 January 1869, Special WCTU File.

62. Willard to Caroline I. Whitely, 28 April 1871, WCTU series, reel 11.

63. Smith-Rosenberg, "The Female World of Love and Ritual," 8–9.

64. Vicinus, "One Life to Stand Beside Me." Freedman approaches the question from a more public stance in "Separatism as Strategy."

65. Motz, *Michigan Women and Their Kin*.

66. For descriptions of the Dickinson-Anthony relationship, see Anthony, *Susan B. Anthony*, 176ff.; Lutz, *Susan B. Anthony*.

67. Cook, "Female Support Networks," reprinted in Cott and Pleck, *A Heritage of Her Own*, 430–44. Adrienne Rich, in "Compulsory Heterosexuality and Lesbian Existence," saw a lesbian continuum that is not limited to the body but includes the sharing of joy and work, a continuum that women move in and out of and that is part of all women's lives.

68. Leila M. Rupp, in "Imagine My Surprise," was among the first to argue that identity rather than sexual behavior is the crucial factor. See also Newton, "The Mythic Mannish Lesbian."

69. For a discussion of the roles played by female support networks in women's reform causes, see Davis, *American Heroine*, 91; O'Neil, *Everyone Was Brave*, 141–42; and, especially, Freedman, "Separatism as Strategy," 512–29. Freedman suggests that in the 1920s women lost ground when they abandoned these supportive female friendships for what they hoped would be complete integration into the male world.

70. Diary, February, March 1867.

71. *Glimpses*, 246–47.

72. Diary, 6 January 1868.

73. Ibid., 12 May 1868; *Glimpses*, 250.

74. The scrapbooks in the WCTU series were first assembled by Mary Hill Willard, a task later assumed by Anna Gordon, who eventually was assisted in the 1890s by other members of Willard's secretarial staff. The articles written during the European trip can be found in scrapbook 2, reel 30. Twenty volumes of diaries also cover the European trip.

75. Scrapbook 2, WCTU series, reel 30, frames 68–69.

76. Ibid., frames 72–74.

77. Diary, 7 February 1870. Willard's Egyptian diary is much less romantic than the account in *Glimpses*. However, some of the travel diaries are nearly illegible from water stains or because they were written in pencil, on the run, and were badly smudged.

78. Diary, 1 February 1870, p. 122.

79. Ibid., 9 March 1870, pp. 13, 18–19.

80. Ibid., p. 249. Mary Earhart believed that without her European experience Willard would have remained an unknown schoolteacher. Earhart, *Frances Willard*, 96.

81. Diary, 27–28 November, 3 December 1867; 2 April 1868.

82. Ibid., 11 March 1869.

83. Undated fragment [1870?], WCTU series, reel 11, frame 40ff.

84. *Glimpses*, 269.

85. Diary, 20 March 1868.

86. Ibid., 12–13 March 1869.

87. Willard to Caroline I. Whitely, 28 April 1871, WCTU series, reel 11.

CHAPTER IV

1. Stratton, *Autobiography of Haven*, 175–79. The story of the Woman's College at Northwestern is told in Williamson and Wild, *Northwestern*, 23–30. Frances Willard tells her version of her connection with the college in *Evanston: A Classic Town*, 56–65, and *Glimpses of Fifty Years*, chaps. 8–10 (hereafter cited as *Glimpses*). Scrapbook 3, reel 30, of the *Temperance and Prohibition Papers*, microfilm ed., WCTU series (hereafter cited as WCTU series), is devoted largely to Willard's connection with the Woman's College, and the *Chicago Tribune* reports developments as they occurred. There are no diaries for this period.

2. Stratton, *Autobiography of Haven*, 176.

3. The stair carpet story was the official version, and appears in *Glimpses*, 198. Letters from Willard to Mary Hill Willard, 10 September 1864, 9 March 1870,

show her interest in the job while still in Europe. WCTU series supplement, reel 5.

4. *Chicago Journal*, February 1871, clipped in scrapbook 3, WCTU series, reel 30, frame 79. Willard may well have been the first woman with the title of college president. Vassar, for example, had male presidents until 1914.

5. *Glimpses*, 202.

6. Ibid., 203.

7. Ibid., 205.

8. Williamson and Wild, *Northwestern*, 25.

9. *Chicago Tribune*, 11 April 1871.

10. *Chicago Journal*, undated 1871, clipped in scrapbook 3, WCTU series, reel 30, frame 79.

11. *Glimpses*, 205.

12. Williamson and Wild, *Northwestern*, 28.

13. By the fall of 1870 seven state universities—Iowa, Wisconsin, Kansas, Indiana, Minnesota, Michigan, and Missouri—admitted women. Oberlin, of course, had admitted women in 1837. Pressure on the state universities to admit women usually came from the legislatures and was accepted reluctantly by the trustees and faculty. See McGuigan, *A Dangerous Experiment*, 29–31.

14. For example, in 1870 Michigan (at that time the largest university in the United States with approximately 1,000 students) had only 13 women in its literary department, 18 in medicine, and 2 in law. Ibid., 31. At the time, Northwestern had only 279 students, 38 of whom were women taking university courses.

15. *Glimpses*, 206.

16. Louise Hart to Nettie Cowles Kent, 22 September 1923, Kent Family Papers.

17. See Anna A. Gordon, *The Life of Frances E. Willard*, 61–62 (hereafter cited as Gordon, *Willard*).

18. *Glimpses*, 116. See above, Chapter II.

19. Isabella Parks, quoted in Gordon, *Willard*, 61–63.

20. Ibid., 208–9.

21. James Alton James, "History of Northwestern," unpublished typescript, chap. 8, p. 10, quoted in Williamson and Wild, *Northwestern*, 28.

22. In 1873 these women were Emily Huntington Miller, Mary B. Willard, Jennie Willing, E. M. Greenleaf and K. G. Queal. *Chicago Evening Mail*, 25 June 1873, clipped in scrapbook 3, WCTU series, reel 30, frame 130.

23. Ibid.

24. Ibid. Willard was to receive an increase of $200 a year until the stipend reached $2,400. She may well have been one of the highest paid women educators in the United States.

25. Williamson and Wild, *Northwestern*, 28.

26. *Chicago Tribune*, 25 June 1873.

27. Unidentified clipping (probably from *Evanston Index*), June 1873, in scrapbook 3, p. 59, WCTU series, reel 30.

28. Stratton, *Autobiography of Haven*, 175.

29. *Chicago Tribune*, 22 March 1871, clipped in scrapbook 3, WCTU series, reel 30, frame 80.

30. *Glimpses*, 226.

31. Ibid., 229–31.

32. Ibid., 231. Sapolio was a popular cleaning agent.

33. Unidentified clipping in scrapbook 3, WCTU series, reel 30, frame 100. Elizabeth Cady Stanton became involved in the rules imbroglio. See below, Chapter VII.

34. The contrast between Soulé and Willard is discussed in Williamson and Wild, *Northwestern*, 30.

35. *Glimpses*, 232.

36. *Chicago Tribune*, 24 June 1874, 2.

37. *Glimpses*, 232.

38. A manuscript draft of Willard's leave-taking to the faculty, dated 13 June 1874, can be found in the WCTU series, reel 11, frame 218ff. Willard's version of this document in *Glimpses*, 233–36, is almost identical with the original.

39. *Glimpses*, 239.

40. Ibid., 243.

41. See Rorabaugh, *The Alcoholic Republic*; Tyrrell, *Sobering Up*; Dannenbaum, *Drink and Disorder*.

42. See Dannenbaum, "Origins of Temperance Activism."

43. See Bordin, *Woman and Temperance*, chap. 2, for an account and assessment of the Crusade and a bibliography on the movement. See also Epstein, *Politics of Domesticity*, chap. IV; Blocker, *Give to the Winds Thy Fears*.

44. *Chicago Tribune*, 14–16 March 1874.

45. *Glimpses*, 336.

46. Ibid., 334–36.

47. On 14–16 March 1874 the *Chicago Tribune* provided front-page coverage, reporting in detail every move in the unsuccessful petition campaign and the mass meetings and marches organized around it. The story on 16 March ran to over six full columns.

48. In *Glimpses*, 31–32, Willard makes much of her family's temperance adherence, but in 1881 she queried her mother, "When did father quit using tobacco? Did you ever use beer or strong cider? And when did *you* quit snuff?" (10 October 1881, WCTU series, reel 12). Though always temperate, the Willard parents were not extreme in their views.

49. *Glimpses*, 334.

50. Ibid., 219.

51. See, for example, clippings of press accounts of her lecture "Everybody's War" delivered in 1876. Scrapbook 4, WCTU series, reel 30, frames 203, 207.

52. *Glimpses*, 128, 551.

53. "The New Chivalry," reproduced in ibid., 576.

54. Ibid., 589.

55. Willard, *Evanston: A Classic Town*, 366–67.

56. *Glimpses*, 692.

57. See Hibben, *Henry Ward Beecher*; Waller, "Beecher-Tilton Adultery Scandal"; Clifford Clark, *Henry Ward Beecher*, chap. 10.

58. History of the Congress of Women, in *Papers Read at the Fourth Congress of Women*, 121–23.

59. For some reason Willard seems not to have read the paper herself. The *Woman's Journal*, 1 November 1873, 352, reports that Willard's paper was read by Caroline Corbin, another Evanstonian, who also read a paper of her own

and was elected to the executive committee of the association. In *Glimpses* Willard states that her paper, part of which is reproduced, was on "School Government" (p. 218).

60. The governing board of the congress was composed of a vice-president and director from each of the states. See Julia Ward Howe, *Reminiscences*, 386. Howe was president of the congress for many years.

61. *Glimpses*, 337. Boole later married a WCTU leader, Ella Alexander, who was president of the WCTU from 1925 to 1933.

62. See ibid., 337. Willard described the gathering in a dispatch she wrote for the *Chicago Post and Mail*, 14 September 1874. Scrapbook 4, WCTU series, reel 30, frame 166.

63. Comment on Murphy to Willard, 7 March 1883, WCTU series, reel 13. Murphy married another WCTU woman.

64. *Glimpses*, 338.

65. Ibid.

66. Gordon, *Willard*, 88–89.

67. *Glimpses*, 339.

68. Ibid. Presumably she was also offered a position at Wellesley by Henry Durant, whom she had met at Orchard Beach. Ibid., 526.

69. Gordon, *Willard*, 100–101. A legend was to grow later that Willard resigned from Northwestern to crusade for temperance. Sometimes Willard attempted to set the record straight, as in her autobiography. At other times she seemed to welcome the distortion. While introducing her as World Woman's Christian Temperance Union president at a great mass meeting in London in 1892 (see below, p. 198), Lady Henry Somerset said, "It was a crucial moment in Miss Willard's life when she deliberately relinquished the brilliant position of dean of the first woman's college connected with a university in America, to go out penniless, alone, and unheralded, because her spirit caught the rhythms of the women's footsteps as they bridged the distance between the home and the saloon." Quoted in Gordon, *Willard*, 195.

CHAPTER V

1. Willard, *Glimpses of Fifty Years*, 342 (hereafter cited as *Glimpses*). There are no diaries for this period, although they seem once to have existed because they are quoted extensively in *Glimpses*.

2. Account book of Frances Willard, 1874–75, *Temperance and Prohibition Papers*, microfilm ed., WCTU series, reel 11, frame 281ff. (hereafter cited as WCTU series). Earhart's assumption that Jackson was not sympathetic to the temperance cause seems to have been in error. See Earhart, *Frances Willard*, 81.

3. Journal in *Glimpses*, 344.

4. Willard's father was an antislavery Whig, then a Free Soiler, and finally a Lincoln supporter. The Oberlin environment of Willard's early childhood was strongly antislavery.

5. Journal in *Glimpses*, 345.

6. Ibid., 345–46.

7. See Chapter IV, p. 42.

8. Unidentified clipping, 6 February 1875, in scrapbook 4, WCTU series, reel 30, frame 172.

9. *Glimpses*, 342–43.

10. Memorandum book, 1874, WCTU series, reel 11, frame 281ff.

11. Ibid.; *Glimpses*, 343–48.

12. Mrs. C. H. Case to Willard, 11 February 1875, WCTU series, reel 11.

13. *Chicago Tribune*, 16 October 1874. Willard herself apparently believed she was less welcome at the congress in 1874 in her temperance role than she had been in 1873 as an educator (see *Glimpses*, 348). But her election to office would seem to belie this.

14. *Minutes of the National Woman's Christian Temperance Union*, 1874 convention, 34–35.

15. Ibid., 36–37.

16. Willard to Wittenmyer, 12 December 1874, WCTU series, reel 11.

17. Willard to Wittenmyer, 29 December 1874, ibid.

18. Willard to Wittenmyer, 16 September 1875, ibid.

19. Willard to Wittenmyer, 8, 25 October 1875, ibid.

20. Willard to Wittenmyer, 11 December 1874, ibid.

21. Willard to Wittenmyer, 19 January 1875, ibid. See also Bordin, *Woman and Temperance*, 49–50.

22. Willard to Wittenmyer, 9 April 1875, WCTU series, reel 11.

23. Willard to Wittenmyer, 14 April 1875, ibid.

24. *Historical Statistics of the United States* (U.S. Government Printing Office, 1960), 91.

25. Eventually this publication became *Our Union*; in 1883 it merged with the Chicago *Signal* to become the *Union Signal*.

26. Unidentified clipping, July 1875, in scrapbook 4, p. 60, WCTU series, reel 30.

27. Correspondence, Summer, Fall 1875, WCTU series, reel 11.

28. Correspondence, 9–10 October 1876, ibid.

29. Memorandum, 1875, ibid., frame 423ff.

30. *Chicago Times*, 25 October 1874.

CHAPTER VI

1. There are sketches of Dickinson in James and James, *Notable American Women*, 1:475–76, and Willard and Livermore, *Woman of the Century*, 241–42.

2. Correspondence, April–May 1871, *Temperance and Prohibition Papers*, microfilm ed., WCTU series, reel 11 (hereafter cited as WCTU series).

3. Diary of Frances Willard, 17 May 1863 (hereafter cited as Diary).

4. Diary, 5 March 1866.

5. Willard, *Glimpses of Fifty Years*, 570 (hereafter cited as *Glimpses*).

6. In 1876 Anna Dickinson made her stage debut in Boston in "A Crown of Thorns," written by herself. She wrote her only successful play, "The American Girl," for the well-known actress, Fanny Davenport.

7. Quotations in this paragraph are from Willard to Wittenmyer, 26 June 1875, WCTU series, reel 11.

8. Dickinson to Willard, 20 July 1875, ibid. All of Dickinson's letters to Willard, at least for this period, seem to have been preserved and are available through the microfilm edition of the *Temperance and Prohibition Papers*. The Anna Dickinson Papers in the Library of Congress contain no letters from Willard to Dickinson. Apparently they did not survive.

9. Dickinson to Willard, 7 August 1875, WCTU series, reel 11.

10. For example, Willard provided support for Dickinson and her family in the 1890s when Dickinson suffered a bout of mental illness that resulted in much unfavorable press attention. See correspondence, March–April 1891, WCTU series, reel 17.

11. WCTU series, reel 27, folder 114, frame 53. Robert L. Cunnock was her teacher. R. L. Cunnock to Anna Gordon, 2 April 1898, WCTU series, reel 27, frame 54. Willard continued to be interested in voice training throughout her life. In 1897 she was investigating the Frenchman Delacourte's system of dramatic expression. Willard to Clara Colby, 4 June 1897, Clara Colby Papers.

12. Unidentified clipping, 1876, in scrapbook 4, WCTU series, reel 30, frame 207.

13. Scrapbook 4, WCTU series, reel 30.

14. Vincent to Willard, 6 June 1877, WCTU series, reel 11. See also Vincent, *John Heyl Vincent*, 122–23, 146. Willard and Vincent continued to spar over the role of women on the Chautauqua platform. Vincent wrote Willard in 1877, when he was trying to lure her to do a repeat performance, "I do want you at Chautauqua this summer. You think I do not deserve you. You think that I hamper and slight the lady-lecturers so much that I deserve to be snubbed by them without exception. Miss Willard, are you not an exception? Are you not womanly and yet are you not determined to talk?" Vincent to Willard, 7 January 1877. WCTU series, reel 11.

15. Scrapbook 4, p. 103, WCTU series, reel 30.

16. Livermore to Willard, 20 November 1876, WCTU series, reel 11.

17. Findlay's *Dwight L. Moody* is the most recent biography of Moody. The sketch of Moody in Johnson and Malone, *Dictionary of American Biography*, 7:103–6, is written by Lawrence C. Wroth.

18. *Glimpses*, 354–55; *Chicago Tribune*, 23 September (p. 9), 24 September (p. 8) 1876; Diary, 6 August 1867.

19. *Glimpses*, 356–57.

20. *Boston Journal*, undated, clipped in scrapbook 6, WCTU series, reel 30, frame 350. One of Willard's revival addresses is fully reported in *Our Union*, May 1877, clipped in WCTU series supplement, reel 3.

21. *Chicago Tribune*, 27 May 1877; see also scrapbooks 6 (frame 347ff.) and 7 (frame 398), WCTU series, reel 30.

22. *Glimpses*, 358–59.

23. Willard to Emma Moody, 5 September 1877 (draft), WCTU series, reel 11. This letter, essentially unchanged, appears in *Glimpses*, 359–60. Her relationship with Moody is discussed in Willard to the editor of the *Chicago Alliance*, 14 July 1877, and Willard to the editor of the *Boston Advertiser*, 25 July 1877, clipped in scrapbook 59, WCTU series, reel 11, frame 377. That scrapbook also contains clippings from the *Boston Globe*.

24. Willard to Emma Moody, 5 September 1877 (draft), WCTU series, reel 11.

25. Emma Moody to Willard, 20 August 1877, ibid.

26. Willard to Vincent, 27 September 1877, Frances Willard Papers, Schlesinger Library of Women's History, Radcliffe College.

27. *Glimpses*, 361.

28. Ibid., 358.

29. Bonner was the notorious publisher of the *New York Ledger* and Maud S. was a horse he used as a successful sulky racer.

30. *Glimpses*, 363.

31. Willard and Livermore, *Woman of the Century*, 326.

32. *Glimpses*, 676.

33. Gordon to Mary Hill Willard, 16 November 1880, WCTU series, reel 11.

34. See Cook, "Female Support Networks."

35. Diary, 27 October 1893, scrapbook 6, WCTU series, reel 30. In 1867 Oliver wrote Frances a long letter in which he reported that he was "in great financial trouble. But she commented that he was brave and true and freed from his great danger which we so bewailed" (Diary, 18 April 1867). As usual, however, this optimism was misplaced, for Frances's diary records on 10 June 1867: "Received a letter from Oliver's wife that smote my heart." This letter enclosed one from Oliver who was in Omaha and wrote that he hoped "God would pity my weakness and come to my aid." Willard's diaries from 1866 to 1868 frequently refer to Oliver's problems, but usually in an oblique way. I have not been able to trace a story told me in 1982 that Oliver Willard accidentally shot a man during a skeet shoot in Denver. The resulting emotional trauma was so intense that he took to drink, and his many troubles began. No account of such an incident appears in the *Rocky Mountain News* for the period. During Frances's European trip, Oliver and his family moved back to Evanston and lived part of the time with Mother Willard, who reported him "fully sustained in his self-denials." M. H. Willard to F. Willard, 14 July 1868, Evanston file, Willard Memorial Library.

36. *Glimpses*, 366.

37. Ibid., 367.

38. Ibid., 503–4.

39. *Chicago Post*, 17 May 1878, clipped in scrapbook 8, WCTU series, reel 30, frame 498.

40. *Chicago Post*, 27 April 1878, clipped in scrapbook 6, WCTU series, reel 30, frame 372.

41. Unidentified clipping, 27 April 1878, in scrapbook 8, WCTU series, reel 30, frames 439–40.

42. *Glimpses*, 505.

43. See Marzolf, *Up from the Footnote*, chap. 1. The one other woman who edited a metropolitan daily was Eliza Poitevant (after her husband's death) at the *New Orleans Daily Picayune*; she held the position from 1876 until 1878 when she married the paper's business manager. Poitevant was an editorial force, but did not attempt to handle business matters. Ibid., 18.

44. *Glimpses*, 506.

CHAPTER VII

1. Willard, *Glimpses of Fifty Years*, 351 (hereafter cited as *Glimpses*). Much the same account appeared earlier in Willard's *Woman and Temperance*, 450ff.

2. Willard to Wittenmyer, 27 May 1876, *Temperance and Prohibition Papers*, microfilm ed., WCTU series, reel 11 (hereafter cited as WCTU series).

3. *Zion's Herald*, August 1876, clipped in scrapbook 4, p. 101, WCTU series, reel 30.

4. Ibid.

5. Anthony to Willard, 18 September 1876, WCTU series, reel 11.

6. Anthony to Willard, 28 September 1876, ibid.

7. Ibid.

8. *Glimpses*, 401.

9. Willard stated in her autobiography that she first used the phrase "home protection" at a lecture on 4 July 1877 in New York City (ibid.). However, the phrase was used in drafting a resolution at the 1876 convention (see *Minutes of the National Woman's Christian Temperance Union*, 1876 convention, 119—hereafter cited as *Minutes*). And she titled her lecture at Beecher's church in November 1876, "Home Protection" (clipping in scrapbook 4, p. 103, WCTU series, reel 30). Willard's chronology in *Glimpses* is unreliable.

10. *Woman's Journal*, 14 October 1876, 1.

11. Willard's address, quoted in ibid. A version of her home protection address appears in Willard, *Woman and Temperance*, 451ff.

12. By the 1890s the WCTU had adopted the natural rights argument, at a time when the suffrage movement proper was moving in the direction of social expediency. See Bordin, *Woman and Temperance*, 57–58, 120–21, 204 (n. 14). The idea of giving women a special temperance ballot had a long history. For example, Stanton and Anthony had used it in appealing for passage of the Maine Law in 1853. See DuBois, *Stanton and Anthony*, 41.

13. WCTU series, reel 27, folder 116, frame 343. Willard may have prepared this document while writing *Glimpses* in 1889 when she frequently dictated to a secretary, although she nowhere uses in that volume the material as put together in this chronology.

14. See above, Chapter V, p. 62.

15. *Chicago Tribune*, 25 November (p. 7), 26 November (p. 4), 27 November (p. 2), 29 November (p. 3) 1873.

16. *Woman's Journal*, August 1876, clipped in scrapbook 4, p. 99, WCTU series, reel 30.

17. Resolution presented to Illinois WCTU convention in 1876, quoted in Earhart, *Frances Willard*, 153; also reproduced in Anna A. Gordon, *The Beautiful Life of Frances Willard*, 119.

18. Clipping from Newark newspaper, October 1876, in scrapbook 4, pp. 121–23, WCTU series, reel 30.

19. *Glimpses*, 352.

20. See Buhle, "Politics and Culture in Women's History."

21. See DuBois, "Politics and Culture in Women's History," for a formulation of this concept.

22. *Minutes*, 1876 convention, 114.

23. Banner, *Elizabeth Cady Stanton*, 45; see also Griffith, *In Her Own Right*.

24. Anthony and Harper, *History of Woman Suffrage*, 4:124–27, 140–42.

25. *The Morning and Day of Reform*, 24 November 1877, clipped in scrapbook 7, WCTU series, reel 30, frame 404.

26. Livermore to Stone, 11 November 1877, National American Woman Suffrage Association Papers.

27. *Minutes*, 1877 convention, 162.

28. Apparently Willard first withdrew, then reentered the presidential race when two other women were also nominated for president. Willard explained that she had vowed never to be part of a two-way race against Wittenmyer. *Chicago Tribune*, 27 October 1877, 3.

29. Willard discusses her differences with Wittenmyer in *Glimpses*, 368–69.

30. Willard to Wittenmyer, 8 September 1878, WCTU series, reel 11.

31. *Minutes*, 1878 convention, 27–35. The state unions officially supporting Willard were Iowa, Illinois, Indiana, and Minnesota from the Midwest, as well as Massachusetts, long a stronghold of suffrage sentiment.

32. *Minutes*, 1878 convention, 35.

33. Willard to Wittenmyer, 20 January 1879, WCTU series, reel 11.

34. Mary Lathbury in Willard, *Woman and Temperance*, 33.

35. Willard's *Woman and Temperance*, 362–70, contains a full account of the campaign.

36. *Chicago Tribune*, 7 March 1879, 6.

37. Clipping from Lewiston, Maine newspaper, 24 September 1881, in scrapbook 5, WCTU series, reel 30, frame 305.

38. *Washington Evening Star*, 26 October 1881, clipped in scrapbook 5, ibid.

39. Willard, *Evanston: A Classic Town*, 13–14.

40. Lillian Whiting in the *Boston Times-Democrat*, 2 August 1891, clipped in scrapbook 57, p. 63, WCTU series, reel 39.

41. See Davis, *American Heroine*, xi, 200–201. According to Davis, Willard and Addams used many of the same techniques.

42. *Toronto Citizen*, 1881, clipped in scrapbook 5, WCTU series, reel 30, frame 303.

43. Presidential address, *Minutes*, 1880 convention, 24.

44. *Minutes*: 1879 convention, 11–18; 1880 convention, 9–25.

45. *Minutes*, 1881 convention, 43.

46. Ibid., 51.

47. Willard to Gordon, 14 October 1881. Wittenmyer remained in the Union when defeated for the presidency, but withdrew with a few followers to form a rival organization after passage of the suffrage resolution. The split involved few people and did not attract a following; also, it was not permanent. In the 1886 minutes Wittenmyer is listed as legislative superintendent of the Pennsylvania union, although she was not a delegate to the national convention.

CHAPTER VIII

1. In *Glimpses of Fifty Years* (hereafter cited as *Glimpses*), Willard dated this venture 1878 (pp. 362–63), but her correspondence with Slayton indicates that it was November 1879 (*Temperance and Prohibition Papers*, microfilm ed., WCTU series, reel 11—hereafter cited as WCTU series).

2. *Glimpses*, 372–73.

3. Diary of Frances Willard, 4 April 1881 (hereafter cited as Diary). Overall, the diaries paint a less rosy picture of the southern tours than *Glimpses*.

4. Gordon to Mary Hill Willard, 18 March 1881, WCTU series, reel 12.

5. Diary, 1896.

6. Letter to the editor from Sallie Chapin, *Our Union*, 1881, clipped in scrapbook 5, WCTU series, reel 30, frame 285.

7. Reproduced in the *Evanston Index*, 16 July 1881, ibid., frame 289. Women preachers, if hardly the rule, were not uncommon in the antebellum South, but acceptance of women in that role sharply declined after the Civil War. See Sweet, *The Minister's Wife*.

8. Willard to Gordon, 11 April 1881, WCTU series, reel 12.

9. Willard to Gordon, from Kentucky, 24 November 1884, ibid., reel 13.

10. *Glimpses*, 373.

11. Presidential address, *Minutes of the National Woman's Christian Temperance Union*, 1881 convention, lxxv (hereafter cited as *Minutes*).

12. *Glimpses*, 373.

13. Gordon to Mary Hill Willard, 8 November 1881, WCTU series, reel 12. For a graphic description of travel on behalf of women's causes, see Anna Howard Shaw Papers, box 18, folder 420. Shaw was campaigning in South Dakota for woman suffrage, riding handcars to make connections when her train was late, fighting off bedbugs and mice while trying to sleep in stifling hot eight-by-seven-foot rooms, meanwhile thinking of rich eastern suffragists fanning themselves at watering places along the New England coast.

14. "A Card from Miss Willard," *Union Signal*, 14 March 1884, 3.

15. Willard to Gordon, 19 March 1885, WCTU series, reel 13. Gordon was not with Willard on this trip. Willard was accompanied by another WCTU officer.

16. Interview with Frances Willard in the Chicago magazine *Our Day*, May 1896, 258, clipped in scrapbook 71, WCTU series, reel 42, frame 530. See also correspondence, December 1888–January 1889, WCTU series, reel 15.

17. Report of the Woman's Christian Temperance Publishing Association in *Minutes*, 1889 convention, cxxviii.

18. Lathbury to Willard, 2 April 1883, WCTU series, reel 13.

19. Her defense of women's right to preach was not, of course, the first. Hardesty, *Women Called to Witness*, 162–64, contains a partial list of nineteenth-century American treatises defending women's ministry.

20. *Woman in the Pulpit* has been analyzed by Hardesty, "Minister as Prophet? Or as Mother?," 1:88–101.

21. See scrapbook 35 in the WCTU library in Evanston for material on *A Great Mother*.

22. Willard published *Occupations for Women* in collaboration with Helen Winslow and Sallie White. For an evaluation of its importance, see Frankfort, *Collegiate Women*, 90–91.

23. Douglas, *The Feminization of American Culture*, 226.

24. Presidential address, *Minutes*, 1886 convention, 79.

25. *New Orleans Daily Picayune*, 23 September 1886, clipped in scrapbook 30, WCTU series, reel 39, frame 8.

26. Willard to Mrs. A. G. Thorp, 11 July 1890, WCTU series, reel 16. The

"sky parlor" and the rest of Willard's home are maintained as a museum in Evanston by the National WCTU, and her library is on the shelves just as she left it.

27. Willard's column in the *Union Signal*, 25 February 1885, 6.

28. Diary, 29 November 1893.

29. Quoted in Gordon, *The Life of Frances E. Willard*, 9.

30. *Glimpses*, 695–96.

31. Memoir of Judge S. H. Beauchamp, 1898, WCTU series, reel 27, folder 114, frame 55.

32. *Chicago Record*, 3 September 1894, clipped in scrapbook 71, WCTU series, reel 42.

33. Reminiscences of Joseph L. Walker, 1898, WCTU series, reel 27, folder 114, frame 125.

34. Sarah K. Bolton, "Some Successful Women," in *Wide Awake*, February 1887, clipped in scrapbook 57, p. 18, ibid.

35. Scrapbook 19, WCTU series, reel 33, frame 333.

36. *Our Day*, May 1896, clipped in scrapbook 71, WCTU series, reel 42, frame 530.

37. Diary, 26 April 1867.

38. Gordon to Mary Hill Willard, 3 October 1882, WCTU series, reel 12.

39. Marie Mayfield, "Frances Willard as Woman and Worker," in *New Orleans Men and Matters* 2 (March 1896): 3, clipped in scrapbook 71, WCTU series, reel 42, frame 468.

40. See correspondence, April 1883, WCTU series, reel 13.

41. Willard to Mary Hill Willard, 7 April 1883, ibid.

42. Charles Bunting to Willard, 7 June 1889, WCTU series, reel 16.

43. Ruby to Anna Gordon, 14 December 1888, WCTU series, reel 15.

44. Willard to Mary Hill Willard, 26 March 1887, WCTU series, reel 14.

45. Earhart's *Frances Willard* contains a full account of the pertinent correspondence (pp. 312–19), and the nephews are fully discussed in the diaries and correspondence. Anna Gordon does not mention the family's problems in her biographies of Willard.

46. Unidentified clipping in scrapbook 71, WCTU series, reel 42, frame 360.

47. See Chambers-Schiller, "The Single Woman."

48. Willard to Mary Hill Willard, 3 July 1880, WCTU series, reel 12.

49. For example, see Willard to Dickinson, 6 October 1875, WCTU series, reel 11.

50. *New York Times*, 20 October 1888, 2.

51. Willard to Mary Hill Willard, 20 October 1888, WCTU series, reel 15.

52. Fisk to Mary Hill Willard, 22 October 1888, ibid. The *New York Times* also reported that there was standing room only and that many were turned away (21 October 1888, 6).

53. Memoir of Mary Hill Willard, WCTU series, reel 11, frame 329ff.

54. The convention is described in *Glimpses*, 454–57. The scrapbook for this convention is in the Willard Memorial Library, Evanston, and it is described in the correspondence. See also the *New York Times*, 20–24 October 1888.

55. *New York Times*, 24 October 1888, 2. For a discussion of this conflict see below, Chapter IX, and Bordin, *Woman and Temperance*, 125–29.

56. The *New York Times*'s accounts of the sessions are straightforward and factual. One headline had a baiting ring, "Free whiskey at temperance convention" (21 October 1888, 6), but the story itself made no mention of any such event. The *New York Herald* found the meetings to show that "women are more eloquent than men" (scrapbook 36, p. 46, in the Willard Memorial Library, Evanston).

CHAPTER IX

1. *Minutes of the National Woman's Christian Temperance Union*, 1880 convention, 18 (hereafter cited as *Minutes*).

2. Ibid., 9–25.

3. Lyman Abbott to Willard, 22 January 1879, *Temperance and Prohibition Papers*, microfilm ed., WCTU series, reel 11 (hereafter cited as WCTU series).

4. See Bordin, *Woman and Temperance*, 99–100. Freedman, *Their Sisters' Keepers*, discusses in detail women's organizations' special affinity for work with women prisoners and delinquents.

5. In *Woman and Temperance*, chap. 6, I did not quite understand how her use of this term changed over the years.

6. Presidential address, *Minutes*, 1882 convention, 64–66.

7. See Furner, *Advocacy and Objectivity*, chap. 1; Haskell, *Emergence of Professional Social Science*.

8. Presidential address, *Minutes*, 1883 convention, 634.

9. Ibid., 50.

10. These schemes long antedate Bellamy's arrangements in *Looking Backward* and Charlotte Perkins Gilman's approach in *Woman and Economics*. See Hayden, *Grand Domestic Revolution*.

11. Presidential address, *Minutes*, 1883 convention, 51–52.

12. See Pivar, *Purity Crusade*, 51. Pivar's book is the best account of the whole social purity movement including the role played by the WCTU, and provides comprehensive information on age of consent laws (pp. 141–43). However, Pivar states that early WCTU women were repelled by the social purity crusade (p. 85). I believe this is in error.

13. *Minutes*, 1883 convention, 39; Willard, *Glimpses of Fifty Years* (hereafter cited as *Glimpses*), 418–42; Bordin, *Woman and Temperance*, 110. Epstein, *Politics of Domesticity*, 125–28, discusses in some detail the social purity movement and Willard's relation to it. Epstein gives Willard too much credit for the program and not enough to membership initiative.

14. *Glimpses*, 419; *Minutes*, 1885 convention, 62.

15. Willard's presidential address, 1885, quoted in *Glimpses*, 20.

16. Pivar, *Purity Crusade*, 132–34; Rachel Strachey, *The Cause*, 218–21.

17. Frances Willard Papers, Schlesinger Library of Women's History, Radcliffe College.

18. Presidential address, *Minutes*, 1885 convention, quoted in *Glimpses*, 421.

19. Epstein, *Politics of Domesticity*, 125, 128.

20. *Glimpses*, 611–12, and *How to Win*, Willard's book of advice for young girls.

21. For discussions of why social reforms could result in strengthening male

control, see Vicinus, "Sexuality and Work," 143, and Walkowitz, *Prostitution and Victorian Society*, 210–13.

22. DuBois and Gordon, "Seeking Ecstasy on the Battlefield."

23. See Vicinus, "Sexuality and Work," 151.

24. *Minutes*, 1885 convention, 37–39.

25. The concept of "lending influence" as used by nineteenth-century women is discussed by Douglas, *The Feminization of American Culture*, chap. 2. Douglas sees this practice of "influence" as the mother of advertising and consumerism (p. 80), but also as the way women were able to use power. Ellen DuBois has regarded the moral reform societies of the antebellum period as the first practitioners of political influence in their use of the petition to promote an antiseduction law in the New York legislature. DuBois believes that petitioning was seen as an extraordinary activity and therefore pursuable by women without risking their womanliness. See her introduction to her collection, *Stanton and Anthony*, 6–7.

26. Willard to Mary Hill Willard, 26 August 1881, WCTU series, reel 12.

27. See Bordin, *Woman and Temperance*, 124–25; *Glimpses*, 382.

28. Presidential address, *Minutes*, 1882 convention, lxxxiv.

29. *Minutes*, 1882 convention, 28.

30. See Bordin, *Woman and Temperance*, 123–31, for a discussion of the split and its effects on the WCTU.

31. *Glimpses*, 437–53.

32. Fink, *Workingmen's Democracy*.

33. *Union Signal*, 3 June 1886, 20; Powderly, *Thirty Years of Labor*, 601.

34. The classic study of the Haymarket affair is David's *History of the Haymarket Affair*, first published in 1938. Avrich's *Haymarket Tragedy*, published in 1984, is the most recent account.

35. See Foner, *History of the Labor Movement*, 2:61–64.

36. See Destler, *Henry Demarest Lloyd*, 156–57; Jernigan, *Henry Demarest Lloyd*, 19–20; Thomas, *Alternative America*, 207–14.

37. Fink, *Workingmen's Democracy*, 19.

38. *Glimpses*, 522–25; Archie Jones, "Elizabeth Flynn Rodgers," in James and James, *Notable American Women*, 3, 187–88; Ann D. Gordon, "Alzina Stevens' Long Road to Hull House"; Lawrence Hobbs to Willard, 3 January 1887, WCTU series, reel 14.

39. Presidential address, *Minutes*, 1886 convention, 85–87.

40. Ibid., 85.

41. *Minutes*, 1886 convention, 138–39.

42. The address is reproduced in *Glimpses*, 413–15, and in scrapbook 12, WCTU series, reel 31, frames 478–80.

43. Powderly to Willard, 12 December 1886, WCTU series, reel 14.

44. *Union Signal*, 3 February (p. 1), 10 February (p. 8) 1887.

45. *Glimpses*, 423; Willard's column in the *Union Signal*, 17 February 1887, 4.

46. Earhart, *Frances Willard*, 75.

47. Willard to Mary Hill Willard, 22 February 1887, WCTU series, reel 14.

48. Stone to Willard, 28 March 1887, correspondence file in the Willard Memorial Library, Evanston.

49. Presidential address, *Minutes*, 1887 convention, 91.

50. See, for example, *Union Signal*, 22 December 1887, 5.

51. Willard to Lloyd, 4 January 1894, Henry Demarest Lloyd Papers.

52. See especially Smith-Rosenberg, *Religion and the Rise of the American City.*

53. See Rothman, *Discovery of the Asylum.*

54. For example, B. F. Skinner, who saw the world's problems as solvable via behavioral psychology in *Walden II* (New York: MacMillan Company, 1948) and *Beyond Freedom and Dignity* (New York: Alfred A. Knopf, 1971), was quoted in the *New York Times* (15 September 1981, 21) as saying that we were not really going to solve our problems, and that he was currently very pessimistic.

55. Quoted in Leach, *True Love and Perfect Union*, 337. Leach (chap. 11) presents a comprehensive analysis of late nineteenth-century women reformers and I am heavily indebted to his formulation. I am also indebted to Judy Papichristou and her comments at the session on Elizabeth Cady Stanton at the Fifth Berkshire Conference on the History of Women, Vassar College, 16–18 June 1981.

56. Lasch, *The New Radicalism in America*, xiii–xiv, believed this commitment to big government came later. Lasch saw American reformers embracing statist solutions around 1900.

57. *Glimpses*, 18.

58. Bellamy to Willard, 24 October 1887 and 3 January 1888, WCTU series, reel 15.

59. Presidential address, *Minutes*, 1888 convention, 53.

60. Buhle, *Women and American Socialism*, 74–82, has the best account of the relationship of Bellamyism and the woman movement. Leach, "Looking Forward Together," points up the dilemma Bellamyism posed for a movement that was essentially democratic and egalitarian. Lipow, in *Authoritarian Socialism*, a recent comprehensive study of the Nationalist movement, views Bellamy as a forerunner of twentieth-century totalitarianism. Lipow's study is marred by the fact that he does not analyze or explain the importance of the movement to women or the importance of women in the growth of the movement. Thomas, in *Alternative America*, also pays little heed to the importance of women in late nineteenth-century "alternative" movements.

61. Leach, "Looking Forward Together."

62. Wallace to Willard, 17 December 1889, WCTU series, reel 16. Bellamy defended his endorsement of wine and tobacco in a letter to Willard, 7 August 1888 (WCTU series supplement, reel 5). Bellamy himself was a tippler, but his female followers seem to have been unaware of this failing (see Thomas, *Alternative America*, 153–54). On the other hand, Willard was never able to support Eugene Debs because of his penchant for drink.

63. Bellamy to Willard, 1 February 1889, WCTU series, reel 16.

64. See below, Chapter XI.

65. Presidential address, *Minutes*, 1889 convention, 95–98, 116.

66. Ibid., 114–15, 145–46.

67. One of the best brief descriptions of Chicago in the last quarter of the nineteenth century, although it does not elaborate on women in Chicago, can be found in Wade, *Graham Taylor*, chap. 3.

68. *Woman's Journal*, 20 September 1890, 304.

69. Ruegamer, "Chicago Women Reformers," explores the Chicago wom-

en's network, especially in relation to the Woman's Club, in considerable detail. A more recent comprehensive study of Chicago philanthropy is McCarthy's *Noblesse Oblige*.

70. See above, Chapter IV, p. 56.

71. Ann D. Gordon, "Alzina Stevens' Long Road to Hull House." See also Buhle, *Women and American Socialism*, 71–73, for a brief discussion of Chicago women in the labor movement. A longer account can be found in Tax, *Rising of the Women*, chaps. 2–3.

72. Information on Elizabeth Morgan can be found in Ritter, "Elizabeth Morgan," and Scharnaw, "Elizabeth Morgan"; there is also a sketch of Elizabeth Rodgers in *Glimpses*, 522–25.

73. Ruegamer, "Chicago Women Reformers."

74. Ibid.

75. Ibid.

76. Leila C. Bedell to Willard, 12 June 1888, WCTU series, reel 15.

77. *Union Signal*, 11 October 1888, 8. The *Union Signal* is one of the best sources on the organization of the league and the alliance.

78. *Union Signal*, 1 March–5 April 1888; Willard's address, 1891, scrapbook 70, WCTU series, reel 37.

79. See below, Chapter X.

80. *Union Signal*, 23 August 1888, 1; Tax, *Rising of the Women*, chap. 4.

81. *Union Signal*, 11 October 1888, 8. The *Chicago Tribune*, 7 October 1888 (pp. 4, 25), reported this meeting in detail and reproduced Willard's address verbatim.

82. *Union Signal*, 1 November 1888, 1.

83. For a discussion of the work of the IWA, see Buhle, *Women and American Socialism*, 72; Tax, *Rising of the Women*, chap. 4.

84. See DuBois, "Limitations of Sisterhood"; Leach, *True Love and Perfect Union*.

85. Editorial, *Union Signal*, 12 April 1888, 4.

86. Goldmark, *Impatient Crusader*, 22.

CHAPTER X

1. See above, Chapter III, for an account of Willard's early religious rebellion and her conversion.

2. Willard to Dora Smith, 20 January 1864, Dora Smith Papers.

3. Diary of Frances Willard, January–March 1866 (hereafter cited as Diary).

4. Willard's testimony in Garrison, *Forty Witnesses*, 97–98. Two recent accounts of the holiness revival are Jones's *Perfectionist Persuasion* and Dieter's *Holiness Revival*.

5. Diary, January–March 1866.

6. See above, Chapter V.

7. Willard to Mary Hill Willard, 1 June 1882, *Temperance and Prohibition Papers*, microfilm ed., WCTU series, reel 12 (hereafter cited as WCTU series).

8. Diary, 6 July 1857.

9. Ibid., 17 March 1862.

10. Ibid., 23 March 1862.

11. Cones to Willard, 14 April 1888 (WCTU series, reel 15), arranging a meeting with Willard when Cones was to be in Chicago.

12. See Willard to Clara Colby, 4 June 1897 (Clara Colby Papers), expressing the depth of her interest in Besant and her ideas, although they had not met. For a thorough analysis of the appeal of spiritualism to the nineteenth-century American public, see Moore, *In Search of White Crows*, pt. 1.

13. See Porterfield, *Feminine Spirituality*, 106–7.

14. See ibid., chap. 6.

15. New York: Harper and Brothers. Winchell, prominent Methodist layman and early adherent of Darwinian theory, argued that reason is the only criterion of truth and that divine revelation must be subjected to rational authentication. In this volume he professes a growing belief in Darwinian theories.

16. Winchell to Willard, 7 September 1878, WCTU series, reel 11.

17. *Glimpses of Fifty Years*, 627–28 (hereafter cited as *Glimpses*).

18. Presidential address, *Minutes of the National Woman's Christian Temperance Union*, 1893 convention, 77–78, 114–15 (hereafter cited as *Minutes*). In the late nineteenth century, Christianity was surprisingly accepting of the other great religions. Perhaps the epitome of this acceptance was reached at the World's Parliament of Religions at the Columbian Exposition of 1893. For a recent analysis of American Protestantism in the 1880s and 1890s, see Szasz, *Divided Mind of American Protestantism*. The conservative response to the ecumenical challenge was muted until the early twentieth century.

19. Quoted in Anna A. Gordon, *The Life of Frances E. Willard*, 149–51.

20. Ibid., 266.

21. For example, James, *Women in American Religion*, uses this fact as the first statement in her introduction to that volume.

22. See ibid., 10.

23. Willard to Mary Hill Willard, 10 May 1880; Willard to General Conference, 14 May 1880; Gordon to Mary Hill Willard, 17 May 1880; F. J. Stanley to Mary Hill Willard, 18 May 1880. WCTU series, reel 12.

24. Clippings from the *Chicago Inter Ocean*, *Cincinnati Gazette*, and *Illinois Signal* (among other newspapers) can be found in scrapbook 14, pp. 34–36, WCTU series, reel 32.

25. *Illinois Signal*, May 1880, clipped in scrapbook 14, p. 36, ibid.

26. *Daily Christian Advocate*, 16 May 1880, clipped in scrapbook 14, WCTU series, reel 32, frame 328.

27. *Glimpses*, 616–17.

28. Gordon to Mary Hill Willard, 27 May 1880, WCTU series, reel 12.

29. *Chicago Tribune*, 24 May–1 June 1880, covered the assembly sessions in detail.

30. For example, see Buckley to Willard, 3 October 1887, WCTU series, reel 14.

31. Presidential address, *Minutes*, 1880 convention, 13.

32. For an analysis of *Woman in the Pulpit* see Hardesty, "Minister as Prophet? Or as Mother?," 1:88–101. I am less convinced than Hardesty that woman as mother was Willard's goal. Willard used that language from time to time, but her whole attitude was to push women forward in new ways.

33. *Woman in the Pulpit*, chap. 1.

34. Ibid., 45.

35. Gordon to Mary Hill Willard, 5 October 1887, WCTU headquarters file, Willard Memorial Library. See also *Glimpses*, 617.

36. *Glimpses*, 618.

37. Hamilton to Willard, 12 March 1888, WCTU series, reel 15.

38. Extensive clippings from the Methodist press in 1888 can be found in scrapbook 38 in the Willard Memorial Library, WCTU headquarters. Unfortunately this scrapbook was not found until after the microfilm edition was completed.

39. *New York Times*, 29 April 1888, 11.

40. Ibid., 3 May 1888, 9.

41. Willard to Gordon, 30 April 1888, WCTU series, reel 15.

42. Willard to Gordon, 4 May 1888, ibid.

43. Mary Earhart (*Frances Willard*, 300–301) believed Willard used her mother's illness to avoid personally exposing herself to an unpleasant and wounding fight. I do not agree. Willard clearly wished to be in New York directing the battle firsthand, but she believed duty demanded she be at her mother's side. In *Glimpses* she protests that after the bishops showed their hostility to women on the opening day she "would have nothing to do with the controversy" (pp. 620–21), but her correspondence belies this later interpretation of her feelings.

44. *New York Times*, 29 April 1888, 11.

45. Ibid., 1 May 1888, 4.

46. Ibid., 4 May 1888, 9.

47. Ibid., 8 May 1888, 9. Interestingly, when the first woman delegate was elected to the British General Synod (1894), she was accepted as eligible to serve. *Woman's Journal*, 22 June 1895, 196.

48. *New York Times*, 8 May 1888, 9.

49. Elwood Starr Harris in Johnson and Malone, *Dictionary of American Biography*, 2:231–32.

50. Presidential address, *Minutes*, 1888 convention, 42–45.

51. *Union Signal*, 19 February 1891, 13.

52. Editorial, ibid., 16 April 1891, 8; *Woman's Journal*, 25 April 1891. Examples of such criticism appear in clippings from the *Pacific Methodist Advocate* and *Zion's Herald*, scrapbook 50, WCTU series, reel 37, frame 157.

53. Clippings in scrapbook 38, Willard Memorial Library, WCTU headquarters.

54. *Christian Advocate*, 24 September 1891.

55. *The Church Union*, 15 October 1891.

56. For an analysis of the fight within Methodism over women's place in church councils, see Keller, "Creating a Sphere for Women," 246–60. Keller discusses the long battle for women to participate in church governance within this context, although she does not discuss Willard's experience in 1888 in any detail.

57. See Bordin, "Upon This Rock"; Blocker, *Give to the Wind Thy Fears*.

58. Diary, 2 July 1855.

59. *Zion's Herald*, August 1876, clipped in scrapbook 4, WCTU series, reel 30.

60. Reported in the *Union Signal*, 10 November 1881, 2.

61. Willard's column in ibid., 3 March 1887, 4.

62. Livermore to Mrs. Smith, 30 July 1888, National American Woman Suffrage Association Papers.

63. The convention did not vote directly on this issue. Instead, it empowered the general officers to present the WCTU cause to what they called "influential bodies." *Minutes*, 1890 convention, 18.

64. Willard to Gordon, 4 August 1891, WCTU series, reel 16. This letter is misplaced and can be found under that date in the 1890 correspondence.

65. Willard to Gordon, 5 August 1891, WCTU series, reel 17; *Washington Post*, 6 August 1891.

66. Willard to Gordon, 6 August 1891, WCTU series, reel 17.

67. Clipping, September 1891, in scrapbook 56, p. 70, WCTU series, reel 56.

68. Clipping, 4 November 1891, in scrapbook 56, pp. 75–76, WCTU series, reel 38.

69. Parkhurst to Willard, 17 August 1891, WCTU series, reel 17.

70. *Union Signal*, 20 August 1891, 5.

71. Ibid., 27 August (p. 5), 3 September (pp. 2–3) 1891.

72. *Minutes*, 1891 convention, 96.

73. Ibid., 181–82.

74. See ibid., 1895 convention, 22, 38.

75. Ibid., 50.

76. Ibid., 38.

77. *Bridgeport Evening Farmer*, 29 November 1895, clipped in scrapbook 70, WCTU series, reel 42, frame 143.

78. Katherine Stevenson to Willard, 7 January 1896, WCTU series, reel 23.

79. *Chicago Tribune*, 3 March 1898, 8.

80. See McLoughlin and Bellah, *Religion in America*, xvi.

81. Ibid.

82. Scrapbook 13, WCTU series, reel 32, deals with *The Woman's Bible* and contains a large variety of clippings as well as other sources. See also Banner, *Elizabeth Cady Stanton*, 161–65, and Griffith, *In Her Own Right*, 210–13, for a discussion of *The Woman's Bible*.

83. See DuBois, "Limitations of Sisterhood"; Banner, *Elizabeth Cady Stanton*, 157.

84. *Union Signal*, 30 May 1895, 1.

85. Willard to Stanton, 1 August 1895, scrapbook, vol. 2, Elizabeth Cady Stanton Papers, Vassar College Library. Willard and Susan Anthony had long since agreed to respect each other's views on religion. To affirm their laissez-faire attitude, Anthony had written, "Let's you and I—my dear—stick together on this point—that neither *knows* she's right." Anthony to Willard, 23 May 1888, WCTU series, reel 15.

86. See Welter, "The Feminization of American Religion."

87. Miller, "Frances Elizabeth Willard," analyzes the relationship of Willard to the Social Gospel movement.

88. See Buhle, *Women and American Socialism*, 64.

89. Ibid.

90. Gutman, *Work, Culture and Society*, chap. 2.

91. Buhle, *Women and American Socialism*, xvi.

1. For a discussion of the Prohibition party in the 1890s see Blocker, *Retreat from Reform*, 68–92. Blocker points out that Prohibitionists claimed that in local elections in nineteen states they pulled 1,676,603 votes for their cause at a time (1892) when they obtained only a quarter of a million votes for their presidential candidate (p. 69). But the growing strength of the farmers' movement was eroding their ranks.

2. The two most comprehensive studies of Populism pay no attention to the attempt in 1890 to organize a reform coalition that included women, Prohibitionists, and Populists. Goodwyn's *Democratic Promise* does not discuss the efforts from 1891 to 1896 to bring Prohibitionists and Populists together. His account of the machinations of 1891–92, which led to the formal organization of the People's party and the fielding of a presidential slate, ignored Willard's and the Prohibitionists' overtures to the Populists both in Chicago in January 1892 and the St. Louis Industrial Congress that followed. Hicks, in *The Populist Revolt*, chap. 8, mentions the presence of Prohibitionists at the Cincinnati conference and reports that Willard headed a small WCTU delegation in St. Louis, but he does not discuss these developments fully. However, Blocker in his study of the Prohibition party, *Retreat from Reform*, describes in detail the effort to arrange a union between Prohibitionists and the new party.

3. Willard's papers do not indicate why she did not attend. Helen Gougar, the Prohibition party's most active woman leader, found Willard a problem and conversely; they certainly did not admire each other. Gougar may not have wanted her there so Willard may not have been invited. Or Willard may have been too busy. She kept no diary that year.

4. *Chicago Tribune*, 20–21 May 1891, 1–2.

5. Willard to Henry Demarest Lloyd, 22 October 1891, Henry Demarest Lloyd Papers; Willard correspondence, Fall 1891, *Temperance and Prohibition Papers*, microfilm ed., WCTU series, reel 17 (hereafter cited as WCTU series).

6. *Chicago Tribune*, 28 January 1892.

7. Ibid. Donnelly's biographer merely mentions this meeting. See Ridge, *Ignatius Donnelly*, 294. Willard and Donnelly first began to correspond in April 1889 when she wrote him on publication of *The Great Cryptogram*, in which he attempted to prove Francis Bacon had written Shakespeare's plays. See Willard correspondence, April 1889, WCTU series, reel 16. The Donnelly Papers in the Minnesota Historical Society do not throw light on the conference, although they contain Willard's letters to Donnelly.

8. *Chicago Tribune*, 28 January 1892, 2; Blocker, *Retreat from Reform*, 54.

9. *Chicago Tribune*, 28 January 1892, 2; Blocker, *Retreat from Reform*, 55.

10. Hannah Whitall Smith to Willard, 2 February 1891, WCTU series, reel 17.

11. Fitzpatrick's *Lady Henry Somerset* is the major biographical study of Lady Henry and includes the most detail. Anna Gordon, who of course knew her well, also discusses Lady Henry and her relationship with Willard in her *Life of Frances E. Willard* (hereafter cited as Gordon, *Willard*). There are many clippings about Somerset in the Willard scrapbooks, and Hooper, *Reigate*, gives genealogical information and material on the family's property holdings. Lady Henry was a dedicated philanthropist, reformer, and political activist

who exercised considerable influence in both Britain and the United States. She deserves a new biography that properly assesses that influence.

12. Fitzpatrick, *Lady Henry Somerset*, 100–107.

13. *Our Message* (Boston), April 1892, clipped in scrapbook 55, pp. 49–50, WCTU series, reel 38.

14. Dow to Willard, 3 May 1892, WCTU series, reel 18.

15. Gordon, *Willard*, 188–89.

16. Blocker, *Retreat from Reform*, 56. The minutes of the executive committee of the Prohibition party do not mention the St. Louis conference and the maneuvering for fusion that went on there. Minutes, Prohibition Party Executive Committee, 23 February 1892, *Temperance and Prohibition Papers*, microfilm ed., Prohibition party series, reel 1.

17. *Chicago Evening Post*, 26 February 1892, and *Springfield* (Ill.) *Liberator*, 23 February 1892, clipped in scrapbook 54, pp. 75, 77, WCTU series, reel 38; Blocker, *Retreat from Reform*, 57.

18. *Chicago Tribune*, 24 February 1892, 2; *Chicago Interocean*, 23 February 1892, clipped in scrapbook 54, p. 72, WCTU series, reel 32.

19. *Chicago Tribune*, 23 February 1892, 10.

20. Blocker agrees with this assessment; see *Retreat from Reform*, 56.

21. *Chicago Tribune*, 25 February 1892, 2.

22. Ibid.; Blocker, *Retreat from Reform*, 56–58; *Union Signal*, 3 March 1892, 8. Scrapbook 54, pp. 71–76, 95, WCTU series, reel 38, contains the details of this battle.

23. *Chicago Evening Post*, 26 February 1892, clipped in scrapbook 54, p. 75, WCTU series, reel 38.

24. *Union Signal*, 3 March 1892, 8.

25. Wheeler to Lady Henry Somerset, 4 March 1892, scrapbook 71, WCTU series, reel 42, frame 473.

26. *Union Signal*, 16 June 1892, 1.

27. Ibid., 7 July 1892, 8–9.

28. Willard herself wrote the account of the convention in ibid., 7 July 1892, 8–9.

29. *Minutes of the National Woman's Christian Temperance Union*, 1892 convention, 57.

30. *New York World*, 17 November 1892, clipped in scrapbook 57, WCTU series, reel 39, frame 276.

31. *Chicago Herald*, 18 July 1894, clipped in scrapbook 71, WCTU series, reel 42.

32. Preface by Lady Henry Somerset to Gordon, *Willard*, xi.

33. See above, p. 19.

34. *Chicago Herald*, 18 July 1894, clipped in scrapbook 71, WCTU series, reel 42.

35. *Union Signal*, 7 July 1892, 9.

CHAPTER XII

1. Quoted in Anna A. Gordon, *The Life of Frances E. Willard*, 153 (hereafter cited as Gordon, *Willard*). Italics mine.

2. See Brumberg, "Zenanas and Girlless Villages." Said, in *Orientalism*, analyzes the attraction of the East for the Western world.

3. Margaret Lucas, president of the B W T A, to Willard, 25 January 1887, *Temperance and Prohibition Papers*, microfilm ed., W C T U series, reel 14 (hereafter cited as W C T U series).

4. *Union Signal*, 14 November 1891, 2.

5. The best overall treatments of the women's movement in England are still the works of two of Britain's leading feminists of the 1920s: Rachel Strachey's *The Cause, Group Movements in the Past*, and *Millicent Garrett Fawcett*; and Vera Brittain's *Lady unto Woman*. Brian Harrison, in *Separate Spheres*, has provided a more recent picture of the movement, although from the opposite side.

6. See Rachel Strachey, *The Cause*, 277–79.

7. See Harrison, *Drink and the Victorians*.

8. J. R. Greenway, "Bishop, Brewers, and the Liquor Question," unpublished paper made available by the author; see also Harrison, *Drink and the Victorians*, 101, chap. 2, and Winskill, *The Temperance Movement*, vol. 1.

9. Francis P. Weisenburger in James and James, *Notable American Women*, 3:376–77.

10. Accounts of Hannah Smith's life and work appear in Logan Pearsall Smith's *Unforgotten Years* and *Philadelphia Quaker*, and in Barbara Strachey's *Remarkable Relations*. The Hannah Whitall Smith Papers are in the possession of her great-granddaughter, Barbara Strachey [Halpern] of Oxford, England.

11. Thistlethwaite's *America and the Atlantic Community* is the classic essay on the Anglo-American connection. Although he deals with an earlier period, much of what Thistlethwaite has to say about "the Anglo-American world of humanitarian endeavor" also applies later in the century. Hall's essay, "The Victorian Connection," is the best recent account of this well-developed Anglo-American community. Hall also concentrates on an earlier time and an earlier group, but, again, many of the characteristics he points to continue to appear throughout the century. Marcus, "Transatlantic Sisterhood," discusses the later transatlantic connections of the suffrage movement.

12. Rachel Strachey, *The Cause*, 166–69.

13. Banner, *Elizabeth Cady Stanton*, 23–27.

14. Daniel Walker Howe, "Victorian Culture in America," 4.

15. Grant to Willard, 18 April 1896, W C T U series, reel 24.

16. Merrick, *Old Times in Dixieland*, 148.

17. Smith, *Philadelphia Quaker*, 113.

18. Ibid.

19. Lady Henry to Countess Somers, 2 November 1891, quoted in Fitzpatrick, *Lady Henry Somerset*, 172.

20. Smith, *Philadelphia Quaker*, 115.

21. Ibid. The originals of these letters reproduced and abstracted in the *Philadelphia Quaker* are in the Hannah Whitall Smith Papers.

22. Lady Henry Somerset, Introduction to Anna A. Gordon, *The Beautiful Life of Frances Willard*, 15 (hereafter cited as Gordon, *Beautiful Life*).

23. *Woman's Herald*, 17 December 1892; *Review of Reviews* (U.K.), 15 October 1892; *Pall Mall Gazette*, September 1892, clipped in scrapbook 57, W C T U series, reel 39.

24. Lady Henry Somerset's Introduction to Anna A. Gordon, *The Life of Frances E. Willard*, ix, x (hereafter cited as Gordon, *Willard*).

25. Ibid., x, xiii.

26. Diary of Frances Willard, 8 January 1893 (hereafter cited as Diary).

27. Ibid., 1 November 1893.

28. Ibid., 7 January 1893.

29. Ibid., 1896.

30. Ibid., 18 August 1896.

31. Ibid., 18 October 1896.

32. Ibid., 9 October 1893.

33. Ibid., 19 October 1893.

34. Fitzpatrick, *Lady Henry Somerset*, 184.

35. Diary, July–August 1893.

36. *Chicago Evening Post*, 8 November 1892, clipped in scrapbook 57, pp. 133–34, WCTU series, reel 39; Diary, 1 January, 13 October 1893.

37. Willard, quoted in Gordon, *Beautiful Life*, 272. I am grateful to Regina Moranz for sharing with me an unpublished manuscript on Greene.

38. Palmer's speech was reproduced in full in the *Chicago Tribune*, 2 May 1893. For a general account of women's role in the fair, see Badger, *The Great American Fair*.

39. Palmer to Willard, 15 December 1891, WCTU series, reel 17.

40. Diary, 2 November 1893. This entry is misplaced on the page for 26 October.

41. *Chicago Evening Post*, 8, 14 November 1892, clipped in scrapbook 57, pp. 133–34, WCTU series, reel 39.

42. Fitzpatrick, *Lady Henry Somerset*, 184–90. Hannah Smith's circular letter to her American friends, #62, 26 May, 6 June 1892, Hannah Whitall Smith Papers.

43. An annotated copy of the BWTA plan of work, 1893–94, delineates the two points of view. WCTU series, reel 19, frame 78.

44. Diary, 16 January 1893.

45. Ibid., 24 January 1893.

46. Ibid., 14 February 1893.

47. Ibid., 28 May–1 June 1893.

48. See scrapbook 57, WCTU series, reel 39, for the press clippings that document Willard's triumphal journey through the British Isles in 1893.

49. For example, in her diary for 14 February 1893 Willard records that absurd implications were being made that she wanted to carry off the BWTA, by which I assume she meant, take over its leadership.

50. *Chicago Tribune*, 4 May 1893, 5; Winskill, *The Temperance Movement*, 4:260.

51. Diary, 18 February 1893.

52. For a detailed account of the Temple crisis and the attendant personality conflicts, see Bordin, *Woman and Temperance*, 140–48.

53. Diary, 18 February 1893.

54. Ibid., 25 February 1893.

55. Ibid., January–April 1893.

56. Barker to Stevens, 25 February 1893, WCTU series, reel 19.

57. Katherine Stevenson to Willard, 8 April 1893, ibid.; *Chicago Tribune*, 4 May 1893, 5.

58. Diary, 9 April 1893. Because of ill health Willard was absent for one full day of the 1890 convention; she was ill for some weeks in late December and early January 1891, after the death of her young friend and colleague, Julia Ames. But both times she appeared to recover fully, and her illness did not persist or seriously limit her activities until 1893.

59. Hannah Smith circular letter, 30 September 1892, Hannah Whitall Smith Papers.

60. Memorandum, April 1893, WCTU series, reel 19, frame 1186; Hannah Smith to Willard, 20 April 1893, WCTU series, reel 19.

61. Anna Gordon to Mary Woodbridge et al., 26 April 1893, WCTU series, reel 19.

62. Diary, June 1893.

63. Ibid., 23 July 1893.

64. Ibid., 6 August 1893.

65. Ibid., 4 May 1893.

66. Ibid., 22 September 1893.

67. Ibid., 14 August 1893.

68. Ibid., 21 July 1893.

69. See Higham, "American Culture in the 1890s," in his *Writing American History*, 80–81.

70. Correspondence, Summer 1892, WCTU series, reel 18.

71. Diary, 6 September 1896.

72. Clipped in scrapbook 75, p. 29, WCTU series, reel 44.

73. Rachel Strachey, who was Hannah Smith's granddaughter, made an interesting comment in the margin of an early Willard diary. Strachey wrote above the entry for 21 February 1863 (Willard was twenty-four at the time and teaching in Pittsburgh), "observe F *never* arranges for rest and exercise. Oh the pity of it." Strachey knew Willard in England as a child, and may well have observed both her illness and her valiant attempts to change its course through exercise, rest, and diet.

74. Diary, 19 July 1893.

75. Ibid., 3, 12 April 1893.

76. Ibid., 3 April 1893. The Webbs had been friends of the Pearsall Smiths at least since 1890 before the Webbs were married. Webb, *My Apprenticeship*, 410.

77. Harrison, *Drink and the Victorians*, 395–96.

78. Diary, 1 August 1893. The diary is clear about both women joining the Fabians at that time. On 21 March 1894, however, Edward R. Pease wrote Anna Gordon that, although Willard was a member of the society, Lady Henry was not "duly and formally joined." Special WCTU Correspondence File, Willard Memorial library.

79. Diary, 24 July 1893. The Fabian Society was founded in 1883. The strong initial influence of Marxism on the movement as well as the liberal tradition of John Stuart Mill was responsible for its members embracing a definitely socialist position, which put Fabianism in the mainstream of worldwide social democracy. See McBriar, *Fabian Socialism*, chap. 1; MacKenzie and MacKenzie, *The First Fabians*.

80. Diary, 1 August 1893.

81. Ibid., 13 May 1893.

82. Ibid., 10 May 1893.

83. Until her diaries became available, it was not clear how ill Willard was, and whether ill health was excuse as well as reason for her absence from the 1893 convention (see Bordin, *Woman and Temperance*, 141–42). The problem of motive was complicated by the fact that reassuring reports were given out in both correspondence and the press to hide the seriousness of Willard's condition, and she did considerable traveling but only under optimal conditions. She did not speak or meet the public, although she was sometimes quoted in the press.

84. Diary, 26 July 1893.

85. Ibid., 5 September 1893.

86. Ibid., 5, 22 September 1893.

87. *Minutes of the National Woman's Christian Temperance Union*, 1893 convention, 104–5 (hereafter cited as *Minutes*).

88. Diary, 3 October 1893. Alys Smith, Hannah Smith's daughter and first wife of Bertrand Russell, accompanied Lady Henry, whose son was in America to hunt near Hudson Bay.

89. Ibid., 7–8 October 1893.

90. Correspondence among Anna Gordon, Willard, and Lady Henry, September, October 1893, WCTU series, reel 20; Diary, September, October 1893.

91. Diary, 20 October 1893.

92. Anna Gordon to Willard, 29 October 1893, WCTU series, reel 20.

93. Flyleaf of 1893 diary.

94. Diary, 21 October 1893.

95. *Minutes*, 1893 convention, 17.

96. Diary, 5 November 1893.

97. Ibid., 2 December 1893.

98. Fitzpatrick, *Lady Henry Somerset*, 196.

99. Memorandum, April 1894, WCTU series, reel 21.

100. Willard to Brother Fitch, 24 April 1894, ibid.

CHAPTER XIII

1. *Chicago Tribune*, 21 June 1894, 2.

2. Correspondence, June–September 1894, *Temperance and Prohibition Papers*, microfilm ed., WCTU series, reel 21 (hereafter cited as WCTU series).

3. *Union Signal*, 5 January 1893, 1; 16 November 1893, 8–9.

4. Presidential address, *Minutes of the National Woman's Christian Temperance Union*, 1893 convention, 138 (hereafter cited as *Minutes*).

5. Wells-Barnett, *On Lynchings* (see *Southern Horrors*, pp. 7–8).

6. Ibid., *A Red Record*, chap. VIII.

7. Ibid.

8. The letter is in scrapbook 13, WCTU series, reel 32, which also contains a telegram from Garrison to Willard denying Wells's accusation that he had later withdrawn his signature. This scrapbook (frame 218ff.) contains correspondence, clippings, and other materials on the lynching controversy.

9. Convention problems are discussed in the 1894 correspondence, WCTU series, reel 21. The press reports of the convention are in scrapbook 11, reel 31.

10. *Cleveland Leader*, 22 November 1894, clipped in scrapbook 70, pp. 6–7, WCTU series, reel 42; *Minutes*, 1894 convention, 49–51.

11. Presidential address, *Minutes*, 1894 convention, 104.

12. *Union Signal*, 27 December 1894, 4.

13. T. R. Carksadon to Willard, 2 February 1895, WCTU series, reel 21.

14. Bain to Willard, 17 August 1893, WCTU series, reel 20.

15. *Illinois Watch Tower*, 15 October 1895, clipped in scrapbook 70, WCTU series, reel 42, frame 191.

16. *Evanston Index*, 26 October 1895, clipped in scrapbook 70, WCTU series, reel 42, frame 142.

17. *New York World*, 18 November 1894, clipped in scrapbook 70, p. 2, WCTU series, reel 42.

18. *Florida Reporter*, January 1895, clipped in scrapbook 70, WCTU series, reel 42, frame 14.

19. *Union Signal*, 7, 14, 21 March 1895.

20. Ibid., 21 February 1895, 1.

21. Undated memorandum, 1895 correspondence, WCTU series, reel 21, frame 455.

22. *Christian World*, August 1895, clipped in scrapbook 13, WCTU series, reel 32, frame 220.

23. *Bonds of Brotherhood*, June 1895, clipped in ibid.

24. Hannah Smith to her daughter, 13 March 1895, Hannah Whitall Smith Papers. Scrapbook 13, WCTU series, frame 218ff., contains not only clippings but also correspondence pertaining to this struggle. Willard's letter defending herself to William Lloyd Garrison is in the Garrison Family Papers.

25. *Woman's Journal*, 25 May 1895, 163.

26. *The Kentucky White Ribbon*, November 1895, clipped in scrapbook 70, WCTU series, reel 42, frame 148.

27. Diary of Frances Willard, 2 March 1896 (hereafter cited as Diary).

28. *Chattanooga Times*, 20 December 1895, clipped in scrapbook 72, WCTU series, reel 42, frame 77.

29. Diary, 22 February 1896.

30. Ibid., Palatka, Fla., 12 February 1896.

31. Diary, 15 March 1896.

32. Ibid., 1 March 1896.

33. Ibid., 23 February 1896.

34. Ibid., 28 March 1896.

CHAPTER XIV

1. Diary of Frances Willard, 27 February, 19 April 1896 (hereafter cited as Diary).

2. Ibid., 19 April 1896. See also clippings, scrapbook 72, *Temperance and Prohibition Papers*, microfilm ed., WCTU series, reel 43 (hereafter cited as WCTU series).

3. Diary, 1 March 1896.

4. Ibid., 30 April 1896.

5. Ibid., 1 May 1896.

6. Ibid., 14 October 1893.

7. Ibid., 28 June 1896.

8. Ibid., 4 June 1896.

9. Lang's *Armenia* is a brief recent account of Armenian history, culture, and religion. Greene's *Armenian Crisis in Turkey* was an influential contemporary account of the Armenian question. Greene had been a missionary in Van for many years.

10. Scrapbook 75, WCTU series, reel 44, is devoted to the Armenian question and Willard's activities in its behalf, and contains clippings from a number of American and British newspapers. The *Woman's Journal* also covered the London protest (1 June 1895, 174–75).

11. See scrapbook 70, WCTU series, reel 42, frame 254, and correspondence, April 1896, ibid., reel 24; *Minutes of the National Woman's Christian Temperance Union*, 1895 convention, 54 (hereafter cited as *Minutes*).

12. See Brumberg, "Zenanas and Girlless Villages" and "The Ethnological Mirror."

13. *Union Signal*, 23 January (p. 1), 30 January (p. 9) 1896; *Woman's Journal*, 8 February 1896, 44.

14. *Union Signal*, 26 November 1896, 4.

15. Diary, 7 February 1896.

16. Ibid., 10 July 1896.

17. Correspondence, September 1896, WCTU series, reel 24; Diary, Fall 1896.

18. The full story of the Marseilles relief effort is told in clippings from a variety of newspapers in scrapbook 75, WCTU series, reel 44. Anna Gordon has a chapter entitled "Answering Armenia's Cry" in her memorial volume, *The Beautiful Life of Frances Willard* (hereafter cited as Gordon, *Beautiful Life*). Willard's diary, 1896, describes the efforts day by day.

19. Diary, 22 October 1896.

20. Among the newspapers expressing these sentiments were the *Detroit Tribune* (29 September 1896), *Buffalo Times* (24 September 1896), and *Rochester Chronicle* (28 September 1896).

21. *Chicago Observer*, 17 October 1896, clipped in scrapbook 75, WCTU series, reel 44.

22. Diary, 20–21, 31 October 1896.

23. See Brumberg, "Zenanas and Girlless Villages," for an analysis of the relationship of foreign missionary work to American women's perceptions of their own favored position in contrast to that of women in much of the world. Patricia R. Hill's *The World Their Household* is the most recent account of the missionary movement and concentrates on the women missionaries themselves.

24. *Woman's Journal*, 6 July 1895, 214.

25. Quoted in Gordon, *Beautiful Life*, 266.

26. Presidential address, *Minutes*, 1893 convention, 114–15.

27. Diary, 10 January 1896.

28. *Union Signal*, 4 June 1896, 1.

29. Willard to Stevens, 29 June 1896, WCTU series, reel 24.

30. *Union Signal*, 11 June 1896, 1.

31. Stevenson to state presidents, undated 1896, WCTU series, reel 24. See other correspondence between Willard and the Chicago office, 1896, ibid.

32. *Minutes*, 1896 convention, 72.

33. Gordon to L. M. N. Stevens, 29 May 1896, WCTU series, reel 24.

34. Diary, 5 June 1896.

35. Ibid., 11 July 1896.

36. Mary Hill, *Charlotte Perkins Gilman*, chap. 3.

37. Diary, 26 July 1896.

38. Gordon to L. M. N. Stevens, 6 May 1897, WCTU series, reel 24.

39. Gordon to L. M. N. Stevens, 1 January 1897; Willard to L. M. N. Stevens, 15 February 1897; Bessie Wilberforce to Willard, 9 March 1897. Ibid.

40. Lady Henry to L. M. N. Stevens, 7 September 1897, ibid.

41. Willard to Mary Lowe Dickenson, 1 December 1896, ibid.

42. Willard to Shaw, 7 June 1897, Anna Howard Shaw Papers.

43. Two recent studies of the Contagious Diseases Acts that take quite different points of view are Walkowitz's *Prostitution and Victorian Society* and McHugh's *Prostitution and Victorian Social Reform*. Walkowitz treats the Contagious Diseases Acts as part of Victorian reformers' enthusiasm for intervening in the lives of the poor and stresses their importance as a feminist issue. McHugh's study, instead of emphasizing the feminist position on the legislation, is concerned with pointing out its place in the movement toward preventive medicine and actual reduction in the incidence of venereal disease. See also DuBois and Gordon, "Seeking Ecstasy on the Battlefield," 14–15, for a discussion of the feminist response to licensing.

44. The fullest, if highly sympathetic, account of Lady Henry's position on the Contagious Diseases Acts is still to be found in Fitzpatrick, *Lady Henry Somerset*, 198–209.

45. Hannah Smith circular letter, 28 May 1897, Hannah Whitall Smith Papers.

46. Fitzpatrick, *Lady Henry Somerset*, 198–209.

47. Gordon, *Beautiful Life*, 180–87, reproduces some of the key speeches and documents that figured in the Contagious Diseases Acts controversy.

48. Open letter, Mary C. Leavitt, 27 September 1897, WCTU series, reel 24, frame 578.

49. Gordon, *Beautiful Life*, 182.

50. Willard to Blackwell, 21 June 1897, Blackwell Family Papers, Schlesinger Library, box 3, folder 87.

51. Fitzpatrick, *Lady Henry Somerset*, 207–9. Gordon, *Beautiful Life*, 202–3, reproduces the letter in which Lady Henry outlined her revised position. Leavitt did not cease her vendetta against Lady Henry. She was still calling for her resignation as world president in the summer of 1898, but had shifted her charges to accusing Lady Henry of serving wine at her table and owning pubs (*Union Signal*, 1 June 1898, 8). Leavitt was only sixty-seven years old and should not have been senile, but during the past few years she had been behaving toward the leadership of the Union in very strange and paranoid ways. Her attitude seemed to sadden rather than anger Willard and her colleagues. Nonetheless, she was a source of considerable trouble.

52. Gordon, *Beautiful Life*, 284. Gordon is the best source for the details of Willard's last illness, although her account is tailored to what she saw as the WCTU's needs at the moment of its publication.

53. Willard to L. M. N. Stevens, 24 December 1897, WCTU series, reel 24.

54. Typescript of interview with "Bushy" (probably Mrs. Westover Alden, editor of the woman's department of the *New York Tribune*), WCTU series, reel 27, folder 114, frame 175ff.

55. Gordon, *Beautiful Life*, 291. This custom is mentioned in Willard's *Glimpses of Fifty Years*, 55–56; *Nineteen Beautiful Years*, 223–24; and Diary.

56. Gordon, *Beautiful Life*, 292.

Bibliography

This bibliography is organized as follows:
1. Manuscript Collections
2. Newspapers
3. Published Works
4. Unpublished Dissertations and Other Manuscripts

I. MANUSCRIPT COLLECTIONS

Cambridge, Massachusetts
  Schlesinger Library, Radcliffe College
    Anna Howard Shaw Papers, Dillon Collection
    Blackwell Family Papers
    Frances Willard Papers
Evanston, Illinois
  Willard Memorial Library
    Anna Gordon Papers
    National Woman's Christian Temperance Union Papers
    Frances Willard Diaries
Madison, Wisconsin
  Division of Archives and Manuscripts, State Historical Society of Wisconsin
    Clara Colby Papers
    Kent Family Papers
    Henry Demarest Lloyd Papers
    Dora Smith Papers
Northampton, Massachusetts
  Sophia Smith Collection, Smith College
    Garrison Family Papers
Oxford, England
  Barbara Strachey Family Collection
    Hannah Whitall Smith Papers
Poughkeepsie, New York
  Vassar College Library
    Elizabeth Cady Stanton Papers

St. Paul, Minnesota
   Minnesota Historical Society
      Ignatius Donnelly Papers
Washington, D.C.
   Department of Archives and Manuscripts, Catholic University
      Terence Powderly Papers
   Library of Congress
      Anna Dickinson Papers
      National American Woman Suffrage Association Papers

2. NEWSPAPERS

Chicago Tribune, 1873–1894   *Union Signal*, 1883–1900
New York Times, 1880–1898   *Woman's Journal*, 1874–1900
Our Union, 1878–1882

3. PUBLISHED WORKS

Anthony, Katherine. *Susan B. Anthony: Her Personal History and Her Era*. Garden City, N.Y.: Doubleday, 1954.

Anthony, Susan B., and Harper, Ida H., eds. *History of Woman Suffrage*, vol. 4. Rochester, N.Y.: Susan B. Anthony, 1881.

Avrich, Paul. *The Haymarket Tragedy*. Princeton, N.J.: Princeton University Press, 1984.

Badger, Reid. *The Great American Fair: The World's Columbian Exposition and American Culture*. Chicago: University of Chicago Press, 1979.

Banner, Lois. *Elizabeth Cady Stanton: A Radical for Woman's Rights*. Boston: Little, Brown and Company, 1980.

Basch, Norma. *In the Eyes of the Law: Women, Marriage, and Property in Nineteenth Century New York*. Ithaca, N.Y.: Cornell University Press, 1982.

Bellamy, Edward. *Looking Backward: 2000–1887*. New York: Modern Library, 1917.

Berg, Barbara. *The Remembered Gate: Origins of American Feminism*. New York: Oxford University Press, 1978.

Blair, William Henry. *The Temperance Movement: Or the Conflict between Man and Alcohol*. Boston: William E. Smythe Co., 1888.

Blocker, Jack S., Jr. *Retreat from Reform: The Prohibition Movement in the United States, 1890–1913*. Westport, Conn.: Greenwood Press, 1976.

———. *Alcohol, Reform, and Society: The Liquor Question in Social Context*. Westport, Conn.: Greenwood Press, 1979.

———. *Give to the Winds Thy Fears: Woman's Temperance Crusade, 1873–1874*. Westport, Conn.: Greenwood Press, 1985.

Blumberg, Dorothy. *Florence Kelley: The Making of a Social Pioneer*. New York: Augustus M. Kelley, 1966.

Bordin, Ruth. *Woman and Temperance: The Quest for Power and Liberty, 1873–1900*. Philadelphia: Temple University Press, 1981.

Brittain, Vera. *Lady unto Woman: A History of Women from Victoria to Elizabeth II*. New York: MacMillan, 1953.

Brooks, Evelyn. "The Feminist Theology of the Black Baptist Church, 1800–1900." In *Class, Race, and Sex: The Dynamics of Control*, edited by Amy Swedlow and Hanna Lessinger. Boston: G. K. Hall and Company, 1983.

Brumberg, Joan Jacobs. *Mission For Life: The Judson Family and American Evangelical Culture*. New York: The Free Press, 1980.

———. "Zenanas and Girlless Villages: The Ethnology of American Evangelical Women, 1870–1910." *Journal of American History* 69 (September 1982): 347–71.

———. "The Ethnological Mirror: American Evangelical Women and Their Heathen Sisters, 1870–1910." In *Women and the Structure of Society*, edited by Barbara J. Harris and Jo Ann K. McNamara. Durham, N.C.: Duke University Press, 1984.

Buhle, Mari Jo. "Politics and Culture in Women's History." *Feminist Studies* 6 (Spring 1980): 37–41.

———. *Women and American Socialism, 1870–1920*. Urbana: University of Illinois Press, 1981.

Burstyn, Joan N. *Victorian Education and the Ideal of Womanhood*. London: Croom Helm, 1980.

Chambers-Schiller, Lee. "The Single Woman: Family and Vocation among Nineteenth Century Reformers." In *Woman's Being, Woman's Place: Female Identity and Vocation in American History*, edited by Mary Kelley, 334–50. Boston: G. K. Hall Co., 1979.

Clark, Clifford. *Henry Ward Beecher: Spokesman for a Middle-Class America*. Urbana: University of Illinois Press, 1978. Chap. 10.

Clark, Norman. *Deliver Us from Evil: An Interpretation of American Prohibition*. New York: W. W. Norton and Company, 1976.

Clifford, Deborah Pickman. *Mine Eyes Have Seen the Glory: A Biography of Julia Ward Howe*. Boston: Little, Brown and Company, 1979.

Cook, Blanche Wiessen. "Female Support Networks and Political Activism: Lillian Wald, Crystal Eastman, Emma Goldman." *Chrysalis* 3 (1977): 43–61.

Cott, Nancy. *The Bonds of Womanhood: "Woman's Sphere" in New England, 1790–1835*. New Haven: Yale University Press, 1978.

———, and Pleck, Elizabeth. *A Heritage of Her Own*. New York: Simon and Schuster, 1979.

Dannenbaum, Jed. "The Origins of Temperance Activism and Militancy among American Women." *Journal of Social History* 15 (December 1981): 235–54.

———. *Drink and Disorder: Temperance Reform in Cincinnati from the Washington Revival to the WCTU*. Urbana: University of Illinois Press, 1984.

David, Henry. *The History of the Haymarket Affair*. New York: Collier Books, 1963. First published in 1938.

Davis, Allen. *American Heroine: The Life and Legend of Jane Addams*. New York: Oxford University Press, 1973.

DeBenedetti, Charles. *The Peace Reform in American History*. Bloomington: University of Indiana Press, 1980.

Destler, Charles McArthur. *Henry Demarest Lloyd and the Empire of Reform*. Philadelphia: University of Pennsylvania Press, 1963.

Dieter, Melvin Easterday. *The Holiness Revival of the Nineteenth Century.* Metuchen, N.J.: Scarecrow Press, 1980.

Douglas, Ann. *The Feminization of American Culture.* New York: Alfred A. Knopf, 1977. Reprint. Avon Books, 1978.

DuBois, Ellen Carol. "The Radicalism of the Woman Suffrage Movement: Notes toward the Reconstruction of Nineteenth Century Feminism." *Feminist Studies* 3 (Fall 1975): 63–71.

_____. *Feminism and Suffrage.* Ithaca, N.Y.: Cornell University Press, 1978.

_____. "Politics and Culture in Women's History." *Feminist Studies* 6 (Spring 1980): 28–36.

_____, ed. *Elizabeth Cady Stanton and Susan B. Anthony, Correspondence, Writings, Speeches.* New York: Schocken Books, 1981.

_____, and Gordon, Linda. "Seeking Ecstasy on the Battlefield: Danger and Pleasure in Nineteenth Century Feminist Sexual Thought." *Feminist Studies* 9 (Spring 1983): 7–25.

Earhart, Mary. *Frances Willard: From Prayers to Politics.* Chicago: University of Chicago Press, 1944.

Elshtain, Jean Bethke. *Public Man, Private Woman: Women in Social and Political Thought.* Princeton, N.J.: Princeton University Press, 1981.

Engelmans, Larry. *Intemperance: The Lost War against Liquor.* New York: Free Press, 1979.

Epstein, Barbara Leslie. *The Politics of Domesticity: Women, Evangelism, and Temperance in Nineteenth Century America.* Middletown, Conn.: Wesleyan University Press, 1981.

Faderman, Lillian. *Surpassing the Love of Men: Romantic Friendships and Love between Women from the Renaissance to the Present.* New York: William Morrow and Co., 1981.

Findlay, James F. *Dwight L. Moody.* Chicago: University of Chicago Press, 1969.

Fink, Leon. *Workingmen's Democracy: The Knights of Labor and American Politics.* Urbana: University of Illinois Press, 1983.

Fitzpatrick, Kathleen. *Lady Henry Somerset.* London: Jonathan Cape and Boston: Little, Brown and Company, 1923.

Foner, Philip. *History of the Labor Movement in the United States.* 2 vols. New York: International Publishers, 1955.

Frankfort, Roberta. *Collegiate Women: Domesticity and Career in Turn of the Century America.* New York: New York University Press, 1977.

Freedman, Estelle. "Separatism as Strategy: Female Institution Building and American Feminism, 1870–1930." *Feminist Studies* 5 (Fall 1979): 512–29.

_____. *Their Sisters' Keepers: Women's Prison Reform in America, 1830–1930.* Ann Arbor: University of Michigan Press, 1981.

Friedan, Betty. *The Second Stage.* New York: Summit Books, 1981.

Furner, Mary. *Advocacy and Objectivity: A Crisis in the Professionalization of American Social Science.* Lexington: University Press of Kentucky, 1975.

Garrison, Stephen Olin. *Forty Witnesses, Covering the Whole Range of Christian Experience.* New York: Hunt and Eaton, 1888.

Gilman, Charlotte Perkins Stetson. *Women and Economics: A Study of the Economic Relation between Men and Women as a Factor in Social Evolution.* New

York: Harper and Row, 1966. First published in 1898.

Gladden, Washington. *Applied Christianity: Moral Aspects of Social Questions.* Boston: Houghton Mifflin Company, 1886.

Goldmark, Josephine. *Impatient Crusader: Florence Kelley's Life Story.* Urbana: University of Illinois Press, 1953.

Goodwyn, Lawrence. *Democratic Promise: The Populist Movement in America.* New York: Oxford University Press, 1976.

Gordon, Anna A. *The Beautiful Life of Frances Willard.* Chicago: Woman's Temperance Publishing Association, 1898.

————. *The Life of Frances E. Willard.* Evanston, Ill.: National Woman's Temperance Publishing Association, 1914.

Gordon, Elizabeth Putnam. *Women Torchbearers: The Story of the Woman's Christian Temperance Union.* Evanston, Ill.: Woman's Temperance Publishing Association, 1924.

Grant, Mary H. "Domestic Experience and Feminist Theory: The Case of Julia Ward Howe." In *Woman's Being, Woman's Place: Female Identity and Vocation in American History*, edited by Mary Kelley. Boston: G. K. Hall & Co., 1979.

Greene, Frederick Davis. *The Armenian Crisis in Turkey: The Massacre of 1894, Its Antecedents and Significance.* London and New York: G. P. Putnam, 1895.

Griffith, Elizabeth. *In Her Own Right: The Life of Elizabeth Cady Stanton.* New York: Oxford University Press, 1984.

Gusfield, Joseph. "Social Structure and Moral Reform: A Study of the Woman's Christian Temperance Union." *Journal of Sociology* 61 (November 1955): 221–32.

————. *Symbolic Crusade.* Urbana: University of Illinois Press, 1963.

Hall, David. "The Victorian Connection." In *Victorian America*, edited by Daniel Walker Howe, pp. 81–94. Philadelphia: University of Pennsylvania Press, 1976.

Hardesty, Nancy. "Minister as Prophet? Or as Mother?" In *Women in New Worlds: Historical Perspectives on the Wesleyan Tradition*, 2 vols., edited by Hilah Thomas and Rosemary Skinner Keller. Nashville, Tenn.: Abingdon Press, 1981–1982.

————. *Women Called to Witness: Evangelical Feminism in the Nineteenth Century.* Nashville, Tenn.: Abingdon Press, 1984.

Harding, Susan. "Family Reform Movements: Recent Feminism and Its Opposition." *Feminist Studies* 7 (Spring 1981): 57–75.

Harrison, Brian. *Drink and the Victorians: The Temperance Question in England, 1815–1872.* Pittsburgh: University of Pittsburgh Press, 1972.

————. *Separate Spheres: The Opposition to Women's Suffrage in Britain.* London: Croom Helm, 1978.

Haskell, Thomas. *The Emergence of Professional Social Science: The American Social Science Association and the Crisis of Authority.* Urbana: University of Illinois Press, 1977.

Hayden, Delores. *The Grand Domestic Revolution: A History of Feminist Designs for American Homes, Neighborhoods and Cities.* Cambridge: MIT Press, 1981.

Hibben, Paxton. *Henry Ward Beecher: An American Portrait.* New York: Readers Club, 1942.

Hicks, John D. *The Populist Revolt*. Minneapolis: University of Minnesota Press, 1931.

Higham, John. *Writing American History*. Bloomington: Indiana University Press, 1970.

Hill, Mary. *Charlotte Perkins Gilman: The Making of a Radical Feminist*. Philadelphia: Temple University Press, 1980.

Hill, Patricia R. *The World Their Household: The American Woman's Foreign Mission Movement and Cultural Transformation, 1870–1920*. Ann Arbor: University of Michigan Press, 1985.

Hooper, Wilfrid. *Reigate: Its Story Through the Ages*. Guildford: Surrey Archeological Society, 1945.

Horowitz, Helen. *Alma Mater: Design and Experience in the Women's Colleges from Their Nineteenth Century Beginnings to the 1930s*. New York: Alfred A. Knopf, 1984.

Howe, Daniel Walker. "Victorian Culture in America." In *Victorian America*, edited by Daniel Walker Howe. Philadelphia: University of Pennsylvania Press, 1976.

Howe, Julia Ward. *Reminiscences, 1819–1899*. Boston: Houghton Mifflin Co., 1899.

James, Edward T., and James, Janet, eds. *Notable American Women, 1607–1950*. 3 vols. Cambridge: Harvard University Press, 1971.

James, Janet Wilson, ed. *Women in American Religion*. Philadelphia: University of Pennsylvania Press, 1980.

Jernigan, E. Jay. *Henry Demarest Lloyd*. New York: Twayne Publishers, 1976.

Jimerson, Randall C.; Blouin, Francis X.; and Isetts, Charles A., eds. *Guide to the Microfilm Edition of the Temperance and Prohibition Papers*. Ann Arbor: University of Michigan, 1977. Supplement, 1982.

Johnson, Allen, and Malone, Dumas, eds. *Dictionary of American Biography*. New York: Charles Scribner, 1930, 1931.

Jones, Charles Edwin. *Perfectionist Persuasion: The Holiness Movement and American Methodism, 1867–1936*. Metuchen, N.J.: Scarecrow Press, 1974.

Kearney, Belle. *A Slaveholder's Daughter*. New York: Abbey Press, 1900.

Keller, Rosemary Skinner. "Creating a Sphere for Women." In *Women in New Worlds: Historical Perspectives on the Wesleyan Tradition*, edited by Hilah E. Thomas and Rosemary Skinner Keller, pp. 246–60. Nashville, Tenn.: Abingdon Press, 1981.

Lang, David Marshall. *Armenia, Cradle of Civilization*. 3rd ed. London: George Allen and Unwin, 1980.

Lasch, Christopher. *The New Radicalism in America, 1889–1963: The Intellectual as a Social Type*. New York: Alfred A. Knopf, 1965.

Leach, William. *True Love and Perfect Union: The Feminist Reform of Sex and Society*. New York: Basic Books, 1980.

———. "Looking Forward Together: Feminists and Edward Bellamy." *Democracy* 2 (January 1982).

Lender, Mark, and Martin, James Kirby. *Drinking in America: A History*. New York: Free Press, 1982.

Lipow, Arthur. *Authoritarian Socialism in America: Edward Bellamy and the Nationalist Movement*. Berkeley: University of California Press, 1982.

Longmate, Norman. *The Water Drinkers: A History of Temperance*. London: Hamish Hamilton, 1968.

Lutz, Alma. *Susan B. Anthony: Rebel, Crusader, Humanitarian*. Boston: Beacon Press, 1959.

McBriar, A. M. *Fabian Socialism and English Politics 1884–1918*. Cambridge: Cambridge University Press, 1962.

McCarthy, Kathleen D. *Noblesse Oblige: Charity and Cultural Philanthropy in Chicago, 1849–1929*. Chicago: University of Chicago Press, 1982.

McDowell, John Patrick. *The Social Gospel in the South: The Woman's Home Mission Movement in the Methodist Episcopal Church South, 1886–1939*. Baton Rouge: Louisiana University Press, 1982.

McGuigan, Dorothy Geis. *A Dangerous Experiment: One Hundred Years of Women at the University of Michigan*. Ann Arbor: University of Michigan Press, 1970.

McHugh, Paul. *Prostitution and Victorian Social Reform*. London: Croom Helm, 1980.

McLoughlin, William G., and Bellah, Robert N., eds. *Religion in America*. Boston: Beacon Press, 1968.

MacKenzie, Norman, and MacKenzie, Jeanne. *The Diary of Beatrice Webb: Glitter Around and Darkness Within, 1873–1892*. vol. 1. Cambridge: Harvard University Press, 1982.

———. *The First Fabians*. London: Weidenfield and Nicolson, 1977.

———. *The Letters of Sidney and Beatrice Webb*. London: Cambridge University Press, 1978.

Marcus, Jane. "Transatlantic Sisterhood: Labor and Suffrage Links in the Letters of Elizabeth Robins and Emmeline Pankhurst." *Signs* 3 (Spring 1978): 744–55.

Marzolf, Marion. *Up from the Footnotes*. New York: Hastings House, 1976.

Meintzes, Johannes. *Olive Schreiner: Portrait of a South African Woman*. Johannesburg: Hugh Keartland, 1965.

Melder, Keith. "Ladies Bountiful: Organized Women's Benevolence in Early Nineteenth Century America." *New York History* 48 (1967): 231–54.

Merrick, Caroline. *Old Times in Dixieland: A Southern Matron's Memories*. New York: Grafton Press, 1901.

Minutes of the National Woman's Christian Temperance Union, 1874–1899. Chicago: Woman's Temperance Publishing Association, 1882–99.

Moore, Robert Laurence. *In Search of White Crows: Spiritualism, Parapsychology, and American Culture*. New York: Oxford University Press, 1977.

Morison, Theodore. *Chautauqua: A Center for Education and Religion and the Arts in America*. Chicago: University of Chicago Press, 1974.

Motz, Marilyn. *Michigan Women and Their Kin*. Albany: State University of New York Press, 1983.

Newton, Esther. "The Mythic Mannish Lesbian: Radclyffe Hall and the New Woman." *Signs* 9 (Summer 1984): 557–75.

O'Brien, Sharon. "Tomboyism and Adolescent Conflict: Three Nineteenth Century Case Studies." In *Woman's Being, Woman's Place: Female Identity and Vocation in American History*, edited by Mary Kelley. Boston: G. K. Hall, 1979.

O'Neil, William. *Everyone Was Brave*. New York: Quadrangle Press, 1971.

Papers Read at the Fourth Congress of Women. Washington, D.C.: Todd Brothers, 1877.

Pivar, David. *The Purity Crusade: Sexual Morality and Social Control*. Westport, Conn.: Greenwood Press, 1973.

Porterfield, Amanda. *Feminine Spirituality in America: From Sarah Edwards to Martha Graham*. Philadelphia: Temple University Press, 1980.

Powderly, Terence. *The Path I Trod*. New York: Ames Press, 1968. Reprinted from the 1940 edition.

_____. *Thirty Years of Labor, 1859–1889*. Columbus: Excelsior Publishing House, 1890.

Rauschenbush, Walter. *Christianity and the Social Crisis*. New York: Macmillan Company, 1907.

Rich, Adrienne. "Compulsory Heterosexuality and Lesbian Existence." *Signs* 5 (Summer 1980): 631–60.

Ridge, Martin. *Ignatius Donnelly: The Portrait of a Politician*. Chicago: University of Chicago Press, 1962.

Ritter, Ellen M. "Elizabeth Morgan: Pioneer Female Labor Agitator." *Central States Speech Journal* 22 (Winter 1971): 242–51.

Roberts, James S. *Drink, Temperance, and the Working Class in Nineteenth Century Germany*. Winchester, Maine: Allen and Unwin, 1984.

Rorabaugh, William. *The Alcoholic Republic: An American Tradition*. New York: Oxford University Press, 1979.

Rossi, Alice. "A Biosocial Perspective on Parenting." *Daedalus* 106 (Spring 1977).

Rothman, David. *The Discovery of the Asylum: Social Order and Disorder in the New Republic*. Boston: Little Brown and Company, 1971.

Rupp, Leila M. "Imagine My Surprise: Women's Relationships in Historical Perspective." *Frontiers* 5 (Fall 1980): 61–70.

Ryan, Mary P. *Cradle of the Middle Class: The Family in Oneida County, New York, 1790–1865*. New York: Cambridge University Press, 1981.

Said, Edward W. *Orientalism*. New York: Vintage Books, 1979.

Scharnaw, Ralph. "Elizabeth Morgan, Crusader for Labor Reform." *Labor History* 14 (Summer 1973): 340–51.

Scott, Ann Firor. *The Southern Lady: From Pedestal to Politics*. Chicago: University of Chicago Press, 1970.

Sheldon, Charles. *In His Steps: What Would Jesus Do?* Chicago: Advance Publishing Company, 1898.

Sicherman, Barbara. "American History." *Signs* 1 (Winter 1975): 475.

Sklar, Katherine Kish. *Catharine Beecher: A Study in American Domesticity*. New Haven: Yale University Press, 1973.

Smith, Logan Pearsall. *Unforgotten Years*. Boston: Little Brown and Co., 1939.

_____, ed. *Philadelphia Quaker: The Letters of Hannah Whitall Smith*. New York: Harcourt Brace, 1950.

Smith-Rosenberg, Carroll. *Religion and the Rise of the American City: The New York City Mission Movement, 1812–1870*. Ithaca, N.Y.: Cornell University Press, 1971.

_____. "The Female World of Love and Ritual: Relations between Nineteenth Century Women." *Signs* 1 (Autumn 1975): 1–29.

Solomon, Barbara Miller. *In the Company of Educated Women: A History of Higher Education in America*. New Haven: Yale University Press, 1985.

Stacey, Judith. "The New Conservative Feminism." *Feminist Studies* 9 (Fall 1983): 559–83.

Stowe, Steven M. "The Thing Not Its Vision: A Woman's Courtship and Her Sphere in the Southern Planter Class." *Feminist Studies* 9 (Spring 1983): 113–30.

Strachey, Barbara. *Remarkable Relations*. New York: Universe Press, 1982.

Strachey, Ray [Rachel Costelloe]. *Frances Willard: Her Life and Work*. London: Jonathan Cape, 1913.

———. *Millicent Garrett Fawcett*. London: J. Murray, 1931.

———. *Group Movements in the Past and Experiments in Guidance*. London: Faber and Faber, Ltd., 1934.

———. *The Cause*. Port Washington, N.Y.: Kennikat Press, 1969. First published in 1928.

Stratton, C. C., ed. *Autobiography of Erastus O. Haven*. New York: Phillips and Hunt, 1883.

Sweet, Leonard. *The Minister's Wife: Her Role in Nineteenth Century American Evangelism*. Philadelphia: Temple University Press, 1983.

Szasz, Ferenc Morton. *The Divided Mind of American Protestantism, 1880–1930*. Montgomery: University of Alabama Press, 1982.

Tax, Meredith. *The Rising of the Women: Feminist Solidarity and Class Conflict, 1880–1917*. New York: Monthly Review Press, 1980.

Teichman, Harold. *Alice: The Life and Times of Alice Roosevelt Longworth*. Englewood, N.J.: Prentice Hall, 1979.

Temperance and Prohibition Papers. Joint Ohio Historical Society–Michigan Historical Collections–Woman's Christian Temperance Union microfilm ed. See Randall C. Jimerson, Francis X. Blouin, and Charles A. Isetts, eds., *Guide to the Microfilm Edition of the Temperance and Prohibition Papers* (Ann Arbor: University of Michigan, 1977), and Supplement, 1982.

Thistlethwaite, Frank. *America and the Atlantic Community: Anglo American Aspects, 1790–1850*. New York: Harper Torchbooks, 1963.

Thomas, Hilah, and Keller, Rosemary Skinner, eds. *Women in New Worlds: Historical Perspectives on the Wesleyan Tradition*. 2 vols. Nashville, Tenn.: Abingdon Press, 1981–82.

Thomas, John L. *Alternative America: Henry George, Edward Bellamy, Henry Demarest Lloyd and the Adversary Tradition*. Cambridge: Harvard University Press, 1983.

Tyrrell, Ian R. *Sobering Up: From Temperance to Prohibition in Antebellum America, 1800–1860*. Westport, Conn.: Greenwood Press, 1979.

Vicinus, Martha. "Sexuality and Work: A Review of Current Work in the History of Sexuality." *Feminist Studies* 8 (Spring 1982): 133–56.

———. "One Life to Stand Beside Me: Emotional Conflicts in First Generation College Women in England." *Feminist Studies* 8 (Fall 1982): 603–28.

Vincent, Leon H. *John Heyl Vincent: A Biographical Sketch*. Freeport, N.Y.: Books for Libraries Press, 1925. Reprint, 1970.

Wade, Louise. *Graham Taylor: Pioneer for Social Justice, 1851–1938*. Chicago: University of Chicago Press, 1964. Chap. 3.

Walkowitz, Judith. *Prostitution and Victorian Society: Women, Class, and the*

State. New York: Cambridge University Press, 1980.

Webb, Beatrice. *My Apprenticeship*. London: Longmans, Green and Co., 1926.

Wells-Barnett, Ida. *On Lynchings: Southern Horrors, A Red Record, Mob Rule in New Orleans*. Facsimile ed. New York: Arno Press, 1960.

Welter, Barbara. "The Cult of True Womanhood, 1820–1860." *American Quarterly* 18 (Summer 1966): 151–74.

_____. "The Feminization of American Religion, 1800–1860." In *Clio's Consciousness Raised: New Perspectives on the History of Women*, edited by Mary Hartman and Lois Banner, pp. 134–57. New York: Harper Torch Books, 1974.

Wiener, Carolyn. *The Politics of Alcoholism: Building an Arena around a Social Problem*. New Brunswick, N.J.: Transaction Books, 1981.

Willard, Frances E. *Nineteen Beautiful Years*. New York: Harper and Bros., 1864.

_____. *Woman and Temperance*. Hartford, Conn.: Park Publishing Co., 1883.

_____. *How to Win*. New York: Funk and Wagnalls, 1886.

_____. *Woman in the Pulpit*. Chicago: Woman's Christian Temperance Publishing Association, 1888.

_____. *Glimpses of Fifty Years: The Autobiography of an American Woman*. Chicago: Woman's Christian Temperance Publishing Association, 1889.

_____. *Evanston: A Classic Town: The Story of Evanston by an Old Timer*. Chicago: Woman's Christian Temperance Publishing Association, 1891.

_____. *A Great Mother*. Chicago: Woman's Christian Temperance Publishing Association, 1894.

_____. *A Wheel within a Wheel: How I Learned to Ride the Bicycle*. New York: F. H. Berell Co. and London: Hutchinson and Company, 1895.

_____, and Livermore, Mary, eds. *A Woman of the Century*. Buffalo: Charles Wells Mouton, 1893.

_____; Winslow, Helen; and White, Sallie; eds. *Occupations for Women*. New York: Success Company, 1897.

Williamson, Harold F., and Wild, Payson S. *Northwestern University: A History, 1850–1975*. Evanston, Ill.: Northwestern University Press, 1976.

Winskill, R. T. *The Temperance Movement and Its Workers*. 4 vols. London: Blackie and Co., 1892–93.

4. UNPUBLISHED DISSERTATIONS AND OTHER MANUSCRIPTS

Bordin, Ruth. "Upon This Rock: Women's Church Networks and the Mass Organization of Women into the WCTU." Paper presented at the Fifth Berkshire Conference on the History of Women, Vassar College, 16–18 June 1981.

DuBois, Ellen. "The Limitations of Sisterhood: Stanton's Political Leadership, 1875–1902." Paper presented at the Fifth Berkshire Conference on the History of Women, Vassar College, 16–18 June 1981.

Giele, Janet Zollinger. "Social Change in the Feminine Role: A Comparison of Woman's Suffrage and Temperance, 1870–1920." Ph.D. dissertation, Radcliffe College, 1961.

Gordon, Ann D. "Alzina Stevens' Long Road to Hull House." Paper presented at the Fifth Berkshire Conference on the History of Women, Vassar College, 16–18 June 1981.

Lee, Susan Dye. "Evangelical Domesticity: The Origins of the WCTU under Frances Willard." Ph.D. dissertation, Northwestern University, 1980.

Mezvinsky, Norton. "The White Ribbon Reform, 1874–1920." Ph.D. dissertation, Wisconsin, 1959.

Miller, Ida Treatault. "Frances Elizabeth Willard: Religious Leader and Social Reformer." Ph.D. dissertation, Boston University, 1978.

Ruegamer, Lena. "Chicago Women Reformers, 1863–1893: The Development of an Elite Network." Paper presented at the Conference on Female Spheres, New Harmony, Indiana, October 1981.

Unger, Samuel. "History of the National Woman's Christian Temperance Union." Ph.D. dissertation, Ohio State University, 1933.

Waller, Altine L. "The Beecher-Tilton Adultery Scandal: Family, Religion, and Politics in Brooklyn, 1865–1875." Ph.D. dissertation, University of Massachusetts, 1980.

Index

Addams, Jane, 75, 151, 154
Alcohol: nineteenth-century use of, 7
American Methodist Ladies Centenary Association, 42–43
American Prison Association, 174
American Social Science Association, 130–31, 145
Ames, Julia, 169
Anglo-American connection, 194–97, 212, 227, 236–37
Anthony, Susan B., 5, 46, 70, 99–100, 101, 154, 157, 189, 223, 233; and Columbian Exposition, 233
Armenian relief mission, 78, 228–31
Arthur, Chester, 111
Association for the Advancement of Women, 71
Auburndale, Massachusetts, 93

Bain, George, 135, 219
Baldwin, Katherine Willard, 126, 224, 238
Baldwin, William Woodward, 126
Balgarnie, Florence, 221, 222
Bannister, Henry, 48
Barker, Helen, 205
Barnard College, 57
Barton, Clara, 8, 154
Beecher, Catharine, 15, 23, 103, 158, 245
Beecher, Henry Ward, 70, 86
Bellamy, Edward, 145–49, 157, 175, 178, 180, 262
Berenson, Bernard, 194
Besant, Annie, 157
Beveridge, Albert, 6
Bicycling, 117, 208
Bidwell, John, 185
Birney, James G., 135
Blacks, 113, 216–18, 221–22, 223
Blackwell, Antoinette, 71
Blackwell, Elizabeth, 132, 196, 237

Blackwell, Henry, 154
Blake, Lillie Devereux, 214
Boole, William H., 71
Booth, Maud Ballington, 214
Brigham, Ada, 224
British temperance movement, 102, 193–94. *See also* British Woman's Temperance Association
British woman's movement, 192–93
British Woman's Temperance Association (BWTA), 181, 182, 192, 194, 227; Cantonment Acts position, 236–37; convention of 1895, 221–22; factions within, 202–3; lynching issues, 221–22; *See also* Somerset, Isabel
Brockway, Zebulon, 130
Brown, Corinne, 151
Brown, Martha McClelland, 66, 78, 79
Bryan, William Jennings, 223
Buckley, James M., 160–61, 164, 165, 166, 167
Buell, Caroline, 211
Buhle, Mari Jo, 8, 9
Burnham, Daniel, 150
Butler, Josephine, 132, 143, 236
Butler, Lucy, 103

Cantonment Acts, 236
Catholic temperance movement. *See* Temperance movement: Catholic
Catholic Total Abstinence Society, 168, 169
Centennial Exposition of 1876, 86, 90, 101, 190
Channing, William Ellery, 27
Chant, Laura Orme, 230
Chapin, Sallie, 114
Chautauqua Assembly, 86, 161; founding of WCTU, 78
Chicago, Illinois: in 1873–74, 74–75; fire, 60, 61, 74, 75; the Loop, 80, 83; wom-